# STATE OF THE UNION

# STATE OF THE UNION

## America in the 1990s

### VOLUME ONE: ECONOMIC TRENDS

REYNOLDS FARLEY

*Editor*

RUSSELL SAGE FOUNDATION • NEW YORK

## The Russell Sage Foundation

The Russell Sage Foundation, one of the oldest of America's general purpose foundations, was established in 1907 by Mrs. Margaret Olivia Sage for "the improvement of social and living conditions in the United States." The Foundation seeks to fulfill this mandate by fostering the development and dissemination of knowledge about the country's political, social, and economic problems. While the Foundation endeavors to assure the accuracy and objectivity of each book it publishes, the conclusions and interpretations in Russell Sage Foundation publications are those of the authors and not of the Foundation, its Trustees, or its staff. Publication by Russell Sage, therefore, does not imply Foundation endorsement.

**Library of Congress Cataloging-in-Publication Data**

State of the union : America in the 1990s / Reynolds Farley, editor.
    p.  cm.—(The 1990 census research series ; 1–2)
    Includes bibliographical references and index.
    Contents: v. 1. Economic trends—v. 2. Social trends.
    ISBN 0-87154-240-4 (v. 1).—ISBN 0-87154-241-2 (v. 2)
    1. United States—Economic conditions—1981–   2. Economic
Forecasting—United States.  3. United States—Census, 21st, 1990.
I. Farley, Reynolds, 1938–   .  II. Russell Sage Foundation.
III. Series.
HC106.8.S7352  1995
303.4′0973—dc20                                        94-40284
                                                                               CIP

Text design by John Johnston.

RUSSELL SAGE FOUNDATION
112 East 64th Street, New York, New York 10021

10 9 8 7 6 5 4 3 2 1

# Contents

# Acknowledgments

MAJOR SUPPORT for the 1990 census research project was provided by the Russell Sage Foundation, the Ford Foundation, the Andrew W. Mellon Foundation, the Spencer Foundation, the National Science Foundation, and the National Institutes of Aging, with special additional assistance from the Social Science Research Council, the Bureau of the Census, and the Population Studies Center of the University of Michigan. The project was under the guidance of a National Advisory Board chaired by Eric Wanner, President of the Russell Sage Foundation.

The following were the members of the Board:

William Butz: U.S. Bureau of the Census
Jorge Chapa: University of Texas
Richard Easterlin: University of Southern California
Reynolds Farley: University of Michigan
David Featherman: Social Science Research Council
James Johnson: University of North Carolina at Chapel Hill
Evelyn Kitagawa: University of Chicago
Karen Mason: East-West Center
Charles Westoff: Princeton University

# Contributors

Suzanne Bianchi          Department of Sociology
                         University of Maryland at College Park

John D. Kasarda          Kenan Institute of Private Enterprise
                         University of North Carolina

Frank Levy               Department of Urban Studies and Planning
                         Massachusetts Institute of Technology

Robert D. Mare           Center for Demography and Ecology
                         and Department of Sociology
                         University of Wisconsin—Madison

Dowell Myers             Department of Urban and Regional Planning
                         University of Southern California

James R. Wetzel          Economic consultant

Jennifer R. Wolch        Department of Geography
                         University of Southern California

# Introduction

REYNOLDS FARLEY

And the Lord spake unto Moses in the wilderness of Sinai in the tabernacle of the congregation, on the first day of the second month in the second year after they were come out of the land of Egypt, saying, take ye the sum of all the congregation of the children of Israel, after their families, by the house of their fathers, with the number of their names, every male by their polls; from twenty years old and upward, all that are able to go forth to war *(Numbers, Chap. 1:1–3).*

CENSUSES have been taken throughout recorded history, primarily to calculate how many men could be mobilized for battle or how much property could be taxed. The gospel of Luke tells us that Christ was born in Bethlehem because Caesar Augustus decreed that all be enrolled and taxed in their home cities. Just after invading England, the Normans carried out a census, henceforth referred to as the Domesday Book, which told them whom they conquered and where they might find tax revenue. Censuses taken in the United States serve purposes other than those of Moses or the Normans. With great ingenuity, the founders of this country decided that population size would determine democratic representation. Therefore, Article I of our Constitution mandates that Congress carry out an enumeration once every 10 years. Thomas Jefferson, serving as secretary of state, supervised the first count, but his report of 3.9 million Americans in 1790 disappointed President Washington, who had already told European heads of state that the new nation exceeded 4 million.

Fifty years ago issues of census undercount interested a few demographers and statisticians. But then, in 1962, the Supreme Court declared that the "one person, one vote" rule applied to all offices in our democracy down to the lowest local level. Suddenly, the importance of census-taking increased. Since Latinos and African Americans are typically missed more often than whites, census enumeration became an important civil rights issue. Each census—and even the planning of the enumerations—now triggers controversy about the mechanics of counting and the constitutionality of adjusting for undercount. Inevitably, numerous lawsuits are filed by local governments and advocacy groups claiming that errors and omissions in the census reduce their fair share of representation and benefits.

Censuses serve another vital purpose in our democracy. Since the early 1800s, they have been much more than head counts: they tell us about the state of our union. They are the primary sources of information about ourselves, about our jobs and our earnings, our prosperity or poverty, where we live and with whom, what kinds of homes we own or apartments we rent, our skin color, the languages we speak, and our ethnic origins. The 1990 census reports how people are now adapting—some with great success and others not very well at all—to the massive social and economic trends that make the United States of this decade extremely different from what it had been in generations past. And by informing us about where we are as a nation today and how we got here, censuses provide the crucial information we must have if we are to continue our efforts to reduce poverty; to increase the productivity of our work force; to eradicate crime; and to provide equal opportunities for women, for African Americans, and for those Native Americans whose ancestors lived here long before Christopher Columbus sailed from Spain.

In the late 1950s, just about a generation ago, a young white man with a high school education, a dedication to hard work, and a strong back could likely find a good blue collar job with a prosperous manufacturing firm, a job with comprehensive fringe benefits, including health insurance for his family and provisions for retirement. In view of sustained economic growth and low rates of inflation, he knew that if he came to work regularly and pleased his boss, his wages would rise year after year. He could afford to marry while he was in his early 20s and, with assistance from a federally backed mortgage, he could buy a starter home in the suburbs before his 30th birthday. Although some women in the high school graduating classes of the 1950s attended college, most of them married by the time they were old enough to vote or buy Scotch in a tavern. Divorces occurred but were relatively rare, and women expected that their husbands would remain with them and support them quite adequately while they stayed home taking care of the three or four children they had while still in their 20s. Few couples lived together before marrying, and childbearing by single white women was unusual. A young woman aspiring to be a U.S. Senator, a police officer, a corporate executive, or an advocate of equal rights for lesbians was an oddity in the 1950s. Few blacks went beyond high school, and those with college degrees were pretty much limited to preaching, teaching, or low-level clerical jobs in civil service.

Fast-forward to the late 1980s. A young man graduating from high school with a strong back and a dedication to steady work may find a job, but the odds are not in his favor. And if he is successful, the job will pay a modest wage and may have no fringe benefits. A young woman might marry her high school sweetheart right after graduation but, if she does, she realizes that their chances for middle-class prosperity and a nice home in the suburbs are slim. Their earnings will be meager and their financial state precarious unless both of them work full time and at least one of them gets advanced training. Divorce is probable, since more than one-half of recent marriages are terminated in that way. Realistically, a young married woman must plan for the possibility that, in her 30s, she will be heading her own family with a child or two.

Young people have adjusted to these pervasive social and economic changes. They now stay in school longer and typically delay marriage until they are much older. In fact, recent trends suggest that a substantial proportion may not marry at all. And compared with the 1950s, young people have adapted by reducing their number of children. But other changes provide young people with possibilities unknown—almost unthought of—four decades ago. We have made much progress in expanding opportunities for women, we have reduced some of the barriers that denied rights to blacks, and, to a large degree, we have changed laws and our values about personal living arrangements and sexuality. Women increasingly stay in school longer than men. As recently as the 1970s, just a handful of women earned advanced degrees in medicine, law, and business administration. Now thousands do every year.

Censuses reveal the social trends and economic shifts that are producing a new and different country. They reflect how we adapted to one array of changes in our values and norms—symbolized by events of the 1960s—and another set of macroeconomic changes dating from the 1970s. In the span of one generation, the social landscape of the country has been drastically rearranged, providing recent birth cohorts with a broader range of decisions and possibilities as they pass through adolescence and become adults. Dr. Martin Luther King, Jr., led an effective movement capped by the March on Washington in August 1963. The next year Congress enacted and President Johnson signed the most effective civil rights legislation since Reconstruction, thereby overturning those centuries-old practices of discrimination that denied blacks citizenship rights and economic opportunities. Importantly, Title VII of the 1964 Civil Rights Act prohibited discrimination in the labor market on the basis of both *gender* and *race*. In 1965, after decades of litigation and then the successful but bloody marches in Selma, Alabama, Congress finally put the Fifteenth Amendment into operation in all 50 states with the encompassing Voting Rights Act. By 1993, 40 African Americans were serving in Congress, and four were selected by President Clinton for his cabinet. While blacks still have extremely high poverty and unemployment rates as compared with whites, opportunities for recent generations are much improved and, in all major metropolises, there are now moderate to large middle-class black populations.

The new immigration law, also enacted in 1965, ended those discriminatory policies that favored the English, Irish, Germans, and Scandinavians. It had the unforeseen and unintended consequence of permitting 7 million Latin Americans and 5 million Asians to legally enter the United States after 1968. Censuses—more than any other sources—tell us how and why this nation's racial and ethnic composition is changing as we move toward the middle of the next century, when non-Hispanic whites will become a minority.

Other changes have given us more options about our personal lives. Until the late 1960s, divorce was possible in New York State only if adultery were proven, and until 1964 states had the right to prevent doctors from providing birth control information even to married couples. In the late 1960s, matters of personal sexuality—that is, sexual activities of almost all types among consenting adults—were pretty much privatized as restrictive laws were declared unconstitutional. And then, in January 1973, the Supreme Court ruled that abortion was primarily a matter for pregnant women to decide. No longer could a state force a woman to bear a child if she did not wish to do so. These developments occurred at a time when technological advances provided women with greater control over their childbearing. As a consequence of these shifts in our values, norms, and laws, as baby boom cohorts approached maturity, they could choose among a variety of socially acceptable alternatives about living their personal lives.

Cohabiting couples are now common, and they are not seriously censured in most circumstances. Persons preferring lesbian or gay relationships have opportunities to live as they wish in some communities. By the late 1980s, there were about four abortions performed for every ten births. The responsibilities of child rearing have gradually shifted away from the two-parent activity it had been in the 1950s to an increasingly female activity done in mother-only families. The marital status of women when they become mothers has also changed such that, by the early 1990s, almost three of every ten births were to single women.

The choices people make are strongly influenced by the economic climate. Declining employment opportunities for semiskilled workers and expanded opportunities for skilled crafts workers or health care professionals result from specific policies and decisions. In 1973, finance ministers of the oil-producing nations greatly increased their prices, a decision that shocked Americans as the cost of their gasoline soared from less than 30 cents a gallon to a dollar and a quarter. This dramatic and totally unexpected jump in energy costs divides an earlier period of sustained economic growth, increasing labor productivity, persistently growing wages, and reduced income inequality from the more recent span. Since 1973, the average weekly wage for all employed workers (in constant dollar amounts) has changed little. It was actually lower in the early 1990s than in 1973, but this masks divergent trends. There have been many winners whose economic status greatly improved, but other losers whose earnings stagnated and then declined. The earnings of women—especially those with an associate's degree or more—rose sharply. The earnings of men with more than a college education also increased, but for men with a high school education or less, earnings have fallen since the 1970s. Three trends—the emphasis on greater productivity in manufacturing; the long-run consumer shift toward purchasing more services and fewer durable goods, that is, more health club memberships or vacations and fewer second or third cars; and the increasingly unfavorable balance of trade for manufactured goods—curtailed employment opportunities and earnings for those millions of men with high school educations or less. By almost all important economic indicators, inequality grew during the 1980s as the gap between the prosperous and the poor widened. But in one area the shift was clearly toward greater equality: for the first time, the earnings of women rose faster than those of men. The 1990 census documents these pervasive shifts in how we earn our living and tells us clearly who is "riding high" and who is "just hanging on."

Since the 1900 census, cogent interpretative books—often given the less-than-felicitous name of census monographs—have interpreted what the enumerations revealed about overarching social and economic trends. As a collection, they portray the evolution of the nation during this century: the movement from farms to cities; the growth of the West; the aging of the population; the disappearance of streetcar conductors from the occupational distribution; and the appearance of systems programs and financial analysts as well as the slow emergence of equal opportunities and equal outcomes for women and blacks. Since 1950, the Russell Sage Foundation has supported these census research volumes. The ambitious *Population of the United States in the 1980s* series produced 17 books derived from the 1980 enumeration, covering topics from children to the elderly, from American Indians to Pacific Islanders. This project, based on the 1990 census, is more modest, offering an authoritative but concise interpretation of recent social trends. It is the first of two edited volumes.

Each chapter in this volume focuses on a specific aspect of *economic* life in the United States, but all chapters approach the task by describing the decisions that birth cohorts—that is, all people born within a particular 10-year period—made at different points in their life. Between the ages of 15 and 29, individuals decide how much schooling to obtain, what career path to pursue, whether to get married or to live with someone, whether to have children, and where to live. They make their decisions in view of what is economically feasible but are influenced by society's norms that specify what is possible, permissible, or desirable. How young people navigate those few years determines, in most cases, how they will live as adults and whether they will be prosperous homeowners when they reach retirement or renters close to the poverty line. People who came to late adolescence when good blue collar jobs were available to men and when premarital cohabitation and premarital pregnancies were severely censured, made different decisions than did later cohorts who faced a much tighter job market but a more permissive social structure.

In the first chapter, Frank Levy provides a stimulating overview of macroeconomic patterns in the decades since our armed forces defeated the Germans and the Japanese. He delineates four economic periods, describing trends in each and their causes. He lucidly portrays the increasing inequality of the 1980s by carefully outlining the forces that led to much greater earnings and wealth for those already toward the top of the income distribution but lower earnings for those at the bottom. If we are to have rising real earnings and more economic equality in this decade and the next, Levy argues, we need to not only increase labor productivity but also to address three pressing challenges: the mismatch between the skills of persons graduating from school and the needs of our increasingly technical and sophisticated labor market; the concentration of the poor in inner cities that now lack the resources to provide excellent schools or the extensive social services these people require; and, finally, the growing proportion of children reared in families headed by women whose incomes are near or below the poverty line.

James Wetzel tells us who is working and who is not, what they are doing on the job, and how much they earn. He begins by directing our attention to the fundamental macroeconomic shifts of recent decades, shifts that have been favorable to the employment and earnings of women but quite unfavorable to men with limited educations. For example, increases in health care spending created many good jobs for women, but reengineering industrial production reduced the need for machine operators and assembly line workers. He stresses that despite persistent economic growth throughout the 1980s, albeit at a moderate rate, there was not one month in that decade when the unemployment rate fell to 5 percent—a rate that would have been considered rather high by the standards of the 1950s and 1960s. The link between poverty and unemployment, Wetzel shows, is different from what it was. Creating more good jobs for men and increasing their earnings will reduce the poverty rate, but only by a very small amount, because poverty, much more so today than in the past, involves women and their children.

The most dramatic news from the 1990 census centers around the economic progress made by women. Suzanne Bianchi shows that during the 1960s and 1970s women made substantial progress in closing the educational gap that separated them from men. In the 1970s, women also gained on men in occupational achievement, since women filled many jobs in management. But prior to 1980, there was no evidence that women were catching up with men in terms of how much they got paid. This changed between 1980 and 1990, but the process was largely a cohort one; that is, women in the late baby boom cohorts—born 1956–1965 and at ages 25–34 in 1990—have educational attainments at least equal to those of men and have occupational and labor force careers quite similar to those of their brothers; and, compared with earlier cohorts, their earnings are more like those of men. As new birth cohorts enter the labor market in the future, we expect further declines in the gender gap in paychecks. But there is also reason for caution in her findings. During the 1980s, as college-educated men in their 30s aged into their 40s, their earnings rose somewhat faster than did the earnings of comparably educated women in the same birth cohorts.

Because job opportunities for persons with limited educations contracted, one might expect that young people would remain in school longer. Robert Mare demonstrates that this happened during the 1980s. He describes an important gender difference in this trend toward greater attainment: women, much more so than men, continued their enrollments and now statistically dominate the pool of recent college graduates. We are witnessing something of a "feminization" of higher education and of many of the traditionally male-dominated professions. But racial differences remain large, since Asians and whites stay enrolled much longer than do Hispanics or blacks and thus get a large share of the advanced degrees that lead to the best jobs and highest pay. On an optimistic note, Mare reports about the rising scores of African Americans on standardized tests. While our educational system provides opportunities for the poor to get the credentials needed to prosper, it also reenforces social inequities by passing them from one generation to the next. Using an innovative approach with census data, Mare demonstrates that during the 1980s highly educated parents continued to transmit their advantages to their children, both by sending them to preschools and by encouraging their school enrollment in late adolescence.

John Kasarda describes significant geographic consequences of industrial restructuring. There has been a development of "edge cities," as employment complexes at the periphery of many metropolises boomed in recent years, attracting a large share of the new high-technology jobs. In several metropolises, these edge cities are now more important than the old downtowns in terms of employment, office space, hotels, financial services, and other amenities. At the same time, the closing of smokestack industries means that employment prospects have gotten much worse for inner-city residents. Because of persistent residential segregation, older cities of the Northeast and Midwest now have large impoverished minority populations. However, both the tax base and tax revenue in such cities have contracted. The needs of a population left behind by industrial restructuring and by racial residential segregation overwhelm the meager resources of older cities.

We spend more time in our homes or apartments than anywhere else. More than just protecting us from the elements, they reflect the choices we make about our style of life, who our neighbors will be, what kind of police protection we get, and what kind of schools our children will attend. At least since the Depression, it has been the American Dream to own a home, and young Americans assumed that the labor and housing markets would provide them with the opportunity to do so when they started to raise their children. Dowell Myers and Jennifer Wolch point out that three types of polarization in the housing market developed in the last decade. First, young people—those late baby boom cohorts under age 35 in 1990—were much less likely to own homes than earlier birth cohorts at the same ages. But homeownership increased among those beginning their retirements in the 1980s. Second, during the 1980s there was an increase in both the precariously housed (i.e., low-income renters who devote such a large share of their small incomes to shelter that they are at possible risk of homelessness) and the generously housed (i.e., people who pay a small share of their substantial incomes to obtain spacious and attractive housing). Third, home prices skyrocketed along the Atlantic and Pacific coasts but plunged in economically stagnating midwestern states. Surprisingly, homeownership increased most where prices rose the fastest.

While this volume describes economic trends, in doing so the authors frequently refer to social changes. The second volume focuses on social trends and includes the following chapters: "Growing Diversity and Inequality in the American Family" (Sara McLanahan and Lynne Casper); "The Older Population" (Judith Treas and Ramon Torrecilha); "Children and Youth: Living Arrangements and Welfare" (Dennis P. Hogan and Daniel T. Lichter); "Racial and Ethnic Diversity" (Roderick J. Harrison and Claudette Bennett); "The New Immigrants" (Barry R. Chiswick and Teresa A. Sullivan); and "The New Geography of Population Shifts" (William H. Frey).

A subsequent book by Margo J. Anderson and Stephen Fineberg will describe undercount issues in the 1990 census along with the fierce political controversies and protracted legal battles that they generated. A companion book in this series, by Francisco Rivera-Batiz and Carlos Santiago, describes the population of Puerto Rico.

Throughout the 1990s there will be vibrant debates—in Congress, on the editorial pages, and particularly on the ever-expanding networks of talk radio—about the condition of our country; that is, about the state of the nation. Are the themes that helped unify this country in its first two centuries threatened by increasing economic gaps separating the rich from the poor and two-parent families from those headed by one parent? What policies, if any, should be adopted to guarantee that all Americans have adequate incomes and shelter? Do affirmative action programs benefit minorities and help to integrate them fully into the union we know as the United States or are they divisive? Will the millions of immigrants now arriving from Asia and Latin America lead to a much stronger and more diverse nation or do they take jobs away from natives? These two volumes, *State of the Union: America in the 1990s,* provide basic information about how new social and economic trends emerged in the last several decades, thereby helping us to understand which programs might succeed or fail as we get closer to the millennium year—when the next census will give us a fresh picture of ourselves.

# 1

# Incomes and Income Inequality

FRANK LEVY

TWO MAJOR ECONOMIC goals of an industrialized nation are rising earnings and increased income equality.[1] In terms of growth and equality, U.S. economic history since World War II divides into four economic periods:

- The first quarter-century—1947–1973—saw rapid earnings growth and moderating income inequality.

- From 1974 through 1979, earnings growth slowed to the point of stagnation (though living standards continued to rise)[2] while income inequality grew slightly.

- From 1980 through 1989, *average* earnings continued to stagnate, but income inequality increased sharply. Inequality increased along most dimensions except gender, and the majority of changes worked against the less-educated workers.

- From 1990 through at least 1993, the economy passed through an extended recession in which job losses and wage declines now reached white collar workers, particularly older, college-educated men.

A full history of these 46 years would take more space than this chapter permits. Six years ago, I wrote in detail about the years from the end of World War II through the mid-1980s (Levy 1987). There is little I would add to my description of the 1950s and 1960s—years when median family income almost doubled. But my understanding of the 1970s and 1980s has changed since I think I have a better idea of why productivity growth slowed in the 1970s. I also have a better understanding of the 1980s growth of inequality.[3] For these reasons, this chapter will focus on the years since 1970 and, in particular, since 1973—the year in which productivity and wages entered a period of prolonged stagnation.

The 1950s and 1960s will still appear here as a yardstick. But increasingly they look like a bad yardstick, an aberrational period in U.S. life. Some of the aberrations are obvious. In 1950, the United States accounted for about one-

1

half of the world's output, and so international trade could offer little competitive pressure.[4] But the 1950s and 1960s were also unusual in that productivity and incomes could grow in a relatively balanced way. While the mechanization of agriculture displaced large numbers of workers, many of those same workers could move into factory jobs. The corresponding movement today—from displaced factory worker to computer repairman or lab technician—appears to be more difficult.[5]

The 1950s were also an aberration in the life of the family. As demographer Andrew Cherlin (1988:3–4) writes, the 1950s were

> the only period in the past 150 years when the birthrate rose substantially; in the 1950s young adults married at earlier ages than in any twentieth-century decade before or since; and the increase in divorce was unusually low. Although many people think of the 1950s family as "traditional," the falling birthrates, rising divorce rates, and increasing age at marriage of the 1960s and 1970s [and most of the 1980s] were more consistent with long-term historical trends. (brackets added)

Cherlin's point is relevant to our discussion because the household and family income distributions are shaped by these demographics—for example, by increases in families headed by single women—as well as by the economy per se.

Bad yardsticks make bad measurements. In the 1950s and 1960s, we had both a dynamic computer industry and lifetime job security at IBM. Today, we have a dynamic computer industry but job security is much lower. Are we failing today? Or were the 1950s and 1960s a time that offers few lessons for the present?

Getting the answer right affects our sense of the possible and so affects our mental health. The right answers also give clues to sensible economic behavior—both public and private. When most workers had long careers with large, established firms, we reasonably could assume that their employers would provide their health insurance. In today's economy, when established firms are laying off longtime employees, the assumption becomes untenable. A similar logic applies to the proportion of income that persons save, a proportion that fell sharply in the mid-1970s. In all likelihood, the lower savings rate reflected the replacement of older generations, made cautious by the Great Depression, by younger persons who had known the more tranquil 1950s and 1960s (Bernheim 1991). But if the 1950s and 1960s were unusually tranquil, a cautious outlook and a higher savings rate would be far more realistic.

The tensions among growth, equality, and security in normal economic life are one theme of this chapter. A second, related theme is the extent to which the nation experienced rising inequality over the 1980s. Inequality rose in each of the distributions with which we are concerned: the distributions of male and female earnings, of family incomes, and of household incomes.[6]

In the case of individual earnings, one aspect of inequality was the "college–

high school" earnings gap, a broad-gauge split in the middle of the earnings distribution based on workers' levels of education (Levy and Michel 1987). A second aspect was the growing incomes of "supernovas," the top 250,000 tax-payers (out of 113 million) who received a dramatically larger share of taxable income over the decade (Slemrod 1991; Feenberg and Poterba 1992). The supernovas were part of a third and more subtle "within-group" inequality in which apparently similar persons—persons of the same age, education, gender, and race—received increasingly dissimilar earnings over time for reasons that are not obvious from census data.[7]

When we turn from individual to family incomes, earnings inequality has been exacerbated by changes in family structure. The bottom of the family income distribution has been reshaped by the growing number of families headed by women, most of whom have low incomes. The highest fifth of the distribution is increasingly dominated by high-income, two-earner couples. The household income distribution (which includes all living units, not just families) also contains these changes, but inequality here has been moderated by the growing number of working age persons who live alone.

The 1980s inequality did not apply to every domain: The earnings gap between women and men closed significantly during the decade. And the trend toward inequality did not begin in the 1980s. Within-group earnings inequality began to increase in the early 1970s; the supernova phenomenon first appeared in the 1970s as well; and the growth in families headed by single women has been a topic of discussion (and avoidance) since at least the mid-1960s. But during the 1980s, these different kinds of inequality reinforced each other in ways that made both earnings inequality and family and household income inequality very visible.

More precisely, the visible trend was the combination of inequality with stagnant average earnings and slow-growing family incomes. When average family income grows quickly, greater inequality means that the poor are getting richer while the rich get richer faster, something that may escape public attention. When average family income grows slowly, the case since the early 1970s, inequality means that the rich are getting richer while the poor get poorer, something that certainly will attract attention. When we compare income distributions for 1970 and 1990, we will see that the proportion of high-income families grew faster than the proportion of low-income families, suggesting more people gained than lost over the period.[8] But the experience has been well short of a great rising tide that lifts all boats—the experience of the 1950s and 1960s.

The story that follows is divided into eight sections. In section 1, I address a question that frames the rest of the discussion: What has happened to our standard of living over the last two decades? In section 2, I discuss the distributions of male and female earnings, beginning with the macro- and microeconomic forces that shaped these distributions. The section closes with a geographic perspective on the same data: the ups and downs of the bicoastal economy. In section 3, I discuss the distributions of family and household incomes beginning with a review of demographic changes in household and family structure. This section also closes with a geographic look at the data: the way in which poverty has increasingly become a central-city problem. In section 4, I extend the discussion into several areas that standard census data do not cover: the impact of fringe benefits and taxes, the details of the extreme upper tail of the income distribution, and the distribution of household wealth. In section 5, I summarize the statistics of the previous sections by describing the experience of three broad income groups: the rich, the middle class, and the poor. In section 6, I briefly trace the economic status of four demographic groups that crosscut income levels: children, the elderly, blacks, and Hispanics. In section 7, I focus specifically on the post–1989 period and the "white collar recession," a period that seems to run against the widening college–high school earnings gap described above. In section 8, I return to the issues of income growth and income equality, this time speculating about the future.

## ARE WE GETTING POORER?

Begin with a simple question. What has happened to U.S. living standards since the early 1970s? For at least a decade, we have been told that we are becoming a poor nation, confronted by declining incomes and a growing list of things we want but cannot afford (e.g., Newman 1993). The truth, or exaggeration, in this assertion shapes the rest of this chapter.

By the standard economic yardstick, we are getting richer. Disposable (after-tax) income per capita—the economist's measure of living standards—stood at $10,541 in 1969, $13,212 in 1979, and $15,369 in 1989, before falling to $15,238 in the recession year of 1991. (Uness otherwise noted, all income numbers are adjusted to 1989 dollars using the Personal Consumption Expenditure deflator.)[9] But the robust increase—46 percent over two decades—says more about demographics than about a strong economy.

We can see this by looking at a different statistic—disposable income per *employed person*, that is, earnings plus fringe benefits. This statistic stood at $27,230 in 1969 and $31,005 in 1973, on the eve of the first OPEC oil price shock. Thereafter, it declined to $30,095 in 1979 and rose to $32,380 in 1989 and $32,948 in 1991, an increase of 8 percent per decade.

Income per capita could grow significantly faster than income per employed person because of three demographic/behavioral trends:

- Large numbers of women, eventually including women with very young children, entered the labor force. Between 1970 and 1990, women's labor force participation rate rose from 43.3 to 57.5 percent.[10]

• The biggest baby boom cohorts, born in the late 1950s, entered their 20s and began their careers.

• Unlike their older brothers and sisters, the late baby boomers married relatively late, a fact that helped to postpone and ultimately reduce the number of children they had.

These trends combined to lower the ratio of dependents to workers in the population from 1.44 in 1973 to 1.24 in 1979 and to 1.05 by the late 1980s. Income per capita (per man, woman, and child) could rise, despite stagnant paychecks, because each paycheck was divided among fewer mouths.

Some part of these trends were an adaptation to slow earnings growth, but the part is hard to measure. How many women went to work because their families needed their income? How many went to work as part of women's redefined role in society? Women's labor force participation also rose in the 1950s and 1960s when incomes were growing quickly, a fact that points to redefined roles. But a bad economy might cause roles to be redefined more than they otherwise might have been.

However one deals with this puzzle, one point is clear: Income per capita could not grow faster than income per worker indefinitely. For example, between 1970 and 1987, we saw the growth of "young singles," as the median age of first marriage rose from 20.6 to 23.6 for women and 22.5 to 25.3 for men. Many young singles lived well because they lived alone and had only themselves to support (high per capita income).[11] But eventually, young singles become older. They get married and have children and the slow growth of paychecks becomes more apparent. In a similar way, a family that increases its income by moving from one earner to two cannot so easily move from two earners to three. By 1988, women's labor force participation had leveled off, the baby boom was absorbed in the work force, and the birthrate had turned up again.[12] The ratio of dependents to workers stabilized at about 1.05, and growth in per capita income (living standards) was increasingly tied to the slow growth of individual earnings.[13]

The story of disposable income per capita and income per worker gives one clue to our economic anxiety: Material consumption per person continued to increase after 1973, but the increases required us to make substantial adjustments in our lives. And, as is now clear, these adjustments could take us only so far.

The slow growth of earnings contained a second source of anxiety: the shrinking of an economic safety net. In any period, the economy favors some groups over others. In the early 1970s, oil field workers were in high demand and young college graduates were a glut on the market. In the early 1980s, their positions were reversed. When average earnings grow quickly, a group in low demand can still see its purchasing power rise—the poor getting richer while the rich get richer faster. When average earnings are stagnant, a group in low demand will lose in absolute as well as relative terms. As we will see, this happened to many less-educated men in the 1980s.

In sum, more work and rearranged household structures have allowed the average person to command 46 percent more income today than her 1970 counterpart commanded. But a significant minority has not done as well. And many of those who do live well and who remember more tranquil times are justified in being cautious about the future. I speculate on the future in the final section. In the following section, I begin to explain the present by discussing the economic forces that have shaped earnings since 1970.

## THE DISTRIBUTIONS OF MEN'S AND WOMEN'S EARNINGS

### The Productivity Slowdown

In the nation's economic accounts, wages, salaries, and self-employment income—earnings—constitute about two thirds of all personal income.[14] Thus, men's and women's earnings are a good place to start the discussion. Roughly speaking, an individual's earnings are determined through a two-step process. First, the nation's productivity determines the economy's average wage level in absolute terms. Then, supply and demand determine the individual's wage vis-à-vis the average.

As noted earlier, one measure of the economy's average wage level—disposable income per employed person—grew quite rapidly from World War II through 1973 and much more slowly thereafter. The suddenly slow growth of the average wage reflected the suddenly slow growth of labor productivity.[15] Labor productivity is a technical term with a simple definition:

$$\frac{\text{Gross Domestic Product}}{\text{Total Hours Worked in the Economy}}$$

Written in this way, the importance of productivity is apparent. In the long run, we can consume and invest only the goods that we produce.[16] We can increase everyone's wages—the purchasing power exchanged for an hour of work—only if we increase the value of goods and services that we produce in an hour. On a farm, increased labor productivity comes through better seeds and machinery, improved irrigation, and new patterns of planting. In a warehouse, increased productivity comes from logging orders on a scanner linked to a central computer rather than logging orders on a long paper trail.

Tables 1.1 and 1.2 summarize labor productivity growth after World War II and compare the roughly parallel pattern of growth in the earnings of middle-

TABLE 1.1   Nonfarm labor productivity growth since World War II.

|  | Total (%/year) | Manufacturing Only | Nonmanufacturing[a] |
|---|---|---|---|
| 1947–1973 | +2.6% | +3.0% | +2.3% |
| 1973–1979 | +0.1 | +1.4 | −0.2 |
| 1979–1990 | +0.8 | +2.7 | 0.0 |
| 1990–1992 | +1.2 | +2.5 | +0.7[b] |

SOURCE: Unpublished tabulations from the U.S. Bureau of Labor Statistics.

[a] Excludes government sector.
[b] Author's estimate.

TABLE 1.2   Median annual income of male full-time, year-round workers aged 45–54: 1946–1991.

|  | Median Money Income | Annual Growth Rate | Median Money Income Plus Estimated Fringes | Annual Growth Rate |
|---|---|---|---|---|
| 1946 | $19,012[a] |  | $20,038 |  |
|  |  | +2.5% |  | +2.8% |
| 1973 | 37,247 |  | 42,478 |  |
|  |  | +.3 |  | +1.0 |
| 1979 | 37,958 |  | 45,208 |  |
|  |  | +.2 |  | +.3 |
| 1989 | 38,810 |  | 46,455 |  |
|  |  | −2.1 |  | −1.8 |
| 1991 | 37,198 |  | 44,852 |  |

SOURCE: U.S. Bureau of the Census, *Current Population Reports*, various issues.

Note: The value of fringe benefits is approximated as "Supplements to Wages and Salaries" in the National Income and Product Accounts.

[a] Urban men only. Amount shown in constant 1989 dollars.

aged men. Even when the value of fringe benefits is included, the growth of earnings (like the growth of productivity) slowed dramatically after 1973. The data raise an obvious question: If innovations are so ubiquitous, why did this slowdown occur?[17] Why, in the 1980s, did productivity revive in manufacturing but not in services? And why does productivity now appear to be reviving slowly on an economy-wide basis?

These questions lack definitive answers,[18] but I will sketch a theory that is consistent with the facts. It begins with Landes's description of technological change (1965):

Technological change is never automatic. It means the displacement of established methods, damage of vested interests, often serious human dislocations. Under the circumstances, there usually must be a combination of considerations to call forth such a departure and make it possible: (1) a need or opportunity for improvement

due to inadequacy, present or potential, of prevailing techniques; and (2) a degree
of superiority such that the new methods pay sufficiently to warrant the cost of
change.

Put differently, we know it is straightforward to purchase a set of personal
computers and to put them on employees' desks. It is more difficult to think
through a reorganization of work to take advantage of the computers. It is more
difficult still to actually undertake the reorganization: to redefine responsibilities,
to require employees to learn new skills, to lay employees off. In a world of
imperfect information, these changes involve substantial risk and they give the
status quo a strong appeal.[19]

When markets are growing rapidly and firms are adding capacity, innovation
can be restricted to the new plants and so can be less disruptive.[20] But when
innovations are made to existing capacity they can be very painful. Often, the
biggest motivation for change is pressure from competitors or from declining
markets that put the firm's future in doubt. Managers and line personnel may
prefer the status quo to any reorganization. But if the status quo is untenable,
work reorganization becomes more acceptable.[21]

In the years following 1973, three factors undercut pressures that might have
forced organizational change and productivity growth. The first was inflation.
While inflation had been building in the late 1960s, it accelerated in the early
1970s driven first by a worldwide food shortage and then by the 1973 OPEC
oil price increase (Levy 1987: Chap. 4). Between 1973 and 1979, both the
consumer and producer price indices rose by more than 100 percent. Inflation
increased the uncertainty associated with long-range investments and, equally
important, distorted incentives facing managers within large corporations. In
many cases, these incentives understated inflation's impact on the cost of capital. A bad project (or inaction) might look good on the basis of an operating
profit even as it lowered the firm's asset value.[22] And while inflation created
some cost pressures, employers could hold wage costs in check as long as "cost-
of-living" pay raises lagged behind actual price increases.

A second factor undercutting pressure for change was the declining international value of the dollar. Between 1973 and 1979, the dollar fell by 31 percent
against the mark, 20 percent against the yen, and 15 percent against a trade-
weighted average of currencies (U.S. Council of Economic Advisers 1993: Table B-107). The falling exchange rate meant that a small U.S. printing press
that cost $8,000 here could be sold in Europe as if it cost $6,800. The same
falling exchange rate meant foreign sellers to the United States had to raise their
dollar prices to cover their costs. Both price movements undercut competitive
pressure from foreign firms and our merchandise trade account remained in balance despite stagnant productivity (Krugman and Obstfelt 1987).

A final shield from pressure for change came from the demographic trends mentioned above, which kept markets expanding at moderate rates despite the collapse of wage growth. (For brevity, I will use the term *demographic trends* to included increases in women's labor force participation as well as changes in marriage ages, birthrates, and family structure.) In the booming 1960s, aggregate consumption expenditure, adjusted for inflation, grew by 53 percent. Between 1973 and 1979, aggregate consumption still grew by 33 percent per decade, despite now-stagnant wages, because the number of workers was increasing so fast. From the perspective of a state tax collector, an automobile manufacturer, or an appliance store, more paychecks were substituting for richer paychecks in supporting revenues. But, as we have seen, consumers in the 1970s were also richer in the sense of having higher per capita income, a reflection of fewer dependents per paycheck. The fast-growing labor force and rising per capita income (despite stagnating wages) provided additional protection against long-run contractions that could have forced firms to change.

One partial byproduct of these forces deserves mention—the collapsing earnings premium for a college diploma. On the supply side, the well-educated baby boom cohorts born between 1946 and 1955 moved into the work force in the late 1960s and 1970s and sharply increased the supply of college graduates. On the demand side, economic developments largely favored blue collar workers. Worldwide crop failures and the 1973 OPEC price shock stimulated agricultural and energy production, both industries that provided blue collar jobs. At the same time, the falling value of the dollar stimulated demand for U.S. manufactured goods and slowed manufacturing restructuring that might have eliminated blue collar jobs. Thus, the number of persons employed in manufacturing was 6 percent higher in 1980 than in 1970.

These supply and demand movements translated into a falling earnings premium for a college diploma. In the late 1960s, a 30-year-old male college graduate earned 25 to 30 percent more than his peer with a high school education. By the late 1970s, the college earnings premium at age 30 had shrunk to about 15 percent (Freeman 1976; Levy and Murnane 1992). Taken by itself, the narrowing college–high school earnings gap would have increased earnings equality. But as I noted earlier, there was a second, offsetting force: a growing earnings inequality *among* workers with a high school education, among workers with a college education, and so forth. I return to this point below.

Inflation, demography, and the falling dollar could ease pressure for change, but they could not eliminate it. Since World War II, we had seen family incomes double, and we believed that we could purchase much of what we wanted:[23] a middle-class living for most of the population, expanded Social Security and health benefits for the elderly, sending a man to the moon, a war on poverty. The world after 1973—rapid inflation, slow-growing real earnings—could be partially offset by delaying marriage, reducing fertility, and having a wife go to work, but it still came as quite a shock.

One reaction to the shock was the taxpayers' revolt of the late 1970s, a political movement that culminated in the election of Ronald Reagan (Sears and Citrin 1982). Today, President Reagan's fiscal policies are properly blamed for our large budget deficits. But we should remember how popular those policies were at the time. After seven years of stagnant earnings, tax cuts had enormous political appeal since they would put money into people's pockets. By the same logic, expenditure cuts would have been counterproductive since any cut—in defense, in Social Security, in farm subsidies—would have taken money *out* of someone's pocket. The combination of big tax cuts and much smaller expenditure cuts was what most people wanted at the time. The resulting deficits would have important consequences in the decade that followed.

### The Restructuring of Manufacturing

In one sense, the restructuring of manufacturing began on July 25, 1979, the date on which President Carter appointed Paul Volcker to chair the Federal Reserve. Volcker's appointment was part of a larger set of personnel moves in which William Miller, then chairman of the Fed, was nominated to be secretary of the treasury. The moves were President Carter's response to rapidly worsening economic conditions. Although the country was entering recession, inflation was approaching 10 percent per year and financial markets were scared. Inflation was becoming an economic way of life, and the markets worried that Miller cared less about reducing inflation than about reducing unemployment to prepare for President Carter's reelection campaign. The worries were summarized in the rising price of gold. In the mid-1970s, gold stood at $160 per ounce. The day before Volcker's appointment, gold stood at $307 per ounce. President Carter could calm the fear only by installing an anti-inflation hawk at the Fed, Paul Volcker.

As financial markets expected, Chairman Volcker invoked a severe tight money policy. Interest rates on three-month Treasury bills rose from an average 6.24 percent in 1977–1978 to 11.5 percent in 1980. The rate on a 30-year mortgage rose from 9 percent to 12.7 percent and showed no signs of stopping. Tight money accelerated the economy's slide into recession. The addition of high interest rates to inflation and the deepening recession further undermined Carter's presidency and helped to elect Ronald Reagan. But when Reagan took office, he made it clear that he was willing to tolerate high interest rates and a deep recession to break inflation.[24] December to December inflation fell from 13.3 percent in 1979 and 12.5 percent in 1980 to 8.9 percent in 1981 and 3.8 percent in 1982, a much more rapid decline than most economists had expected.

Other things being equal, the end of inflation should have meant the end of high interest rates. But the end of inflation coincided with the beginning of the Reagan fiscal policy and its big budget deficits. The Treasury's need to borrow large amounts of money and the market's fear that deficits would spur future inflation kept interest rates high. By 1982, the *real* interest on three-year gov-ernment securities rate—the interest rate adjusted for inflation—exceeded 6 per-cent, three times its normal postwar level.

High real interest rates made U.S. securities very attractive both at home and abroad. When foreign investors purchased these securities, they first had to con-vert their own currencies into U.S. dollars. The resulting demand for dollars quickly reversed the currency's falling value, which, as we saw, had kept for-eign competition at bay. By 1984, the average value of the dollar in terms of foreign currencies was 55 percent higher than it had been five years earlier (U.S. Council of Economic Advisers 1993: Table B-107).

Manufacturing firms were already weakened by the deep recession. High real interest rates and the high dollar weakened them further by making U.S. exports very expensive overseas and by making foreign imports cheap. As a result, U.S. manufacturing faced restricted opportunities for expansion. Simultane-ously, high real interest rates raised investors' standards for an acceptable rate of return, a standard that many manufacturers now could not meet.[25] The result was a wave of downsizing and reorganization within manufacturing including mergers and takeovers, outsourcing production to foreign countries, and the in-troduction of new technology.

Together, these changes helped to revive manufacturing productivity growth over the 1980s.[26] The immediate beneficiaries were stockholders, managers, in-vestment bankers, and, in some cases, skilled labor. The financial industry also benefited from the growing number of government bonds that had to be sold.[27]

The losers were semiskilled labor, men and women who had not gone beyond high school and who held jobs that paid $10–$18 per hour. Among men aged 25–55 who had not gone beyond high school, 23 percent were employed in durable manufacturing in 1979 and more than half of these men were earning more than $30,000 per year (i.e., $15 per hour).

During the 1980s, total durable goods employment declined by 1 million workers, and within this total the decline in semiskilled blue collar labor—machine operators, assemblers, and inspectors—was 1.4 million (Table 1.3). Higher-skilled precision production workers—machinists, mechanics, and vari-ous technicians—actually grew by 440,000 while "all other occupations"—managers, sales representatives, engineers, accountants, and other white collar occupations—remained roughly stable.

The loss of semiskilled jobs was not confined to firms that faced import com-petition (Berman, Bound, and Griliches 1993). But it is reasonable to speculate that firms facing foreign competition were among the first forced to make such changes, and the examples they set diffused through other firms via imitation.[28]

In the language of supply and demand, reorganized work was a demand-side change that hurt semiskilled labor. But semiskilled labor was also hurt by two supply-side changes. One was increased competition from immigration. Abowd and Freeman (1991) estimate that legal and illegal immigration represented 23

TABLE 1.3    Selected occupational categories in durable
manufacturing (in thousands).

|  | 1979 | 1989 | % Change (1979–1989) |
|---|---|---|---|
| Precision Production Workers | 2,641 | 3,081 | + 17% |
| Machine Operators, Assemblers, Inspectors | 5,341 | 3,933 | − 26 |
| All Other Occupations | 6,509 | 6,330 | − 3 |
| Total employment | 14,491 | 13,344 | − 8 |

SOURCE: Author's tabulation of the Current Population Survey.

percent of labor force growth in the 1980s, up from 12 percent in the 1970s. The second supply-side change was the steady decline in union membership from 25 percent of agricultural workers in 1970 to 16 percent in 1989, a trend that further weakened the bargaining power of industrial workers (Freeman 1993).

Declining demand for semiskilled workers was one of three new occupational trends that emerged in the 1980s.[29] The others were the accelerated growth of managers and administrators and of sales occupations. Managers and administrators accounted for about 10 percent of jobs in 1979. But they accounted for 20 percent of net jobs added during the 1980s, the "decade of the M.B.A." As Wetzel shows in his chapter on the labor force and Bianchi shows in her chapter on women, many of these new managerial positions went to women, one aspect of women's increased economic mobility during the 1980s.

Sales occupations grew at a similar rate, spurred by both the growth in retail trade and the rapid expansion of the financial sector in which stockbrokers and similar positions are counted by the census as sales personnel. Like managers and administrators, sales positions accounted for 10 percent of all jobs in 1979, but 22 percent of net jobs added over the next 10 years.[30] Just as many of the eliminated machine operator jobs were held by high school graduates, most of the managerial occupations and a significant number of the sales occupations (particularly in finance) went to persons with higher education.

The resulting changes in labor demand were a sharp reversal of the 1970s. Recall that by the end of the 1970s, college graduates were a glut on the market and a college–high school earnings gap for men aged 25–34 had shrunk to about 20 percent—$27,900 for college versus $23,100 for high school (Table 1A.1). During the 1980s, the earnings of male college graduates rose slightly but the earnings of male high school graduates collapsed so that by 1989 the earnings gap had expanded to 47 percent—$28,700 for college graduates aged 25–34 and $19,500 for high school graduates. It was, as a result, much harder for younger high school graduates to buy a home and in other ways enter the middle class. I look at these patterns in more detail in a later section.

## The Next Step

What changes once can change again. As this chapter is being written, the 1980s explosion of managers, administrators, and sales personnel appears to have been a precursor to the "white collar recession" of the early 1990s, a new management mind-set in both manufacturing and service sector firms that focuses on restructuring work and eliminating middle management positions to improve productivity.[31] If these developments are as extensive as their publicity, they have the power to cause the college–high school earnings gap to shrink once again. I return to the white collar recession and the events that underlie it in a later section.

## What Census Data Say about Male and Female Earnings

Figures 1.1 and 1.2 compare the distributions of male earnings for 1969–1979 and 1979–1989 (in 1989 dollars). The distributions are limited to men aged 25–54 (hereafter, prime working age men) to eliminate the artificially low

FIGURE 1.1    Earnings of men aged 25–54: 1969 and 1979.

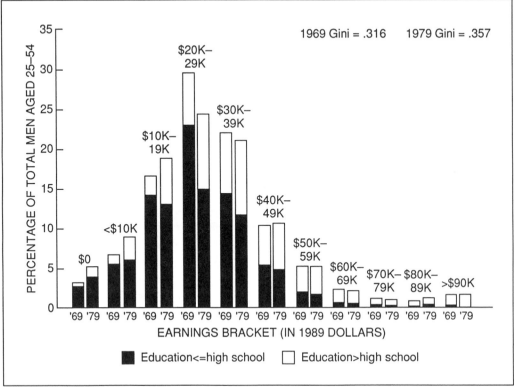

FIGURE 1.2 Earnings of men aged 25–54: 1979 and 1989.

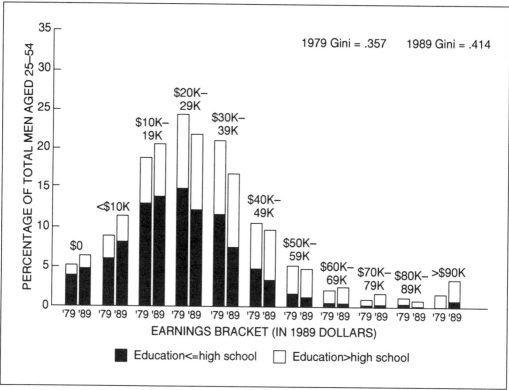

earnings of young men still in school and of older men who are moving into retirement. They include men who reported no earnings in 1969, 1979, or 1989. Shifts in the distributions over time mirror the history just presented.[32] Note that the height of each bar shows the total percentage of men in each income category. The dark portion shows the percentage with a high school education or less, while the open portion shows the percentage with more than a high school education.

Figures 1.1 and 1.2 make three points—two obvious and one hidden. The hidden aspect is the way in which the two distributions have roughly the same midpoint: the previously mentioned slow growth of earnings. In the 1950s and 1960s, real median male earnings grew by about 30 percent per decade (Table 1.2). Had anything like that growth continued over the last 20 years, earnings in 1989 would have been centered close to $45,000, half-again as large as the midpoint for 1969. In fact, the midpoint of the 1989 distribution is about $28,000, a reflection of the sharp slowdown in productivity growth that began in 1973.

A second, more visible feature is the growth of inequality in the distribution, particularly after 1979. Statistically speaking, inequality can increase in many different ways: for example, a stable lower half and an elongated upper tail. Over the 1980s, inequality in the male earnings distribution took the form of a moderate "hollowing out" of the middle, with growing numbers of men both above $50,000 and below $20,000 and fewer men in between. There is no formal definition of a middle-class job, but this hollowing out is consistent with discussions of a shrinking number of middle-class jobs. The Gini coefficient, a standard measure of income inequality, stood at .316 in 1969, .357 in 1979, and .414 in 1989.[33]

The third point is the post-1979 deterioration in the position of men who did not go beyond high school. By 1989, one third of working men aged 35–44 with 12 years of education reported earnings of less than $20,000. Among men aged 25–34, the proportion was over one-half.[34] Thus, a large part of the story of the vanishing middle-class jobs is a story about men who have not gone beyond high school.

This general picture—growing earnings inequality between more- and less-educated workers—was not limited to the United States. Davis (1992) shows that earnings differences between more- and less-educated males also increased in a number of European countries during the 1980s. The growth of earnings inequality was greater in the United States than in Europe, but this means little because European countries experienced greater long-term unemployment—that is, more persons who were not counted in earnings statistics because they had no earnings. More unemployed in Europe and more low-wage work in the United States—in both cases, the root cause was a declining demand for less-educated labor.

Earlier, I noted that growing 1980s inequality in male and female earnings had several aspects: a widening split along educational lines, but also a growing inequality *among* men (or women) of similar age, education, and other observable characteristics. Figure 1.3 contains one example of this increasing "within-group" inequality, the earnings distributions for men aged 25–34 with exactly four years of college for 1979 and 1989. *Median* earnings for the two groups of men were roughly equal (Table 1A.1). But earnings among the 1989 group are more spread out with slight gains at the lower tail and greater gains at the upper tail.

Figures 1.4 and 1.5 show the annual earnings distributions of women aged 25–54, a picture that differs substantially from that of men.[35] In both decades, but particularly in the 1980s, the proportion of working women with annual earnings between $20,000 and $50,000 increased and the proportion with earnings over $50,000 increased slightly. Overall, inequality increased modestly, with the Gini coefficient rising from .344 in 1969 to .367 in 1979 and 0.386 in 1989. These figures exclude women who had no earnings in 1969, 1979, or 1989.

FIGURE 1.3    Earnings of men aged 25–34 with four years of college: 1979 and 1989.

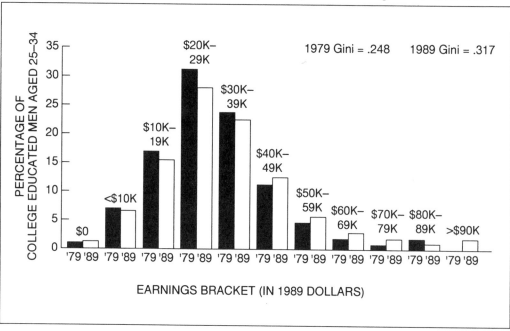

Among female high school graduates and dropouts, increased annual earnings reflected a slight fall in hourly wages and more hours of work per year (Mishel and Bernstein 1993: Table 3.21). College graduates, by contrast, experienced rising wages, driven in part by the previously mentioned movement into managerial, administrative, and professional occupations.

As a group, then, women continued to earn less than men of the same age and education (Table 1A.1), but during the 1980s the gap slowly narrowed. The annual earnings of male high school graduates declined sharply, whereas the earnings of female high school graduates held roughly constant. The annual earnings of male college graduates held constant, whereas the earnings of female college graduates rose significantly.

The result was modest convergence in the female/male earnings ratio, a widely cited indicator of women's economic status, from .597 in 1970 to .716 in 1990.[36] As Blau and Kahn (1992) point out, this limited convergence presents a paradox. United States men and women are closer in education, labor market experience, and occupational status than men and women in many other industrialized countries. Yet compared with those same countries, the United States female/male earnings ratio is quite low.

The authors argue that the problem is not simply discrimination against

FIGURE 1.4  Earnings of women aged 25–54: 1969 and 1979.

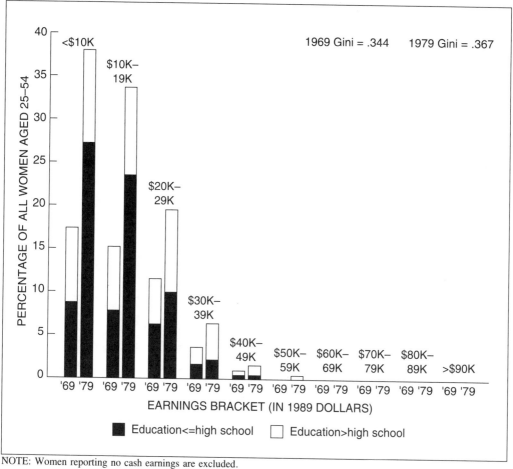

NOTE: Women reporting no cash earnings are excluded.

women, but the very unequal wage structure among United States men. For example, suppose that the characteristics of the average working woman make her "equivalent" to men at the 40th percentile of the male earnings distribution. If the male earnings distribution is very equal, earnings at the 40th and 50th percentiles of the male distribution will be close in dollar terms; thus, the female/male ratio of average earnings will be near 1.0. If the male earnings distribution is very unequal, earnings at the 40th and 50th percentiles will be far apart in dollar terms; thus, the female/male ratio of average earnings will be lower.[37]

As we have seen, the United States male earnings distribution became substantially less equal during the 1980s. This means that while women were gaining on men in terms of characteristics, the dollar penalty for being below aver-

FIGURE 1.5   Earnings of women aged 25–54: 1979 and 1989.

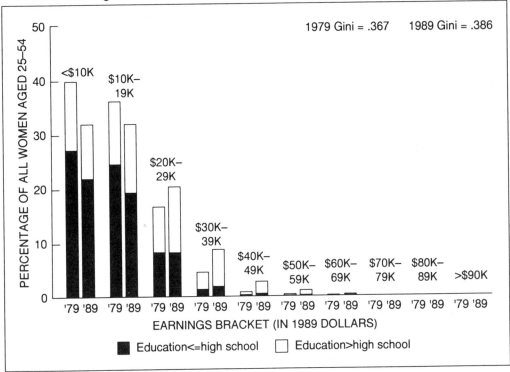

NOTE: Women reporting no cash earnings are excluded.

age was increasing; thus, women were, in essence, swimming upstream. Blau and Kahn estimate that if male earnings inequality had not increased during the 1980s, the female/male earnings gap would have closed by more (to about .75) than actually occurred.[38]

## Earnings and Geography: Bicoastalism

One other dimension of earnings inequality is usefully discussed at this point: earnings inequality across regions. Most economic events—even the falling and rising college premium—have a geographic dimension. Frey's Chapter 6 in Volume 2 describes the nation's changing economic geography. Here, I underline two of those changes—the fall, rise, and second fall of bicoastalism, and, in the next section, growing family income differences between city and suburb.

In the years since World War II, U.S. regional geography has been dominated by two kinds of migration. Among regions, migration flowed out of the North and East and toward the South and West. Within regions, migration flowed toward large metropolitan areas. Movements toward large metropolitan areas reflected rapid gains in agricultural productivity, which meant reduced demand for farm labor. Movements to the South and West had several motivations, including the desire of northern and midwestern manufacturers to move to low-wage, nonunion southern sites and the preference of individuals (and aircraft manufacturers) for a good climate. Eventually, these regional movements became self-reinforcing. As the Pacific coast states grew from 10.4 million persons in 1940 to 26.5 million persons in 1970, it became more efficient to move production to the region rather than, for example, to produce California's automobiles in Michigan. These jobs that followed the population further increased western and southern opportunity, a draw to yet more inmigration.

The "rural renaissance" of the late 1960s and early 1970s marked a temporary reversal of these trends. It was a period in which the populations of rural areas and small metropolitan areas—many in the nation's heartland—grew more rapidly than the populations of large, coastal metropolitan areas.[39] As Frey (1990) notes, the renaissance was driven by the same macroeconomic factors described earlier. The 1972–1973 worldwide food shortage created a boom in agricultural commodities that slowed the migration out of farming areas. The 1973–1974 OPEC oil price rise created an energy boom in Texas, Louisiana, and Oklahoma. The steadily falling dollar helped to limit change in older, smokestack firms—what would soon be called "Rustbelt" firms. Thus, the rural renaissance was the geographic equivalent of the boom for blue collar and semiskilled labor and the falling college–high school earnings gap.[40] Since the coastal areas had generally higher incomes than interior areas, this blue collar boom—a force for individual earnings equality—was also a force for regional income equality.

The rural renaissance attracted substantial media attention, but it was over by 1976 (Forestall 1987; Long and DeAre 1988). By the early 1980s, food and oil were in surplus with falling prices, while the recession and fast-rising dollar was putting significant pressure on traditional smokestack industries. At the same time, the rapidly growing industries of finance, real estate, defense manufacturing, computers, and software were both more intensive in their use of college-educated labor and more concentrated on the Atlantic and Pacific coasts. This was the bicoastal economy, the geographic equivalent of the growing college–high school earnings gap. It increased inequality both within the earnings distribution and among regions (Eberts 1989).

As this chapter is being written, it appears that trends might be reversing again. While the national labor market was beginning to enter a recovery, some coastal areas—particularly the Northeast and Southern California—remained very weak. This, too, was a story of specific industries: shrinkage in real estate, financial services, and defense contractors, the industries that had sustained these regions through the 1982 recession. Thus, the white-collar recession was also a bicoastal recession. I discuss its impact on the college–high school earnings gap in a later section.

## THE DISTRIBUTIONS OF HOUSEHOLD AND FAMILY INCOMES

### Demography

If living arrangements were fixed, shifts in the household and family incomes would simply mirror shifts in earnings patterns.[41] But living arrangements change and these changes have independent impacts on household and family incomes. McLanahan and Casper's Chapter 1 in Volume 2 details trends in households and family structure. What follows is a brief review of these trends as they affect the household and family income distributions. A household, as defined by the Census Bureau, includes one or more persons who share a housing unit. A family is two or more persons who are related to each other by blood, marriage, or adoption and who share a housing unit.

Earlier I quoted Cherlin's description of the historically unusual nature of 1950s households. The television family of the 1950s—Ozzie and Harriet Nelson—represented a division of labor in which the husband earned income while the wife worked at home.[42] But Ozzie and Harriet represented other things, not all of them in the script. They married young and until they married they had probably lived with their parents or in a college dorm. Their first sexual encounter was very likely with each other (Cherlin 1988). Once married, they expected to stay married—slightly more than one in every four 1950s marriages ended in divorce. And the marriage, on average, produced something close to three children. (David and Ricky Nelson constituted less than the average number.)

In sum, marriage, sex, and children occurred together, occurred early in a woman's life, and occurred for most women (and men). The households of this era had three main characteristics:

- Most households were families. Few persons lived by themselves or with unrelated roommates.

- Children were the norm. As late as 1970, 55 percent of families and 45 percent of households contained at least one child under age 18.

- Most families, including most families with children, were husband-wife families in which the wife did not work.

Each of these propositions is far less true today.

- Nearly one-third of households are *not* families. Most of these nonfamily households contain only one person—young persons living on their own, divorced men, and older women who have outlived their husbands.

- Far fewer households (and families) have children—about 34 percent of all households today compared with 45 percent in 1970.

- Households with children are far less likely to be husband-wife families. Twenty-two percent of children now live in mother-only families compared with 8 percent in 1960.[43] And of those children who live in husband-wife families, three-quarters live in a family in which the mother works.

Between the time of Ozzie and Harriet and the time of the Simpsons, then, sex no longer guaranteed children, while neither sex nor children guaranteed marriage.[44] The reasons behind these trends, insofar as they are known, are discussed in Chapter 1 of Volume 2. My more narrow purpose is to point out their implications for a study of living standards and income inequality.

Earlier, I noted that the Census Bureau defines a family as two or more related persons who share a living unit. Since one third of today's households are *not* families, a picture of the population's living standards must include both the household income distribution as well as the family income distribution. At the same time, average household size has fallen sharply from 3.14 persons in 1960 to 2.63 persons in the early 1990s, while average family size has fallen in a similar way. A picture of household and family income that ignores this shrinkage will understate gains in living standards and may mismeasure inequality.[45] Finally, it is risky to assume that children's incomes are similar to incomes in the total population. When only 34 percent of households have children, families with children may differ sharply from families or households without children. I address the specific question of the children's living standards in a later section.

The impact of demography on inequality differs between families and households. Two demographic trends affect family income inequality. One is the growing number of female-headed families. On average, female-headed families have very low incomes; thus, their growing numbers expand the bottom of the family income distribution.

Demographics also affect family incomes through the growing number of working wives, but the story here is more complex. Twenty years ago, working wives typically had husbands with low earnings. Their combined (moderate) family incomes thickened the middle of the distribution. Since then, the proportion of wives who work has grown steadily and recent increases have been concentrated among wives of high-earning husbands. Between 1969 and 1989, among families with incomes between $30,000 and $40,000, the proportion relying on two earners or more rose from .53 to .57. But among families with incomes between $70,000 and $80,000, the proportion rose from .61 to .77. Most wives now work—not just wives of husbands with very low incomes—and the growing number of two-earner, high-income families increased income inequality.[46]

Of course, low-income, female-headed families and high-income, two-earner families appear in the household income distribution, too. But their impact on *household* income inequality is dampened by a third demographic trend: the growing number of persons who live alone. As recently as 20 years ago, single-person households were disproportionately persons with very low incomes—the elderly and the disabled. Had this remained the case, more single-person households would have meant a growing bottom tail of the household income distribution. But the recent growth of single-person households has involved prime working age persons—young persons who delayed marriage and middle-aged persons who are divorced.[47] These were more likely to be persons of moderate-to-middle incomes, located near the middle of the distribution. As such, they moderated the disequalizing effects of female-headed families and two-earner families.

The preceding arguments can be summarized in three points:

- Over the 1980s, both men's earnings and women's earnings became less equal. On the basis of these earnings trends, we should expect, other things constant, that both the family and household income distributions should grow less equal as well.

- Family income inequality has been increased both by less equal earnings and by two demographic factors: more female-headed families (with low incomes) and more two-earner, high-income families.

- The household income distribution contains the disequalizing demographics of the family income distribution and a third factor that works in the other direction: the growing number of moderate-income persons who lived in single-person households.

We should expect, other things being equal, that family income inequality has increased more than household income inequality. We should also expect in both cases that increased inequality had both economic and demographic causes.[48]

### What Census Data Say about Household and Family Incomes

The household and family income distributions for 1969 and 1989 are displayed in Figure 1.6 and 1.7, respectively. In Figure 1.6 the total height of a bar reports the percentage of total households in an income category, while in Figure 1.7 it represents the percentage of total families.

Over these 20 years, the household distribution shifted to slightly higher ground, with median household income rising from $26,402 to $28,906. At the tails of the distribution, the proportion of households with incomes below $20,000 fell by 4.5 percentage points (from 38.2 to 33.7 percent), while the proportion of households with incomes above $60,000 increased by 11.5 percentage points (from 5.0 to 16.5 percent). Because the upper tail increased

FIGURE 1.6    Household income distribution: 1969 and 1989.

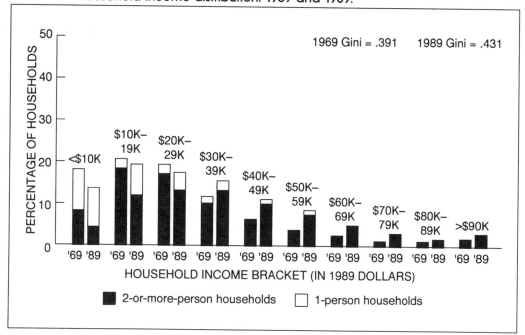

faster than the lower tail declined, the Gini coefficient of the distribution rose from .391 to .431 over the period.

What part of the growing inequality among households reflects less equal earnings and what part reflects changed living arrangements? Several economists who looked at this question have arrived at similar answers: About three fifths of the increased inequality reflects less equal individual earnings and other economic factors,[49] while the remaining two fifths reflects changed living arrangements. For example, Ryscavage et al. (1992) estimate that if household structures had stayed at their 1969 levels, the 1989 Gini coefficient for household incomes would have stood at .411 rather than its actual value of .431. (Recall that the 1969 Gini was .391.)[50]

At first glance, the household income distribution appears to be an example of the "good" inequality, where the poor get richer slowly while the rich get richer a little faster. If we mean this as a statement about the economy, we have to be careful because the pattern owes as much to demography as to economics.

I can illustrate this point by turning to the family income distribution over the same period (Figure 1.7). Between 1969 and 1989, median family income rose from $29,688 to $34,212, with about one half of the increase occurring by 1973. But, as anticipated above, inequality in the family income distribution increased more rapidly than in the household income distribution, with the Gini coefficient rising from .349 to .401. The rise of inequality around a slow-grow-

FIGURE 1.7   Family income distribution: 1969 and 1989.

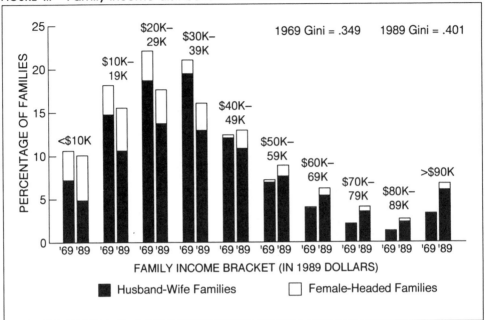

ing median meant that the proportion of families with incomes above $40,000 grew, the proportion of families with incomes below $10,000 stayed roughly constant, and the distribution's middle thinned out substantially (Figure 1.7). This is closer to the "bad" inequality, where the rich get richer while the poor get poorer or just hang on. It is the kind of inequality described by persons who perceive a vanishing middle class.

As Figures 1.6 and 1.7 show, however, both the "good" and "bad" inequality contain a large dose of demographics. In Figure 1.7, the stable proportion of families with incomes below $10,000 was dominated by increased numbers of female-headed families. Without these families, it is plausible that the whole family income distribution would have moved to higher incomes.[51] The household income distribution did shift to higher incomes, but the shift was largely driven by increased numbers of moderate-income persons who lived alone. Without these persons, the household income distribution would have looked more like the family income distribution.

The basic point is that after 1973 average household incomes, family incomes, and earnings all grew at very slow rates. When average growth is slow, demographics (or any other change in inequality) exert a large impact on living standards. In the rapid growth of the 1950s and 1960s, living standards would have risen in the face of almost any demographics.

The impact of growth on living standards can be seen in Table 1.4, which

TABLE 1.4    Shape of the family income distribution, 1949–1991.

| | Share of All Family Income Going to Each One-Fifth (Quintile) of Families | | | | | | | Median |
|---|---|---|---|---|---|---|---|---|
| | Quintile 1 | Quintile 2 | Quintile 3 | Quintile 4 | Quintile 5 | Top 5 Percent[a] | Gini Coefficient | Family Income |
| 1949 | 4.5% | 11.9% | 17.3% | 23.5% | 42.7% | 16.9% | .378 | $15,536 |
| 1959 | 4.9 | 12.3 | 17.9 | 23.8 | 41.1 | 15.9 | .361 | 22,152 |
| 1969 | 5.6 | 12.4 | 17.7 | 23.7 | 40.6 | 15.6 | .349 | 29,687 |
| 1979 | 5.3 | 11.6 | 17.5 | 24.1 | 41.6 | 15.7 | .365 | 32,821 |
| 1989 | 4.6 | 10.6 | 16.5 | 23.7 | 44.6 | 17.9 | .401 | 34,213 |
| 1991 | 4.5 | 10.7 | 16.6 | 24.1 | 44.2 | 17.1 | .397 | 32,719 |

SOURCE: *Current Population Reports,* Series P60 various issues.

[a] Also included in the fifth (richest) quintile's share. Amounts are in 1989 dollars.

presents historical data as displayed in annual Census Bureau publications: with median family income and the share of total family income going to each fifth (quintile) of families. During the 1950s and 1960s, family incomes became only slightly more equal. But family incomes were *rising* throughout the distribution so that most families gained ground. Growth was strong enough to overcome some negative demographics. Recall that the growing number of female-headed households became an issue in the mid-1960s (Rainwater and Yancy 1967). Yet over the 1960s, average income among the poorest one fifth of families grew by about 50 percent.

Another aspect of Table 1.4 requires comment: the lack of a long-run trend in family income inequality. It fell through the 1950s and 1960s and then increased particularly in the 1980s. But family income inequality in 1989 was not radically larger than in 1949, and so it is reasonable to ask whether today's level of inequality should be an issue.

In at least one sense, the answer is yes.[52] In 1949, the poorest fifth of families contained large numbers of farm families with very low cash incomes[53] and large numbers of elderly families, most of whom lacked either Social Security or a private pension. Since 1949, the number of farm families has fallen from about 12 percent to 3 percent of all families. And as Treas and Torrecilha show in their chapter in Volume 2, elderly families since 1970 have gained income at a much faster rate than the national average. Other things constant, these trends should have caused a substantial decline in family income inequality. In reality, other things were not constant and the growing number of female-headed families became the new occupants of the lowest quintile.

A final issue, buried in Table 1.4 (and Figures 1.6 and 1.7), is the shrinking size of households and families and its effect on living standards. When a table or graph simply compares family incomes at two points in time, it conceals the way in which declining family size can raise living standards in some or all parts of the distribution. Does correction for living unit size make a difference?

With respect to the level of income, the answer is clearly yes. A careful analysis by Karoly (1993: Table 2B.1) shows that median family income grew by 15 percent between 1969 and 1989, but the median of family income adjusted for family size[54] grew by 27 percent over the same period. Put simply, today's family (or household) and the family of 20 years ago may have similar dollar incomes. But today's family divides that income among fewer persons.

With respect to inequality, adjusting income for family size makes little difference in the story we have told. Between 1979 and 1989, family income adjusted for family size grew by about 2 percent in the bottom quarter of the distribution and by 15–20 percent in the top quarter.

### Income and Geography: The Isolation of Cities

Earlier, I discussed the relationship between earnings changes and bicoastalism. To conclude this section, I briefly review a geographic dimension of family and household incomes—the growing income difference between city and suburb. The argument sketched here is discussed in more detail by both Frey (in Volume 2) and Kasarda (in this volume).

One of the trends I described was the long-run migration toward large metropolitan areas. *Within* metropolitan areas, a simultaneous migration was the move from the central city to the suburbs. Suburban migration had many origins including the desire for a single-family home. But the migration was reinforced over time by our system of governmental finance in which each jurisdiction relies heavily on its local tax base. In this system, a move to the suburbs often meant a move to lower taxes.

From the perspective of central cities, migration from rural areas had largely offset the city-to-suburb move, allowing central-city populations to hold their own for a decade or more after World War II. But this balance temporarily changed with the rural renaissance of the late 1960s and early 1970s and the redirection of rural migration to smaller metropolitan areas. During the renaissance, most large metropolitan areas grew slowly, and some in the Northeast and Midwest actually lost population, (see Chapter 6 in Volume 2). And when large metropolitan areas grew slowly, their central cities lost population. New York City's population fell from 7.9 million in 1970 to 7.1 million in 1980, Philadelphia's fell from 1.9 million to 1.7 million, and Los Angeles' grew only slightly from 2.8 million to 2.9 million. To the extent that central cities grew in the 1970s, growth occurred in places like Phoenix, San Jose, and Riverside (Frey and Speare 1988: Table 7.3).

The end of the rural renaissance meant a return to longer-run trends and the migration of population toward large coastal metropolitan areas. In some cases—Boston, New York, and San Francisco—central-city populations began to grow again. But even in these cases, the outmigration of middle-class families (now including black middle-class families) continued.

The movement to the suburbs can be summarized in four statistics describing large metropolitan areas (i.e., areas with populations over 1 million). In 1970, 41 percent of the population in these areas lived in central cities. Median family income in these central cities was $33,370, whereas suburban income was $41,880. By 1990, the cities' share of area population had fallen moderately to 35 percent and the income gap had widened: median city income remained roughly constant at $32,918, whereas suburban income, at $47,376, was almost half again as large.

The constant central-city median income did not mean a constant central-city income distribution. As the middle class migrated to the suburbs, city populations tended more toward the rich and the poor. In 1970, poverty was still a rural problem, with almost half of all poor living outside any metropolitan area. Poverty in central cities was real, but manageable: One of every seven central city residents was poor and central-city poor (in all central cities, not only those with populations over 1 million) accounted for about one third of all poor in the nation.

By 1990, poverty was much more of an urban problem. The poverty rate had grown from one-in-seven to one-in-five and central cities now accounted for 42 percent of all U.S. poor. The shift was particularly dramatic for children: Central cities now were home to 45 percent of all poor children and almost one central-city child in three was poor (U.S. Bureau of the Census 1992. "Poverty in the United States: 1991").

The effect was to further reinforce the advantage of the suburbs. Now, a move to the suburbs meant not only an escape from higher taxes but an escape from the violence, bad schools, and other correlates of U.S. poverty. As Edsall (1992:29) writes:

> Just as America's suburbs are becoming functionally independent of center cities . . . suburban voters are also increasingly able to provide for their civic needs through locally based taxes. . . . In the past, public concern over issues such as education, recreation and the quality of municipal services could be taken advantage of, in political terms, to build a national consensus in support of an activist federal government. Now, the growth of suburbia and of suburban government provides a means to address public concerns, while confining services and benefits to local residents.

I return to the connection of poverty and cities in later sections.

## WHAT CENSUS STATISTICS DO NOT SAY

Without Census Bureau data—the decennial census and the annual Current Population Survey (CPS)—research on the U.S. income distribution would be impossible.[55] But these data sets, like all economic data sets, have limitations that reduce their ability to describe the economy. In this section, I review the missing items and ask whether a fuller data set would change the story presented so far.

At the outset, both the census and the CPS undercount the income they purport to measure because persons understate certain types of income—particularly interest and dividends. Also, the two data sets describe income and earnings, but not wealth. While persons often think of income and wealth together, researchers interested in wealth must look to other data sources. I return to the distribution of wealth in a moment.

Other limitations in the census and CPS apply to income data per se:

*Income reporting limits:* In part to protect confidentiality, census forms record incomes only up to fixed limits. In 1992, a person whose wage and salary income exceeded $300,000 was recorded as earning "$300,000 or above."[56] When the Census Bureau calculates distribution statistics for publication, it treats the number as $300,000. If the number of very high earners is growing (as it did in the 1980s), their share of total earnings will be obscured in this calculation.

*Income definition:* Historically, census statistics have measured money income excluding capital gains. The focus on money income misses the growing importance of other kinds of income, such as employer-provided health insurance, Medicaid, Medicare, and food stamps. The exclusion of capital gains potentially blurs income trends in a decade like the 1980s when the stock market and real estate (for part of the decade) did very well.

*Taxes:* The Census Bureau collects data on pretax income. This is a practical decision since few people could quickly tell an interviewer the amount of federal, state, and local taxes they pay. But the convention obscures the effect of taxes on living standards and income inequality.

How important are these omissions for income level and income inequality? The net effect of adding omitted items like the value of insurance and subtracting taxes lowers the level of median household income by about 10 percent but does not affect its trend over time. For example, the census has reestimated median household income correcting for taxes and most omissions except income reporting limits.[57] In 1989, the census estimate of median household income was $32,706. The same estimate adjusted for taxes paid (an income loss) and the value of government programs and employer-provided benefits (an income gain) was $30,451. Under either definition, the growth of median household income between 1979 and 1989 was about 4 percent (U.S. Bureau of the Census 1992. "Measuring the Effect of Benefits and Taxes on Income and Poverty: 1979–1991": Table D).

To determine the effects of omissions on inequality, it is necessary to introduce other data sets. Detailed statistics on very high incomes (above the census reporting limits) are available annually from the U.S. Treasury. These Treasury data have their own limitations[58] but the U.S. Congressional Budget Office (CBO) has made a merge of the two data sets that gives a more complete view of the household income distribution.

The first two rows of Table 1.5 compare usual census estimates and comparable CBO estimates of household income inequality over the 1980s. The CBO estimate differs from the census estimate by including income from capital gains and putting no upper limit on reported income.[59] With these additions, the CBO estimate of 1979 household income inequality is higher than the census estimate for the same year—no surprise there. The relevant fact is that CBO reports a greater increase in inequality over the 1980s than does the Census Bureau. The faster growth of inequality in the CBO estimate indicates that during the 1980s census income cutoffs obscured significant income growth at the extreme upper end of the distribution, a point to which I return in the next section.

The effect of the exclusion of taxes in published statistics is illustrated in the comparison between the second and third rows, CBO estimates of the household income distribution before and after all taxes paid. Taken as a whole, the tax system is mildly progressive, so that after-tax income is more equal than pretax income. But over the 1980s, inequality in after-tax income grew as rapidly as inequality in pretax income. This is consistent with the analysis of CBO data by Gramlich, Kasten, and Sammartino (1993), which indicates that over the 1980s federal taxes became somewhat less progressive, but the tax changes account for only a small part of the growth in household income inequality.

TABLE 1.5   Gini coefficient measures
of household income inequality
under alternative definitions.

|  | 1979 | 1989 |
|---|---|---|
| Standard Census Definition (pretax money income, no capital gains, income reporting limits) | .403 | .429 |
| CBO Definition (pretax money income, includes capital gains, no income reporting limits) | .467 | .526 |
| CBO Definition Less Taxes | .424 | .485 |

SOURCES: U.S. Bureau of the Census (1992. "Measuring the Effect of Benefits and Taxes on Income and Poverty: 1979–1991.") and unpublished tabulations of the Congressional Budget Office.

Census calculations suggest that the remaining omission—the value of noncash income—does not have a significant effect on estimates of income inequality.[60]

To summarize, a more accurate measure of income would change the census story of the 1980s in one key respect: The increase in income inequality would have been greater. The increase would have been driven by the growth of very high incomes that the census caps off for confidentiality reasons. The remainder of the census story, including the slow growth of average household income, would have remained unchanged even when items like health insurance are included in income.

## The Distribution of Wealth

While income statistics are collected annually by the Census Bureau and the Treasury, the best wealth data are collected only periodically by the Federal Reserve Board in its Survey of Consumer Finances (SCF).[61] A good analysis of these data has been performed by Wolff (1993) using the SCF for 1962, 1983, and 1989.[62] His major focus is on the distribution of "marketable wealth"— roughly, the market value of a household's real estate and financial assets less its outstanding debts.[63]

As Wolff shows, the distribution of household wealth in any year is far more unequal than the distribution of household income (Table 1.6), with Gini coefficients in the range of .80 (where the Gini coefficient of household income is about .40). Between 1962 and 1983, wealth increased by 17–22 percent per decade in all parts of the distribution and the Gini coefficient of the wealth distribution remained unchanged at .80. Between 1983 and 1989, growth across the distribution was far less equal. Average wealth per household in the top 1 percent of the distribution grew at a rate of 66 percent per decade, average wealth per household in the bottom 80 percent of the distribution did not grow, and the Gini coefficient increased from .80 to .84. Thus, wealth inequality, like income inequality, increased in the 1980s.

Earlier in this section, I noted evidence of rapid income growth in the extreme upper tail of the distribution. In this connection, it is reasonable to ask whether those who are richest in income are also richest in wealth. While the two groups overlap substantially, they are not identical. For example, the *wealthiest* 1 percent of households had average net worth of $8.5 million, while the 1 percent of households with *highest income* had average net worth of $2.8 million. Similarly, the bottom 80 percent of households ranked by wealth averaged $42,000 in net worth while the bottom 80 percent of households ranked by income averaged $86,550 in net worth. (Both averages are from unequal distributions where significant fractions of households had no net worth.) The imperfect correlation between income and wealth is partially driven by life-cycle effects in which some retired families have substantial assets without large

TABLE 1.6    Distribution of wealth across households (households ranked by wealth rather than income).

| | Mean Marketable Wealth within Wealth Classes | | | | | |
| | Top .5 Percent | Next .5 Percent | Next 9 Percent | Next 10 Percent | Bottom 80 Percent | Gini Coefficient |
|---|---|---|---|---|---|---|
| 1962 | $6,284,000 (21%) | $1,820,000 (20%) | $451,000 (22%) | $169,000 (17%) | $29,500 (18%) | .80 |
| 1983 | $9,311,000 (90%) | $2,674,000 (41%) | $680,000 (34%) | $233,000 (26%) | $42,000 (0) | .80 |
| 1989 | $13,704,000 | $3,276,000 | $809,000 | $267,000 | $42,000 | .84 |

SOURCE: Adapted from Wolff (1993).

NOTES: Figures in parentheses are rates of growth per decade. Marketable wealth includes the market value of real estate and financial assets less household debt. It excludes the value of consumer durables (e.g., cars) and financial assets like Social Security that cannot be converted into cash in the present.

incomes. But among the wealthiest households, the sources of net worth are heavily concentrated in real estate and the assets of unincorporated businesses (including professionals, etc.), suggesting that most of these households are not simply coupon clippers.

## THE RICH, THE MIDDLE CLASS, AND THE POOR

The data presented so far give a statistically accurate picture, but they are not the stuff of day-to-day conversation. For this reason, it is useful to recapitulate in everyday language what happened to the rich, the middle class, and the poor.

### The Rich

Common wisdom has it that the rich did very well in the 1980s. Substantial evidence supports the case. For example, Joskow, Rose, and Sheppard (1992) tracked compensation of chief executive officers (CEOs) using a sample of about 800 firms per year from 1973 through 1991. From 1973 through 1980, average annual compensation in the sample (including stock options, etc.) grew from about $750,000 to $910,000 (in 1989 dollars), a growth rate of 2.8 percent per year. Over the 1980s, the growth of compensation of CEOs accelerated to 5.2 percent per year, so that by 1991, annual compensation averaged $1,590,000, this during a period when average earnings in the economy were stagnant.[64]

Do such trends extend beyond 800 CEOs, a few athletes, and some movie stars? As I noted in the previous section, U.S. Treasury data on the adjusted gross income (AGI) of individual tax returns are better suited than census data to answer the question. Feenberg and Poterba's analysis of these data (1992) support the common wisdom. Consider the share of total AGI reported by the top .5 percent (.005) of taxpayers. In 1989, the top .5 percent of tax filers[65] reported 11 percent of all AGI, up from 6 percent in 1979. In 1989, the group in question totaled about 558,000 tax filers (out of 113,000,000). AGI within the group began at $276,000, and average AGI for the group was about $900,000.[66] Since these numbers are "snapshots" at different points in time, it is possible that the top earners differ from year to year and that there is less inequality over time than these numbers imply. Slemrod (1991) found that while there is turnover in the very top of the distribution, few persons who leave the very top fall very far.

What caused this growth of extremely high incomes? Recent discussions have centered on two explanations. The first was the growth of "winner-take-all" markets in such fields as investment banking, specialty medicine, and law (Kaus 1992; Frank and Cook 1993). A person buying a banana will price shop in part because little is riding on the purchase: If a banana is bad, another one can be bought. But a corporate takeover or open heart surgery is a one-time affair that must be performed well. In such cases, investment bankers and surgeons with outstanding reputations can command extremely high fees without fear of price competition from less experienced competitors. Frank and Cook argue that for a variety of reasons, such markets became more numerous in the 1980s.

The salaries that result from winner-take-all may be extremely high, but they are set in a competitive market. A second explanation for high salaries focuses on persons who exploit situations that are *insulated* from the competition (Crystal 1992; Bok 1993). The archetypical example is a corporate executive who is not closely monitored by his stockholders and whose compensation is set by a board of directors beholden to him. It is, as one corporate observer told me, "like Congress voting themselves a pay raise." In this explanation, a less beholden board member or stockholder would work to hold down compensation to the level necessary to attract a qualified replacement.

The two explanations are quite different, but they contain a common element. Both assume that a person will fully exercise any power he or she has to command a high salary. The assumption is not obvious. Most of us are concerned with making money. But most of us are also concerned with our reputation, which depends in part on adhering to community norms. A person who makes "too much money," like a six-time divorced man, runs a reputational risk. "Too much money" is, of course, a subjective standard. But it appears (to me) that whatever the standard had been, it was revised upward during the 1980s. Popularizers of President Reagan's supply-side policies argued that the rich saved and invested for the rest of us.[67] More generally, the President and the people around him seemed to be saying that richer was unambiguously better and so persons felt less restraint in making as much as they could while they could.

Less restraint encouraged more positive risk taking and innovation in, for example, the provision of venture capital to new firms. But less restraint also promoted other kinds of risk taking—looting savings and loans, dismantling firms for immediate gain while ignoring long-run consequences, disregarding simple fairness. The effects influenced incomes throughout the distribution, not just the top. An example is the decline in union membership and bargaining power, noted earlier, which owes something to the changed climate in which management felt it could take on unions without presidential interference.[68]

As Feenberg and Poterba show, the increased share of very high incomes actually began in the late 1970s. Moreover, some of the increase in the 1980s reflected reduced tax rates (which encouraged people to declare income) rather than changes in the underlying distribution. But it will be hard to write a history of the decade without perceiving a strong dose of what might be called Woody Allen economics: take the money and run.

### The Middle Class

The United States has a dollar definition of poverty (see below), but there is no equivalent standard for the middle class. We know, however, that the mass middle class was a product of the 1950s and 1960s. As late as 1952, only 37 percent of the population identified themselves as middle class or higher while the remainder saw themselves as working class or lower. These attitudes were consistent with the occupational distribution. In 1950, only one-third of white men—the best-educated demographic group in the labor force—held white collar occupations (Levy 1987: Chaps. 4 and 6).

As prosperity continued, the outlook shifted. By 1964, 44 percent of respondents described themselves as middle class and the proportion continued to climb. In the process, the middle class had become an expression of the American dream of upward mobility accessible to everyone. But within two decades, books and articles would begin to appear suggesting that the middle class was vanishing (Kuttner 1982; Bluestone and Harrison 1982).

To make sense of these changing perspectives, it is necessary to consider why people in the 1950s and 1960s saw the middle class as growing. At least two different movements were involved. One was the rapid growth of white collar and office work—"clean" work that did not involve manual labor in factories or on farms. The other was the rise in real incomes that allowed families to purchase a middle-class lifestyle—a single-family home, car(s), major appliances, air conditioning—items that were pictured (along with a helicopter) on the cover of *Life* magazine (November 26, 1946). But a growing middle class did not mean the incomes were converging at the middle of the family income distribution. To appreciate the point, look again at Table 1.4: During the 1950s and 1960s, real family income grew rapidly, but income inequality improved only modestly.

In the same way, being in the middle class did not mean being in the middle (e.g., the third quintile) of the family income distribution. In 1991, the middle quintile ran from $29,111 to $43,000 (U.S. Bureau of the Census 1992:

"Money Income of Households, Families, and Persons in the United States: 1991: Table 15; figures in 1991 dollars). But many families with higher incomes—in particular, incomes above the $62,991 that begins the top quintile— see themselves as middle class. The apparent contradiction reflects the groups with whom we compare ourselves. When we speak of a middle-class family, we implicitly mean a family in its prime earning years—their 30s, 40s, and 50s. The family income distribution includes both these families and many others— retired couples, young married college students—whose current income may not accurately reflect their long-run status.

It follows that if we are to make sense of the vanishing-middle-class issue, we should focus on families in their prime earning years. To conform with standard census age groupings, we focus on families in which the head is aged 25–54. Figure 1.8 compares the income distributions of such families for 1969 and 1989. The figure displays the kind of hollowing out we have seen in earlier distributions: a general stagnation of average income over the period,[69] a shrinking proportion of families with incomes between $20,000 and $49,000, and growing proportions of families with incomes under $10,000 and incomes of $50,000 and over. Earlier, we noted that the upper tail of the distribution was shaped by both growing numbers of men with high earnings and the increasing number of high-income husbands with working wives. In Figure 1.8, we see how the growing proportion of families with incomes under $10,000 is driven by the increasing proportion of families headed by single women.

What, then, is one supposed to make of the vanishing middle class? The most important element is the slow growth of average incomes that undermined the process of mass upward mobility—coupled with actual falls in incomes for less-educated workers.

The stagnation can be illustrated through a simple example: If a father aged 30 in 1949 had the average income of men his age, he would have been making about $17,200 (in 1989 dollars). In 1969, the father, now aged 50, would have been making about $28,100, a 63 percent increase over his career. If a son aged 30 in 1969 earned the average of men his age, he would have been making about $26,000, enough to put him at the bottom rung of the middle class. But the son would spend most of the next 20 years in a period of slow growth and at age 50 would be earning about $31,000, a gain of only 19 percent over his career.

Had the son been a college graduate, he would have done much better than this average: $32,200 in 1969 moving to $44,000 in 1989 (+38 percent as he aged from 30 to 50). But if the son had stopped at high school, he would have begun at about $25,200 and climbed to only $28,000, 20 years later; and if this son had turned 30 in 1989 rather than 1969, he would have been making about $19,500 at the age when he would be expecting to have children and start thinking about buying a house.[70] This weak growth of average wages and declining incomes for less-educated men goes a long way toward explaining fears of a vanishing middle class.

FIGURE 1.8    Incomes of families headed by persons aged 25–54: 1969 and 1989.

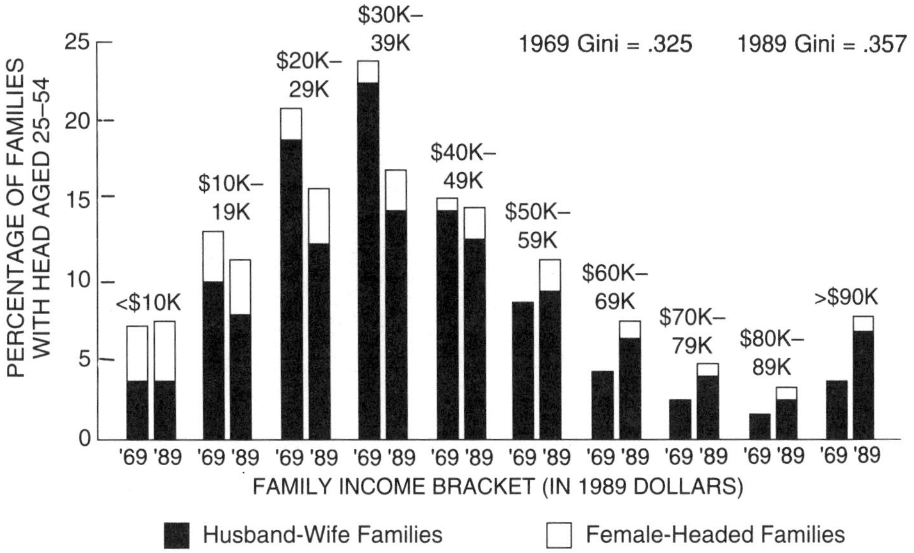

The Poor

Unlike the middle class, America's poor are defined using an official dollar standard. In 1989, a family of three was poor if its money income fell below $9,893, while the corresponding standard for a four-person family was $12,674. The standards were developed in the early 1960s and are annually adjusted to reflect inflation but are otherwise unchanged; that is, they remain fixed in terms of purchasing power.

Since 1970, the most obvious feature of poverty is its apparent stability. In 1970, 12.6 percent of the population was poor. Over the next 21 years, that proportion fell to 11.1 percent in the business cycle peak of 1973 and rose to 15.2 percent in the recession year of 1983, but the rate again stood at 12.8 percent in 1989 before rising in the subsequent recession.

A stable summary statistic often implies no change in underlying structure, which is not the case here. Over the last two decades, there have been substantial changes in the nature of poverty, including its relationship to the national economy.

Given the recessions of the 1970s, the stable poverty rate during the period was no surprise. But the economy experienced a sustained increase of employment from 1982 through 1989. Had past relationships held, the increased number of jobs should have driven the poverty rate down to 9.3 percent by 1989 (Blank 1991). The fact that the poverty rate fell to only 12.8 percent in 1989 was both disappointing and puzzling.

Some observers argue that the problem lies in the government's measurement of poverty. For historical reasons, the poverty standard applies to money income and does not count in-kind benefits such as food stamps, Medicare, and Medicaid.[71] Counting these benefits as income, the argument goes, would show a different result. The argument is largely wrong. Counting in-kind benefits as income raises the incomes of many families and so lowers the poverty rate in a single year. But applying this adjustment year by year produces an equally weak reduction during the 1980s expansion: a fall from 15.2 to 12.8 percent under the official definition or from 12.7 to 10.4 percent under the definition counting in-kind benefits (U.S. Bureau of the Census 1992. "Measuring the Effect of Benefits and Taxes on Income and Poverty: 1979–1991": Table 1). Thus, poverty rates are lower if one counts in-kind benefits but the trend is the same.

A number of other arguments have been advanced to explain the poverty rate's slow decline.

*Demographics.* One explanation for the stagnant poverty rate is that it reflected the growing proportion of the poor who were in female-headed households, which were unable to take advantage of an improving economy (Table 1.7). This argument has been examined by Blank (1991), who estimates that

TABLE 1.7   Composition of the poverty population (in millions).

|  | 1969 | 1979 | 1989 |
|---|---|---|---|
| Persons in Families Headed by Someone Aged 65 or Over and Unrelated Individuals Aged 65 or Over | 5.7 | 4.4 | 4.1 |
| Persons in Husband-Wife Families Headed by Someone Under Age 65 | 9.4 | 8.8 | 10.7 |
| Persons in Female-Headed Families Headed by Someone Under Age 65 | 6.0 | 9.2 | 11.6 |
| Persons in Male-Headed Families (no spouse) Headed by Someone Under Age 65 | .3 | .4 | 1.3 |
| Unrelated Males Under Age 65 | .8 | 1.5 | 2.2 |
| Unrelated Females Under Age 65 | 1.4 | 1.8 | 2.4 |
| Total | 24.1 | 26.1 | 31.5 |
| Percentage of the Population in Poverty | 12.2% | 11.6% | 12.8% |
| Proportion of the Poor Who Are |  |  |  |
| Black | .30 | .31 | .29 |
| Hispanic | n.a. | .11 | .17 |
| Living in central cities | .32 | .37 | .43 |
| Poverty Rate by Age |  |  |  |
| Children Under Age 18 | .15 | .16 | .19 |
| Persons Aged 65 and Over | .25 | .15 | .12 |

SOURCES: *Current Population Reports,* various issues, and author's tabulation of Current Population Survey tapes.

NOTE: Numbers may not add to 100 due to rounding.

without the increase in female-headed households, the 1989 poverty rate would have been about 12.3 percent rather than 12.8 percent. The difference, while significant, explains only a fifth of the decline in poverty that should have resulted from the 1980s expansion.

*Underclass Behavior.*    Over the 1980s, a number of authors explored the growing concentration of poverty in urban areas, a phenomenon that worked at two levels. There was, first, the increasing concentration of the poverty population in central cities described earlier. Within central cities, there was a growing concentration of the poor in certain areas—"underclass areas"—noted by Wilson (1987), Ricketts and Sawhill (1988), and others. These areas, apparently cut off from the mainstream economy, had large concentrations of low-income households with dysfunctional culture: high proportions of female-headed families, persons who had not finished high school, young persons neither employed nor in school, persons dependent on welfare, and so on.

Underclass areas clearly exist. But if they are to explain the weak 1980s decline in poverty, they must have been *growing* during the 1980s in a way that offset economic expansion; that is, that increasing numbers of persons were isolated (by geography and behavior) from the mainstream economy. Kasarda examines underclass areas in Chapter 5 in this volume and arrives at a mixed conclusion. He finds that the proportion of the population in high-poverty urban census tracts has grown since the 1980s. But the proportion of the population living in urban census tracts with high levels of dysfunction remain at their 1980 levels. This suggests that an increasing underclass is not a good explanation for the slow decline in poverty.[72]

*Changes in the Labor Market.*    Over the decade, researchers advanced both supply-side and demand-side hypotheses involving poverty and labor market behavior. The major supply-side hypothesis argued that growing income transfers had undercut people's willingness to work (Murray 1984); thus, people would not take the jobs that became available in an expansion.[73] Blank (1991) examined labor supply directly and concluded that both unemployment rates and labor supply among low-income families were as responsive to the economy in the 1980s as they had been in the 1960s.

The major demand-side hypothesis rests on the stagnation of average wages and, in particular, the fall in real wages for less-educated workers. In earlier expansions, workers rose above the poverty line because they could find work and because their real wages were rising.[74] As we saw earlier, the growth of GNP in the 1980s reflected increased numbers of workers more than rising earnings per worker, and the earnings of less-educated workers actually fell in real terms. Put differently, the incomes of the poor benefited as the expansion created jobs, but the same incomes were hurt as real wages per hour fell. As a result, the expansion pulled the incomes of relatively few people above the poverty line. Blank (1991) and Blank and Card (1994) show how these two offsetting forces—more jobs but falling wages for the less educated—largely explain the failure of the expansion to lower the poverty rate.

At the beginning of the 1980s, supply-side economists argued that Reagan policies would produce what I have called the "good" inequality: the rich would get richer but ultimately the poor would get richer, too, albeit at a slower rate. In practice, this happened to only a small extent. The argument failed in part because, contrary to supply-side theory, tax reductions for the well-to-do did not cause a dramatic surge in funds for investment. More important, neither supply-siders nor their liberal critics foresaw that productivity growth in the 1980s, unlike the 1950s and 1960s, would differentially eliminate jobs for less-educated workers, a situation which meant that few of these workers would share in prosperity.

## THE ELDERLY, CHILDREN, BLACKS, AND HISPANICS

Describing the income distribution in one chapter is like a one-week tour of Europe. The trip, however rapid, should cover certain landmarks. Similarly, a tour of the U.S. income distribution should touch on four groups who cut across income lines: the elderly, children, blacks, and Hispanics.

### The Elderly and Children

The circumstances of both the elderly and children are described in detail by Treas and Torrecilha and by Hogan and Lichter, respectively, in Volume 2. Here, I briefly describe each group in the context of the income distribution.

Since the early 1970s, children and the elderly have followed moderately different paths (Preston 1984). For the elderly, the story is clear: Most of today's elderly are better off than their 1970 counterparts. For children, the story is more complex because there are more high-income children *and* more low-income children today than there were two decades ago.

Figure 1.9 compares the 1969 and 1989 income distributions of households headed by an elderly person (age 65 or over). The picture is one of uniform increases. In 1989 there were proportionally fewer households in the under $10,000 income category than in 1969, but at all higher income categories there were proportionally more households in 1989 than 20 years earlier. The most important reason for these increases was the 1971 revision of the Social Security program. Prior to 1971, a person's Social Security benefit was fixed unless Congress voted to increase the benefit schedule. During the 1950s and 1960s, rising real incomes and a growing ratio of workers to recipients gave the Social Security trust fund consistant, unanticipated surpluses. Congress would respond to these surpluses by passing large benefit increases just before elections.

FIGURE 1.9    Incomes of elderly households: 1969 and 1989.

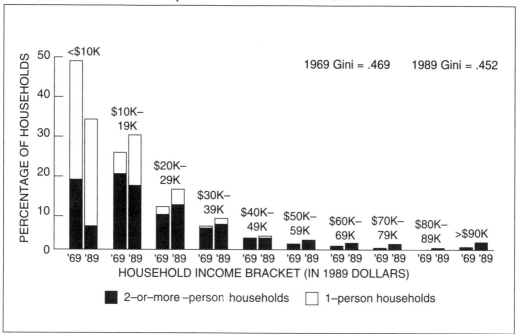

To undercut this process, the Nixon administration and Congress agreed to legislation in 1971 that immediately raised benefits by 20 percent and, thereafter, indexed benefits to the rate of inflation to keep real benefits constant. Since earnings and family incomes had risen *faster* than the rate of inflation since World War II (Tables 1.2 and 1.4), the proposal appeared to be both prudent and inexpensive. In fact, the stagnant wages that began two years later made indexation far more generous (vis-à-vis wages) than Congress had intended.[75]

Beyond Social Security, many elderly benefited from the growing system of private pensions and an increase in wealth driven by a rapid rise in housing prices, all of which contributed to rising incomes. Thirty years ago, elderly families were concentrated in the bottom quintile of the income distribution. Today, they are relatively more likely to be found in the lower middle quintile. While the absolute number of elderly poor has fallen only modestly (Table 1.7), the *proportion* of the elderly who are poor (the poverty rate) fell from .25 in 1969 to .12 in 1989.

The poverty rate of children under age 18, by contrast, rose from 15 percent in 1970 to 19 percent in 1989. During these years, the poverty rate among white children rose from 11 to 14 percent, and the poverty rate among black children remained unchanged at about 42 percent. As Danziger and Gottschalk (1993) show, the slowly rising child poverty rate obscures large changes that worked in offsetting directions.

Two factors, other things being equal, reduced child poverty over the period: low birthrates and increased parental education. As late as 1970, 70 percent of all children lived with two or more siblings.[76] By 1990, only 44 percent of children lived in families this large and more than 50 percent of all children lived with one sibling or as an only child (Hernandez 1993). Since the income needed to be above the poverty line increases with family size, smaller families, other things being equal, meant fewer children in poverty. Among children born in the 1960s, only one quarter had mothers who had gone beyond high school and nearly one third had mothers who had not finished high school. Among children born in the 1980s, nearly two fifths had mothers who had completed college and fewer than one fifth had mothers who had not finished high school. Given the increasing association between education and earnings and the growing proportion of working mothers, mothers' increased education, other things being equal, worked to raise the incomes of children's families and reduce the poverty rate.

Offsetting both trends is the increasing proportion of children who live outside two-parent families. In 1970, 11 percent of all children were living in a mother-only family. By 1990, 23 percent were living in a mother-only family and another 5 percent were living in a father-only family or with neither parent. Among whites, the proportion of children living with two parents fell from 90 to 73 percent. Among blacks, the proportion fell from 59 to 38 percent.

A growing literature documents the negative effects for children of being raised in mother-only families. In their forthcoming book, McLanahan and Sandefur conclude that growing up in a female-headed family "doubles the risk of dropping out of high school [to about .25], triples the risk of having a teen premarital birth [to about .15], and increases the risk of being idle [to about .12]" (brackets added; "idle" refers to young men who are both out of school and not working). As the demand for labor shifts toward better-educated workers, dropping out of high school and similar outcomes exact increasingly high penalties. One of the mechanisms generating these negative outcomes is low income for the children in such families: In 1989, 55 percent of all black children and 41 percent of all white children in mother-only families had family incomes of less than $11,000 per year.[77]

As is clear from Figure 1.10, the increase in child poverty is only half of the story. The other half is the increased proportion of children in higher-income families—in particular, families with incomes of $50,000 and over. Notice that the bars for children in families with incomes of $50,000 and more are higher for 1989 than for 1969. As we saw earlier, the split in children's incomes parallels a split in geography in which poor children are increasingly concentrated in central cities while better-off children increasingly live in suburbs. When these

FIGURE 1.10   Income distribution of families with children: 1969 and 1989.

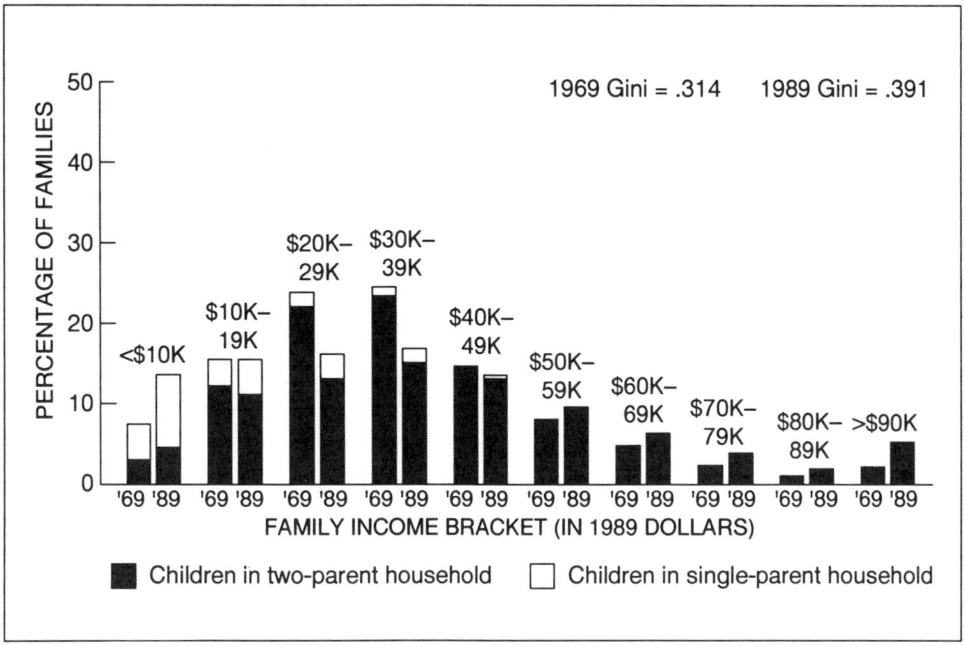

disparities in condition are combined with a third fact—that only about one-third of all households now have a child—they point to the difficulty in developing a national consensus around children's issues.

### Blacks and Hispanics

The economic status of blacks and Hispanics is covered in detail in Chapter 4 in Volume 2. Here I briefly connect the status of these groups to this chapter's themes.

Earlier, I showed how the 1970s were a good period for semiskilled labor. The 1960s and 1970s were also a time of substantial black progress. Black-white gaps in earnings and in family incomes had closed steadily. By the mid-1970s, black and white women and young men with similar educations had fairly similar earnings (Freeman 1973; Smith and Welch 1986). While some of the convergence reflected the strong demand for blue collar labor, convergence also came from the effects of the civil rights movement in achieving more equal hiring practices (Donohue and Heckman 1991).

This earnings convergence peaked in the mid-1970s. Since then, black-white earnings ratios have widened (Table 1A.1) and black to white and Hispanic to white family income ratios have, at best, remained constant (Table 1.8). Behind this stalled progress lie factors ranging from the declining demand for less-

TABLE 1.8  Comparison of white, black, and Hispanic family incomes.

|  | White | Black | Hispanic |
|---|---|---|---|
| All Families |  |  |  |
| 1969 median family income | $31,389 | $19,419 | n.a. |
| Ratio to white family income | 1.000 | .612 |  |
| 1979 median family income | $34,634 | $24,611 | $23,743 |
| Ratio to white family income | 1.000 | .566 | .693 |
| 1989 median family income | $35,975 | $20,209 | $23,446 |
| Ratio to white family income | 1.000 | .562 | .652 |
|  |  |  |  |
| Families with Head Aged 25–34 in 1989 |  |  |  |
| All families | $32,804 | $16,849 | $21,324 |
| Ratio to white family income | 1.000 | .513 | .650 |
| Husband-wife | $36,180 | $27,914 | $25,323 |
| Ratio to white family income | 1.000 | .772 | .700 |
| Female-headed | $12,446 | $ 8,974 | $ 9,208 |
| Ratio to white family income | 1.000 | .721 | .740 |
|  |  |  |  |
| Families with Head Aged 35–44 in 1989 |  |  |  |
| All families | $41,648 | $28,245 | $26,325 |
| Ratio to white family income | 1.000 | .678 | .632 |
| Husband-wife | $46,074 | $40,054 | $31,707 |
| Ratio to white family income | 1.000 | .869 | .688 |
| Female-headed | $19,517 | $15,822 | $11,939 |
| Ratio to white family income | 1.000 | .811 | .612 |

SOURCE: *Current Population Reports,* various issues.

skilled labor to a relaxation of equal employment efforts to the growing number of minority female-headed households.

As Mare shows in his chapter in this volume, educational attainments among both blacks and Hispanics, while increasing, remain below those for whites. This means that the growing earnings–education gap had a racial dimension. Among young men, black–white earnings differences grew most rapidly in the Midwest, a reflection of the region's rapid loss of high-paying jobs in smokestack industries (Bound and Freeman 1992).

There was, however, more to the story as black–white earnings differences grew between workers of similar age and education. In the 1970s, for example, recent black and white college graduates received roughly equal wages.[78] By the 1980s, a substantial earnings gap had reopened reflecting, at least in part, a surge in the numbers of black college graduates (increased supply) and a weakening of government antidiscrimination efforts (Bound and Freeman 1992). Data on Hispanics are more difficult to interpret because immigration is constantly changing the relevant population, but Hispanic earnings followed a generally similar pattern.

The stalled convergence in black–white and Hispanic–white earnings carried over to family incomes where here, particularly among blacks, earnings trends

FIGURE 1.11   Incomes of black families headed by persons aged 25–54: 1969 and 1989.

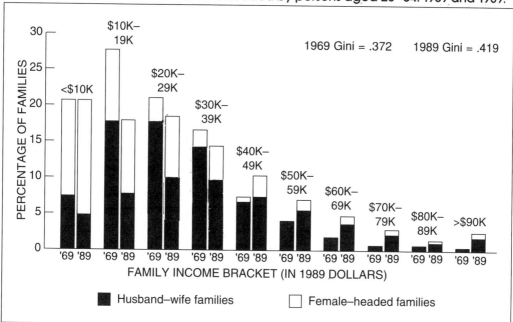

were compounded by differences in family structure. The result, as shown in Table 1.8 (for both groups) and in Figure 1.11 (for prime working-age black ·families), is another version of the polarization we have seen in some earlier distributions: for example, a significant number of prime working-age black families with incomes above $40,000 and a significant number of black families with incomes below $10,000. Notice the increase between 1970 and 1990 in the height of the bars showing black families with incomes of $40,000 or more compared to the unchanged proportion with incomes under $10,000. In this kind of polarization, simple statistics on median family income lose their meaning.

## THE WHITE COLLAR RECESSION OF 1991–1993

As this chapter is being finished, media reports suggest a central trend of the 1980s—declining earnings for less-educated workers (particularly men)—is reversing. According to these reports, the country is in the middle of a period of restructuring, in which significant numbers of college-educated, middle-class professionals are being laid off. Taken to their limit, these reports imply that it is the better-educated worker who is now at a disadvantage. How true is this idea?

Let us begin with some background. The bulk of restructuring has taken place during the current, unexpectedly long recession. Its length has been explained by cutbacks in defense, the overbuilt real estate market, and the simultaneous recessions in Europe and Japan. One more factor belongs on this list: the end of favorable demographics. Earlier, I described how the rapid growth of the labor force has kept aggregate expenditures increasing in the late 1970s despite stagnant paychecks. By the late 1980s, labor force growth had declined from 3 percent per year to little more than 1 percent per year.[79] Since average wages remained stagnant, a business looking into the future could well project a slow growth of sales and believe that it was time to retrench.

The result was a white collar recession, which did *not* mean that white collar unemployment rates were higher than blue collar unemployment rates. It did mean three things:

- White collar and blue collar unemployment rates are now closer than they were in earlier recessions. Traditionally, the blue collar rate is about three times as large as the white collar rate. In the current recession, the blue collar rate is only twice as large as the white collar rate (Groshen and Williams 1992).

- The numbers of white collar and blue collar newly unemployed are relatively equal. White collar workers now constitute about 59 percent of the labor force; blue collar workers constitute 29 percent.[80] Because of this size difference, white collar and blue collar unemployed have increased by roughly equal *numbers* even though the blue collar unemployment *rate* was twice as high (Groshen and Williams 1992; Mishel and Bernstein 1993).

- In earlier recessions unemployment fell most heavily on the young and uneducated. *Relative to these recessions,* current unemployment is falling relatively more heavily on older and more educated workers (Farber 1993).

Since white collar workers have a wide variety of educational attainments, it is necessary to ask what this description means for high school and college graduates. A review of the data (not reported here) shows a similar picture. In this recession, the typical college graduate was far less likely to be unemployed than the typical high school graduate. But the unemployment gap between them was smaller than it had been in earlier recessions. And because there are relatively more college graduates today than there were, say, in 1982, there are more unemployed college graduates today than there were in 1982.

For the most part, then, "white collar recession" is a relative term: today's white collar (or educated) workers are suffering relatively more unemployment than they suffered in earlier recessions, but not more unemployment than today's blue collar workers. But there was one group for whom the white collar recession had absolute meaning: older men with one to four years of college. These are men in their late 40s and early 50s, who were "earning their age" in management and administrative positions. Traditionally, these workers earned more than younger workers because their experience made them more valuable, particularly as managers of others. In the current wave of restructuring, this logic was overturned. The new logic argued that (1) organizations should be flatter, with fewer layers of management; and (2) employees should be adept at working with computer technology. In the new logic, older middle managers suffered on three counts: They were doing jobs that no longer needed doing, their experience could not offset their lack of recent training, and their salaries were suddenly high relative to the salaries of younger workers. They and their jobs became obvious targets for cutting.

The results showed up not so much in high unemployment rates as in low earnings. Annual figures from the Current Population Survey indicate that men aged 45–54 with four years of college earned an average (median) of $42,590 in 1989. By 1992, median earnings for the comparable group had fallen to $38,439 (in 1989 dollars), a decline of 10 percent in just three years. This decline was far larger than the earnings decline for younger men with a college degree.

Thus, the white collar recession has fallen with particular severity on older, well-educated middle managers. But older male high school graduates also experienced earnings declines; thus, even in this age group, the college–high school annual earnings premium closed only slightly. Among younger men, the college–high school premium continued to widen through the recession.

It is this last point which suggests that the white collar recession, like the blue collar rural renaissance of the 1970s, is a temporary break in trend. In the longer run, I would expect earnings differences by education to, at best, remain constant.

## CONCLUSION

I opened this chapter by arguing that two goals of an industrialized society are growth and equality. From the perspective of 1993, the prospects for faster growth look better than the prospects for reduced inequality. If the continued restructuring in services and manufacturing lives up to anything like its billing, it is plausible that we should return to annual productivity growth approaching 2 percent a year, a rate sufficient to return us to a path of rising real wages.

The question is, "Whose wages?" If I am right that the white collar recession is a temporary adjustment, then the trends of the 1980s will dominate and the falling unemployment rate will tighten the market for better-educated labor even as the market for less-educated labor remains slack.[81] Wage gaps may not widen further, but their chances of closing appear to be weak in the near term. If my picture is correct, productivity growth will benefit living standards in the upper half of the distribution more than in the lower half.

Persons familiar with economic writing can be excused for laughing. Over at least 17 years, economists have been preaching the virtues of higher productivity growth as the key to rising living standards (Thurow 1976; Levy 1987). Unanimity was such as to raise a good manager's first question: "If this idea is so good, why hasn't somebody tried it?"

As we see the economic turbulence around us, we now know the answer. Higher productivity growth produces long-run gains, but it also produces substantial short-run displacement (see Landes's quotation earlier). There is the cost of greater inequality as some persons' skills become obsolete and other persons take advantage of new opportunities. And there is the cost of greater individual insecurity as established job patterns are uprooted. These costs first appeared a decade ago in manufacturing where the principal casualties were blue collar men and women. The costs have now spread to the service sector and the casualties include workers at every level. Most of these people played by the rules, but the rules changed in the middle of the game.

If few economists (including me) predicted these costs, it was because we focused too heavily on the 1950s and 1960s. The 1950s and 1960s were also a period of high productivity growth, but productivity grew then in an unusually balanced way. The people displaced by the mechanization of agriculture had the skills to move into the expanding manufacturing sector. The bulk of the people who graduated from high school (and many who dropped out) had the skills to take a variety of good jobs. Put simply, the economic pieces fit. Today the pieces no longer fit, and it will take time to put them back together. There is, first, an oversupply of semiskilled workers—those who have the equivalent of a high school education with no other skills. The result is the fall in wages, particularly for men, that we saw earlier. But we also have a set of institutions—schools, a structure of health insurance and pensions—that in many ways are no longer suited to our situation.

I discussed one of these institutions earlier—how workers and their families are supposed to obtain health insurance through their employers. In the current environment, this is a bad arrangement. Consider health insurance coverage for semiskilled workers. If my arguments are correct, the market for semiskilled labor is likely to remain weak even as the market for more-educated labor recovers. Worker competition for jobs will bid down earnings, and a shrinking number of semiskilled jobs will include health insurance. Beyond this, the current wave of restructuring means that firm-to-firm movement of employees at all educational levels is likely to remain high. Over the last decade, insurers have become increasingly restrictive about accepting enrollees with preexisting conditions, and these restrictions, combined with high mobility, are also likely to increase the number of uncovered persons. In a similar way, upheavals in the economy point to the need for higher savings. But our current pension system is not well adapted to persons who frequently change jobs.

Institutional reform applies equally to our educational system. During the last year, how many high school teachers had a conversation with an employer of recent high school graduates? I do not have an answer, but my own contact with school systems suggests the number is not high. This should not surprise us. When high school graduates could move easily into long, stable careers, there was no need for employers and teachers to talk, just as there was no need for health insurance beyond what employers provided. Eliminating the conversation was an efficient use of time. Today, teachers and employers have a serious need to talk to help teachers and students better understand what employers need. This means establishing connections that have not existed for a long time. Similarly, the United States job training system has never been strong, but its weakness was not as obvious when far fewer workers needed training to move into new jobs.

Attempts to improve institutions are often attempts to compensate the losers in a period of change. Compensating losers is not something the United States does well, but the idea is important. Economists justify higher productivity growth, and the restructuring behind it, on the basis of greater national output. The justification assumes that if output grows enough, the winners can compensate the losers and still be better off. If we honor this idea in the breach—if we welcome changes but fail to compensate the losers—we are creating a coalition to oppose further changes, for example, a coalition against free trade. And we are flirting with social disintegration.

Better health insurance, pensions, training, and schools cannot guarantee more equality, but they can help to level the playing field. They can reduce the penalty to a man or woman forced to switch jobs or to a child who would otherwise graduate from high school with no skills. In leveling the playing field, two issues deserve particular attention.

The first is the city-suburban split described earlier. When the poor are heavily concentrated in central cities and when cities have to rely heavily on their own tax base for revenues, we are creating a strong incentive to improve the schools and other services that serve the better-off while saving money on the rest.

The other dimension involves family structure. As this chapter is being completed, about 23 percent of all children live in mother-only families while more than 25 percent of all children are born to unwed mothers. As we saw earlier, being raised in a mother-only family has real consequences in terms of living standards, but also in terms of educational attainment and other aspects of life. In a society that places increasing weight upon skill and education, a child born to an unmarried woman begins life at an enormous disadvantage. Twenty years ago, attempts to address this problem through public policy—for example, by precluding teenage welfare recipients from establishing their own homes—would have been heavily criticized as "blaming the victim."[82] That is not true today, and I expect it to be less true in the future. While public policies may have little impact on the formation of female-headed households, the issue will be increasingly discussed in analyses of the nation's future.

———————————

First thanks go to Michael Cook of the University of Maryland Department of Economics who compressed a year's worth of research assistance into five months. Lijian Chen of MIT's Department of Urban Studies and Planning also provided extensive computational assistance. A second debt of gratitude goes to Kathy Swartz, my wife, and to Richard Murnane, my coresearcher for the last four years. Many of the ideas in this chapter grew out of long and frequent conversations with each of them.

A number of other friends, relatives, and colleagues shared their ideas and their data and, in some cases, read draft pieces of this work. An incomplete list includes Suzanne Bianchi, Bill Butz, Margaret Blair, Jaci Coleman, Ed Dean, Dick Easterlin, Tom Edsall, William Frey, Ren Farley, Peter Gottschalk, Nick Lemann, Dan Levy, Sara McLanahan, Larry Mishel, Lisa Niedert, Jim Poterba, Ricardo Rodriguez, Nancy Rose, Paul Ryscavage, Frank Sammartino, Bob Samuelson, Bob Solow, Peter Temin, David Warsh, David Wessell, and Ed Wolff. Despite their help, mistakes remain and the mistakes belong to me.

Financial support from the Russell Sage Foundation, the Social Science Research Council, the Spencer Foundation, the University of Maryland Computer Science Center, and the Rose Chair in Urban Economics are gratefully acknowledged.

This chapter is dedicated to the memory of Aaron Wildavsky, a friend and teacher for more than a quarter-century.

## ENDNOTES

1. I focus on individual earnings as a better measure of economic welfare than a nation's gross domestic product (GDP). During much of the 1980s, average U.S. earnings were stagnant but U.S. GDP grew briskly because the number of workers was growing briskly.

   The term *income inequality* will be used in this chapter to cover a number of items including the inequality of individual earnings, of family and household incomes, and so on. Another goal—particularly today—is economic security, an individual's ability to construct a career out of several long jobs rather than many short ones. I discuss economic security at various points in this chapter.

2. Economists usually measure living standards in terms of income per capita, which continued to grow after 1973, despite stagnant earnings, because the number of employed persons was growing faster than the number of dependents. I discuss this movement in the next section.

3. My earlier book (Levy 1987) downplayed the 1980s inequality for two reasons. First, most of my data ended in 1984–1985 when growing inequality seemed to be a temporary result of the 1980–1982 recession. More important, I wanted to focus on the role of income growth and stagnation. Between World War II and 1973, incomes in all parts of the distribution had roughly doubled in purchasing power terms. Beginning in 1973, income growth collapsed. I believed that the shift from rapid income growth to stagnation went a long way toward explaining our perceptions of a "vanishing middle class" and related ideas.

4. Thus, international trade was unimportant not only compared with today, but compared with the early part of this century. In 1929, the sum of U.S. imports and exports equaled 12.5 percent of GNP. In 1955, imports and exports equaled 9.8 percent of GNP (U.S. Bureau of Economic Analysis 1981: Tables 1.1 and 4.1).

5. An important example is offered by Kevin Murphy (personal communication), who notes that many of the agricultural jobs held by blacks in the 1940s were eliminated by mechanization. And yet black incomes rose substantially over the next 30 years, a reflection of their ability to move into other industries.

6. Roughly speaking, the Census Bureau defines a family as two or more related persons who share a living unit and a household as the persons living in an occupied living unit. Thus, all families are households, but a household can also be a person living alone, two or more unrelated roommates, and so on. See McLanahan and Casper's Chapter 1 in Volume 2 for a full discussion.

7. Within-group inequality is a statistical term; in this case, the "group" refers to persons of the same age, educational attainment, gender, and race. To economists, within-group inequality is a surprise since competitive market theory holds that two persons with the same characteristics should earn the same wage. Some researchers have argued that the theory is right and that these earnings differences reflect characteristics that census data do not capture, such as intelligence and motivation. There are, however, many other explanations for the growth of within-group earnings inequality. See Levy and Murnane (1992) and Sattinger (1993).

8. See Figure 1.6 for households and Figure 1.7 for families. When I say that more persons won than lost, it is a rough summary because there is no simple way to talk about specific individuals over 20 years' time. Persons who were 25 in 1970 were 45 in 1990 and we would expect their earnings to rise through promotions, even if average wages in the period were stagnant—that is, even if a 45-year-old made the same in 1990 as a 45-year-old had made in 1970. Conversely, persons who were 50 in 1970 would be 70 in 1990 and we would expect their earnings to fall owing to retirement.

9. Statistics on per capita income come from U.S. Council of Economic Advisers (1993:Table B-25). This measure, based on GDP accounts, includes the value of noncash income such as employer-provided health insurance, Medicare, and food stamps.

10. U.S. Council of Economic Advisers (1993:Table B-34). The figure refers to the proportion of women aged 16 and over who work at a point in time. As Mishel and Bernstein note (1993:Table 1.30), as married women move into the labor force, the official increase in disposable income per capita exaggerates the rise in living standards. Official income statistics measure transactions. Thus, they measure mother's wages from her new job, but they do not measure the reduction in childcare, cooking, cleaning, and other services that she used to perform in the home "for free." The family can purchase substitutes for these lost services—for example, a daycare center—but if they do, their living standard will have risen by less than their measured change in per capita income suggests.

11. Though by the end of the decade this trend had leveled off as some young adults— particularly men—remained single but chose to live with their parents instead of establishing homes. McLanahan and Casper examine this reversal in their chapter in Volume 2.

12. On women's labor force participation, see U.S. Council of Economic Advisers (1993:Table B-34). On birthrates, see U.S. Bureau of the Census (1992. *Statistical Abstract of the United States for 1992:*Table 84). Some of the late 1980s birthrate increase reflected the previously postponed births of women who were now in their 30s.

13. This is perhaps one reason why Clinton's 1992 campaign statements about stagnant earnings were taken more seriously than Dukakis's similar statements four years earlier.

14. Other major components are interest income, 15 percent; net government transfer payments (Social Security, Medicaid), 11 percent; fringe benefits on wages, 6 percent (U.S. Council of Economic Advisers 1993:Table B-23).

15. As I suggested above, the full productivity-wage relationship is more complex than this description. *Average* wages grow with productivity, but the wages of specific groups can grow faster or slower than the average depending on supply and demand. During the 1950s and 1960s, productivity evolved in ways that kept demand and supply in balance for most groups leading to wage gains for most groups. In the 1980s, productivity evolved in ways that favored more-educated labor over less-educated labor and many semiskilled workers saw their wages fall.

16. We can trade with other nations, of course, but over the long run the value of our imports cannot exceed the value of our exports.

17. More detailed figures would show that from 1947 to 1966, labor productivity grew at 3.25 percent per year, well above its historical trend; that from 1966 to 1973, labor productivity growth averaged 2.25 percent per year, something like its historical trend; and productivity growth after 1973 averaged well below its long-run historical trend.

18. As careful scholars of the subject have shown, it is far easier to reject causes of the productivity slowdown than to accept them. For example, the fact that the slowdown occurred so suddenly rules out an explanation such as the shift of employment to the service sector, which had proceeded gradually over many years. Similarly, other industrialized countries also experienced productivity slowdowns after 1973, a fact that throws doubt on uniquely U.S. explanations like the glut of baby boom workers. See Denison (1985) and Baily and Blair (1988) for fuller discussions.

    Complicating matters is Robert Samuelson's observation (personal communication) that the high earnings and family income levels of 1973 may have been an artifact of President Nixon's wage and price controls which were lifted in that year. Samuelson argues that without wage and price controls, the move from growth to stagnation would have been more gradual.

19. Less painful investment alternatives include (a) "working around" existing employees by hiring additional people to run the new technology and (b) adding new technology by acquiring other companies that use that technology.

20. It is plausible that the rapid expansion of consumer markets after World War II eased the introduction of new technology in this way.

21. For example, during the 1980s, the credible threat of plant closings caused the United Auto Workers to agree to substantially modify work rules and job classifications in a number of automobile plants.

22. I am indebted to Dan Levy for this insight. Consistent with this story is Mueller

and Reardon's finding (forthcoming) for a sample of 700 U.S. corporations that the rate of return on investment was typically well below the effective cost of capital.

23. But see the 1969 preface to Riesman (1976) in which he describes his membership on a task force on national goals that easily constructed a list of projects that would have broken the then booming economy.

24. An early sign of Reagan's attitude was his firing of federal air traffic controllers, whose union had supported him, when they went on strike in 1981. In 1982, the national unemployment rate passed 10 percent, but Reagan made it clear he would not pressure the Fed to loosen the money supply, propose an emergency jobs bill, and so on.

25. See Blair and Schary (1993). As they note, high real interest rates help explain the start of the leveraged buy-out boom, but deals continued, pushed by a process of imitation and encouragement by investment bankers, long after interest rates subsided.

26. I recognize that this conclusion runs against the official data of the Bureau of Labor Statistics. Those data hold that manufacturing productivity gains were heavily concentrated in one industry—nonelectrical machinery (principally computers). But census data show that the elimination of semiskilled labor occurred throughout manufacturing, and anecdotal evidence suggests that these changes led to productivity gains in automobiles, steel, and a variety of other industries.

27. Between 1985 and 1990, *net* U.S. borrowing per year was nearly three times what it had been in 1981. See U.S. Council of Economic Advisers (1993:Table B-70).

28. In an Economics 1 course, firms act in similar ways—for example, they all eliminate semiskilled jobs—because each has independently made the same profit-maximizing calculations and has arrived at the same conclusion. More realistic theory suggests that patterns of job reduction and job growth contain a large element of imitation in which each firm relies on other firms' actions both for evidence on what is feasible and as protective cover in case the action is a failure. On the role of "cover" in investment decisions, see Scharfstein and Stein (1990).

29. Another decline in demand for semiskilled labor occurred in transportation, communications, and utilities—a group of industries that, until the late 1970s, could pay high wages because they were heavily regulated and protected from competition. In 1979, these industries employed about one in every eight men aged 25–55 who had not gone beyond high school. Of these men, 60 percent earned more than $30,000 per year.

30. I calculate net jobs added by subtracting the number of persons in an occupational category in April 1980 from the corresponding number of persons in April 1990. Over this period, managers and administrators grew from 11.3 million to 15.6 million, sales positions grew from 10.4 million to 16.6 million, and total employment grew from 109.2 million to 132.6 million.

31. I emphasize again the role of interfirm imitation in adopting ideas such as process reengineering. Until the late 1980s, a firm might have feared that employment reductions would be seen by the financial markets as a sign of weakness rather than of effective management. Clearly, that fear no longer exists.

32. Data are drawn from the decennial census for 1970, 1980, and 1990, and the Current Population Survey for March 1970, 1980, and 1990, both of which report

earnings and incomes for 1969, 1979, and 1989, respectively. 1969, 1979, and 1989 are all business cycle peaks, which means that comparisons among them reflect long-term trends more than different points in the business cycle.

33. The Gini coefficient lies between 0 and 1. A Gini of 0 corresponds to complete equality in which all persons have the same income. A Gini of 1 corresponds to complete inequality in which one person has all the income and everyone else has nothing. See Levy (1987:App. E) for a fuller description.

34. Both fractions exclude the 2–3 percent of each cohort who report no earnings at all.

35. Whereas Figures 1.1 and 1.2 include men with no earnings, Figures 1.4 and 1.5 include only women with at least $1 of earnings during the year. Prime-age men are expected to work. The proportion of men who report no earnings is of interest because many of these men are, at best, working episodically at very low wages. A significant proportion of prime working age women choose to work in the home. The fact that they report no earnings contains little evidence of what they might earn if they were working in the market, and a distribution that includes such women confounds economic conditions for working women with the decision to stay at home.

36. The ratio refers to the median money earnings of men and women who work year-round and full-time.

37. You can think about difference between two persons drawn from the same income distribution in two ways; either the dollar amount of income separating their incomes or the fraction of the population situated between them in the income distribution. These are known as the dollar distance and the people distance. The two measures do not necessarily provide the same picture of income inequality.

38. Fuller discussions of the female/male earnings gap are contained in the chapters by Wetzel and Bianchi in this volume.

39. Here, large metropolitan areas are defined as having 1 million persons or more at the beginning of the period under study.

40. Industry demand patterns were reinforced because college graduates were *not* concentrated in interior states. In the coastal states of California, New York, Washington, and Connecticut, 23–28 percent of adults were college graduates compared with 14–23 percent in the interior states of Iowa, Texas, Illinois, Indiana, and Oklahoma.

41. Household incomes would also be shaped by changes in income sources other than earnings, such as interest payments, dividends, and Social Security benefits.

42. And while Harriet's work was hard, it was arguably easier than the work of a farmer's wife a century earlier. Thus, Harriet may have had historically large quantities of time to devote to her children.

43. Another 3 percent of children live in father-only families.

44. I owe this way of seeing the problem to Cherlin (1990).

45. I thank Richard Easterlin for making this point in his discussion of an earlier draft of this work. The problem is similar to the different view one gets when looking at the growth of income per worker versus the growth of income per capita, a problem I discussed earlier.

46. On balance, working wives still equalized the income distribution among *husband-wife* families, though the equalizing effect was smaller than it had been in earlier decades. The different effects on husband-wife incomes and all family incomes arise because working wives' earnings "pull up the bottom" of the distribution of husband-wife family incomes, making them more equal. But this same "pulling up the bottom" increases the income gap between husband-wife families and female-headed families. See Cancian, Danziger, and Gottschalk (1993).

47. Although, as I noted earlier, the most recent data show a growing proportion of young singles who live with their parents rather than in independent households. See McLanahan and Casper's Chapter 1 in Volume 2.

48. The separation of economic and demographic causes is admittedly tricky. For example, Easterlin would argue that the rising age of first marriage was an adaptation to the slow growth of wages and so was as much economic as it was demographic.

49. For example, changed levels of welfare payments, private pensions, and other income beyond earnings.

50. This calculation is based on constant proportions of single-person households, female-headed households, and so on, but it is based on the actual increase in working wives. In a separate calculation, Ryscavage et al. (1992) assume actual changes in household structures but hold the level of wives' work at its 1969 level. In this case, the Gini coefficient would have been .420 rather than .431. Karoly (1993) estimates a slightly larger effect of changed household structures on income inequality.

51. "Without these families" fails to specify the counterfactual situation. Wilson (1987) and others argue that the growth of female-headed families reflects the growing number of men with very low wages—a situation that would provide a low family income even if the woman were married. Other researchers (e.g., Mare and Winship 1990) dispute this claim and argue that the increase in out-of-wedlock births and the resulting female-headed families are an independent trend that does not reflect the substantial growth of low-income men.

52. I thank Richard Easterlin for pointing this out to me.

53. These cash incomes may have understated farmers' living standards, but they are what the census counted.

54. Specifically, Karoly adjusts family income by the poverty standard for a family of that size. I discuss the poverty standard below.

55. In fairness, not everyone believes that this would be a bad thing. See Irving Kristol's discussion of Alan Blinder's essay on the income distribution (Kristol 1982).

56. Beyond confidentiality, there is an issue of accuracy since many high-income recipients refuse to give information to census interviewers.

57. Recall that median household income is defined such that half of all households have higher incomes and half have lower incomes. While the census estimates retain reporting limits on the incomes of high-income families, these families remain at the top of the income distribution and so leave the calculation of median income unchanged.

58. The Treasury data deal with confidentiality by providing literally no information on the persons in the tax filing unit (e.g., the age or education of the household head).

In addition, since the data are based on tax returns, they exclude any observations on persons with very low incomes who do not file.

59. The two distributions also differ in that CBO weighs each household's income by the number of persons in that household while the Census Bureau counts each household's income only once. This difference may lead to divergent inequality estimates in a single year, but it is unlikely to cause significant divergent estimates of the *change* in inequality over the 1980s.

60. In 1989, for example, census estimates suggest that including the value of employer-provided health insurance in household income would leave the Gini coefficient unchanged (since it is received throughout the distribution), whereas including the value of noncash government benefits would lower the Gini coefficient by .03. See U.S. Bureau of the Census (1992c:Table 1).

61. A second source of wealth data is the Census Bureau's Survey of Income and Program Participation (SIPP), but its small number of observations, particularly among high-income households, makes it the less useful of the two data sets in examining inequality.

62. In order to perform this analysis, Wolff had to make a number of adjustments to the three data sets to make them consistent with one another and to reconcile them with the Federal Reserve Board's annual Flow of Funds accounts, which estimate the level of various assets in the economy (e.g., savings accounts, real estate holdings) but do not examine the distribution of the assets across households.

63. This definition excludes the value of cars and other consumer durables. Assets like life insurance and pension plans are treated through their cash surrender value. The projected value of Social Security payments is not counted since it has no immediate market value.

64. I base these calculations on the authors' fixed effects reported in Table 1A.1. The calculations adjust for the changing composition of the sample over time.

65. Since individuals can file separately or jointly, there is no neat correspondence between tax filing units and households. In the early 1990s, there were about 113 million tax filing units compared with about 95 million households. Since many of these households had too little income to file taxes, the discrepancy between tax filers and households is larger than these numbers suggest.

66. As Feenberg and Poterba show, the change in the upper tail of the distribution is more skewed than these data suggest, with the biggest gain in the share of the top .50 percent of tax filers coming from the top .25 percent of tax filers.

67. I have in mind such economists as Jude Wanniski, Paul Craig Roberts, and Lawrence Kudlow. For a recent example, see Kudlow's assessment of the Clinton tax increases on high-income taxpayers as quoted in Harper (1993).

68. The Reagan administration's signals in this regard included the previously mentioned firing of the air traffic controllers as well as a positive attitude toward striker replacement legislation.

69. Recall that had incomes been growing at reasonable rates, the 1990 distributions would have been centered around median incomes perhaps 45 percent higher than the 1970 distribution.

70. In this connection, Mishel and Bernstein (1993:Table 8–17) summarize data from

the Joint Center for Urban Studies, which show that homeownership rates among household heads aged 30–34 declined from 61.1 percent in 1980 to 53.6 percent in 1989.

71. Counting food stamps as part of income is straightforward and should be undertaken. Converting Medicaid and Medicare as income is a more difficult process. In actuarial terms, it is reasonable to say that Medicaid is equivalent to, say, a $5,000 insurance policy. But if we counted the $5,000 as income, it would mean that taking $5,000 from poor persons and giving them Medicaid coverage leaves them equally well off, which is not necessarily true.

72. The counterargument focuses on the stunning increase in murders of black males in their late teens. This rate more than doubled between 1986 and 1991 such that a 15-year-old black male now has about a 1-in-200 chance of being murdered before he turns 21. I have not seen an analysis on whether these murders coincide with already existing underclass areas or whether they represent something more widespread.

73. The hypothesis makes more sense in the late 1960s and early 1970s when many states increased Aid to Families with Dependent Children (AFDC) cash benefits, and the cash benefits were supplemented by newly enacted Medicaid health insurance benefits. During the 1980s, however, AFDC per person cash benefits declined in real terms by about 10 percent (U.S. House of Representatives 1993:pp. 666–667, 668).

74. Recall that the poverty line is constant in real terms and so rising real wages would raise earnings vis-à-vis the poverty line.

75. This was doubly true since the original legislation overindexed for inflation, a fault that was subsequently remedied. See Derthick (1979) for a full discussion.

76. These numbers are calculated from the perspective of the child: A family with five children will generate five observations in the calculation. Thus, the percentage of all children in five-child families will be larger than the percentage of all *families* who have five children.

77. As the authors note, these effects are upper bounds because they do not control for unobserved problems (e.g., a bad marriage) that caused the formation of the female-headed family in the first place. The authors' estimates do *not* control for family income because, as they argue, in today's society, low income is usually one of the consequences of being in the female-headed household.

78. This was a significant change from, say, the 1950s, when black male college graduates typically earned less than white male high school graduates.

79. Slower labor force growth also meant that the labor force no longer was growing faster than the population, thus, the number of persons dividing each paycheck stopped falling.

80. The missing third category is service workers: guards, cooks, janitors, and so on.

81. I use the term "better-educated" to describe not only college graduates but persons with particular skills—for example, radiology technicians and auto mechanics.

82. This nondiscussion is best illustrated by the [treatment] "Moynihan Report." See Rainwater and Yancy (1967) for a discussion.

TABLE 1A.1  Median annual earnings of men and women, by age, education, and race (in 1989 dollars).

| Educational Attainment | 1969 | | | 1979 | | | 1989 | | |
|---|---|---|---|---|---|---|---|---|---|
| | Ages 25–34 | Ages 35–44 | Ages 45–54 | Ages 25–34 | Ages 35–44 | Ages 45–54 | Ages 25–34 | Ages 35–44 | Ages 45–54 |
| **Men** | | | | | | | | | |
| < High school | $19,396 | $22,602 | $22,602 | $16,898 | $21,652 | $23,654 | $13,500 | $17,000 | $20,000 |
| High school | $25,167 | $29,014 | $29,014 | $23,114 | $30,410 | $31,171 | $19,500 | $25,000 | $28,000 |
| Some college | $26,129 | $32,220 | $32,220 | $24,330 | $33,620 | $33,788 | $22,000 | $29,334 | $33,000 |
| 4 years of college | $32,220 | $42,960 | $45,044 | $27,876 | $42,233 | $45,679 | $28,700 | $37,000 | $44,000 |
| > 4 years of college | $31,579 | $45,044 | $49,853 | $28,553 | $42,233 | $47,300 | $33,000 | $45,000 | $50,000 |
| **Women** | | | | | | | | | |
| < High school | $ 6,572 | $ 9,137 | $ 9,778 | $ 8,352 | $ 9,670 | $10,142 | $ 7,560 | $ 9,500 | $10,000 |
| High school | $10,420 | $11,381 | $12,984 | $11,738 | $11,831 | $13,183 | $11,000 | $12,000 | $13,000 |
| Some college | $12,984 | $12,664 | $14,908 | $13,520 | $13,858 | $15,007 | $14,100 | $16,000 | $16,933 |
| 4 years of college | $17,793 | $16,511 | $20,679 | $16,898 | $16,898 | $18,452 | $20,383 | $21,400 | $22,000 |
| > 4 years of college | $20,358 | $24,205 | $27,091 | $19,431 | $22,810 | $25,343 | $24,453 | $28,000 | $30,000 |
| **Non-Hispanic White Men** | | | | | | | | | |
| < High school | $20,999 | $24,205 | $23,564 | $18,587 | $23,732 | $25,343 | $15,000 | $19,800 | $22,000 |
| High school | $25,808 | $29,014 | $29,014 | $23,722 | $30,410 | $32,099 | $20,000 | $25,000 | $29,000 |
| Some college | $26,770 | $32,220 | $33,182 | $25,343 | $33,788 | $35,351 | $23,000 | $30,000 | $34,212 |
| 4 years of college | $32,220 | $43,441 | $46,006 | $28,586 | $42,233 | $47,300 | $29,600 | $38,000 | $45,000 |
| > 4 years of college | $31,900 | $45,364 | $51,296 | $28,721 | $43,027 | $48,314 | $35,000 | $46,032 | $50,000 |
| **Non-Hispanic White Women** | | | | | | | | | |
| < High school | $ 6,893 | $ 9,778 | $10,099 | $ 7,913 | $ 9,720 | $10,480 | $ 7,500 | $ 9,900 | $10,000 |
| High school | $10,098 | $11,381 | $12,984 | $11,426 | $11,831 | $13,183 | $11,000 | $12,000 | $13,000 |
| Some college | $12,343 | $12,343 | $14,908 | $13,520 | $13,520 | $14,796 | $14,454 | $15,800 | $16,536 |
| 4 years of college | $17,152 | $16,190 | $20,358 | $16,898 | $15,209 | $16,898 | $20,500 | $20,968 | $21,840 |
| > 4 years of college | $20,358 | $23,884 | $26,770 | $19,195 | $21,965 | $25,343 | $24,500 | $28,000 | $30,000 |

|  | | | | | | | | | |
|---|---|---|---|---|---|---|---|---|---|
| **Non-Hispanic Black Men** | | | | | | | | | |
| < High school | $14,587 | $16,190 | $16,190 | $13,520 | $16,898 | $16,898 | $10,000 | $13,345 | $16,000 |
| High school | $19,396 | $21,320 | $20,197 | $16,898 | $22,810 | $24,773 | $14,000 | $19,000 | $24,000 |
| Some college | $21,320 | $24,205 | $24,045 | $18,672 | $25,707 | $27,032 | $17,000 | $24,000 | $27,312 |
| 4 years of college | $24,045 | $29,014 | $25,808 | $23,705 | $32,099 | $28,996 | $23,833 | $30,908 | $32,583 |
| > 4 years of college | $27,411 | $33,564 | $32,220 | $23,654 | $33,788 | $37,166 | $27,000 | $37,000 | $40,500 |
| **Non-Hispanic Black Women** | | | | | | | | | |
| < High school | $ 6,572 | $ 6,893 | $ 6,572 | $ 8,453 | $10,142 | $ 9,670 | $ 7,499 | $ 9,800 | $10,000 |
| High school | $10,740 | $11,702 | $11,702 | $12,203 | $13,520 | $13,183 | $10,400 | $13,103 | $14,226 |
| Some college | $14,267 | $14,587 | $14,587 | $14,872 | $16,898 | $16,485 | $14,000 | $18,000 | $19,000 |
| 4 years of college | $19,396 | $20,678 | $16,190 | $18,587 | $22,810 | $23,654 | $20,000 | $25,000 | $26,000 |
| > 4 years of college | $21,320 | $25,808 | $29,335 | $21,121 | $25,597 | $28,688 | $25,000 | $30,000 | $32,000 |
| **Hispanic Men** | | | | | | | | | |
| < High school | | | | $15,159 | $18,250 | $18,503 | $12,000 | $14,000 | $15,600 |
| High school | | | | $20,276 | $25,343 | $25,495 | $16,000 | $20,000 | $23,000 |
| Some college | | | | $21,121 | $28,992 | $29,144 | $19,000 | $25,000 | $28,000 |
| 4 years of college | | | | $25,343 | $33,864 | $33,788 | $24,827 | $32,000 | $36,000 |
| > 4 years of college | | | | $24,499 | $38,855 | $38,855 | $25,000 | $38,635 | $42,000 |
| **Hispanic Women** | | | | | | | | | |
| < High school | | | | $ 8,453 | $ 9,180 | $ 9,281 | $ 7,600 | $ 8,500 | $ 9,000 |
| High school | | | | $11,544 | $11,831 | $12,625 | $11,520 | $12,191 | $12,390 |
| Some college | | | | $13,520 | $14,297 | $14,449 | $14,000 | $16,000 | $15,600 |
| 4 years of college | | | | $16,898 | $18,587 | $18,452 | $20,000 | $23,000 | $22,000 |
| > 4 years of college | | | | $18,309 | $21,965 | $25,343 | $24,000 | $29,000 | $30,000 |

NOTE: The reader may be surprised that many 1989 medians end in 000 or 500, while medians for 1969 and 1979 do not. The difference is artificial. When persons fill out census forms, they often report their family income and earnings rounded to the nearest $500 or $1,000. As a result, medians will often be round numbers as well. The 1969 and 1979 medians lost their "roundness" when they were adjusted for inflation to 1989 dollars.

57

# 2

# Labor Force, Unemployment, and Earnings

## JAMES R. WETZEL

SHORTLY AFTER THE 1980 census, national media attention centered briefly on the cheerful, 83-year-old innkeeper of the Spirit Lake Lodge. Living hard abreast the northern slope of Mount St. Helens, Harry Truman earned his 15 minutes of fame by steadfastly ignoring the rumbling signals of geophysical change deep below the mountain. On May 18, 1980, at 12:32 P.M., the signals of change gave way to a full-scale volcanic eruption. Within moments, Harry Truman and the Spirit Lake Lodge were swept into oblivion. Just as Mount St. Helens loomed above Harry Truman's inn, the nation's economy looms above our everyday lives. Generally a comforting presence, it is always changing, usually quietly, but sometimes dramatically. During the 1980s, economic change was exceedingly dramatic. The first few years of the decade were marked by the worst economic contraction and highest unemployment since the Great Depression. The middle years brought a prolonged period of junk-bond-funded corporate merger and buy-out activity and speculative building activity. That speculative frenzy was largely responsible for the savings and loan debacle at decade's end. Like Harry Truman, some people and institutions did not adapt and were destroyed. Most adapted, of course, but the shock waves of change reached virtually every nook and cranny of the nation.

Unpredictable global imbalances during the 1970s set the stage for the economic developments of the 1980s. Worldwide crop failures and the OPEC oil embargo drove food and energy prices sharply higher early in the 1970s. Because energy is instrumental in the provision of virtually all goods and services, steep increases in energy costs gave rise to a 10 percent jump in consumer prices. The consequent shrinkage of real incomes, coupled with the deflationary effects of prevailing high interest rates, triggered a severe recession.

**59**

Unemployment soared to 9 percent of the labor force near the recession trough in 1975—a figure almost triple the jobless rates of the late 1960s and an unprecedented high for the post–World War II era. *That recession marked the end of 30 years of sizable, widely distributed advances in workers' real earnings and ushered in two decades of challenging economic times.* Inflation continued high after the recession of 1975 and accelerated sharply late in the decade. Two successive recessions in the early 1980s, brought on by anti-inflationary monetary policy, caused even more severe unemployment. The national jobless rate reached a post–Depression high of 11 percent and averaged almost 10 percent during 1982 and 1983. Employment rose considerably as the decade progressed, but there were important differences by industrial sector. Restructuring in the goods-producing industries to enhance competitiveness in the face of fierce foreign competition continuously reduced labor requirements for any fixed level of goods output. The limited additional hiring by goods producers that did take place during the 1980s was confined largely to skilled workers with the flexibility and adaptability necessary to make effective use of sophisticated machines and complex processes. Simultaneously, the changing tastes and needs of an aging population stimulated relatively more spending on services, especially on those provided by highly educated workers. Reflecting these changes, demand for labor was strong in occupations that require self-direction, command of language, and good quantitative skills.

Favored by strong demand, persons with high levels of education improved their relative position in the good-jobs, high-earnings sweepstakes. Those with less education, especially high school dropouts, found employment conditions grim. Even educated youths fared less well during the 1980s than the middle-aged, who apparently enjoyed some advantage based on prior job attachments with seniority protection. Encouraged by strong demand for skilled white collar and technical workers, women substantially widened and deepened their commitment to work for pay or profit. They realized significant gains in absolute and relative earnings. By contrast, men's labor force participation eroded somewhat and, on average, growth of their annual earnings barely exceeded inflation. Employment and earnings outcomes for the more- and less-educated, for women and men, and for youths versus their parents were especially influenced by the differential effects of technological advances, by the labor-saving properties of the modernization of industrial production processes, and by changing spending patterns and their derivative labor requirements. Using as little technical jargon as possible, this chapter describes labor market trends that influenced the demographic and social developments analyzed in this book and its companion volume.

## The Organization of the Chapter

This chapter is divided into five broad subject areas: labor supply, employment and work experience, total compensation and earnings, unemployment, and labor market–related economic hardship. The average labor market experiences of women and men by education, age, occupation, and industry are summarized as are differential trends among whites, blacks, and Hispanics. Because the size and composition of the nation's armed forces were little changed over the decade, I focus entirely on the civilian economy.

Labor market conditions are highly sensitive to the various stages of business cycles, so I mainly use measures of employment, unemployment, and earnings during 1989 and 1979 when cyclical conditions were similar. The national unemployment rate averaged 5.8 percent in 1979, just before the economy reached a business cycle peak in January 1980, and 5.3 percent in 1989, just before the economy reached a cyclical peak in July 1990.

Decennial censuses and the Current Population Survey (CPS) are the primary sources of the data presented.[1] They measure labor market developments from two complementary perspectives. Each month, the government uses the CPS to develop a cross-sectional portrait of labor market conditions. It provides the well-known *monthly unemployment rate.* Analyzed in conjunction with related measures of employment and hours of work, the jobless rate is a critical macroeconomic indicator: a timely, reliable index of current business conditions and the cyclical health of the economy. When the rate is dropping and employment is rising, more of the nation's human resources are being used to produce needed goods and services. A tightening labor market—that is, decreasing unemployment—is consistent with rising earnings and consumer spending, lending additional strength to an expansion. The monthly labor market measures are averaged over the calendar year to provide annual estimates. The monthly figures and their annual averages are static measures; that is, they capture how many persons are in a particular labor force status at a particular time, but they do not capture movements of people among various situations. Thus, an annual unemployment average of 1 million could be composed of a group of 1 million people pounding the bricks month after month all year in search of work. Or that same 1 million figure could be composed of 12 million different people each of whom experienced one short episode of joblessness during the year. The two extreme possibilities present quite different social, economic, and public policy implications.

To assess labor market dynamics, data are collected on work experience during the entire prior year in the March CPS. The work experience data tell us how many weeks of work, how many weeks of unemployment, and how many weeks outside the labor force workers experienced during the year as well as their annual earnings, educational attainment, family status, and occupation/industry attachment. These data provide a quite different view of labor market conditions. The incidence of unemployment—that is, the number of persons who had at least one spell of joblessness during the year—is usually two and one-half to three times as large as the average monthly unemployment figure. The average incidence of employment—that is, people who worked at some time during the year—typically is 10 to 15 percent greater than the monthly average of employed persons. Usually, 5 to 10 percent more persons have some labor market experience—that is, either worked or looked for work—during the year than are in the labor force in an average month. Similar work experience data also are collected in decennial censuses. Because decennial census samples are much larger than CPS samples, they permit accurate analysis of small subpopulations and geographic areas with modest-size populations.

### Definitions Used

Definitions in this chapter are those used in the CPS and censuses, but they may be somewhat inconsistent with the reader's appreciation of the specific terms. For example, any work for pay or profit, even one hour, during a survey's reference period automatically classifies a person as *employed. Full-time, year-round employment* is defined as usually working 35 hours or more per week and working at least 50 weeks of the year. Circumstances of no work for pay or profit (not even one hour), but with job-seeking activity or being on layoff from a job, and being available for work are required to classify a person as *unemployed.* The sum of employment and unemployment is the *labor force.* The *unemployment rate* is the ratio of the unemployed to the labor force times 100. The *labor force participation rate* is the ratio of the civilian labor force to the civilian noninstitutional population times 100.

In this chapter, persons aged 16–64 are referred to as the *working age* population. Within the working age population, persons aged 16–24 are referred to as *youths* and persons aged 25–64 are *prime working age adults.* Persons aged 65 and over are the *retirement age* population. The terms *labor force* and *work force* are treated as synonymous as are *unemployed* and *jobless,* and *poor* and *poverty.* Also, all references to the poverty rate and the poverty status of workers or potential workers are based on official government estimates and definitions.

### LABOR SUPPLY

Labor force growth accelerated in the late 1960s and continued strong through the 1970s, mostly because of the large number of baby boomers (persons born between 1946 and 1965) moving through the early working ages (by 1990, they all were aged 25 and over). Because of substantial reductions in childbearing during the late 1960s and early 1970s, the net number of American youths declined steadily during the 1980s and was smaller by 4.8 million at decade's end. The small size of the Depression–World War II generations meant that the population aged 45–64 increased by only 2.2 million over the

TABLE 2.1  Sources of labor force growth: 1979–1989 (thousands of persons).

| Gender and Age | Labor Force Change Attributable to | | | |
| | Population Change | Participation Rate Changes | Interaction | Total |
| --- | --- | --- | --- | --- |
| Men, Total | +8,281 | −1,171 | −64 | +7,046 |
| 16–24 years | −1,760 | −343 | +51 | −2,052 |
| 25–44 years | +8,971 | −267 | −95 | +8,609 |
| 45–64 years | +1,070 | −561 | −20 | +489 |
| Women, Total | +4,955 | +5,524 | +1,047 | +11,526 |
| 16–24 years | −1,567 | +389 | −44 | −1,222 |
| 25–44 years | +5,938 | +3,328 | +999 | +10,265 |
| 45–64 years | +584 | +1,807 | +92 | +2,483 |
| Total, Both Sexes | +13,236 | +4,353 | +983 | +18,572 |

SOURCE: U.S. Department of Labor (1991; 1988).

decade. In stark contrast, persons aged 25–44 increased by 18.7 million as the huge baby boom generation matured into the prime working ages. In all, the civilian noninstitutional population aged 16–64 increased by 16.1 million during the 1980s.

With the prime working age population soaring and the number of youths declining, demographic circumstances were optimal for sharp population-induced labor supply increases. If labor force participation rates by gender, race, and ten-year age group had remained constant over the decade, the age composition of population growth by itself would have produced a net labor force increase of 13.2 million, as is shown in Table 2.1 (column 1). In fact, the labor force increased by 18.6 million (column 4), fully 5 million more than anticipated on the basis of population growth. Rising participation rates accounted for the "extra" 5 million workers.

Participation in the labor force was essentially stable at 59–60 percent of the working age population from the end of World War II through the early 1970s. Within the overall average, women were increasing their participation and men were reducing theirs, largely via earlier retirement. Women's commitment to market work intensified early in the 1970s. During the 1980s, adult women of *all* ages, races, and Hispanic ethnicity boosted their labor force activity sharply (Table 2A.1). If labor force participation rates had stabilized at 1979 levels, the rise for women would have been less than half as large as the actual increase of 11.5 million. The average labor force participation rate of women aged 16–64 rose almost 9 percentage points from 1979 to nearly 68 percent in 1989. *Women cut the average labor force participation gap with men by one third during the 1980s.*

Men of *all* ages, races, and Hispanic ethnicity had lower participation rates

TABLE 2A.1  Labor force participation rates (percentage of the civilian noninstitutional population in the labor force).

| Gender and Age | 1989 Level | | | | Change from 1979 | | | |
|---|---|---|---|---|---|---|---|---|
| | Whites | Blacks | Other Races | Hispanics | Whites | Blacks | Other Races | Hispanics |
| Men | | | | | | | | |
| 16–19 | 61.0% | 44.7% | 43.1% | 55.6% | −3.7% | −0.1% | −3.2% | −1.2% |
| 20–24 | 86.8 | 80.1 | 70.8 | 89.5 | −0.8 | −0.5 | −3.0 | −0.7 |
| 25–34 | 95.4 | 89.8 | 87.3 | 94.0 | −0.6 | −0.9 | −1.1 | −0.1 |
| 35–44 | 95.3 | 88.7 | 91.8 | 92.8 | −1.1 | −1.8 | −0.5 | −1.1 |
| 45–54 | 92.2 | 82.5 | 89.3 | 87.1 | −0.1 | −2.1 | −1.4 | −2.6 |
| 55–64 | 68.3 | 55.4 | 75.0 | 66.3 | −5.1 | −9.4 | −3.5 | −5.9 |
| Women | | | | | | | | |
| 16–19 | 57.1 | 40.5 | 42.0 | 38.5 | −0.3 | +3.8 | −3.7 | −5.2 |
| 20–24 | 74.0 | 65.5 | 63.7 | 59.3 | +3.5 | +3.9 | +2.9 | +0.4 |
| 25–34 | 73.8 | 73.6 | 66.2 | 61.4 | +10.7 | +3.4 | +2.8 | +8.8 |
| 35–44 | 75.9 | 78.0 | 72.5 | 66.0 | +12.9 | +10.0 | +7.2 | +12.4 |
| 45–54 | 70.6 | 70.0 | 69.3 | 58.8 | +12.5 | +10.4 | +5.7 | +9.2 |
| 55–64 | 45.2 | 42.4 | 48.9 | 39.6 | +3.7 | +0.1 | +3.6 | +5.3 |

SOURCES: U.S. Department of Labor (1991; 1988).

NOTE: Hispanics may be of any race and are included under the appropriate race category.

in 1989 than in 1979. Lower participation by men meant a shortfall in their labor force growth of 1.2 million compared with the level anticipated on the basis of 1979 participation rates (see column 2 in Table 2.1). Participation of young men declined significantly, especially among teenagers who had dropped out of high school and had few marketable skills. The largest reductions, however, were among men aged 55–64. Early retirement incentives at troubled firms and permanent job losses at failed firms doubtless stimulated more early retirements than would have been the case in more economically ebullient times. In an average month of 1989, 17.8 million persons said they were not in the labor force because of retirement. The comparable figures for 1979 and 1969 were 10.4 million and 4.9 million, respectively. Thus, the retired population rose by 70 percent over the decade, while the working population rose a little less than 20 percent and the total population rose only 10 percent.

## Minorities in the Labor Force

The nation's absolute labor supply was significantly bolstered by immigration during the 1980s. Of the 7.2 million working age immigrants who arrived in the United States during the 1980s, 4.9 million were in the labor force at the time of the 1990 census.[2] Thus, recent immigrants accounted for about one of every four net additions to the labor force over the decade. Because male immigrants have labor force participation rates close to those of native-born men, they had little effect on overall labor force participation trends for men. Female immigrants of recent vintage have lower labor force participation rates than native-born women, so they slightly damped the rise of women's labor force participation.

The work experience of new immigrants strongly influenced average labor market outcomes for minority groups. Indeed, immigration had to directly and importantly influence the averages for minorities since about two thirds of Asians and more than two fifths of Hispanics living in the United States in 1990 were born abroad (see Chiswick and Sullivan's chapter in Volume 2). Because most immigrant workers of the 1980s were from nonindustrial, non–English-speaking countries and had limited educational exposure, they contributed substantially to growth of the less-educated, low-skilled work force. By the standards of native-born Americans, such immigrants face an uninviting labor market future of low-wage, no-fringe-benefit, temporary work in an economy that places an increasing premium on the skills learned in school. By the standards of immigrants, however, such outcomes may look extremely inviting in light of conditions in their country of birth and the comparative success of prior immigrants after extended periods in the United States (Meisenheimer 1992).

Whites generally have higher labor force participation rates than blacks, other races,[3] or Hispanics for comparable gender and age groups (see Table 2A.1). The gap is especially large among youths—about 15 percentage points higher for white teenagers than for black and other races teenagers, for example. Lower participation by men during the 1980s was pervasive by age, race, and ethnicity, but rates fell most sharply for mature black men, who already had the lowest rates among adult males. Disability is a significant factor in the lower participation rates of black men. Fully 10 percent of black men and 5 percent of white men aged 16–64 reported a severe work disability in 1989.[4] Regardless of race, only about one in every eight severely disabled men had any employment during that year. Thus, about 9 percent of black men and 4 percent of white men aged 16–64 did not participate in the labor force during 1989 owing to a severe work disability. If the frequency of severe work disability were comparable among whites and blacks, other things remaining the same, the black-white participation gap of men would have been smaller by about 5 percentage points.

Participation rates of white, black, other races, and Hispanic women rose for all adult age groups during the 1980s. The largest increases were among white women aged 25–54. For most of the post–World War II years, black women were more likely to be in the labor force than white women. During the 1970s, however, rates began to converge as the labor market commitments of white women intensified. By 1989, rates for white women were generally a trifle higher than rates for black women of the same ages. Hispanic women, many of whom are recent immigrants, have much lower participation rates than white, black, or other races women, but their rates rose considerably during the 1980s.

### Women in the Labor Force

Despite generational differences in the scale of the increases, women of every cohort born since the turn of the century have shown an increased propensity to be in the labor force at any age than had their mothers or grandmothers. After World War II, gradual changes in the industrial structure of the economy and concentration of the population in urban areas provided job opportunities and access to labor markets. At the same time, labor saving devices for the home and greatly expanded access to personal transportation facilitated job market entry. Attitudes about women working, especially after marriage and childbearing, shifted gradually from widespread disapproval in the 1950s to the proactive public policy support of today. However, the change in attitudes seemed to trail behind advancing participation and certainly does not explain the intensification of the upward trend during the most recent decade.

Women in all marital and motherhood categories boosted their labor force participation during the 1980s. Women of the Depression generation had reduced their participation during their early childbearing years. As Figure 2.1 shows, the early baby boom generation (born 1946–1955) started with much higher participation in their early 20s and increased their participation at each stage of the marriage, childbearing, and child-rearing years. The late baby boomers (1956–1965) started participating at a higher level than their elder sisters and showed an even higher propensity to continue working during the childbearing years. Thus, the behavioral change in the labor market commitment of women, particularly of wives and mothers, has been most pronounced among baby boomers. The room for increases was largest for wives with children, and they recorded the largest absolute and relative increases (DaVanzo and Rahman 1994). The baby bust cohort (born 1966–1975) still is too young for a significant number to be mothers, but they have participated in the labor force at an even higher rate in the initial stages of the work-life cycle than did the baby boomers.

Increases in the labor market commitment of women as pervasive, sustained, and sizable as those of the past two decades must be an outgrowth of some identifiable set of social, economic, or perhaps even demographic conditions that help explain the behavioral shift. Why has women's participation risen so sharply? Although it is impossible to quantify, attitudes regarding the rights and

FIGURE 2.1   Women's participation rates, by birth cohort and age.

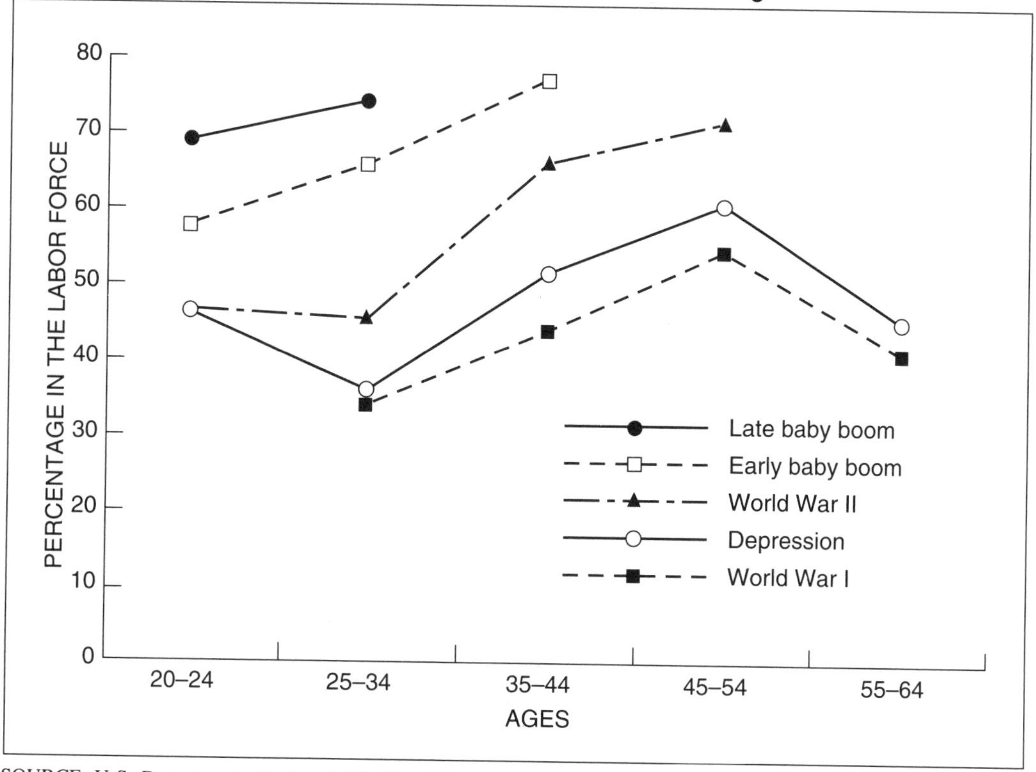

SOURCE: U.S. Department of Labor (1991:164–167; 1988).

opportunities that should be available to women in all aspects of life dramatically shifted for large segments of the population during the 1960s. Paralleling the drive to provide equal opportunity for minorities, the attitude shift with regard to women's labor market opportunities appears to have most noticeably influenced the thinking and behavior of middle-class white women. Subsequent social and economic trends strongly reinforced the labor market "equity" shift, as did earlier fertility trends that generated a relative surplus of marriage-age women from the late 1960s through the early 1980s.

An important feature of the social change that swept the nation during the turbulent 1960s was a pronounced breakdown of the marital compact between women and men. While never fully observed, the compact (which required the husband to be the economic provider, *forever*, and the wife to care for the family and the home, *forever*) still was firmly in place in the 1950s (see Bianchi's chapter in this volume). Since then, however, the portion of adult life spent in marriage has been declining steadily. We now marry later, and a larger share never marry. For those who do marry, the likelihood of divorce is much higher than it was for earlier generations. Moreover, for a person who is divorced now, the chances of remarriage are smaller than they were a decade or two ago.[5] Steeply rising divorce rates during the 1960s and 1970s (Wetzel 1990) doubtless contributed to a shift in the mind-set of many women and men who came of age in that era. Finally, because women live longer than men and tend to marry men who are a few years older, the average woman whose final marriage is not terminated by divorce faces a long period of widowhood during which her economic well-being depends largely on her own earnings and pension entitlement. Thus, an important incentive for women's increased participation is the basic need for economic support before and after marriage.

Maintenance of future earning power also provides an incentive for women to stay in the labor force. Wage premiums are associated with longer tenure that provides specialized knowledge acquired on the job in a particular establishment; consequently, those who move into and out of the labor force diminish their future earning power (Mincer 1974). The relative cost of not working also is an important incentive for women to stay in the labor force. Baby boom women achieved high levels of education at considerable costs in terms of both out-of-pocket expenditures and forgone earnings, but they command higher wages. Thus, time spent on nonmarket activities is more expensive in terms of forgone earnings than for their peers with less education.

Unsurprisingly, consumption goals probably are the most important incentive for women's market work. Baby boomers expect a rising standard of living based on their experience while growing up in the prosperous 1960s and relatively prosperous early 1970s (Jones 1980). With their average real wage rate almost stagnant since the middle 1970s, few men have sufficient earning power to provide an ever-rising standard of living (see Levy's chapter in this volume). Hence, during the 1970s a more widely shared view emerged of the family as an economic unit in which both husband and wife should contribute market earnings and more equally share household and family duties, although the latter seems to have lagged considerably behind the former.

Finally, particular areas of inflationary pressure on families may be especially important in influencing wives' participation. Most Americans regard homeownership as an essential element of a middle-class lifestyle. Because housing costs rose particularly sharply during the 1970s and most of the 1980s, many couples felt it essential for the wife to be in the labor force in order to buy and maintain a family home (Myers 1985). (See Myers and Wolch's chapter in this volume.) Also, most baby boomers intend that their children go to college. College costs have risen much faster than general price levels. With as few as two closely spaced children only a small minority of single-earner families can afford to put their children through even a less-costly state college. Responding to all of these pressures and incentives, wives and mothers flocked into the labor force. There were 6 million more married-couple families with the wife in the paid labor force in 1989 than in 1979, while the number of married-couple families with the wife not in the labor force declined by 2.8 million.

## Increases in the Educational Endowment of the Labor Force

Reflecting ever-larger investments of time and tuition, the educational preparation of each successive cohort of young Americans has increased relative to its immediate predecessor (see Mare's chapter in this volume). Among persons aged 25–29 the percentage of high school dropouts fell from 62 percent in 1940 to 39 percent in 1959 and to about 14 percent in 1979. College training of youths rose more rapidly after the Soviet Union orbited Sputnik in 1958, and more young women chose to enter college. Women constituted less than one third of college students in the late 1950s. During the 1960s, young women's paths through the school-to-college-to-work transition began to converge with those of young men. The proportion of young women going on to college after high school graduation approached that of young men in the late 1970s, and, by 1990, women held a majority of college slots and were slightly more likely than men to be enrolled.[6] Also, their college completion rates rose faster than men's. In the late 1950s, young men (aged 25–29) were twice as likely as young women to have completed four years or more of college training—15 versus 7.5 percent. In 1991, they were equally likely to have four years of college—about 23 percent each.[7] To achieve higher and higher levels of education, of course, youths must spend more time in the classroom and less in other pursuits, including full-time labor force activity, but also, apparently, in early marriage, childbearing, and child rearing (see McLanahan and Casper's chapter in Volume 2).

Full-scale labor force entry of adult college-trained baby boomers coupled with steady retirements of less-educated persons who reached working age during the 1930s and 1940s resulted in quantum increases in the average educational endowment of the labor force. Prime working age participants with four years or more of college training rose by 64 percent to 25.5 million during the 1980s, and those with one to three years rose by 58 percent to 20.8 million. Absolute and relative increases were larger for women than for men (Figure 2.2). Labor force participation for high school graduates increased by 9.5 million, while participation for those who did not complete high school *declined* by 3.3 million, almost one fifth, to 13.2 million. Although participation increases were largest among the college trained, women in each educational category boosted their rates. At the same time, labor participation rates of men in all education categories edged lower over the decade.

FIGURE 2.2    Prime working age labor force, by education:
1980 and 1990 (persons aged 25–64).

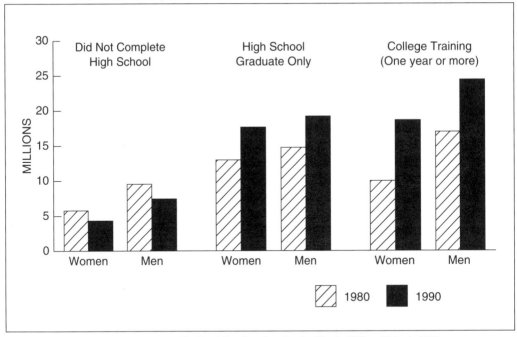

SOURCE: Current Population Survey Public Use Microdata Samples for March 1980 and March 1990.

### Nonparticipation in the Labor Force

About 55 million persons aged 16 and over did not participate in labor market activities at all during 1989. Thirty million were aged 60 and over. Of those, about two thirds were fully retired (i.e., they did not work for pay or profit at all during the year) and living on social security, deferred compensation in the form of pensions, and their personal savings (see Treas and Torrecilha's chapter in Volume 2). An additional 1 million younger persons were outside the labor force all year because they had retired "early." Home and family responsibilities were given as the reason for nonparticipation by 12 million women, many with young children at home, while school was given as the reason by 6.5 million youths (mostly teenagers). The disabled, who accounted for most remaining nonparticipants, are of particular social and public policy concern. Their number is much larger than commonly presumed. According to the 1990 census, 8.7 percent of prime working age persons had a severe work disability. Few of them were employed at the time of the census (McNeil 1993). During 1989, almost 4.5 million persons aged 16–59 reported that they were not in the labor force at all, and 2.6 million persons were out of the labor force part of the year owing to disability or serious illness. Annual survey data for the 1980s showed no basic change in the prevailing rate of work disability or its effects on the employment and earnings circumstances of the disabled. Compared with persons who do not have a work disability:[8]

The work-disabled were less than half as likely to be in the labor force;

If in the labor force, they were twice as likely to be unemployed;

If employed, they were only about two-thirds as likely to be in a full-time job;

Consequently, the annual earnings of those who worked were extremely low; and

Their poverty rates were (and continue to be) very high.


## EMPLOYMENT AND WORK EXPERIENCE

The decade opened on a dreary note as the economy reached a cyclical peak in January 1980 and drifted into recession during the spring and summer. There was a temporary uptick in net hiring late in the year; then labor demand weakened dramatically as real spending on consumer goods, structures, and capital equipment plummeted. Cyclical and permanent job losses mounted as the economy fell precipitously into the most severe recession since 1938. A record 26.5 million workers experienced at least one spell of unemployment during 1982. More important, 5.1 million workers with at least three years of seniority lost their jobs permanently over the 1979–1984 period owing to plant closures, shift elimination, or insufficient work to justify the continuation of permanent positions (Herz 1991). Although manufacturing accounted for only about one fifth of total employment at its 1979 peak of 22 million, almost half of the permanent job displacements took place in factories. Permanent job losses were concentrated among blue collar men, who held the lion's share of higher-wage factory production jobs.


### "Good" Jobs and "Bad" Jobs

Employment gains were very large during the initial cyclical recovery period (4.2 million in 1984 alone) and continued to be sizable until late in the decade. Despite the rapid growth, an intense "good jobs–bad jobs" controversy developed and was played out in the media (see, e.g., Kuttner 1983 and Thurow 1987) and public policy forums during the remainder of the decade. Participants in the debate agreed that job creation was rapid. Indeed, total employment increased about 18 percent over the decade, and the percentage of the population with jobs rose significantly. The dispute centered on the quality of newly created jobs: that is, about the capacity of the new jobs to ultimately provide middle-income, middle-class lifestyles to fully committed workers. In part the debate rested on the dual labor market theory that emerged during the 1970s. Dual market theorists contend that the labor market really comprises two large sub-markets with very different characteristics (Doeringer and Piore 1971). Specifically, a primary labor market provides "good" entry jobs that, via internal promotion, ultimately provide high wages, year-round work, fringe benefits (e.g., health insurance), on-the-job training, opportunities for advancement, and generous retirement benefits. A secondary market provides "bad" jobs with low wages, episodic work, few or no benefits, no training, and no real chance for advancement.

In provocative testimony and a widely distributed report for the Joint Economic Committee of the Congress (1986) and in *The Deindustrialization of America* (1982), Bluestone and Harrison argued that most of the jobs created after 1975 were in the secondary labor market and would not provide the upward mobility needed to sustain the middle-income, middle-class core of our society. At the time, job growth appeared to be quite different than it had been earlier. In particular, young men were not finding "good" jobs and their real earnings were declining steadily. Actual and perceived poor prospects of young men were seen as contributing to a variety of social trends of considerable public policy concern. Among others, lack of good jobs for young men was seen as contributing to declining marriage rates, rising out-of-wedlock birthrates, higher poverty rates, and growing participation by young men in crime (Johnson, Sum, and Weill 1989).

The crucial substantive issue of the "good jobs–bad jobs" debate is how different job creation was during the 1980s. If trends were decidedly different, are the changes temporary? If not, what is the appropriate public policy response? Gittleman and Howell (1992) provided quantitative answers to the first question. In a carefully executed analysis, they classified about 600 different occupations covering virtually all civilian employment into six, about equally sized, homogeneous groups. The job groups were objectively classified from good to bad on the basis of 17 measures of job quality (e.g., wage rates, fringe benefits, skill requirements). Using criteria based solely on the good/bad characteristics of occupations, the authors analyzed growth between the cyclical peak of 1979 and 1988, the latest data available to them. They found that "middle-class" jobs *declined* relative to total employment, and "good" and "bad" jobs increased about equally. Inevitably then, added workers were concentrated in the best and the worst jobs. They also discovered that the quality of the least desirable jobs declined; wages were relatively lower, there was more involuntary part-time work, and even less in the way of fringe benefits in 1988 than in 1979. When the distribution of job occupants by gender and race ethnicity in 1988 was compared with the 1979 distribution, it showed that white women were the principal beneficiaries of the increase in the best jobs. Black and Hispanic women and white men were about evenly distributed between the best and worst jobs. Hispanic and black men increased their presence only in the two least desirable job groups. Why did this pattern of job growth evolve, and why did it eventuate in this set of winners and losers?

Labor market imbalances sometimes are characterized in the media as situations in which "the economy *failed* to generate sufficient jobs for all who wish to work." Such perceptions betray deep misunderstanding of basic economics. The economy is not a benign presence that casually generates jobs merely because we are here and want work. Jobs are created by purchases of the services and goods produced by workers. The numbers and types of jobs created or destroyed at any given time are solely a function of the labor requirements of the production techniques in place in the particular sectors in which purchases are rising or falling. If there is insufficient purchasing of domestically produced goods and services for any reason—cyclically driven uncertainty, foreign competition, or changing preferences of consumers—there will be fewer jobs than job seekers. Even with sufficient overall demand, there will continue to be employment shortfalls if workers searching for jobs do not have needed skills or are in the wrong locations. At the same time, workers or prospective workers who have skills in key occupations in sectors that are experiencing growth may find that there are more job openings than workers. In that circumstance, their hours of work per week and their weeks of work per year are likely to increase. If a demand shift is strong enough relative to the supply of workers with needed training and work experience, wages will be bid up (Gamber and Joutz 1993). Workers in these sectors will realize higher annual earnings arising from both more work time and from higher wage rates, while workers without the requisite skills remain jobless or must accept menial jobs. In this context, Gittleman and Howell infer that growth of spending decisively favored sectors or occupations primarily staffed by highly educated workers, especially white women. Since middle-range jobs *declined,* demand conditions left mainly poor jobs (that were getting poorer) for those whose education ended after completing high school and particularly for those who dropped out before completing high school. Did the composition of labor demand result in the outcomes described by Gittleman and Howell and, if so, why?

## Employment Growth for Women and for Men

Demographic, socioeconomic, and public policy developments powerfully influence the composition and growth of purchases and, consequently, job creation and destruction. Characterized by sweeping scientific and technological advance, intense international competition, and major demographic changes, the 1980s provide particularly good examples of the labor market effects of changing patterns of demands for goods and services. For example, because of an aging population's health care needs, extensions of health insurance coverage,

TABLE 2.2  Experienced workers, by industry (thousands of persons).

| Industry Group | 1989 Level | | Change from 1979 | | |
|---|---|---|---|---|---|
| | Men | Women | Total | Men | Women |
| Professional services | 9,383 | 20,526 | +7,812 | +2,181 | +5,631 |
| Retail and wholesale trade | 14,942 | 14,284 | +5,391 | +2,700 | +2,691 |
| Finance, insurance, and real estate | 3,481 | 5,264 | +2,274 | +850 | +1,424 |
| Business and repair services | 4,016 | 2,516 | +1,842 | +1,029 | +813 |
| Construction | 7,759 | 864 | +1,464 | +1,192 | +272 |
| Transportation and public utilities | 6,411 | 2,685 | +1,365 | +621 | +744 |
| Entertainment and recreation | 1,242 | 949 | +794 | +446 | +348 |
| Personal services | 1,286 | 2,301 | +762 | +303 | +459 |
| Public administration | 3,510 | 2,622 | +344 | +142 | +202 |
| Mining | 698 | 120 | −322 | −303 | −19 |
| Manufacturing | 15,105 | 7,908 | −1,791 | −1,346 | −445 |
| Total | 67,833 | 60,039 | +19,935 | +7,815 | +12,120 |

SOURCE: Decennial census Public Use Microdata Samples (5 percent) for 1980 and 1990.

NOTE: Private household, farming, forestry, and fishery workers are excluded from this table.

and development of highly effective but costly medical procedures and medicines, overall expenditures on health care tripled during the 1980s to 14 percent of all purchases in 1989 (U.S. Council of Economic Advisers 1993:362). Purchases of services and goods other than health care about doubled over the decade. Thus, health care purchases grew about 50 percent faster than spending on products and services of all other sectors taken as a group.

The growth of employment paralleled the growth of spending.[9] From 8.1 million during 1979, employment of health care workers rose steadily to 10.6 million during 1989—a 31 percent increase versus a 17 percent rise for employment exclusive of health services. Conventional hospitals, operating 24 hours a day, seven days a week, provided employment for 750,000 more Americans during 1989 than during 1979. The number living in nursing homes rose by 350,000 in 1980 to 1.7 million in 1990, as about 6,700 nursing homes were added to the nation's stock (almost 34,000 in 1990) during the decade.[10] Staffs of nursing homes and posthospitalization care facilities rose, and there were especially large increases in the offices of medical practitioners. Strong growth of health services purchases, driven by demographic and public policy trends, translated directly into continually expanding job opportunities for educated workers, particularly those with associate degrees in technical health specialties or bachelor's degrees in health sciences specialties. What were the job distribution implications of this growth? More than 95 percent of the nation's registered and licensed practical nurses are women, as are about 90 percent of all health service support workers (dental assistants, health aides, and nursing aides). Similarly, about 75 percent of all health technologists (clinical laboratory workers, dental hygienists, and radiologic technicians) are women. In large part because of gains in such professional specialty occupations, women landed four times as many additional jobs as did men in health services during the 1980s (2 million versus 500,000).

Medical services are part of the professional services industry group, which also encompasses educational, social, and other professional services. Teachers in elementary and secondary schools constitute the bulk of educational employment, in which women hold almost three of every four jobs and virtually all jobs require a college education. Women employed in educational services rose by 17 percent to more than 7 million, while employment of men rose by only 10 percent to 3.5 million. Growth in social services amounted to more than 1 million, as social welfare programs administered by governments expanded services across a broad range of demographic groups. In all, the professional services industry group provided 7.8 million additional jobs, or about 38 percent of the net gain of total employment for the decade (Table 2.2). Women landed 5.6 million of the new jobs compared with only 2.2 million new jobs for men.

Were these "good" jobs? Professional services are labor-intensive, and the sector has a high and rising ratio of skilled to unskilled workers. Thus, most of the growth was in areas that require college training, and most of the new jobs were year-round, full-time, permanent appointments. Wages are above average in the professional services, and jobs in the sector are cyclically stable. In the language of the 1980s controversy, they are "good" jobs. Moreover, they got better. Applications of advanced technologies required higher-level technical skills and, correspondingly, provided better pay. A similar pattern occurred in the finance, insurance, and real estate industry group, where employment of women rose by 70 percent to 5.3 million. Half a million of the new jobs filled by women were in the executive and professional ranks where pay is higher and benefits are generally excellent.

Professional services and finance, insurance, and real estate accounted for half of all net new jobs created during the 1980s, and an even larger portion of the "good" jobs. Which group was waiting in the wings to fill such jobs? The baby boom generation, of course, and particularly the women, who had acquired much more college training and were much more career-oriented than earlier generations of women. New entrants found their training for the traditionally female-dominated health care and education occupations supported by strongly rising demand. Also, more women advanced into executive and senior managerial positions as their sustained work experience, educational preparation, and career orientation readied them for leadership roles.

Women also became much more competitive in high-earnings, male-dominated specialty occupations. Female physicians, for example, rose from almost 11 percent of all physicians in 1979 to more than 19 percent in 1989. Similarly, the percentage of female lawyers and judges was almost 21 percent in 1989 up from 12 percent in 1979. More than half of the net job gains for women were in the professional specialty and executive-managerial groups compared with less than two fifths for men. Less than one third of gains for women were in the lower-earnings retail sales and services occupations versus almost half the gains for men (Table 2.3). Not only did women fill three jobs for each two filled by men, but the jobs they won were more concentrated in the higher-earnings and better-benefits echelon of the occupational hierarchy.

If strong growth in particular industries and occupations was important in explaining why women fared relatively well, what explains the poorer outcomes for men? Before 1975, spending on domestically produced goods stimulated rapid job growth in goods-producing industries and provided "middle-class" jobs with comparatively low educational requirements for millions of Americans. As illustrated in the top panel of Figure 2.3, final purchases of goods (e.g., cars and clothing) and structures (e.g., houses and commercial buildings) grew much less rapidly than purchases of the output of service-producing industries (e.g., medical services, retail trade, and financial services) during the 1980s. More-over, owing to the continuation of a very tight monetary policy, foreign producers enjoyed considerable pricing advantages in both U.S. and international markets through most of the 1980s. Consequently, domestic and export sales of domestically produced heavy manufacturing goods, such as motor vehicles and machinery, weakened in the face of intense foreign competition based largely on prices (Bunda and Gerlach 1992). As sales of domestically produced, big-ticket hard goods dropped, there was considerable downsizing in manufacturing (largely plant closures) to reduce domestic production capacity to the level of demand for domestically produced goods. In factories that remained open, there was considerable reengineering to improve quality and to enhance productivity. In essence, reengineering means getting rid of production workers and lower-level managers either by maximizing robotics applications or by "outsourcing" labor-intensive operations to newly industrialized countries. Because productivity gains essentially matched the growth of the additional purchases of domestically produced goods that did occur, employment in goods-producing industries showed no net growth over the decade. Within the goods-producing total, construction employment rose, while employment in manufacturing and mining, where men outnumber women three to one and wages are high relative to the schooling levels of workers, was considerably lower in 1989 than it had been in 1979 (Table 2.2).

In short, the domestic economy was in a position to satisfy final demand for domestically produced goods with far fewer semiskilled blue collar workers, and their job count was cut by 1.1 million. Gains for skilled and unskilled blue collar workers were insufficient to offset losses among the semiskilled, and the overall blue collar group declined. The still incomplete downsizing and reengineering of the domestic auto industry was instrumental in the weakness of demand for blue collar workers. Cities highly dependent on the auto industry for

FIGURE 2.3   Final purchases and employment, by sector (indexes, 1979=100).

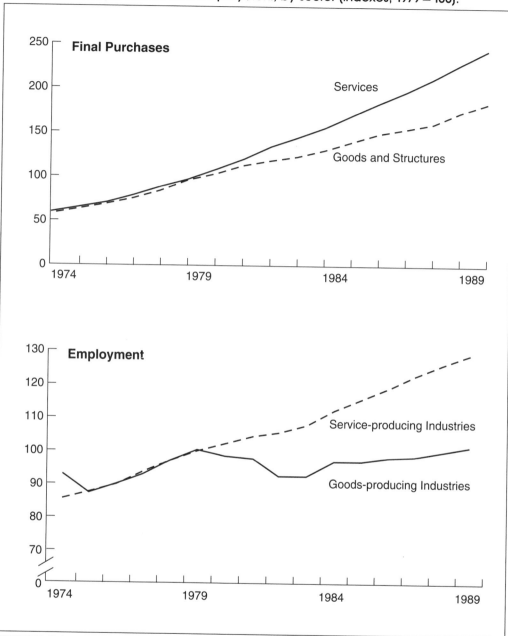

SOURCES: U.S. Council of Economic Advisers (1993) and Current Population Survey quarterly historical files.

TABLE 2.3  Experienced workers, by occupation (thousands of persons).

| Occupation Group | 1989 Level | | Change from 1979 | | |
|---|---|---|---|---|---|
| | Men | Women | Total | Men | Women |
| White Collar | 31,990 | 43,078 | +17,397 | +6,543 | 10,854 |
|   Executive and managerial | 8,799 | 6,512 | +4,528 | +1,401 | +3,127 |
|   Professional specialty | 8,085 | 9,642 | +4,667 | +1,624 | +3,042 |
|   Technical specialty | 2,475 | 2,154 | +1,369 | +668 | +702 |
|   Sales | 7,771 | 8,189 | +4,518 | +2,245 | +2,273 |
|   Administrative support | 4,860 | 16,580 | +2,315 | +605 | +1,710 |
| Services | 7,603 | 10,316 | +3,105 | +1,467 | +1,639 |
| Blue Collar | 28,312 | 6,977 | −366 | −76 | −290 |
|   Precision crafts and repair | 13,350 | 1,458 | +665 | +370 | +295 |
|   Semiskilled operatives | 10,304 | 4,336 | −1,149 | −557 | −592 |
|   Laborers | 4,658 | 1,183 | +118 | +111 | +7 |

SOURCE: Decennial census Public Use Microdata Samples (5 percent) for 1980 and 1990.

NOTE: Private household, farming, forestry, and fishery workers are excluded from this table.

jobs and local taxes, such as Flint and Detroit, Michigan, typify the severe socioeconomic and civic consequences of the massive adjustments taking place as a result of globalization of industrial production and innovation in production techniques (see Kasarda's chapter in this volume).

Of course, as Gittleman and Howell found, not all men fared badly during the 1980s. As shown in Table 2.3, there were large net gains among college-educated, white collar men, largely in the professional services industries but also in the executive and managerial ranks in other industries. However, a relatively large share of the overall gain for men was in retail sales and service occupations where wage rates generally are well below the average for men holding blue collar jobs in factories.

## Self-Employment

The allure of independence and economic self-determination is deeply embedded in American folklore. Entrepreneurial success stories are celebrated in our media and, in a practical vein, the self-employed report much higher levels of job satisfaction than those who work for others. The increasing uncertainty of wage and salary work for big organizations apparently induced more Americans to create their own opportunities, and thus the growth of self-employment was considerably faster than the growth of wage and salary positions during the 1980s. Women started businesses and added to the ranks of the self-employed at a much faster rate than men. Four women became self-employed during the 1980s for every three men who did so. As of the 1987 economic censuses,

businesses owned by women had increased twice as fast as the overall comparable total from 1982 for individual proprietorships and more than half again as
fast for partnerships.[11] But even with the sharp rise, women are considerably
less likely than men to be self-employed. The gender difference probably reflects the physical labor requirements in the male-dominated agriculture and
construction industries, which together account for about 30 percent of total
self-employment. In retail trade, by contrast, women accounted for nearly half
of the 1.5 million self-employed, as was the case in the higher-earnings professional services industry group that had 1.4 million self-employed in 1989. Regardless of gender, the likelihood of being self-employed rises progressively
with age, in part reflecting the accumulation of experience, contacts, and assets
needed to initiate and sustain a personal enterprise. The high educational attainment, career orientation, and rapidly accumulating experience of younger
women now in the work force appear likely to generate even stronger growth
of self-employment among women in the years ahead.

## Work Experience

In all, 132.5 million Americans worked at some time during 1989, an increase of almost 20 million from 1979. Women held six of every ten new work
slots. Their proportion of the total with employment during the year rose to 46
percent as their proportion with jobs continued its seemingly inexorable upward
trend (Figure 2.4). About 121 million Americans worked at wage or salary jobs

FIGURE 2.4   Percentage of the working age population with jobs, by gender.

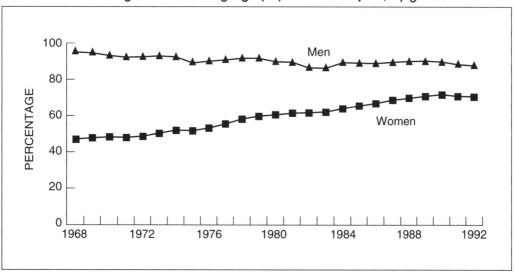

SOURCE: Current Population Survey quarterly historical files.

and 5 million combined that work with some self-employment. Self-employment was the primary work activity of nearly 12 million persons. Large absolute and relative increases were registered by workers with college training, while employment of workers with less than four years of high school training dropped by 4.6 million during the 1980s (Table 2.4).

Demographic and socioeconomic trends collaborated to concentrate growth in full-time, year-round work. Teenagers more often than not work part-time and seldom work all year. Their declining number in the labor force, largely a demographic phenomenon, meant a decrease in the number of voluntary part-time and voluntary part-year workers. Conversely, steep increases in the number of prime working age adults boosted the number of persons seeking to work full-time, year-round. On the economic side, demand was strongest for highly educated professional and technical workers in sectors likely to require full-time work and provide year-round employment (e.g., medical and financial services). Finally, pressures to enhance family income led to substantial increases in the numbers of wives seeking full-time, year-round jobs.

Rates of growth of full-time, year-round employment were decisively faster for women and minorities than for white men (Table 2A.2). Fed by a steady stream of new immigrants and by rising participation of women, the number of Hispanics who worked year-round, full-time about doubled. The number of black women who worked full-time, year-round increased by more than one

**TABLE 2.4   Experienced workers, by education (thousands of persons).**

| Work Experience and Education | 1989 Level | | Change from 1979 | |
|---|---|---|---|---|
| | Men | Women | Men | Women |
| Full-Time, Year-Round, Total | 49,639 | 31,322 | +7,267 | +9,277 |
| College training | | | | |
|   Four years or more | 14,027 | 7,789 | +3,937 | +3,757 |
|   One to three years | 10,069 | 7,128 | +2,394 | +3,010 |
| High school training | | | | |
|   Four years | 19,073 | 13,421 | +2,922 | +2,755 |
|   Less than four years | 6,470 | 2,984 | −1,986 | −245 |
| All Other than FTYR | 20,159 | 27,973 | +67 | +1,656 |
| College training | | | | |
|   Four years or more | 3,144 | 5,072 | +580 | +1,386 |
|   One to three years | 4,315 | 6,566 | +209 | +1,291 |
| High school training | | | | |
|   Four years | 7,396 | 11,956 | +229 | +443 |
|   Less than four years | 5,304 | 4,379 | −951 | −1,464 |
| Total | 69,798 | 59,295 | +7,334 | +10,933 |

SOURCE: Current Population Survey Public Use Microdata Samples for March 1980 and March 1990.

NOTE: Unpaid family workers and persons aged 16 and 17 are excluded.

TABLE 2A.2   Full-time, year-round workers, by race/ethnicity.

| Gender and Age | Employment (thousands) | | | Annual Earnings (1989 $) | | |
|---|---|---|---|---|---|---|
| | 1979 | 1989 | Change | 1979 | 1989 | Change |
| Men, Total | 42,437 | 49,678 | +17% | $31,969 | $33,010 | +3% |
| Whites | 38,272 | 43,736 | +14 | 32,781 | 33,979 | +4 |
| Blacks | 3,319 | 4,353 | +31 | 23,133 | 23,196 | 0 |
| Hispanics | 2,023 | 3,709 | +83 | 23,788 | 22,440 | −6 |
| Women, Total | 22,082 | 31,340 | +42 | 18,203 | 21,039 | +16 |
| Whites | 19,038 | 26,239 | +38 | 18,292 | 21,191 | +16 |
| Blacks | 2,560 | 3,979 | +55 | 17,283 | 19,278 | +12 |
| Hispanics | 1,021 | 2,076 | +103 | 15,999 | 17,570 | +10 |
| Total, Both Sexes | 64,519 | 81,018 | +26 | 27,257 | 28,379 | +4 |

SOURCE: Current Population Survey Public Use Microdata Samples for March 1980 and 1990.

NOTE: Hispanics may be of any race and are included under the appropriate race category.

half, and that of black men by one third. Driven by increasing participation, the number of white women who worked full-time, year-round rose by 7.2 million from 1979, a 38 percent rise. White men, most of whom work full-time, year-round most years, recorded the smallest relative increase of 14 percent. Their proportion of full-time, year-round wage and salary workers fell from almost 58 percent of the total in 1979 to 52 percent in 1989.

Although full-time, year-round work rose sharply over the decade, about 15 million workers were limited to part-time work for economic reasons for at least part of 1989. In an average month, about 2.3 million were able to find only part-time jobs, and 2.4 million who usually worked full-time were on reduced schedules because of slack work. Men were most likely to report short work-weeks because of slack work. The proportion doing so was particularly high for blue collar workers in the goods-producing industries. Compared with the 1970s and particularly with the late 1960s, the relative frequency and increased duration of involuntary part-time work for economic reasons damped growth of blue collar workers' annual earnings.

## TOTAL COMPENSATION AND EARNINGS

Total compensation of employees reached $3.1 trillion in 1989: $2.6 trillion in wages and salaries and $510 billion in fringe benefits. Fringe benefits include direct personal benefits (e.g., health and life insurance) that accrue directly to workers and mandatory public "insurance" programs such as Social Security and Medicare. The fringe benefits portion of workers' compensation has grown at a faster rate than wages and salaries since the end of World War II. There were significant differences in changes in compensation by gender, by age, and, in particular, by education. These were driven by changing labor demand and supply conditions and by differential effects of technological change on workers' productivity.

## Average Annual Earnings

Annual money earnings averaged $20,780 for the 132.5 million Americans who worked for pay or profit during 1989.[12] As shown in Table 2.5, about 71 million men averaged $27,000 and almost 61 million women averaged $14,800. After allowance for rising prices,[13] men's average earning rose by only 4.5 percent over the decade, while women's rose by 24.5 percent. The larger rise for women resulted from faster growth of annual hours of work and average hourly earnings. Women who worked full-time, year-round reported annual earnings of $21,000 during 1989, while men averaged $33,000. Average annual

TABLE 2.5   Average annual earnings, by education (1989 dollars).

| Work Experience and Education | 1989 Level | | Percentage Change from 1979 to 1989 | |
|---|---|---|---|---|
| | Women | Men | Women | Men |
| All Earners | $14,809 | $27,025 | +24.5% | +4.5% |
| College Training | | | | |
| Five years or more | 26,977 | 50,144 | +26.6 | +13.3 |
| Four years | 21,089 | 38,692 | +32.8 | +7.5 |
| One to three years | 14,688 | 25,555 | +21.9 | +3.6 |
| High School Training | | | | |
| Four years | 12,468 | 22,508 | +10.4 | −6.2 |
| One to three years | 8,431 | 15,169 | +1.3 | −17.6 |
| None | 7,901 | 14,014 | +2.4 | −17.6 |
| Full-Time, Year-Round | $21,045 | $33,028 | +15.5% | +3.2% |
| College Training | | | | |
| Five years or more | 33,847 | 55,303 | +19.5 | +11.7 |
| Four years | 26,977 | 42,999 | +21.2 | +5.2 |
| One to three years | 21,237 | 31,792 | +11.1 | 0.0 |
| High School Training | | | | |
| Four years | 17,656 | 26,733 | +5.2 | −6.5 |
| One to three years | 14,181 | 21,457 | −2.5 | −13.4 |
| None | 12,533 | 18,539 | −0.3 | −14.5 |

SOURCE: Current Population Survey Public Use Microdata Samples for March 1980 and March 1990.

NOTES: Unpaid family workers and persons aged 16 and 17 are excluded. Inflation adjustments were made using the Consumer Price Index-U-X1. See footnote 13.

earnings of women who worked full-time, year-round were up 15.5 percent from 1979, while earnings of men were up only 3.2 percent.

Education was instrumental in determining how different groups of workers fared in the earnings sphere during the 1980s. Average annual earnings for full-time, year-round work by men with 4 years and with 5 years or more of college training rose by 5 and 12 percent, respectively (Table 2.5). In vivid contrast, earnings declined about 7 percent for men who had completed only high school, and plummeted about 13 percent for those who did not complete high school. In earnings, just as in employment and labor force participation, women posted much larger gains than men. Gains for college-educated women who worked full-time, year-round ranged from 11 to 21 percent, while annual earnings of those with less than four years of high school education declined slightly.

Most Americans' earnings are a function of their hourly wage (or equivalent salary) rate and the number of hours they work during the year. Within the confines of employers' needs, individual workers can increase their annual earnings by working more hours per week, more weeks per year, increasing their wage or salary rate, or any combination of the three. Because most men are holding or seeking full-time, year-round jobs by the time they reach their middle 20s and continue to do so until they begin to move into the retirement process in their early 60s, there is comparatively little room to raise their earnings by boosting their annual work effort. Mature single women, most of whom have full-time, year-round jobs, face the same constraints as men. For married women as a group, by contrast, there was much more latitude to raise earnings during the 1980s. Wives previously not in the work force could initiate labor market activity, and those who had been working part-year or part-time could boost their annual weeks or weekly hours of work. They did so with gusto! As discussed in the participation section, the percentage of wives in the labor force shot up from 49 to 59 percent, and, as discussed in the employment section, more than 85 percent of the net rise in employment of women was among full-time, year-round workers. Consequently, gross as well as average annual working hours increased much more for women than for men. The increases meant that women provided a growing share of family incomes, especially among the baby boomers whose participation rose so much relative to earlier generations. (See Bianchi's discussion in this volume.)

Highly educated persons work more weeks per year, work more hours per week, and earn more per hour than persons with less education. During the 1980s, those differentials widened significantly. Men's average annual hours worked rose by 1.3 percent to an average of 1,885 hours during 1989.[14] The small increase in men's average annual hours of work primarily resulted from a rising proportion of highly educated men and more annual hours for such men. Men with five years or more of college averaged 2,220 work hours during 1989 compared with 1,940 for those with a high school diploma, and 1,680 hours for men with less than four years of high school. Annual working hours declined over the 1980s for less-educated men, even those with a full-time, year-round job, but rose by the equivalent of a full 40-hour workweek for the highly edu-cated.

Like men, women at each successive education level work more hours annu-ally. During the 1980s, however, trends were distinctly different for women than for men. *Women of all education and racial-ethnic groups increased their annual hours of work.* Their average annual work year rose by 140 hours, a 10 percent increase from 1979. As shown in Figure 2.5, the overall increase re-flected about three additional weeks of work annually (they averaged 43 weeks) and about one more hour in their average workweek (almost 35 hours per week). About two fifths of the improvement in women's average annual earn-ings was attributable to working more hours during the year.

Rising real annual earnings for women relative to men reflected advances for Hispanic women relative to Hispanic men, for black women relative to black men, and for white women relative to white men (Table 2A.2). Damped by the constant additions of less-schooled, new immigrants, the annual earnings of Hispanic women did not grow as rapidly as the earnings of either white or black women. Black women lost ground relative to white women, whose additions to

FIGURE 2.5    Average workweek and weeks worked, by gender: 1979 and 1989.

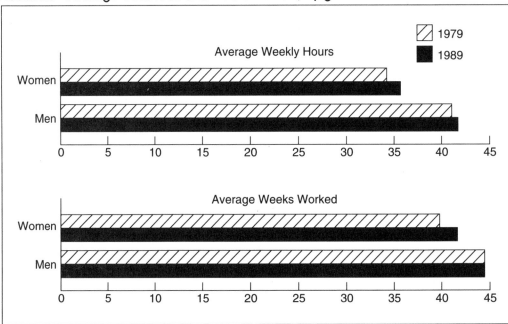

SOURCES: Decennial census Public Use Microdata Samples (5 percent) for 1980 and 1990.

the ranks of full-time, year-round workers were more concentrated among col-lege-educated women who increased their annual hours of work. In contrast to women, the real annual earnings of Hispanic men fell, the earnings of black men were essentially unchanged, and those of white men rose only a trifle. Among men, the ratio of black to white earnings declined somewhat, while the ratios for Hispanic men to both black and white men declined significantly (Card and Krueger 1993).

## Average Hourly Earnings

Reflecting very much stronger demand for highly educated workers, real av-erage hourly earnings of highly educated men and women rose, while those of the lowest education categories registered sharp declines (Table 2.6). Conse-quently, real hourly earnings differentials by education widened dramatically during the 1980s. The hourly earnings of men with five years or more of college

TABLE 2.6   Average hourly earnings, by education (1989 dollars).

| Work Experience and Education | 1979 Level | | 1989 Level | | Percentage Change 1979 to 1989 | |
|---|---|---|---|---|---|---|
| | Women | Men | Women | Men | Women | Men |
| All Earners | $8.75 | $13.91 | $9.87 | $14.35 | +12.8% | +3.2% |
| College Training | | | | | | |
| Five years or more | 13.00 | 20.34 | 15.45 | 22.60 | +18.9 | +11.1 |
| Four years | 10.55 | 17.09 | 12.59 | 18.07 | +19.4 | +5.7 |
| One to three years | 8.91 | 13.36 | 9.66 | 13.54 | +8.4 | +1.4 |
| High School Training | | | | | | |
| Four years | 7.84 | 12.19 | 8.09 | 11.61 | +3.1 | −4.8 |
| One to three years | 8.10 | 12.76 | 7.98 | 11.17 | −1.4 | −12.5 |
| None | 5.90 | 9.63 | 5.88 | 8.34 | −0.3 | −13.4 |
| Full-Time, Year-Round | $8.56 | $13.73 | $9.72 | $14.20 | +13.6% | +3.4% |
| College Training | | | | | | |
| Five years or more | 12.66 | 20.35 | 15.03 | 22.53 | +18.7 | +10.7 |
| Four years | 10.33 | 17.50 | 12.20 | 18.17 | +18.1 | +3.8 |
| One to three years | 9.01 | 13.58 | 9.86 | 13.64 | +9.5 | +0.5 |
| High School Training | | | | | | |
| Four years | 7.97 | 12.33 | 8.26 | 11.65 | +3.6 | −5.5 |
| One to three years | 6.82 | 10.83 | 6.60 | 9.50 | −3.2 | −12.2 |
| None | 5.89 | 9.45 | 5.82 | 8.33 | −1.2 | −11.9 |

SOURCE: Current Population Survey Public Use Microdata Samples for March 1980 and March 1990.

NOTES: Unpaid family workers and persons aged 16 and 17 are excluded. Inflation adjustments were made using the Consumer Price Index-U-X1. See footnote 13.

were 2.7 times those of men with no high school training in 1989, up from just twice as high in 1979. Had wage rates of less-educated men kept pace, their average hourly earnings would have been higher by $2.35 in 1989. The multiple of the most- to least-educated women rose from 2.2 to 2.6 over the decade. To have kept pace, the hourly earnings of the least-educated women would have had to rise $1.15 instead of showing a slight decline.

Why did the earnings gaps by education widen so much? Underlying all economic developments during the 1980s was a huge leap in the application of new technologies in the work place (Bound and Johnson 1992). Although perhaps not the most important, the computerization of virtually everything is a familiar example. When the technology base is changing rapidly, as it was during the 1980s, employers concentrate on hiring workers who can best use the technology coming on stream and who are flexible enough to deal with unforeseeable new developments. Simultaneously, productivity advances inherent in much of the new technology were destroying old, low-skill jobs. In an era of computer storage of records, for example, there is little need for file clerks. Process control systems in factories are much more important, if less familiar, applications. Although the number of low-education workers in the labor force declined sharply (Figure 2.2), their number did not contract as rapidly as demands for less-skilled workers. When supply exceeds demand, prices (in this case wage rates, which are the price of labor) drift down or drop. That is precisely what happened to the wage rates of less-educated workers during the 1980s. Conversely, even though the supply of educated workers rose very rapidly, it rose less rapidly than demand, and the average hourly earnings of highly educated workers rose.

Between genders, women's average hourly earnings rose relative to men's at every educational level during the 1980s. Women and men who worked full-time, year-round averaged $9.11 and $13.06 per hour, respectively, in 1989— a ratio of about .70. While still large, *the hourly earnings gap narrowed about one sixth* from a ratio of .64 in 1979. Women's gains relative to men were large at each educational level and in almost all industry and occupation groups. Why did the gender earning gap narrow as much as it did? For one thing, the strong growth of purchases in sectors such as professional services and finance meant that women's employment grew most rapidly in higher-than-average wage rate occupations, while declines in blue collar jobs in sectors such as mining and manufacturing meant fewer middle-income jobs for men. Within industry groups, women's gains primarily reflected gains within occupations rather than women shifting into higher-wage occupations largely dominated by men. Research by Cotter et al. (1993) shows that only about 15 percent of the relative gain in women's average hourly earning was attributable to shifts among occupations; the rest was due to higher average hourly earnings for women within specific occupations. Thus, *the relative improvement appears to reflect real wage rate gains for women.* Analysts differ on the relative significance of developments that helped narrow the gender wage gap, but agree that continuous work experience is associated with higher productivity levels and higher wage rates.[15] By virtue of sustained participation, baby boom women have accumulated much more work experience than did their mothers (O'Neill and Polachek 1993). Moreover, as women have become more career-oriented, both they and their employers have invested more in training, contributing to their higher productivity and higher wages. Also, demands for women workers were clearly stronger relative to the supply than was the case for men, and their wages apparently were bid up. In part, of course, that may have been a result of the gender wage gap. In a decade of intense competition and systematic corporate efforts to minimize costs, women's wage rates were highly competitive, especially in light of their increased educational preparation, work experience, and career commitments.

The earnings gap between young and mature men with a high school education or less widened significantly during the 1980s, as did the gap between the highest and lowest earners in the same education-age groups for men without any college training. Declining labor demand in manufacturing and mining contributed significantly to these developments. There was little hiring of young men into higher-wage-rate industrial blue collar jobs. The proportion of all employed younger men with jobs in the higher-wage manufacturing and mining industries fell from 26 to 15 percent between 1979 and 1989. This lowered young men's average wages both because there were fewer high-wage workers and because those who landed jobs were more likely to be employed in low-wage retail and service jobs. Among mature men with high school training or less, the widening of the earnings gap partly resulted from sustained high earnings among industrial workers with seniority protection who were fortunate enough to be in a plant not yet downsized and in a job not yet reengineered. Those who were less fortunate and were displaced from higher-wage jobs sustained losses of earnings averaging about 20 percent when they found new jobs. Hence a wider differential.

In summary, strong demands for educated workers overwhelmed an exceedingly large increase in the supply of educated workers, and their real wage rates increased. Although the supply of the least-educated declined, demand for their labor market services declined more and faster. Their real wage rates declined as did their annual hours of work. Consequently, the annual earnings gap between the most- and least-educated segments of the labor force increased sharply, leading to a much less equal distribution of income. In part because of difficult labor market circumstances for men, women had strong reasons to increase their labor force activity and earnings. During the 1980s, women in general, and wives in particular, took most avenues open to them to expand their average annual earnings. Their efforts were successful, partly as a result of preparation and partly because demand was strong in their areas of labor market dominance. The basic outcomes of the efforts of wives to enhance family income are discussed in more detail by Bianchi in Chapter 3 of this volume, and the broader effects on income distribution are discussed by Levy in Chapter 1. On average, men were much less successful than women in increasing their annual earnings. Indeed, men with only high school educations, and particularly those who had dropped out before completing high school, suffered substantial declines in average real earnings—both hourly and particularly annually—over the decade. Their losses reflected outright declines in the amount of work provided by higher-wage industrial employers and relatively large increases in the numbers of young men working in low-wage retail and service jobs.

## UNEMPLOYMENT

The national unemployment rate averaged 7.3 percent during the 1980s, up significantly from the 6.3 percent average for the 1970s. During the prosperous and economically expansive 1960s, strong labor demands held the average rate to only 4.8 percent, and in the tight markets of the 1950s, it averaged only 4.5 percent. *During the 1980s, the unemployment rate never got as low, not even in one month, as the average rates of the 1960s and 1950s.* This set of facts raises two crucial questions. Namely, what combination of economic, social, and demographic developments gave rise to progressively higher jobless rates, and what is the economic and social significance of the increases? To address these questions, one must understand a few details about our official unemployment measures.

Originally developed to meet the needs of an industrial, traditional-family-structure society, the definition of unemployment used in our nation's official labor market yields estimates that are subject to misinterpretation. Although there has been considerable modernization of the CPS, particularly in the methods of collecting and processing, the basic unemployment concept and classification scheme have remained essentially the same.[16] In the early years, unemployment was a sound indicator of workers seeking full-time jobs. In the middle 1950s, for example, almost half of the unemployed were prime working age men, most seeking full-time jobs, and an additional one fifth were young men who had completed their schooling and were searching for permanent jobs. Thus, the unemployment figure gave a good indication of the additional labor supply available to raise production, especially since manual labor made up a much larger portion of total labor requirements in the 1950s than it does today. Unemployment also was a reasonable indicator of economic hardship. A large share of the unemployed were married men, who were highly likely to be the sole earners in their families. When married men were out of work, family incomes generally were low or nonexistent.

As the economy and the society evolved, so did the labor market behavior of individuals and the needs of employers. Both sets of changes altered the relevance of the official measures for macroeconomic policymaking and for assessing likely matches between employers' needs for workers and the types of workers seeking jobs. In the late 1970s, for example, only about 25 percent of the unemployed were prime working age men seeking full-time jobs, and a much larger proportion were youths and women seeking part-time work. Simultaneously, growth of employers' need for high-education, high-skill workers intensified and their need for manual and generally low-skill workers declined steadily. Changes in labor supplies and demands of the 1980s further muddied the waters. Who were the unemployed of the late 1980s, why were they unemployed, and what was the socioeconomic significance of their joblessness?

### The Unemployed in 1989

In an average month of 1989, 6.5 million were unemployed and the jobless rate was 5.3 percent. Over the course of 1989, 17 million individuals experienced at least one spell of joblessness. They represented 13 percent of the 133 million persons who participated in the labor force at some time during the year. That is, more than one labor force participant in eight was out of work at some point in 1989. The likelihood of experiencing unemployment and its duration varied with the conventional stages of the work-life cycle. One of every five youths who were in the work force experienced unemployment at some time during the year. First entry and reentry into the labor force are common causes of unemployment. When schools are dismissed for the summer (an educationally and economically inefficient artifact of our once agrarian economy), millions of youths flood the job market in search of summer jobs. Although millions find employment, hundreds of thousands do not and are counted among the unemployed. Quitting a job to search for a better one also is a common cause of unemployment. Economists generally classify joblessness from such causes as *frictional unemployment,* which occurs frequently for youths at the early stages of the work-life cycle and among previously uncommitted mature women moving into a permanent work force attachment. Unemployment arising from initial entry, reentry, and quits—sources that most economists would classify as normal, unavoidable frictional unemployment—accounted for about half of total joblessness in 1989.

Youths accounted for 29 percent of the persons who experienced unemployment during 1989, although they provided only 18 percent of the persons with labor force activity. The measurable economic costs of youths' unemploy-

ment—the loss of income to the individual and the loss of output to the economy—are comparatively small owing to low entry-level wages and their propensity to work part-time while in school. Because few contemporary youths are
responsible for the economic support of families, their unemployment often is
not regarded as a serious matter. However, there is a more serious, unmeasur-
able cost—the loss of labor market learning. Job-seeking experience, job test-
ing, and the development of realistic expectations regarding earnings, effort,
and mores of the workplace are all investments in later success. In this regard,
the different experiences of majority and minority youths are a matter of social
and public policy concern (see Harrison and Bennett's chapter in Volume 2).
Even after allowances for differences in education, socioeconomic status, and
other variables that are directly observable in large-scale surveys, black and
Hispanic youths experience more frequent and longer spells of unemployment
than white non-Hispanic youths.

The situation did not improve during the 1980s. Indeed, the gap between
young blacks and their white peers widened further. In 1989, jobless rates for
black youths were two and one-half times as high as those for white youths (23
versus 9 percent), despite much lower rates of minority participation in the work
force. Many hypotheses have been advanced to explain the gap, but we do not
have definitive findings or easy solutions (Follett, Ward, and Welch 1993).
There is limited support for arguments that the concentration of black youths in
urban areas far removed from areas with job openings contributes to the gap
(see Kasarda's chapter in this volume). This thinking is somewhat supported by
qualitative, almost anecdotal, evidence that black youths living in middle-income neighborhoods experience labor market transitions and subsequent work
lives somewhat similar to those of majority youths. Discrimination against
young blacks, especially men, is a continuing problem. Indeed, it may have
increased during the 1980s in response to the concerns of potential employers
about high levels of violence and crime among young black men. We do know
that joblessness, nonparticipation, and criminal activity are related, but the relationships are extremely complex (Allan and Steffensmeier 1989). New and
imaginative programs to facilitate the transition from school to work are ur-
gently required, especially for young black men (Commission on Youth and
America's Future 1989a).

Among persons aged 25–44, the incidence of unemployment at some time
during 1989 was 12 percent for women and 14 percent for men. Among persons
aged 45–64, it was 8 percent for women and about 9 percent for men. In an
average month of 1989, jobless rates for men and women aged 25 and over
were 4.1 and 4.4 percent, respectively. Reflecting strong demands in sectors
dominated by women, both the incidence of unemployment during the year and
the average monthly rate of unemployment were lower for women in 1989 than

in 1979. Conversely, both the average monthly rate and the incidence of joblessness during the year were higher in 1989 for men than they were in 1979. Economic hardship arising from unemployment is discussed in the next section. However, looking at the distribution of joblessness within families is instructive in considering the relevance of unemployment as a socioeconomic indicator. The 6.5 million jobless in 1989 included 1.2 million husbands living with their wives and 560,000 women and 125,000 men supporting a family household without the aid of a spouse. Presumably, these 1.8 million householders basically supported their families. However, two thirds of the unemployed husbands had a relative, usually a wife, who was working at the time of his unemployment. Three aspects of the householder unemployment figures are impressive: first, their relatively small share of total unemployment (under 30 percent during 1989); second, the average duration of their unemployment (only about 11 weeks in 1989); and third, the very large proportion of husbands whose wives were working at the time that they were jobless. Persons not responsible for the maintenance of a household constituted a substantial majority of the unemployed (70 percent). Included in the nonhouseholder group in 1989 were 1.1 million wives living with their husbands, 2.4 million relatives, usually living-at-home sons and daughters of householders, and about 2.2 million individuals living in nonfamily households, many of whom were college students.

## Kinds of Unemployment

A major cause of temporary unemployment among experienced adult workers is seasonality arising from weather and seasonal markets. When adverse weather prevents outdoor work, as in construction and agriculture, it causes temporary *seasonal unemployment*. Market-driven seasonality is episodic unemployment arising from a regular pattern of seasonal demand. Resort workers, for example, often experience a spell of unemployment during the off-season. Jobless rates of experienced workers always are highest for those attached to seasonal industries (e.g., construction at 11.1 percent in 1989) and lowest for those in sectors with a more constant flow of work (professional services, 2.6 percent). Within industries, the pattern of unemployment rates favors the more skilled occupations. For example, construction craftspersons, semiskilled operatives, and laborers experienced annual average jobless rates of 8.1, 11.2, and 18.5 percent, respectively. In 1989, about two thirds of experienced workers with a spell of unemployment were out of work for less than 15 weeks. The annual earnings of experienced wage and salary workers with fewer than 15 weeks of unemployment during 1989 (about two thirds of their number with any unemployment) averaged about $11,000 in individual earnings, well above the poverty level for an individual and midway between the poverty thresholds for families of three persons ($9,885) and of four persons ($12,675). Because these short spells generally are accompanied by unemployment insurance payments, they usually do not have severe economic implications for the worker.

*Cyclical unemployment* arises when demand for output falls and workers are laid off from their regular jobs, usually temporarily but perhaps for many months. Business cycles generally eventuate in, and sometimes arise from, shortfalls of spending on hard goods and homes. Because goods production can readily be adjusted by reducing or delaying work, factory workers most frequently encounter cyclical unemployment. During the severe recession of 1981–1982, for example, manufacturing employment fell by over 2.5 million. Total unemployment rose from 7.6 million in 1979 to 10.7 million in 1982, with close to 40 percent of the rise among factory workers who accounted for only one fifth of total employment at the time. Although unemployment rates rose somewhat for workers in service-producing industries, there was some net growth of service jobs during the recession. Although a good number of the layoffs during the recessions of the early 1980s were cyclical and many factory workers were recalled to their old jobs, many were permanently lost owing to plant shutdowns or job eliminations arising from basic structural change in the economy.

*Structural unemployment* is more serious for the economy and is more likely to signify prolonged economic hardship for workers and their families than other kinds of unemployment. It arises when there is a continuing mismatch between the skills of workers who are seeking jobs and the skills sought by employers with vacant jobs. Residing uncomfortably within the structural unemployment category are experienced workers whose old jobs have disappeared because of technological advances or foreign competition. The Bureau of Labor Statistics defines permanently displaced workers as those who lost a job that they had held for at least three years because of a plant closing or its moving to a distant location, the elimination of their type of work, or the elimination of their particular job. During the devastating structural shifts of the 1979–1984 period, more than 5 million workers were permanently displaced as employers' needs for industrial blue collar workers dropped sharply in response to weak demand for domestically produced goods. Although the pace of the cuts slowed, displacement for structural reasons continued through the rest of the 1980s and into the 1990s. Structural unemployment is not entirely concentrated among unskilled and semiskilled workers. The obsolescence of old technology within a firm or industry, or outright failure of a firm because of restructuring or surplus sectoral capacity, almost always is accompanied by the elimination of jobs at all skill levels, including top management and high-level technical jobs (Cohen 1993). The savings and loan debacle, for example, and failures of several large department store chains and the bankruptcy of such major employers as Eastern and Pan-Am airlines, placed many white collar workers on the permanently displaced list. Many of these workers had long job tenure in comparatively large, once-profitable firms. Thus, despite strong growth of total employment after 1984, 4 million more workers were permanently displaced during the last half of the 1980s and a somewhat larger share were drawn from the nonindustrial sector (Table 2.7).

Permanently displaced workers experience large losses of earnings before, during, and after their job loss. Displaced workers often have specialized training and experience that is specific to a particular firm and is associated with wage premiums. Unfortunately, firm-specific specialized knowledge does not appear to be readily transferable, even within the same industry. Consequently, once a worker is displaced, any wage premium based on firm-specific knowledge is lost. In terms of the old job's earnings level, displaced workers who were eventually reemployed, and a significant minority were not, lost an average of 20 percent of their earnings potential. Earnings losses apparently vary only marginally by gender, industry, and the economic circumstances in the worker's local labor market (Jacobson, LaLonde, and Sullivan 1993).

There are no clearly marked boundaries among the four categories of unemployment and we cannot measure them directly. Conditions in one area invariably influence conditions in others. When the economy is very strong and there is little cyclical unemployment, new entrants and reentrants will be able to find jobs faster. Net frictional unemployment will be lower. In seasonal activities, finding a job also will be quicker; and if labor is in sufficiently short supply, employers often stretch the season. Structurally unemployed workers also will have a better shot at finding jobs when the economy is strong. Conversely, when spending is declining and workers are being laid off, all groups of potential workers will experience more and longer periods of unemployment.

TABLE 2.7    Permanently displaced workers, by industry
(thousands of persons).

| Displacing Industry | 1979–1984 | 1985–1990 | Total |
|---|---|---|---|
| Goods-Producing Industries | 3,140 | 2,128 | 5,268 |
| Manufacturing | 2,483 | 1,626 | 4,109 |
| Other goods-producing | 657 | 502 | 1,159 |
| Service-Producing Industries | 1,951 | 2,198 | 4,149 |
| Transportation | 280 | 199 | 479 |
| Trade | 732 | 845 | 1,577 |
| Other service-producing | 939 | 1,154 | 2,093 |
| Total | 5,091 | 4,326 | 9,417 |

SOURCE: U.S. Department of Labor (1991).

## Unemployment Patterns

The evolution of unemployment patterns of the post–World War II era is almost impossible to characterize in easy-to-understand, short passages. Clearly, frictional joblessness rose steeply during the 1970s as the baby boomers moved through the initial stage of the work-life cycle. The rise was exacerbated by a lengthening school-to-work transition period, as an increasingly sophisticated, technology-based economy required and rewarded increased investments in formal education. During the 1980s, the contribution of frictional joblessness undoubtedly declined with the size of the young cohort entering the labor market and because mature women made commitments to year-round work. The contribution of seasonality to total unemployment also appears to have declined considerably, primarily because employers became more sophisticated in managing swings in employment during the 1960s and 1970s and to some extent because the share of the labor force in the most seasonally sensitive industries declined (Rydzewski, Demming, and Rones 1993). Cyclical unemployment was damped during the 1960s and early 1970s by very strong domestic demand and the strong competitive position of U.S. industry vis-à-vis foreign manufacturers.

Beginning in the late 1970s, however, our industrial strength began to unravel as lower-cost, high-quality goods from foreign manufacturers made deep inroads in U.S. markets. Then during the early 1980s, a combination of extremely tight monetary policy and stimulative fiscal policy resulted in an extremely strong dollar, which in turn rendered U.S.-produced hard goods much less price competitive. We sold much less to other nations and bought much

FIGURE 2.6    Unemployment rates, by gender and age: 1979 and 1989.

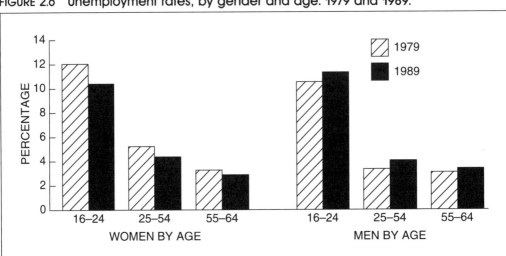

SOURCE: U.S. Department of Labor (1988, 1989).

more from them, particularly from Japan. Our net trade account for durable goods, such as autos and capital goods, swung from a positive 1 percent of gross national product in 1979–1980 to a negative 2 percent in 1985–1986. At the same time, the composition of domestic demand shifted to include more spending on services. With the relative weakening of the industrial sector, structural unemployment rose. *The increase in structural unemployment took the form of higher joblessness for men in general and less-educated men in particular.* The annual unemployment rate for prime working age men (aged 25–64) was higher by almost a full percentage point in 1989 than in 1979, while the rate for women was about half a percentage point lower. As is illustrated in Figure 2.6, the same general pattern of higher joblessness for men was even more striking among youths. Thus, the rise in joblessness over the 1980s was concentrated among men; it occurred largely among those with the least education; it included many men whose earnings once had provided middle-income lifestyles based on jobs in hard-goods manufacturing; and it was associated with a decline in labor force participation for low-education, low-skill men as well (Topel 1993).

## LABOR MARKET–RELATED ECONOMIC HARDSHIP

The long, strong economic expansion of the 1980s did not drive the national poverty rate back down to its earlier low. *In fact, at its lowest point for the 1980s (12.8 percent in 1989), the national poverty rate was higher than it had been in any year of the 1970s.* If the labor market programs of the 1990s are expected to contribute to the alleviation of poverty, we must identify the sources of the rise in poverty relative to the strength of the economy. Identifying those sources requires a brief historical review.

Defending the poverty-fighting properties of proposed stimulative fiscal policies, President Kennedy once remarked that "a rising tide lifts all boats." It was a good analogy that captured both the economic and social circumstances that lent themselves to reductions in poverty. Gains in disposable income during the 1950s and 1960s were more likely than now to be spent on cars, other durable goods, and homeownership. Such spending generated many jobs with modest educational requirements in goods-producing industries, in which productivity and wage growth were rapid. The blue collar jobs created were held primarily by mature family men. At that time more than three fourths of all poor family members were in married-couple families, usually with a single earner. Consequently, creation of full-time, year-round jobs in goods-producing and support industries in the 1960s and early 1970s, coupled with rising real wages, readily lifted families out of poverty. Strong job and real wage growth during the vigorous economic expansion of the 1960s was instrumental in driving down the proportion of the nation's population afflicted by poverty from about 22 percent to about 12 percent. The overall poverty rate declined slightly further to about 11 percent prior to the recession of 1975.[17]

During the years of declining poverty, gradual but cumulatively profound social and economic changes eroded the substantive underpinnings of President Kennedy's analogy. On the social side, the pool of poor families changed in ways that weakened the linkage of job growth to poverty reduction. When President Kennedy spoke, families maintained by a woman without a husband present accounted for less than one of every four poor families. By the late 1970s, the proportion had more than doubled to almost two of every four. The rising proportion of poor families maintained by women reflected both a sharp rise in their proportion of all families—from 10 percent in 1959 to 11 percent in 1969, then more steeply to 15 percent in 1979—and the continuance of very high poverty rates for such families.

The contributions to poverty of changing marital and childbearing behavior continued apace during the 1980s. In all, the number of poor families rose by 1.3 million from 1979 to 1989. More than two thirds of the rise, 850,000, was among families maintained by women without a spouse present. In a particularly deleterious development, an increasing share of poor single-parent families came to be maintained by young, unwed mothers. In 1989, 59 percent of families maintained by a mother with children under age 6 were living in poverty. On the economic side, demand was strong during the 1980s for highly educated workers but extremely weak for those with less education or specialized training. Since we continue to receive less-educated immigrant workers and to produce high school dropouts at a high rate relative to the requirements of the labor market for manual labor, there was upward pressure on poverty rates from the continuing flow of workers who at least initially are unqualified for any but the most menial work.

At 31.5 million in 1989, the poverty population was higher by 5.5 million than it had been in 1979. Almost 40 percent of the nation's poor were children who are unable to work, and 10 percent were aged 65 and over and unlikely to work. However, about 16.6 million of the persons living in poverty in 1989 were aged 16–64 and theoretically able to participate in labor market activities. About 7.7 million of these poor adults did not participate in labor market activity at all during 1989. *Thus, even in a year of comparatively favorable economic activity and excluding retirement-age persons, almost half of the working age poor had no direct connection, not even for one week, to the formal job market and the possibility of generating earnings to help pull them out of poverty.* Why did they not participate? About one third of the total, 2.4 million, were severely work-disabled and presumably were simply unable to work. As depicted in Figure 2.7, more than 3 million poor women, three fourths with children at home, reported that they did not participate because of family responsibilities. More

FIGURE 2.7    Reasons for nonparticipation of the poor, by gender and age: 1989.

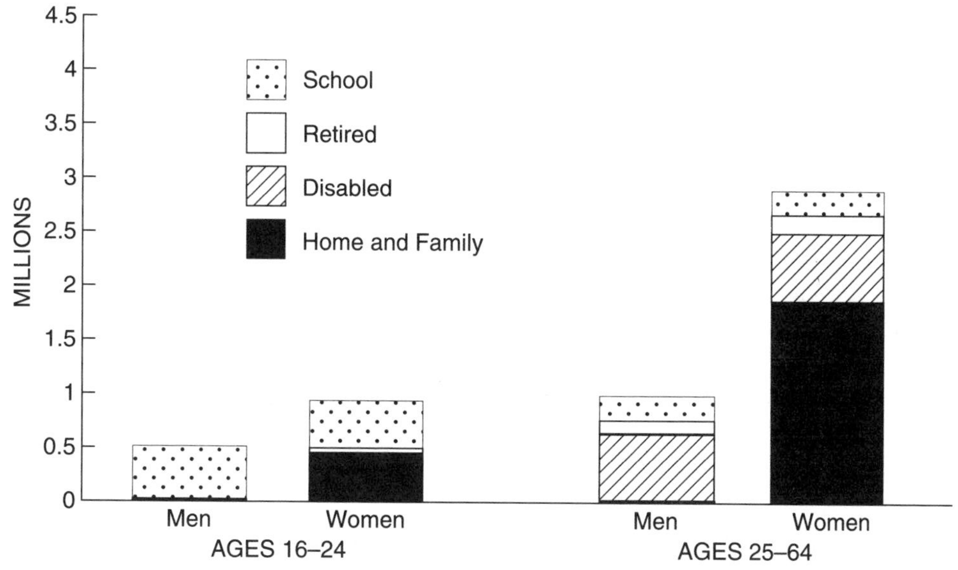

SOURCE: U.S. Bureau of the Census (1991).

than 2 million students, mostly youths, did not participate in the labor market at all because of their concentration on schooling. It is hard to visualize economic conditions that would be sufficiently ebullient to draw many of these nonparticipants into the job market, especially the severely work-disabled and less-educated women with two or three young children at home. Students are a different matter, of course, inasmuch as they likely will move into the labor market upon completion of their studies and be more competitive than if they had not concentrated on their education.

Among the working age poor were almost 1.5 million youths in the early stages of their adult lives who had not completed high school and were not currently enrolled in school. More than half of the dropouts were not in the labor force. Those in the work force were highly likely to be unemployed, 26.5 percent in March 1990, and those who had worked during 1989 generally had only modest earnings. For example, males aged 18–24 with one to three years of high school reported average earnings of only $7,000 during 1989 compared with $16,600 for those with four years of college. Poor persons aged 25–64 who had not completed high school numbered 5.6 million, or more than 40 percent of all prime working age poor persons. Persons who had not completed high school experienced a 23.5 percent poverty rate compared with a 6.9 percent rate for working age persons who had completed high school or more.

While there is nothing magic about completing high school, it is clear that failure to acquire minimal skills of computation and communication usually learned in high school is a powerful predictor of labor market difficulty and a very high risk of poverty.

Only 9 million working age poor persons (aged 16–64) were in the labor force at some time during 1989. Almost 2.8 million were in the labor market less than six months (Table 2.8). As was the case with persons who did not participate at all, school (1.5 million), family responsibilities (1.1 million), and serious illness or disability (1.1 million) were crucial reasons behind part-year participation. About 6.3 million working age adults in poverty were engaged in labor market activity for at least six months of the year. What conditions resulted in their poverty status? Almost 700,000 were self-employed persons who worked full-time for the entire year, but experienced a loss or had only minimal self-employment income during 1989 generally because of adverse business conditions. An additional 1.2 million worked part time *voluntarily*. These two groups probably are subject to high turnover and do not appear to represent core poverty populations.

Exclusive of the self-employed and voluntary part-time workers, 4.5 million workers living in poverty were in the labor force six months or more, and most were in the labor force all year. About one fourth of them could find only part-time jobs though they wanted full-time work, and over 200,000 searched for work but did not land a job, which leaves about 3.2 million poor wage and salary workers who usually worked full-time at a wage or salary job. Close to 1 million of them actually worked full-time, year-round. For 465,000 of the latter group, there were no labor market problems as conventionally defined by the Bureau of Labor Statistics. That is, they worked 50 weeks or more, their workweeks were usually more than 35 hours, and their wage rates were above a minimal standard (Klein and Rones 1989). Their poverty status was rooted in the fact that they were part of a family that simply was too large to get above the poverty threshold despite the earned income of the adults in the family. Because poverty classification is based on family size as well as income, the likelihood of living in poverty is a function of familial as well as employment and earnings characteristics. In 1989, the poverty threshold for a married-couple family of six was $16,921, or about four fifths of the average annual earnings of wage and salary workers. The poverty rate of families of that size was about 20 percent. There were 800,000 family households of that size or larger with a total of 5.4 million members living in poverty in 1989.

Why were the remaining 2.7 million fully committed wage and salary workers, and their dependents, living in poverty? Conditions of work associated with high poverty risk include low wage rates, periods of unemployment, too few hours of work when employed, and various combinations of the three. Low wage rates, arising from low-productivity jobs, are by far the most important

TABLE 2.8    Labor market status of the working poor: 1989
(thousands of persons).

| Labor Force Status or Problem | Total | In the Labor Force During 1989 | |
| | | Less Than Six Months | Six Months or More |
| --- | --- | --- | --- |
| In the Labor Force During 1989 | 9,048 | 2,787 | 6,260 |
| Unemployed only | 698 | 476 | 222 |
| Worked During 1989 | 8,350 | 2,311 | 6,038 |
| Usually worked part-time | 3,351 | 1,202 | 2,149 |
| Voluntarily | 2,039 | 868 | 1,171 |
| Involuntarily | 1,312 | 334 | 978 |
| Usually worked full-time | 4,998 | 1,109 | 3,889 |
| Self-employed | 905 | 230 | 675 |
| Wage and salary | 4,093 | 879 | 3,214 |

SOURCE: U.S. Department of Labor (1993).

contributor to poverty status of the hard-core working poor (Blank 1990). In 1989, 1 million full-time wage and salary workers were poor solely because their wage rate was too low, even with regular work, to keep their households out of poverty (Figure 2.8). Persons in low-skill, low-wage jobs are more likely to experience spells of unemployment, and another 675,000 workers were in poverty because of a combination of low wages and unemployment. As is illustrated in Figure 2.8, involuntary part-time on a usually full-time job, coupled with low wage rates, kept 220,000 workers in poverty, and 240,000 suffered poverty because of all three maladies. Thus, low wage rates figured exclusively, or at least very importantly, in the poverty status of more than two thirds of the poor wage and salary workers with a full-time, year-round commitment to the work force. Most of these workers had less than a high school education and many were recent immigrants.[18]

Less than half a million full-time wage or salary workers who worked at some time during the year, and 200,000 persons who sought but did not find any work, were in poverty solely because of cumulatively long periods of unemployment. Their absolute number was small compared with the 17.4 million workers who experienced joblessness during the year. Indeed, only about one of every 25 workers who experienced unemployment while in the labor force for at least six months during 1989 was living in poverty primarily because of chronic unemployment. The relatively few who were in poverty because of extended unemployment were most likely permanently displaced from earlier career jobs because of structural transformations or they had never managed to land a "good" job because of insufficient education or training (Hill and Corcoran 1983).

In summary, among the working poor are fairly large numbers of persons whose poverty is probably transitory. The self-employed who had a bad year,

FIGURE 2.8    Specific job problems of the working poor: 1989.

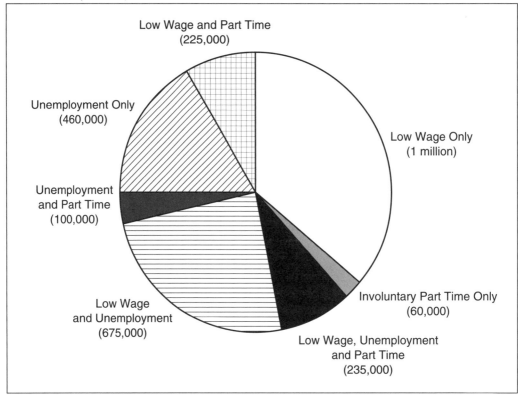

SOURCE: U.S. Department of Labor (1993).

NOTE: Data relate to wage and salary workers who usually work full-time.

students who work while concentrating on completing their education, and some family householders with good training and labor market skills who experienced an illness or other noneconomic setback during the year can be expected to move out of poverty without much in the way of custom labor market support. For the shrinking proportion of the working age poor who do have a strong labor market attachment, the clear need is for skills development among persons whose schooling and work experience are insufficient for the requirements of our increasingly technical economy. For youths, that means at least completing high school, better mechanisms to facilitate the transition from school to work, and preferably specialized technical training (Commission on Youth and America's Future 1989b). For structurally displaced adult workers who fall into poverty, the situation is more complex and likely more costly. Still, their prior labor market success makes them a good bet for training and placement, and their number appears to be small enough to be programmatically addressable even in an era of tight budgets. Indeed, by moving such workers into alternative jobs faster, we might be able to simultaneously reduce the costs of unemployment compensation and increase tax revenues.

## LOOKING AHEAD

Structural change in the national economy and, consequently, in labor markets profoundly influenced the well-being of American workers and their families during the 1980s. Faster growth of spending on services than on goods created many "good" jobs in upscale service occupations dominated by the highly educated as well as some much less desirable jobs in low-wage services. Simultaneously, the structural transformation of manufacturing led to the permanent displacement of hundreds of thousands of blue collar workers. Industrial firms that had prided themselves on lifetime paternalistic commitments to their production workers—largely men with average or below-average educational attainment—slashed employment, and some went out of business. The abrupt contraction struck at the heart of the middle class by drastically impacting mature family men with strong labor force attachments, good work histories, and long job tenure. Such men generally have the lowest incidence of unemployment and, taking into account their educational level, the highest wage rates. Broadly speaking then, during the 1980s labor requirements led to expanding demands for the highly educated and virtually no net gains in middle-income jobs for those with average or below-average educational attainment. The less-educated ended up filling down-scale, lower-wage service jobs and, on average, they suffered declining wages and annual earnings.

Responding to changing socioeconomic conditions, a growing share of women, particularly wives and mothers, chose to participate in the labor force during the 1980s. Women's educational preparedness for market work has risen to equal that of men, and the training of the most recent birth cohorts broadened to encompass preparation in occupational fields long dominated by men. By obtaining more education, work experience, and seniority, women substantially enhanced their earning power. Supported by strong demands in their areas of labor market dominance, a rising share of women found full-time, year-round jobs. Relative to men, women realized significant gains in average hourly earnings, and even larger gains in average weekly and annual earnings as they worked more hours per week and weeks per year. Thus, the 1980s brought a pronounced convergence of the labor market behavior and experience of women and men. The narrowing of employment and earnings differentials by gender was appreciable within race/ethnicity, education, occupation, and major industry groups. Within gender groups, earnings gains for whites and blacks substantially outstripped those of Hispanics, largely as a result of massive additions of young, less-educated immigrants in low-wage occupations. Annual earnings gaps between whites and blacks widened somewhat, reflecting a much sharper rise in the average educational endowment and annual hours of working whites.

Among older men and youths, time outside the work force increased during the 1980s. Older women slightly increased their labor force commitment and relative earnings during the 1980s, while men continued to retire at earlier ages than had been the case in the 1950s and 1960s. Reflecting both earlier retirement ages and increased longevity, retirees living on some form of deferred compensation increased much faster than the total population. Youths experienced lower full-time, year-round employment rates and lower inflation-adjusted earnings than their recent predecessors had at the same stage of their work-life cycle. The decline resulted in part from increased college attendance, when work time and earnings usually are limited, in part from less participation of high school dropouts, but primarily from shrinking demand for less-skilled labor that led to outright severe declines in real wage rates for less-educated workers.

Our individual and collective problems with unemployment were reasonably well handled from the end of World War II through the middle 1970s by temporary income maintenance programs designed to bridge the gap during periods of cyclical or seasonal unemployment. The emergence of heavy structural displacement was not anticipated in the creation of such programs, and they are not responsive to the training and new job placement needs of the structurally unemployed. The majority of permanently displaced industrial workers find new jobs, but almost always after considerable periods of unemployment and at lower wages (and benefits) than they had earned before displacement. We need to revise existing unemployment assistance programs to better serve the needs of the permanently displaced. For older workers with little education and mostly obsolescent industrial skills, extensive retraining often is necessary; and even after they complete retraining, there is little hope of reachieving the wage premiums that many enjoyed in their prior jobs. Redesigning our labor market programs to systematically identify the permanently displaced and to provide intensive transition counseling and skill training would bear much larger collective and individual social and economic benefits than continuing to rely on programs designed for a bygone era of industrial expansion and opportunity.

With respect to labor market–related poverty, policymakers and the public need to understand that long-run changes in the economy and in personal behavior have resulted in a growing adult poverty population that has little labor market connection and is unlikely to be significantly reduced by strong labor demand conditions. Little can be done to alter the frequency or severity of disability or serious illness that is more common for the poor than appears to be generally understood. Similarly, the sustained rise in the numbers of poor persons, and especially poor children, in single-parent families is not particularly amenable to labor market solutions. In particular, attempts to force less-educated, inexperienced workers into entry-level jobs, as has been proposed in recent welfare reform initiatives, seems likely to fail in the context of a low-end labor market that is already awash in surplus workers and simultaneously experiencing shrinking demand. Unfortunately, adaptation of labor market programs to upgrade the skills and develop effective work habits of single mothers, especially those who are young high school dropouts, is extremely costly and appears to provide only marginal payoffs (Gueron, Pauly, and Logy 1991). Solutions in this area reside not in dealing with the current crop, but in reducing the future flow. Policy responses to the essentially social origins of the rise in out-of-wedlock childbearing, for example, need to remove any economic incentives and reinstate strong social and, perhaps, even economic disincentives (Murray 1993).

Nothing about the 1990s suggests a slowdown in the rate of technological change—in fact, it may have accelerated a bit—or in the growth pattern of final demand. Indeed, there is reason to expect a continuation of relatively heavier spending on services as both the now-mature baby boomers and the still rapidly growing retirement age population spend larger shares of their incomes on services. In the industrial sector, cuts in military procurement as we wind down the heavy spending of the cold war virtually guarantee further job losses in heavy manufacturing. Also, there will be fewer opportunities for young men to develop technical skills as the armed forces are downsized. Thus, there is reason to believe that wage and annual income disparities between the more- and less-educated will continue to grow even as the disparities between women and men narrow. Because productivity growth is slow in sectors such as health and education services, and given the probable path of final purchases, sharp jumps in average productivity are unlikely. Hence, there is little reason to expect a resumption of large annual increases in average real earnings.

Since the sectors likely to show the strongest growth require more highly educated workers, few "good" jobs are likely to be available for those with a minimal education. Although high school dropout rates were somewhat lower in the early 1990s than in the 1980s, a significant minority of young Americans still fail to complete high school. Intensified efforts to persuade youths to at least complete a rigorous secondary school program certainly are warranted. Because pregnancy is sometimes the proximate cause of dropping out of school, and out-of-wedlock childbearing is almost always associated with lifetime economic disadvantage, such efforts should embrace very strong social sanctions on pregnancy outside marriage.

Since the 1980s we have been in a period of adjustment to a new economic paradigm. Major economic and social challenges already beset us and others (such as supporting the baby boom generation during their retirement years) are destined to emerge in the years ahead. Those who look to the past when "good" jobs that would support a middle-class lifestyle were available in the nation's factories to men (and some women) who were willing to work hard, came to work on time and regularly, and had a high tolerance for monotony (but not much interest in advanced training) are destined to be disappointed. Indeed, those who ignore the rumblings of a changing economy risk being swept into economic oblivion, but without the publicity that attended Harry Truman's departure from Mount St. Helens.

---

I am grateful to Jack Bregger, Suzanne Bianchi, Bill Butz, Reynolds Farley, and James H. Johnson for helpful comments on earlier drafts and to the Russell Sage Foundation for the opportunity to prepare this chapter. Katharine Wetzel, Cary Bean, and Ricardo Rodriguez provided invaluable programming and processing support. I am indebted to Barbara Anderson, Lisa Neidert, and their colleagues at the University of Michigan's Population Research Center for assistance in processing complex census microdata files.

## ENDNOTES

1. For detailed definitions, methodology, and sampling error information see U.S. Bureau of the Census, *1990 Census of Population and Housing: Public Use Microdata Sample Technical Documentation* (1992); and U.S. Department of Labor, Bureau of Labor Statistics, "Explanatory Notes," *Employment and Earnings,* any issue.

2. U.S. Bureau of the Census, *The Foreign Born Population in the United States: 1990* (1992).

3. Separate labor force data for the constituent parts of the "other races" category are not available annually for the 1980s. The 1990 census data show that Asians have the highest, and Native Americans have the lowest, participation rates within this rapidly increasing component of the overall working age population.

4. U.S. Bureau of the Census, "Poverty in the United States: 1988 and 1989," *Current Population Reports* (1991).

5. U.S. Bureau of the Census, "Marriage, Divorce and Remarriage in the 1990s" (1992).

6. U.S. Bureau of the Census, "School Enrollment—Social and Economic Characteristics of Students" (1993).

7. U.S. Bureau of the Census, "Educational Attainment in the United States, March 1991" (1991).

8. U.S. Bureau of the Census, "Labor Force Status and Other Characteristics of Persons with a Work Disability: 1981 to 1988" (1989).

9. Unlike some countries, the U.S. government does not collect data on jobs looking for workers—job vacancies—to analyze jointly with the high-quality information we have on workers looking for jobs. The one measure available, the index of help wanted advertising, is generally indicative of changing labor demand but has no detail that would permit meaningful analysis of the character, concentration, and intensity of labor demand by skill level. Consequently, assessments of the demand

side of labor market conditions must be based on proxies such as changes in employment and wage rates by industry and occupation.

10. U.S. Bureau of the Census, *Nursing Home Population: 1990* (1993).

11. U.S. Bureau of the Census, *Women-Owned Businesses* (1990); and *Characteristics of Business Owners* (1991).

12. U.S. Bureau of the Census, "Money Income of Households, Families, and Persons in the U.S., 1988 and 1989" (1991).

13. "Real" earnings figures for years other than 1989 were calculated using the Consumer Price Index-U-X1. For the historical series and an explanation, see U.S. Bureau of the Census, "Money Income of Households, Families, and Persons in the U.S., 1988 and 1989" (1991:350–352).

14. Decennial censuses and the March CPS include questions for each worker on the number of weeks worked during the prior year and their usual weekly hours. All references to weeks worked and hours worked per week are averages of those observed values. Annual hours worked are the product of average weeks worked and average usual weekly hours for the particular reference group.

15. For a comprehensive discussion, see Levy and Murnane (1992).

16. As this is being written in the fall of 1993, the Bureau of Labor Statistics is preparing to implement a comprehensive modernization of the measures. See the entire issue of the *Monthly Labor Review,* September 1993.

17. U.S. Bureau of the Census, "Poverty in the United States: 1988 and 1989" (1991:11–12).

18. U.S. Bureau of the Census, "Workers with Low Earnings: 1964 to 1990" (1992).

# 3

# Changing Economic Roles of Women and Men

SUZANNE M. BIANCHI

A CHAPTER ON GENDER roles written in the 1950s would have focused on differences in men's and women's family and labor market roles and whether such specialization was essential for societal well-being.[1] A chapter on gender roles written in the 1990s of necessity must focus on the issue of economic equality between women and men. The fundamental gender question of the past two decades, rising in part out of the civil rights movement of the 1960s and the renewed women's movement of the late 1960s and 1970s, has been: How equal are economic opportunities and outcomes for women and men in U.S. society?

In *American Women in Transition,* Daphne Spain and I asked why there had been so little change in the ratio of women's to men's earnings throughout the 1960s and 1970s (Bianchi and Spain 1986). We noted that the difference in the labor force participation rates of women and men had narrowed steadily and dramatically since World War II. College enrollment rates of women and men were virtually identical by 1980. Between 1970 and 1980, women increased their share of law, medical, and dental school degrees and moved into managerial positions in record numbers. Despite these changes, women's earnings hovered around 60 percent of men's throughout the 1955–1980 period.

During the 1980s, however, the ratio of women's to men's earnings increased significantly. Understanding what caused the wage gap to narrow in the 1980s is a major focus of this chapter. The 1990 census data, in conjunction with data from prior censuses, provide the raw material for an analysis of the economic activity of men and women in the United States between 1980 and 1990. More important, the data provide a perspective on how the experiences of *birth cohorts,* or generations of men and women, have changed.

The narrowing of the gender wage gap in the 1980s is in large part a story about the baby boom generation of young women. As this well-educated group of women moved into mid-career and as their mothers, who had spent many years at home raising children before returning to work, retired from the labor force, the average earnings of women increased and the wage gap narrowed.

Women born after World War II were raised by parents whose ability to finance a college education for their daughters and sons was unprecedented. Baby boom women marched forward to obtain college and advanced degrees in record numbers at the same time that they were protesting the sexism of college course offerings and content. They inundated executive offices, law firms, hospitals, and finally the armed forces, voicing great skepticism as to whether their abilities and credentials would be rewarded to the same extent as those of their male counterparts. Nevertheless, as individuals, they acted as if they would be the exception rather than the rule. If they worked assertively, diligently, *and continuously,* the inherently sexist, unfair system would somehow recognize their individual talent and would promote them as readily as their equally well-trained male counterparts. This chapter is about how the gamble that unfairness and discrimination would not impede their progress—or at least would deter them much less than it had in the past—ultimately paid off.

However, this chapter is also about another group for whom life did not seem so "fair" in the 1980s—young men and women with a high school education or less. The gender wage gap narrowed across the board, but less well-educated women workers succeeded in closing the gap with men only because they worked longer hours and because the wages of men stagnated and then declined. Men with a high school education had in the past been much better able to secure a high-paying job than women, even women with a college education. Increasingly, those high-paying, semiskilled jobs disappeared as massive restructuring occurred in the manufacturing sector. Because men were more concentrated in shrinking job sectors, they were hurt more than women, who more often worked in the expanding service sector jobs, particularly in health care.[2]

Finally, this chapter is about how the individual decisions of workers affect marriage and childbearing patterns. Marital and parental status have become less predictive of which women will be in the labor force, but remain important determinants of how much they participate and how much they earn. Marriage and parenting have in the past meant quite different things for men and women, increasing men's labor supply and reducing women's. How recent decisions away from early marriage and childbearing have influenced gender equality and how differences in responsibility for children keep men's and women's roles differentiated is the third topic addressed in the chapter.

## A NOTE ON COHORTS

Much of this chapter is about the experiences of birth cohorts, or generations of men and women. *Cohort* refers to a group of individuals who have a unique set of experiences throughout life. Although cohorts can be defined by events other than birth, the term is most commonly used to refer to all individuals born in a specified time period. Tables in this chapter present data on ten-year birth cohorts of women and men; Table 3.1 provides a reference for statistics in later tables.

Much of the chapter focuses on comparisons among the three youngest age groups shown in Table 3.1. Those born between 1936 and 1945, referred to as the World War II cohort, typically reached labor force age between the mid-1950s and mid-1960s. They entered adulthood during the ten-year period of increased civil rights activity leading up to the passage of the Civil Rights Act of 1964, which for the first time in U.S. history barred discrimination on the basis of sex. The prescient writings of some of the women of this generation sowed the seeds of the renewed women's movement of the late 1960s and 1970s. However, most of the women (and men) of this cohort completed their education and began their families prior to the widespread questioning of gender and racial stereotypes that typified the 1970s.

The early baby boom cohort of men and women (born between 1946 and 1955), who reached adulthood between the mid-1960s and the mid-1970s, was a relatively large generation of young persons who created serious dislocations as they moved through school and into the labor force. Classrooms bulged as school administrators scrambled to obtain resources needed by such a large co-hort of schoolchildren. Many attended high school on split shifts because of the lack of classroom space. They flooded college campuses as activism was at its height. Men of this cohort made decisions about college attendance that were, in part, influenced by the Vietnam War: By attending college they could defer military service and avoid being drafted.

The late baby boom cohort, those born between 1956 and 1965, reached adulthood and began entering the labor force in the mid-1970s. They trailed the large group of older brothers and sisters, those of the early baby boom, into the labor market and onto college campuses. This created advantages and disad-vantages for them as they settled into adulthood. They entered a labor market in which wage rates were generally stagnating rather than rising as they had

TABLE 3.1  Birth cohorts, by period of labor market entry and age in 1980 and 1990.

| Birth Cohort | Description/ Generation | Labor Force Entry | Age in 1980 | Age in 1990 |
|---|---|---|---|---|
| 1956–1965 | Late baby boom | Mid-1970s through 1980s | 15–24 | 25–34 |
| 1946–1955 | Early baby boom | Mid-1960s through 1970s | 25–34 | 35–44 |
| 1936–1945 | World War II | Mid-1950s through 1960s | 35–44 | 45–54 |
| 1926–1935 | Parents of baby boom | Mid-1940s through 1950s | 45–54 | 55–64 |
| 1916–1925 | Parents of baby boom | Mid-1930s through 1940s | 55–64 | 65–74 |
| 1906–1915 | Grandparents of baby boom | Mid-1920s through 1930s | 65–74 | 75–84 |

during the previous four decades. (See Chapter 1 in this volume on income trends.)

The examination of the behaviors of various cohorts ends with the late baby boom women and men because this was the youngest group to reach the prime working ages (age 25 and over) by 1990 (see Table 3.1). Not much can yet be said about gender equality in employment and earnings among the much smaller birth cohort to come after the late baby boom. The baby bust generation, born between 1966 and 1975, was just beginning to enter adulthood in the late 1980s. Mare's chapter on education in this volume shows that women of the baby bust cohort are spending *more* time in school than men. This suggests that the gender wage gap should continue to narrow, other things being equal.

Any cross-sectional snapshot of the population, such as provided by decennial census data, combines the experiences of different cohorts who are at various ages at the time of the census enumeration. The third and fourth columns of Table 3.1 provide perspective on the birth cohorts moving into various ages in the 1980s. For example, late baby boom men and women were reaching their late 20s and early 30s by 1990 when the early baby boom generation was aging from roughly age 30 to age 40. And during the 1980s, the parents of the baby boom began aging into retirement. This chapter uses the concept of cohort to more clearly illustrate the "facts" of the gender story of the 1980s and ascertain why certain changes occurred in the 1980s rather than earlier.

As noted at the outset, the most important "gender news" of the 1980s was that the earnings of women and men became more equal. Factors affecting the convergence in labor market activity are complex and subject to differing interpretations. To place the increase in relative earnings of women in context requires attention to many factors—the narrowing in gender differences in labor force attachment, educational attainment, and occupational placement as well as the trend toward delayed marriage and childbearing among recent cohorts of women and men. I now turn to these topics.

## WOMEN'S PARTICIPATION IN MARKET WORK

What motivates men and women to work? First, there is economic need: to support oneself, to contribute to family income, or, in many cases, to provide support for dependents. Second, aspects of work other than monetary return make life interesting and enjoyable and provide individuals with a sense of purpose. Finally, wider cultural or societal settings reinforce norms about who "should" be spending their time doing market work.

There is no doubt that the economic activity of women and men has become much more similar in recent decades. Increasingly, it is viewed as "normal" for adult women and men, regardless of parental status, to be employed. The increased participation of women in *market* work is a story that has been un-folding since at least the early nineteenth century, although growth in women's employment has accelerated in recent decades (Goldin 1990). With the shift from an agricultural to an industrial economy, the demand for factory workers grew and women filled some of that need.

As the service sector of the economy expanded in the early twentieth century, the need for clerical workers increased and women again helped fill the demand. Between 1890 and 1920, the employment of single women increased substan-tially; but when the supply of young, single women workers was not sufficient to meet demand, married women became an accepted substitute in the labor force (Goldin 1990; Oppenheimer 1970). Married women's participation in the paid labor force grew steadily but slowly between 1920 and 1940. The Great Depression dampened the increase in employment generally, and bars against the employment of married women also intensified during the 1930s (Goldin 1990; J.G. Robinson 1988). After 1940, however, the increase in married women's employment accelerated.[3]

During the 1950s and early 1960s, older, married women returned to the labor force in great numbers after raising their children. They filled jobs in the expanding clerical and service sectors while younger women were occupied in the home rearing the relatively large baby boom families. In the 1970s and 1980s, younger women's labor force participation increased most rapidly. The demand for workers intensified in the service sector, where women had tradi-tionally been concentrated. In addition, the wages of women—the value of spend-ing time in market work rather than in the home—also rose (England 1992).

Factors other than market demand have facilitated young women's increased participation in the labor force in the last two decades. Changes in marriage and childbearing patterns, along with rising educational attainment, have favored more labor market involvement of women. Table 3.2 provides a summary of these changes for young women in three birth cohorts: World War II, early baby boom, and late baby boom.

As women and men increasingly delay marriage, and divorce more fre-quently, they spend less of their adult lives in marriage. When the World War II cohort of women were aged 25–34 (in 1970), 77 percent were married and living with their husband. This dropped dramatically to 64 percent for the early baby boom women (who were 25–34 in 1980) and to 60 percent for the late baby boom women (who were 25–34 in 1990).

Reductions are equally (if not more) dramatic for men.[4] Given that marriage has historically tended to discourage labor force participation for women and encourage market work among men, the shift toward later marriage (and more divorce) has tended to enhance women's labor force participation and depress men's market involvement at younger ages; thus it serves as a gender-equaliz-ing force.

TABLE 3.2    Marriage, children, and college education at ages 25–34
             for three cohorts of American women and men.

| | World War II | Early Baby Boom | Late Baby Boom |
|---|---|---|---|
| Marriage | | | |
| Percentage married | | | |
| Women | 77% | 64% | 60% |
| Men | 77 | 64 | 54 |
| | | | |
| Children | | | |
| Percentage childless (women) | 19 | 30 | 33 |
| | | | |
| Education | | | |
| Percentage college graduate | | | |
| Women | 12 | 21 | 23 |
| Men | 19 | 26 | 24 |
| Ratio women/men (per 100) | 63 | 81 | 96 |

SOURCE: Decennial census Public Use Microdata Samples (1 in 1,000) for 1970–1990.

At midcentury, the majority of American women left the labor force at the time of marriage. Indeed, substantial discriminatory "marriage bars" to employment of married women existed into the 1950s (and later for some industries such as the airlines). Many employers of clerical workers and public school systems either would not hire married women or dismissed women workers when they married (Goldin 1990: Chap. 6). In recent decades, such overt discrimination based on marital status has become illegal, and marriage per se has become less important in determining which women work. Still, the delay in marriage has been an important component of the increase in young women's labor force participation in the last two decades because it is related to the delay in childbearing, which has far greater import for women.

Recent cohorts have postponed the transition to parenthood—the transition that still differentiates the adult roles of women and men more than any other. As shown in Table 3.2, when the World War II cohort of women were in their late 20s and early 30s, 19 percent of them were childless. Among the early baby boom cohort of women, 30 percent were childless; and among late baby boom women, 33 percent were childless.

Figure 3.1 shows the interrelatedness of childlessness—or at least the postponement of a first birth—and educational attainment. Of the 33 percent of late baby boom women, aged 25–34, who were childless in 1990, the proportion varied from about 15 percent for those who had not finished high school to about 60 percent for those who had completed college or earned a postgraduate degree.

Among women of the early baby boom who had reached ages 35–44 by 1990, the fertility differential was smaller as more of the well-educated had the

FIGURE 3.1  Percentage childless, by educational attainment: 1990.

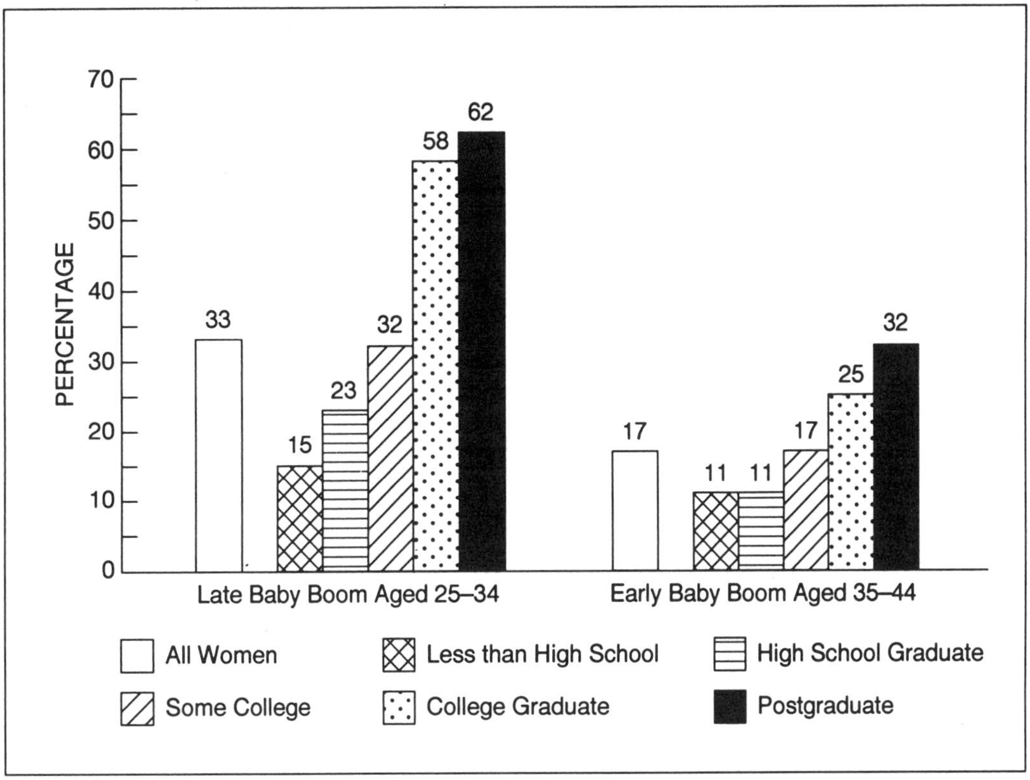

SOURCE: Decennial census Public Use Microdata Samples (1 in 1,000) for 1990.

children they had postponed to obtain their education. Still, the differential remained sizable, with 11 percent of those with a high school education (or less)
childless compared with 25 percent of those with a bachelor's degree and 32
percent of those with an advanced degree.

The increase in childlessness among the college-educated differentiates the
early baby boom and World War II cohorts. At ages 35–44, only 16 percent of
the World War II cohort of college-educated women remained childless compared with 25 percent of the early baby boom women, who were the first cohort
to experience the completion of the contraceptive revolution with the legalization of abortion throughout the 50 states. Although the development of oral
contraceptives and the widespread availability of effective contraceptive methods probably had the greater effect in reducing fertility, the legalization of abortion was symbolically important. It strengthened the notion that having children
was something women could choose to do or not and further expanded the
means by which women could effectively control the number and timing of
births. In 1973, when *Roe* v. *Wade* made the denial of abortion services illegal,
early baby boom women were in their late teens and early 20s, whereas most

of the World War II cohort of women had already begun, if not completed, childbearing. By contrast, the late baby boom women, who were still children in 1973, entered a world in which contraception and abortion were existent, legal, and accessible choices from the beginning of their reproductive years.

With the birth of a first child, mothers have traditionally become focused on providing nurturance to the child while fathers have become more focused on adequately providing financial support. While these gender-specific responses to children may be changing—mothers may increasingly concern themselves with financially supporting children, especially as marriages dissolve, and fathers may be taking a somewhat more active role in the care of children[5]—change is gradual. Historically, the prescribed role for mothers has interfered with market work while the prescribed role for fathers has reinforced the importance of market work.

The delay in childbearing has therefore extended the period in young adulthood in which women concern themselves with the same things that concern men—finishing school, getting a job, and getting established in the labor market. Women and men experience the greatest conflict between market work and competing family responsibilities at later ages. As women postpone childbirth and have fewer children, they also spend less of their adult lives raising a family.

Schooling strongly influences how much women earn and how likely they are to participate in the labor market. Table 3.2 shows that 12 percent of the World War II cohort of women completed college. This figure jumped to 21 percent among the early baby boom women, but rose only to 23 percent for the subsequent late baby boom cohort.

The percentage of women who were college graduates was high relative to men for women born early in this century when college attendance was rare for both sexes.[6] The gender gap in college attendance and completion subsequently widened for those born between 1916 and 1935, the mothers and fathers of the baby boom. Beginning in the 1960s, gender differences again began to narrow, but the bulk of the closing of the gender gap in college enrollment and completion occurred in the 1970s with the baby boom cohorts.

Women in the World War II cohort, most of whom attended college in the late 1950s or early 1960s, increased their college attendance, but much greater gender equality was achieved by the early baby boom cohort. Women's college completion rates were 63 percent of men's among the World War II cohort compared with 81 percent among the early baby boom cohort (Table 3.2). By 1990, when late baby boom women had reached ages 25–34, the proportion of women who were college graduates was 96 percent that of men. It seems likely that women's college completion will actually surpass men's among the baby bust cohorts that will follow the late baby boom into the labor force.[7]

The phenomenal progress in closing the gender educational gap is further illustrated by Table 3.3, which shows the change in the number of degrees in

TABLE 3.3   Degrees in law, medicine, and dentistry, by gender: 1970–1990.

| | Number of Degrees Conferred | | |
| --- | --- | --- | --- |
| | 1970 | 1980 | 1990 |
| Law | | | |
| Women | 801 | 10,754 | 14,519 |
| Men | 14,415 | 24,893 | 21,048 |
| Percentage women | 5.4% | 30.2% | 40.8% |
| Medicine | | | |
| Women | 699 | 3,486 | 5,128 |
| Men | 7,615 | 11,416 | 10,326 |
| Percentage women | 8.4% | 23.4% | 33.2% |
| Dentistry | | | |
| Women | 34 | 700 | 1,108 |
| Men | 3,684 | 4,558 | 3,139 |
| Percentage women | 0.9% | 13.3% | 26.1% |
| Birth Cohort Aged 25–34 | World War II | Early baby boom | Late baby boom |

SOURCE: U.S. Department of Education (1991: Table 172).

law, medicine, and dentistry conferred on women and men in 1970, 1980, and 1990. Arrayed across the bottom of the table is the birth cohort aged 25–34 in each year, the cohort most likely to be in the age range during which advanced professional and graduate degrees are conferred.

Between 1970 and 1980, the number of law degrees granted to women increased dramatically from 800 to over 10,000, from 5 to 30 percent of all law degrees. The trend is similar for degrees in medicine and dentistry, even rarer fields of study for women than law; in the 1970s, the number of such degrees conferred on women increased greatly. The early baby boom cohort was the first to experience this great expansion in the number of female lawyers, doctors, and dentists. In the 1980s, the number of degrees in law, medicine, and dentistry conferred on the late baby boom women continued to increase as the number conferred on men actually declined. By 1990, women received 41 percent of degrees in law, 33 percent of degrees in medicine, and 26 percent of degrees in dentistry.

Individuals who have invested greatly in education typically reap the return for their investment by becoming and staying employed. As women's educational levels have risen, more women remain in the work force even after marrying and having children. Also, women can no longer be overtly discriminated against by their employers for being wives and mothers. The civil rights and women's movements of the 1960s and 1970s embodied the notion that personal and family choices of workers were not legitimate criteria on which to base hiring and promotion decisions, a notion bolstered by protections that were written into law in Title VII of the Civil Rights Act of 1964 and reinforced by far-reaching court cases involving many of the nation's largest employers.

Perhaps as much as 40 percent of the overall increase in women's labor force participation in the 1970s and 1980s might be "accounted for" by the continued shift toward those more likely to be employed—that is, the better-educated, unmarried, and childless (Zhan 1992; Lichter and Costanzo 1987). But behaviors and normative conditions in society were also changing, either as cause or, perhaps more often, as consequence of demographic change, educational upgrading, and market demand. Increasingly, what had differentiated how likely women were to work outside the home—whether they were wives and mothers—came to matter less.

Throughout the 1970s and 1980s, the group with the lowest rate of labor force participation historically—white, married women with young children—increased participation most rapidly (Table 3.4). In 1970, 44 percent of married women with young children worked during the year and only 10 percent worked full-time, year-round. By 1990, 68 percent of married women with young children worked outside the home and 28 percent worked full-time, year-round. By 1990, most married mothers of young children had some involvement in market work, although they still were not usually full-time, year-round workers (Hayghe and Bianchi 1994).

Stresses at the bottom of the income distribution assured that working became more "normal" for all women, not just the college-educated. Women with a high school education or less, who might have discontinued market work when they had children because their wages were relatively low, were married to similarly educated men who increasingly could not support a family on their earnings alone.[8] Having more than one breadwinner became increasingly important to less-educated parents who hoped to own their own home (Myers 1985, 1986). Young wives, even those who could not command high salaries, worked outside the home to supplement the household income, or in some cases provided the majority of it. Also, as more women and men divorced, work for pay became an economic necessity for the growing number of single mothers, many of whom received inadequate child support from absent fathers.

A normative transformation took place in the United States in the 1970s and 1980s, one that was occurring in other developed countries as well.[9] As a society, our view of women's proper place as at home with their young children shifted to one that considered it normal for married women with children to work. The welfare reform debates of the 1980s and early 1990s reflect the pervasiveness of this behavioral and normative change. As more married mothers worked outside the home, the right of single mothers to stay at home with children (and collect welfare) was increasingly called into question. As a nation,

TABLE 3.4  Married mothers' labor force attachment: 1970–1990.

|  | 1970 | 1980 | 1990 |
|---|---|---|---|
| **With Children under Age 18** | | | |
| Percentage who worked last year | 51% | 63% | 73% |
| Percentage who worked full-time, year-round | 16 | 23 | 34 |
| **With Children under Age 6** | | | |
| Percentage who worked last year | 44 | 58 | 68 |
| Percentage who worked full-time, year-round | 10 | 18 | 28 |
| **With Children Aged 6–17** | | | |
| Percentage who worked last year | 58 | 68 | 78 |
| Percentage who worked full-time, year-round | 23 | 29 | 40 |

SOURCE: U.S. Bureau of Labor Statistics, Current Population Survey, unpublished tabulations.

we began to lament what might be happening to the care of children (Presser 1989), but we increasingly viewed as "normal" the participation in the market of all adults, regardless of gender, marital status, or parental status.

## CHANGING LIFETIME WORK EXPERIENCE OF WOMEN AND MEN

Change in labor force participation tells only part of the story of gender equality. To understand whether changes in the earnings of women relative to men in the 1980s represent a sustainable trend, it is necessary to determine the likelihood of women and men working continuously throughout adulthood.

The distinction between the labor force participation rates of men and women and their lifetime work experience helps explain why women's wages failed to increase relative to men's in earlier decades. Goldin has shown that in the first part of this century, married women rarely worked outside the home, but those who did tended to work continuously throughout their adult lives. Although working women had high levels of lifetime work experience, overt discrimination kept their wages low relative to men's. This situation changed after World War II, as married women's labor force participation accelerated and the most blatant forms of discrimination were gradually eradicated.

During the 1950s and 1960s, older, married women, who had been out of the labor force for a considerable number of years while raising their children, returned to the labor force in great numbers (Goldin 1990; Smith and Ward 1989). While out of the labor force rearing children, these women were often not honing skills demanded in the paid labor market. Nor were they accruing seniority or tenure with an employer, another basis for salary or wage increases. The large influx of workers with limited recent experience in the labor market in the 1950s and 1960s effectively diluted the average work experience of the female labor force and held down average wages of working women. Employers paid them relatively low wages when they reentered the labor force.

Beginning in the late 1960s, the increase in female labor force participation was more often accounted for by younger women who entered the labor force after completing school and remained employed even after they married and had children. This increased the average work experience of young women workers relative to their mothers' generation. Measures of cumulative lifetime work experience suggest that the proportion of women with continuous labor force attachment increased during the 1970s and 1980s (O'Neill and Polachek 1993; Hill and O'Neill 1992; and Wellington 1993). However, because young, less experienced workers earn lower wages than older, more experienced workers, the entry of a large cohort of baby boom women beginning in the late 1960s and early 1970s did not immediately raise the relative wages of women workers. It took a number of years in the labor force before the salutary effect of their increased educational attainment and work experience relative to men and relative to previous generations of women began to narrow the wage gap.

Women are working more continuously throughout their adult years partly for the reasons just mentioned—the increase in schooling, delayed childbearing and smaller families, and changes in marriage patterns. But lifetime work experience has increased among women of all educational and family statuses, suggesting that a pervasive behavioral shift has occurred among recent cohorts of women (Hill and O'Neill 1992). As noted in the previous section, being a wife and mother of young children does not deter labor force attachment for baby boom women to the extent that it did for their mothers.

Decennial censuses do not collect employment histories of the population; rather, they collect more limited information on attachment to the labor force in the year preceding the census: Did a person work in the year prior to the census; if so, how many hours per week and how many weeks was he or she employed? The percentage of women employed full-time (35 hours or more per week) and year-round (50–52 weeks per year) gives some perspective on the attachment of those who moved into and out of the labor force in the 1970s and 1980s. It also affords a picture of the increase in work experience of young women and the growing similarity in the labor force attachment of men and women, a picture that is bolstered by longitudinal data with more complete measures of lifetime work attachment.[10]

Table 3.5 shows changes in the percentage who worked full-time, year-round for cohorts born between 1906 and 1915 and 1956 and 1965, as observed in the 1960–1990 censuses. These cohorts are labeled as in Table 3.1. In addition to the baby boom and World War II cohorts, older age groups in the table are classified as either parents or grandparents of the baby boom.

TABLE 3.5   Percentage of women and men who are full-time, year-round workers, by age, sex, and birth cohort.

| | Ages | | | |
|---|---|---|---|---|
| Birth Cohort | 25–34 | 35–44 | 45–54 | 55–64 |
| **Women** | | | | |
| 1956–1965 Late baby boom | 42% | | | |
| 1946–1955 Early baby boom | 29 | 43% | | |
| 1936–1945 World War II | 18 | 30 | 41% | |
| 1926–1935 Parents of baby boom | 14 | 21 | 29 | 25% |
| 1916–1925 Parents of baby boom | | 18 | 25 | 21 |
| 1906–1915 Grandparents of baby boom | | | 20 | 20 |
| **Men** | | | | |
| 1956–1965 Late baby boom | 66 | | | |
| 1946–1955 Early baby boom | 62 | 72 | | |
| 1936–1945 World War II | 68 | 71 | 70 | |
| 1926–1935 Parents of baby boom | 66 | 71 | 68 | 51 |
| 1916–1925 Parents of baby boom | | 70 | 68 | 51 |
| 1906–1915 Grandparents of baby boom | | | 65 | 55 |
| **Ratio Women/Men (per 100)** | | | | |
| 1956–1965 Late baby boom | 63 | | | |
| 1946–1955 Early baby boom | 47 | 60 | | |
| 1936–1945 World War II | 27 | 42 | 58 | |
| 1926–1935 Parents of baby boom | 21 | 30 | 42 | 49 |
| 1916–1925 Parents of baby boom | | 26 | 37 | 42 |
| 1906–1915 Grandparents of baby boom | | | 31 | 36 |

SOURCE: Decennial census Public Use Microdata Samples (1 in 1,000) for 1960–1990.

Each succeeding cohort of women had a higher likelihood of full-time, year-round market work than previous generations, but the pace of change accelerated among baby boom women. For example, whereas 14 percent of the mothers of the baby boom (born 1926–1935) worked full-time, year-round at ages 25–34, 18 percent of the World War II cohort, 29 percent of the early baby boom cohort, and 42 percent of the late baby boom cohort were full-time, year-round workers. Women in the early baby boom cohort had a rate of full-time participation (29 percent) at ages 25–34 that was not achieved by those in the World War II cohort until they were ages 35–44. And at ages 35–44, which still tend to be years in which child-rearing responsibilities are great, 43 percent of the early baby boom cohort compared with 30 percent of the World War II cohort were full-time, year-round workers.

The participation rates shown in Table 3.5 index the increased labor force attachment of women and help one visualize the attachment of women workers who moved into and out of the labor force in the 1970s and 1980s. As the early baby boom cohort of women moved into the prime working ages of 25–34 in 1980, with a full-time, year-round labor force participation rate of 29 percent, they in some sense "replaced" the oldest generation of women shown in the table, grandmothers of the baby boom, who aged out of the labor force completely. In the 1980s, as the early baby boom women reached ages 35–44, they began replacing the oldest of their mothers who were aging out of the prime working ages. So, for example, as early baby boom women turned 35–44, with a full-time, year-round participation rate of 43 percent, they replaced their mothers born in 1916–1925, only 18 percent of whom had been full-time workers when they were in their late 30s and early 40s. A cohort much more firmly attached to the labor force moved into mid-career as much more tenuously attached cohorts of women (parents and grandparents of the baby boom) retired from the labor force.

The result that this "replacement of generations" had on gender equality in labor force attachment is shown in the bottom panel of Table 3.5. Men's full-time participation rates have not changed much over generations: Historically the peak years of labor force participation occur at ages 35–54, when about 70 percent of all men are employed full time. Ironically, women's lower rates of full-time attachment are often implicitly, if not explicitly, measured against a false perception that virtually all men work full-time, year-round.

The acceleration in labor force attachment at young ages among baby boom women—and the lack of change among men—produced profound movement toward gender equality among those in their late 20s and early 30s by 1990. At ages 25–34, the full-time attachment of women of the World War II cohort was only 27 percent that of men of this generation and only a little higher than the comparable number (21 percent) for the cohort before them (see first column, bottom panel of Table 3.5). Among the early baby boom cohort, the full-time attachment of women jumped to 47 percent of men's and then rose to 63 percent for those of the late baby boom generation. Women's full-time labor force participation rates have not yet reached parity with men's, but they are moving in that direction.

Other researchers provide corroborating evidence of a profound shift in labor force attachment of women that occurred around 1970 with the early baby boom generation of women. For example, the overall rate of labor force participation shown in Figure 2.1, in the chapter by James Wetzel, clearly indicates that the increase in labor force participation at ages 25–34 was exceptionally great for the early baby boom cohort compared with the preceding World War II cohort.

Rexroat (1992) has examined longitudinal data on a group of women corresponding roughly to the early baby boom generation shown in Table 3.5. She looks separately at those born between 1944 and 1946, between 1947 and 1949, and between 1950 and 1953 and examines the proportion of years these women worked as they aged from their early 20s to their late 20s. As those born 1944–1946 aged from 23 to 28, they worked about 50 percent of the years in this five-year period, a time in which many of them completed their education, married, and started families. The proportion of years worked rose to over 70 percent for the middle group (born 1947–1949) and to almost 80 percent for the youngest group (born 1950–1953). Those who planned to be employed at age 35 rose from 33 percent to 57 percent to 66 percent across the three subgroups of women (Rexroat 1992).

Between 1968 and 1980, when these groups of women were aging from their early to late 20s, each successive group was exhibiting characteristics more conducive to continuous employment. Sizable compositional shifts accelerated the trend toward more continuous market involvement. For example, the increase in the proportion who had not married, who married but were still childless, or who married and then divorced was most dramatic between those born in 1944–1946 and those born in 1947–1949 (Rexroat 1992). Thereafter, the trend toward continuous market work persisted, propelled by widespread normative and behavioral changes that had taken on a life of their own. Increases in work attachment, in the expectation that one would still be working at age 35, and in the likelihood that a woman would marry a husband supportive of a wife's market involvement continued even after the greatest shifts in educational attainment, delayed marriage, and childbearing had already occurred.

The rapid, unanticipated increase in young women's market work during the past two decades is conveyed by projections contained in *The American Labor Force* (Bancroft 1958). Using labor force data for the early 1950s, Bancroft projected participation rates for women in 1975. Her projections for women over age 45 are within 2 or 3 percentage points of the actual participation rates in these age ranges in 1975. For women aged 25–34, her projections underestimated the actual participation rates in 1975 by 16 percentage points—a projected rate of 39 percent compared with an actual rate of 55 percent (Bianchi and Spain 1986: Table 5.1). By the early 1990s, the comparable labor force participation rate for young women had jumped almost another 20 percentage points and stood at 74 percent.[11]

If young women continue to earn college degrees at the same rate as men, or at a higher rate, and if they continue to narrow the gender differences in labor force participation at young ages and remain attached to the labor market as they age, we should expect gender differences in earnings to decrease. Researchers do not dispute that increased work experience is key to further earnings improvements of women relative to men, but the pace at which the wage gap will be closed remains uncertain. Smith and Ward (1989) project continued narrowing of the wage gap between men and women through the end of the 1990s. Recent work by Wellington (1993) with longitudinal data suggests that the main way that women have narrowed and will continue to narrow the wage gap is to increase their labor market experience, although she finds the earnings return to an actual additional year of experience to be substantially smaller than the estimates used by Smith and Ward.

Although women are closing the educational and experience gap with men, the college majors chosen by men and women are different and the jobs they enter after they complete school continue to be different. These differences—to the extent they are implicated in wage differences between men and women— also lead to uncertainty about the pace of gender equality in earnings. Hence, I turn to an examination of trends in occupational segregation during the 1970s and 1980s.

## TRENDS IN OCCUPATIONAL SEX SEGREGATION

In addition to gender differences in how attached individuals are to the labor force at any given point and how continuously they work over a lifetime, men and women are differentiated by what they do in the labor market and the sectors of the economy in which they perform their work for pay. These differences continue to be of great interest because of the assumption that they at least partly explain women's inability to earn as much as men earn.

Why occupations are so differentiated by gender has been a subject of considerable debate. Human capital theorists within economics have emphasized the role of choice, arguing that women's expectations about spending time outside the labor force to rear children lead them to choose occupations that are compatible with child rearing—occupations such as part-time or temporary clerical or sales jobs that may not penalize them for time out of the labor force. Women are assumed to look for jobs that are less demanding because they anticipate the need for flexibility in their lives in order to rear children. They pay a price for this because they "choose" jobs with lower age-earnings profiles, lower returns to seniority, and little on-the-job training.

Some aspects of the human capital explanation have been debunked; for example, the original formulation argued that women choose jobs with higher starting salaries but a less steep rise in wages with age, but no research has demonstrated the existence of higher starting wages of women in female-dominated jobs (England 1982, 1992). Still, there continues to be the supposition that women contribute to their "ghettoization" in lower-paid, female-dominated occupations because they view job choice and time for child rearing as far more interconnected than do men and act accordingly.

Causes of occupational segregation are also traced to job discrimination, past and present—explanations that point more to constraints than to choice as the reason for the gender segregation in jobs. For example, Bergmann argues that when women are crowded into fewer, female-dominated occupations, it increases the supply of workers for these jobs and ultimately lowers the amount of money an employer has to pay to get workers to fill such positions (Bergmann 1986). An alternative explanation as to why female-dominated occupations have lower age-earnings profiles is that some jobs have strong career trajectories, while others do not, and that women and minorities have been systematically excluded from the former. Perhaps the best circumstantial evidence that occupational "choices" of women are constrained is that predominantly female jobs pay less than male jobs (England 1992). If increased wages motivate market work, it is unclear why women would continue to choose occupations that are relatively low-paid.

If the reason for gender segregation of occupations is choice, England argues, then the choice results from lifelong socialization that leads men and women to find different jobs interesting (England 1992). She notes that the occupational goals of boys tend to be more highly sex-typed than those of girls and that even preschoolers express sex-typed occupational preferences. There is some evidence that men place higher value on status, power, money, and freedom from supervision, and men may be more willing to take risks. Women more often value working with people, helping others, and creativity. Job choice may also reflect a preference for working with one's own sex (England 1992).

Some of the conditions and preferences that have in the past resulted in occupational segregation are presumably changing as more women view labor force participation as a lifelong activity. For example, female high school seniors continue to place much less emphasis than male high school seniors on having lots of money, but the proportion who thought it very important in life tripled from 10 to 30 percent between 1972 and 1992. (The comparable increase for men was from 26 to 45 percent.) By 1992, 89 percent of these young women (87 percent of men) reported that steady employment was very important in life, up from 74 percent (82 percent for young men) in 1972. In fact, in 1992 young women were even more likely to report that steady employment was very important than they were to report that marrying and having a happy family was very important (82 percent) (Green 1993).

How differentiated by gender was the occupational distribution by the end of the 1980s after two decades of increased participation and a growing perception of the importance of market work and high earnings by younger women? Table 3.6 shows the percentage female in the 13 major occupational groupings used to classify workers in the decennial censuses of 1970–1990.[12] Between 1970 and 1990, the experienced civilian labor force increased from 38 to 46 percent female. Women greatly increased their representation in white collar occupations. In particular, the proportion of managers who were women jumped from 19 to 31 percent in the 1970s and then to 42 percent by the end of the 1980s.

Women and men continue to do quite different jobs. In 1990, 77 percent of clerical, administrative support positions were filled by women. In fact, such

TABLE 3.6    Major occupational groups, by percentage women:
1970–1990.

|  | 1970 | 1980 | 1990 |
|---|---|---|---|
| Managers, executives | 19% | 31% | 42% |
| Professional specialty | 44 | 49 | 54 |
| Technicians | 34 | 44 | 46 |
| Sales | 41 | 49 | 49 |
| Administrative support, clerical | 73 | 77 | 77 |
| Private household occupations | 96 | 95 | 95 |
| Protective service | 7 | 12 | 16 |
| Other service | 61 | 63 | 63 |
| Farming, forestry, fishing | 9 | 15 | 16 |
| Precision production, craft | 7 | 8 | 10 |
| Machine operators | 40 | 41 | 40 |
| Transportation workers | 4 | 8 | 10 |
| Handlers, laborers | 17 | 20 | 20 |
| Total percentage female in labor force | 38% | 43% | 46% |

SOURCE: Decennial census for 1970–1990, published tabulations.

positions were more often filled by women in 1990 than in 1970. Service occupations (except protective service) were more often filled by women than men, although the percentage of the male labor force in service jobs has increased as this sector of the economy has expanded. On the other hand, only 10 percent of skilled craft (or precision production) and transportation jobs in 1990 were filled by women.

In the decennial census, workers are classified into about 500 detailed occupations, far more detail than allowed by almost any other data source. A commonly used measure of the segregation of occupations by gender is the index of dissimilarity, which measures what percentage of the male or female labor force would have to change categories in order to have the same distribution of women or men across occupations. An index of 100 means that women and men are completely segregated from each other in different occupations, whereas a measure of 0 means that men and women are equally distributed across all occupational categories.

As shown in Table 3.7, in 1970, the index of dissimilarity stood at 68 percent—two thirds of the women (or men) in the labor force would have had to change jobs to achieve equal representation in all occupational categories. The degree of concentration by gender remained high in 1990 when over one half of the labor force would have had to be redistributed to achieve equal representation of men and women in all occupational categories. However, the decline of almost 15 points in the index of dissimilarity over the 1970–1990 period was quite remarkable, especially in light of changes prior to 1970.

In the 1950s, the index of dissimilarity actually increased slightly and then

TABLE 3.7    Index of occupational dissimilarity of women and men: 1970–1990.

|  | Index Number | Percentage |
|---|---|---|
| 1970 | 67.7 |  |
| Change in 1970s due to |  | 100% |
| Desegregation | −6.7 | 80 |
| Structural shift | −1.7 | 20 |
| 1980 | 59.3 |  |
| Change in 1980s due to |  | 100 |
| Desegregation | −4.3 | 69 |
| Structural shift | −2.0 | 31 |
| 1990 | 53.0 |  |
| Total Change 1970–1990 | −14.7 | 100 |
| Desegregation | −11.0 | 75 |
| Structural shift | −3.7 | 25 |

SOURCE: Decennial census for 1970–1990, published tabulations.

NOTE: Decomposition calculations by Prithwis Das Gupta.

declined by 2 or 3 percentage points during the 1960s (Gross 1968; Blau and Hendrichs 1979). As the early baby boom cohort entered the labor force during the 1970s, the decline in occupational concentration accelerated. Although the decline was not as great in the 1980s when the later baby boom cohort was moving into the labor force, the change was still twice that of the 1960s.

The index of dissimilarity, or occupational segregation, can decline in either of two ways. One source of change is that gender-segregated occupations—for example, machinists, who are primarily men, or clerk-typists, who are primarily women—can grow more slowly than integrated occupations. This is called "structural" shift and occurred throughout both decades. As can be seen in Table 3.7, this component accounted for 20 percent of the decline in the 1970s and 31 percent in the 1980s.[13] This implies that employment in gender-segregated occupations grew more slowly than in more integrated occupations. Relatively slower growth in gender-segregated occupations accounted for 25 percent of the increased integration of men and women in the workplace over the 20-year period; the other source of change—less segregation within specific occupations—accounted for the other 75 percent. Although baby boom women continued to concentrate in different occupations than baby boom men, there was more similarity than there had been for the generations that preceded them.

Even the detailed occupational categories used in the decennial census may not fully capture dissimilarity in the work that men and women do. Women are more likely to be in small firms, industries with labor-intensive production, and relatively low levels of unionization and profit compared with men (England

1992). The 500 detailed occupational categories are aggregations of jobs, within which women often specialize in different fields than men. For example, women doctors tend to concentrate in specialties such as pediatrics, which do not pay as well as surgery or cardiology, fields more often dominated by men. More detailed data on job titles and characteristics of firms would no doubt show more occupational segregation than suggested above (Bielby and Baron 1984). Although the *level* of "true" segregation may be underestimated with census data, the trend seems clear and the change is dramatic relative to previous decades. Hence, the conclusion that there was less segregation in 1990 than in 1970 would likely hold even if more disaggregated data on actual jobs were available.

Recent research with the 1990 census detailed occupational data suggests that the tie between the gender wage gap and occupational segregation may not be strong—the dissimilarity in detailed occupations "explains" only 14 percent of the average earnings difference between men and women (Cotter et al. 1994). As illustrated in the chapter by Wetzel in this volume, women may narrow the gender wage gap but remain occupationally segregated. If relatively high-paying occupations dominated by women, such as nursing, are growing and high-paying jobs dominated by men, such as unionized, semiskilled jobs in manufacturing, are disappearing—as seems to have been the case in the 1980s—the gender wage gap can narrow with relatively little decline in occupational segregation.

On average, however, female-dominated occupations pay much less well than male-dominated occupations. Hence, it would seem that the decline in occupational segregation experienced primarily by recent cohorts of women is necessary to ensure continued, sustained narrowing in the gender wage gap. One of the troublesome aspects of the decline in occupational segregation in the 1970s is that there was a tendency for occupations that desegregated rapidly to resegregate—from mostly male to mostly female.

Roos and Reskin (1992) looked at case studies of occupations that witnessed great increases in the percentage female in the 1970s and suggest that these occupations were often ones in which wages were declining even before women entered. As an occupation became less attractive, men exited and women filled the void. Women who entered occupations that were rapidly desegregating—for example, pharmacists, editors, public relations specialists, insurance and real estate salespersons—earned more than the average woman worker in female-dominated occupations. But their wage increases relative to men were due more to declining earnings for men than to large wage gains for women. For example, Roos and Reskin calculate that four fifths of the increase in the female-to-male earnings ratio among editors in the 1970s was attributable to men's loss in real earnings.

During the 1980s, some of the occupations that were predominantly male in 1970 "tipped" to being predominantly female by 1990. For example, insurance adjusters shifted from 30 to 72 percent female and typesetters from 17 to 70 percent female. In many of the most rapidly desegregating occupations, either women were "ghettoized" in the lower-paying specialties, or firms, or industrial changes were occurring to deskill or make employment less attractive and less financially rewarding than it had been in the past (Roos and Reskin 1992).

To provide some perspective on the level of earnings of women and men and changes during the 1980s, Table 3.8 displays the average hourly earnings for women and men within major occupational groupings. The table is restricted to workers in the prime working ages of 25–64. During the 1980s, across the major occupational groupings, the percentage increase in women's earnings tended to outstrip the increase in men's earnings (or declines in average earnings were not so severe for women as for men. (see Table 3.8). In most instances, women's hourly earnings were closer to men's in 1990 than in 1980. Particularly among managers, women increased their average earnings during the decade by 16 percent, although they earned only 62 percent of men's earnings in these occupations by 1990.

Women achieved the greatest parity with men by 1990 in service and transportation occupations. In these groups, women's average hourly earnings were over 80 percent of men's earnings. However, convergence in earnings in these groups occurred primarily because men experienced real declines in average earnings between 1980 and 1990.

## THE CONVERGENCE IN WOMEN'S AND MEN'S EARNINGS

How much do women earn relative to men? The answer depends on who is included in the comparison (all workers, full-time workers, wage and salary workers) and the measure (annual, weekly, or hourly wages) used to afford the comparison. In 1992, for example, according to Current Population Survey data, the hourly earnings of female wage and salary workers were 79 percent of those of male workers, on average. On the other hand, among all men and women who worked in 1992, the ratio of women's to men's annual earnings was only 61 percent. The most commonly used indicator of the gender wage gap, average earnings of full-time, year-round workers, stood at 71 percent in 1992.

Although the level of equality in earnings of women and men varies widely depending on controls for weeks and hours per week worked, the story told by each time series graphed in Figure 3.2 is the same. Something rather dramatic happened in the 1980s, perhaps beginning in the late 1970s. After at least two decades in which the ratio of women's to men's earnings fluctuated but remained at about the same level, there was a sizable increase in the ratio during the 1980s. Between 1979 and 1992, women's hourly wages as a percentage of

TABLE 3.8 Hourly earnings of workers aged 25–64, by sex and major occupational group: 1980 and 1990 (1989 dollars).

| | Women | | | Men | | | Ratio Women/Men (per 100) | |
|---|---|---|---|---|---|---|---|---|
| | 1980 | 1990 | Percentage Change | 1980 | 1990 | Percentage Change | 1980 | 1990 |
| Managers, executives | $12.27 | $14.27 | +16% | $22.45 | $23.03 | +3% | 55 | 62 |
| Professionals | 14.61 | 15.51 | +6 | 20.72 | 22.85 | +10 | 71 | 68 |
| Technicians | 10.48 | 11.66 | +11 | 17.11 | 17.42 | +2 | 61 | 67 |
| Sales | 9.36 | 10.83 | +16 | 17.59 | 19.32 | +10 | 53 | 56 |
| Administrative, clerical | 10.23 | 10.11 | −1 | 14.64 | 13.51 | −8 | 70 | 75 |
| Protective service | 10.13 | 12.21 | +21 | 14.68 | 14.03 | −4 | 69 | 87 |
| Other service | 8.03 | 7.96 | −1 | 12.16 | 9.70 | −20 | 66 | 82 |
| Farming, forestry, fishing | 7.09 | 7.20 | +2 | 13.07 | 10.95 | −16 | 54 | 66 |
| Precision production, craft | 9.56 | 9.25 | −3 | 15.25 | 14.86 | −3 | 63 | 62 |
| Machine operators | 8.43 | 8.13 | −4 | 13.89 | 12.49 | −10 | 61 | 65 |
| Transportation workers | 10.11 | 10.31 | +2 | 14.78 | 12.57 | −15 | 68 | 82 |
| Handlers, laborers | 9.69 | 8.06 | −17 | 12.86 | 12.65 | −2 | 75 | 64 |
| Total employed workers | 10.44 | 11.20 | +7 | 16.71 | 16.65 | 0 | 62 | 67 |

SOURCE: Decennial census Public Use Microdata Samples (1 in 1,000) for 1980 and 1990.

FIGURE 3.2    Gender gap in earnings: 1960–1990.

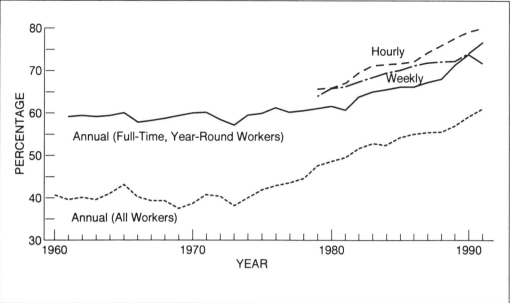

SOURCES: U.S. Bureau of the Census and Bureau of Labor Statistics, published and unpublished tabulations.

NOTE: Median hourly earnings and median weekly earnings of wage and salary workers and median annual earnings of all workers and full-time, year-round workers. Women's earnings as a percentage of men's earnings.

men's increased from 64 to 79 percent, weekly earnings from 63 to 75 percent, annual earnings of full-time, year-round workers from 60 to 71 percent, and annual earnings of all workers from 46 to 61 percent.

Table 3.9 arrays mean earnings of full-time, year-round workers, calculated using the 1960–1990 decennial censuses, for the same birth cohorts of women and men shown earlier. Each succeeding cohort of women tended to earn more at a given age than preceding cohorts (reading the columns for women from bottom to top). For men, on the other hand, the baby boom cohorts earned somewhat less at young ages (25–34) than the World War II cohort that came before them. While it is "good news" for women that their earnings are increasing in real terms, and many would applaud greater equality of outcomes between the sexes, it is not necessarily "good news" for young women that the men they have married or will marry may do less well in the labor market than previous cohorts.

The bottom panel of Table 3.9 shows the ratio of women's to men's earnings. At ages 25–34, the World War II cohort of women who were working full-time, year-round at these ages had average earnings that were about 59 percent those of men, the same as the generation before them. This ratio increased to 65 percent for early baby boom women and to 74 percent for late baby boom

TABLE 3.9   Annual earnings of full-time, year-round workers, by age, sex, and birth cohort (1989 dollars).

| Birth Cohort | Ages | | | |
|---|---|---|---|---|
| | 25–34 | 35–44 | 45–54 | 55–64 |
| Women | | | | |
| 1956–1965 Late baby boom | $21,337 | | | |
| 1946–1955 Early baby boom | 19,004 | $23,876 | | |
| 1936–1945 World War II | 18,024 | 19,641 | $22,965 | |
| 1926–1935 Parents of baby boom | 13,734 | 17,582 | 19,369 | $20,898 |
| 1916–1925 Parents of baby boom | | 13,919 | 18,169 | 19,258 |
| 1906–1915 Grandparents of baby boom | | | 13,784 | 17,892 |
| | | | | |
| Men | | | | |
| 1956–1965 Late baby boom | $28,739 | | | |
| 1946–1955 Early baby boom | 29,407 | $38,210 | | |
| 1936–1945 World War II | 30,506 | 37,943 | $42,904 | |
| 1926–1935 Parents of baby boom | 23,163 | 37,228 | 38,919 | $40,643 |
| 1916–1925 Parents of baby boom | | 26,936 | 36,104 | 35,960 |
| 1906–1915 Grandparents of baby boom | | | 25,871 | 32,487 |
| | | | | |
| Ratio Women/Men (per 100) | | | | |
| 1956–1965 Late baby boom | 74 | | | |
| 1946–1955 Early baby boom | 65 | 62 | | |
| 1936–1945 World War II | 59 | 52 | 54 | |
| 1926–1935 Parents of baby boom | 59 | 47 | 50 | 51 |
| 1916–1925 Parents of baby boom | | 52 | 50 | 54 |
| 1906–1915 Grandparents of baby boom | | | 53 | 55 |

SOURCE: Decennial census Public Use Microdata Samples (1 in 1,000) for 1960–1990.

women, more of whom worked full-time, year-round because fewer of them were married and rearing children at these ages.

For men who settled into mid-career (ages 35–44) during the 1960s when the economy was booming (the fathers of the baby boom born between 1926 and 1935), real earnings increased by a phenomenal 61 percent, on average, as they aged from 25–34 to 35–44. Among the World War II cohort of men who aged into their late 30s and early 40s during the 1970s, a decade of sluggish economic growth, the increase in earnings between age 30 and age 40 still averaged 24 percent in real terms. And for both cohorts of men, the percentage increases realized by full-time, year-round workers greatly outstripped those for women.

Early baby boom men also experienced a sizable increase in average earnings as they made the same transition in the 1980s. Hence, their earnings at ages 35–44 were comparable to, or even slightly higher than, the World War II cohort before them. Late baby boom men had yet not reached their late 30s by 1990, so it is unknown whether their age-earnings profile will be as steep as for men in the early baby boom cohort.

What is different about early baby boom men and women is that as they made the transition from age 30 to age 40, the increase in earnings—the steepness of the age-earnings profile—was more similar for women and men than it had been for previous cohorts. The increase in mean earnings among full-time, year-round workers was greater for men (30 percent), but only a little greater than for women (25 percent). In earlier cohorts, earnings rose much more for men than for women as they aged from their 20s to their 40s. By ages 35–44, the early baby boom cohort of women had earnings that were still only 62 percent of those of men, on average, but this ratio was much higher than for previous cohorts.

As discussed earlier, the continuity of women's labor force attachment over the life course increased greatly among the baby boom cohorts. The movement into mid-career of a cohort of women with educational credentials and work experience much more similar to men's than those of previous cohorts was a potent force affecting the male-to-female earnings ratio during the 1980s. Already in the early 1980s, there were signs that the wage gap was beginning to narrow among young, college-educated workers (Bianchi and Spain 1986: Table 6.2). The question was whether there would be consistent, sustained improvement for these women. Part of what bolstered the relative earnings of women—and resulted in a decade of much greater narrowing in the gender wage gap than previously—was that women were poised by 1980 to advance in the labor force, and the decade turned out to be a phenomenal one in terms of earnings improvement for the well-educated. But it was a very poor decade in terms of earnings for young, unskilled workers, and this fact, somewhat perversely, also contributed to greater gender equality in earnings.

## EARNINGS BY EDUCATION

During the 1980s, as documented in the chapter by Frank Levy, the earnings of less-skilled, less-educated workers declined relative to more-skilled, more highly educated workers.[14] Average wages of younger workers decreased relative to wages for older workers among those with a high school education or less. And, within educational and age groups, earnings inequality increased (Katz and Murphy 1992). During the 1950s and 1960s, the proportion of less-educated men with low earnings—earnings lower than the poverty level for a family of four—declined dramatically, but then rose sharply in the 1970s and 1980s. The trend was similar but not nearly so pronounced for better-educated young men (Danziger and Stern 1990).

Why did the earnings of those with a high school education or less deteriorate relative to those with a college education? The causes, reviewed more thoroughly in the chapters by Wetzel and Levy in this volume, include the large shifts out of low-technology industries and basic manufacturing and into professional and business services, a shift that favored college graduates. The increased demand for highly educated workers was brought about, in part, by the revolution in computer and information technologies and also encouraged by the expanding health care industry (Davis and Haltiwanger 1991; Krueger 1991; Mincer 1991).

Owing to large deficits and the globalization of trade, demand for low-skilled labor declined as production jobs moved overseas (Borjas, Freeman, and Katz 1992; Murphy and Welch 1992). Katz and Murphy (1992) have shown that decreased demand for domestically produced goods due to international competition was quite modest until the dollar strengthened and substantial trade deficits developed in the 1980s. Adverse effects were concentrated among high school dropouts.

Others have investigated the decline in unions, erosion in the real value of the minimum wage, and supply factors such as the slower growth in the number of college graduates in the 1980s than in the 1970s (Blackburn et al. 1991; Katz and Murphy 1992). A large part of the shift in earnings inequality is due to the increase in wage inequality among workers of the same age and educational attainment, an increase that is not well understood (Levy and Murnane 1992).

Given the increase in earnings inequality, the conditions that increased gender equality in the 1980s were distinctly different for those at the bottom than for those at the top of the educational distribution. Table 3.10 arrays mean earnings of women and men aged 25–34, in 1980 and 1990, separately for those with a high school education or less and those with a college education or more.[15]

To summarize 1980 to 1990 changes in earnings by educational attainment, women did well relative to men in the 1980s across the educational spectrum. However, among workers with a high school education or less, women's gains resulted primarily from the deterioration in the real earnings of men rather than from any increase in the wages of women. The average earnings of full-time, year-round workers declined for both sexes, but the percentage change was much greater for men (a 13 percent drop for men and a 2 percent drop for women). Among all workers (part-time and full-time workers), women with a high school education or less did not experience a decline in earnings, primarily because they worked more in 1990 than in 1980.

Among young, college-educated workers, on the other hand, the average earnings of men and women increased, but the percentage increases for women were over three times as large as those for men. Women continued to earn much less than men, but gained on men in relative terms because the rise in their average earnings was so much greater. The ratio of women's to men's

TABLE 3.10    Annual earnings of workers aged 25–34 with a high school or college education: 1980 and 1990 (1989 dollars).

|  | 1980 | 1990 | Percentage Change |
|---|---|---|---|
| High School Graduate (or less) | | | |
| All Workers | | | |
| Women | $10,810 | $11,443 | +6 |
| Men | 22,537 | 20,443 | −9 |
| Ratio women/men (per 100) | 48 | 56 | |
| | | | |
| Full-Time, Year-Round Workers | | | |
| Women | $16,591 | $16,318 | −2 |
| Men | 26,018 | 22,525 | −13 |
| Ratio women/men (per 100) | 64 | 72 | |
| | | | |
| College Graduate (or more) | | | |
| All Workers | | | |
| Women | $17,889 | $22,905 | +28 |
| Men | 31,111 | 33,513 | +8 |
| Ratio women/men (per 100) | 58 | 68 | |
| | | | |
| Full-Time, Year-Round Workers | | | |
| Women | $23,566 | $27,559 | +17 |
| Men | 34,728 | 36,432 | +5 |
| Ratio women/men (per 100) | 68 | 76 | |
| | | | |
| Birth Cohort Aged 25–34 | Early baby boom | Late baby boom | |

SOURCE: U.S. Bureau of the Census, Current Population Survey, published tabulations.

earnings increased for workers with a high school or college education, but the ratio was higher for workers with a college education (68 percent in 1990) than for those with a high school education or less (56 percent in 1990). Among full-time, year-round workers, the differences by educational attainment were not so striking—women with a college education earned 76 percent as much as men, whereas women with a high school education earned 72 percent as much as men.

As can be seen by the cohort note at the bottom of Table 3.10, earnings change in the 1980s among young workers is actually a comparison of gender equality between two cohorts, the early and late baby boom men and women. A somewhat different view is provided by asking what happened to the relative position of comparably educated women and men as the early baby boom cohort aged over the decade of the 1980s.

Table 3.11 shows average earnings for men and women by educational level for those aged 25–34 in 1980 and 35–44 in 1990. That is, the average earnings

TABLE 3.11    Annual earnings of the early baby boom cohort with a high school or college education: 1980 and 1990 (1989 dollars).

|  | Ages 25–34 in 1980 | Ages 35–44 in 1990 | Percentage Change |
|---|---|---|---|
| High School Graduate (or less) | | | |
| All Workers | | | |
| Women | $10,810 | $13,597 | +26 |
| Men | 22,537 | 24,324 | +8 |
| Ratio women/men (per 100) | 48 | 56 | |
| | | | |
| Full-Time, Year-Round Workers | | | |
| Women | $16,591 | $18,269 | +10 |
| Men | 26,018 | 27,563 | +6 |
| Ratio women/men (per 100) | 64 | 66 | |
| | | | |
| College Graduate (or more) | | | |
| All Workers | | | |
| Women | $17,889 | $25,745 | +44 |
| Men | 31,111 | 48,276 | +55 |
| Ratio women/men (per 100) | 58 | 53 | |
| | | | |
| Full-Time, Year-Round Workers | | | |
| Women | $23,566 | $32,185 | +37 |
| Men | 34,728 | 50,945 | +47 |
| Ratio women/men (per 100) | 68 | 63 | |

SOURCE: U.S. Bureau of the Census, Current Population Survey, published tabulations.

of early baby boom men and women with a high school or college education are tracked as they aged from roughly age 30 to age 40 over the decade of the 1980s.

Among workers of the early baby boom cohort with a high school education, men's earnings did not decline between age 30 and age 40, although the percentage increases were small relative to college-educated men of the same cohort. The earnings of women with a high school education rose more than those for men, in part because they increased their likelihood of full-time employment as they aged. This is indicated by the fact that the rise in earnings among workers with a high school education was much more comparable for full-time, year-round workers than for all workers: Women's earnings as a percentage of men's rose as they moved from age 30 to age 40 from 48 to 56 percent among all workers, but only from 64 to 66 percent among full-time, year-round workers.

What about the college-educated of this cohort for whom the cross-sectional picture of Table 3.10 suggested increases for both sexes during the 1980s but improvements for women that far outstripped those for men? Both men and women workers realized sizable percentage increases in earnings as they aged from 30 to 40, but the percentage increases for college-educated men of the early baby boom cohort were greater than those for women.

College-educated men already earned significantly more than college-educated women when this cohort was about age 30. Young women's earnings averaged around $18,000 (in 1989 dollars) compared with young men's earnings of $31,000 in 1980. And as this cohort aged, the relative position of women declined. For example, the ratio of women's to men's earnings among all workers with a college degree was 58 percent in 1980, but only 53 percent in 1990. For full-time, year-round workers, the ratio was 68 percent at age 30 and 63 percent at age 40.

The cross-sectional picture of dramatic improvement in the earnings of women relative to men (shown in Table 3.10) must be qualified in at least two ways. First, in the cross-section, the improvement for women resulted from deterioration for men at the low end of the educational distribution. Second, at the high end of the educational distribution, the relative improvement for women when viewed from a cohort perspective is much less indicative of a rapid move toward gender equality in earnings in the 1980s. What happened during the 1980s was that a cohort of women more equal to men in work experience and educational attainment replaced a cohort of women less equal to men in experience and education. This cohort replacement process had progressed to the point that it was occurring not only at the job entry level but also among workers with as much as 10 to 20 years of labor force experience, a point when earnings are relatively high.

Why did the early baby boom cohort of well-educated women—who gained immensely on men in terms of educational credentials and occupational attainment and who participated in the labor force in far greater numbers and with more continuity than prior generations—lose ground relative to men over the decade of the 1980s? Why were the better-educated among these women not able to sustain earnings improvements vis-à-vis men as they aged from 30 to 40?

As they aged, many of these women married and, more important, had the children they had postponed in order to get their advanced education. Well-educated women tended to marry well-educated men, who on average earned more than they did. Hence, if and when the question arose as to who should cut back on labor force participation to accommodate the needs of children, the women of this generation curtailed their labor force participation more so than did their husbands. During the 1980s, women—even well-educated women—continued to have difficulty sustaining their earnings position relative to men across the life cycle.

Table 3.12 provides perspective on the labor force and earnings differences that continued to distinguish men and women of the early baby boom cohort in 1990. Married men of the early baby boom cohort continued to have higher employment rates, stronger year-round attachment to the labor force, more

TABLE 3.12    Employment and earnings of married and unmarried women
and men aged 35–44 in 1980 and 1990.

|  | 1980 | 1990 | Difference 1990–1980 |
|---|---|---|---|
| **Percentage Who Worked Last Year** | | | |
| Married women | 65% | 77% | +12 |
| Unmarried women | 80 | 84 | +4 |
| Unmarried men | 89 | 87 | −2 |
| Married men | 97 | 96 | −1 |
| | | | |
| **Percentage Who Worked Full-Time, Year-Round** | | | |
| Married women | 27% | 38% | +11 |
| Unmarried women | 47 | 54 | +7 |
| Unmarried men | 61 | 59 | −2 |
| Married men | 78 | 77 | −1 |
| | | | |
| **Annual Hours Worked (including none)** | | | |
| Married women | 951 | 1,250 | +299 |
| Unmarried women | 1,394 | 1,567 | +173 |
| Unmarried men | 1,759 | 1,729 | −30 |
| Married men | 2,124 | 2,138 | +14 |
| | | | |
| **Hourly Earnings (workers)** | | | |
| Married women | $9.84 | $11.60 | +$1.76 |
| Unmarried women | 10.78 | 11.99 | +1.21 |
| Unmarried men | 14.37 | 15.29 | +0.92 |
| Married men | 17.77 | 17.42 | −0.35 |
| | | | |
| Birth cohort aged 25–34 | World War II | Early baby boom | |

SOURCE: Decennial census Public Use Microdata Samples (1 in 1,000) for 1980 and 1990.

hours of work, and higher earnings than other workers. The gap separating the most attached workers (married men) from the least attached workers (married women) shrank compared with the gap that existed for the World War II cohort in 1980. However, the labor force activity and earnings of married women and married men of the early baby boom generation continued to be quite divergent.

For example, the proportion of married men employed in the preceding year was 96 percent compared with 77 percent of married women, a 19 percentage point differential. The full-time, year-round employment rate of married women of the early baby boom cohort in 1990 was 39 percentage points lower than that of married men of the same cohort (38 versus 77 percent). Married women averaged almost 900 fewer hours of market work than married men and earned, on average, $11.60 for those hours of work compared with $17.42 among married men.

It is not easy to determine whether the failure of early baby boom women's labor force involvement and earnings to keep pace with men's of the same cohort as they aged was the result of choices they made about family or of discrimination in the workplace, however subtle. It is also difficult to determine why these women started their labor force career with earnings that were at most 70 percent of earnings of comparably educated men, although choice of college major and occupational selection were no doubt factors.

The census data reveal that the upgrading of women's relative position in the labor market over time has been, and continues to be, a gradual process. Events, such as the entry of large numbers of inexperienced women workers in the 1950s and 1960s or the industrial restructuring of the 1970s and 1980s, can retard or enhance the pace toward gender equality in a given decade. But permanent, enduring change is slow and can occur only when cohorts with more equal earnings replace cohorts with less equal earnings.

The data for the early baby boom cohort also suggest that differences between men and women in their allocation of time to family versus market work continue. Any assessment of the pace of further movement toward gender equality in earnings must consider differences in the family and domestic roles that men and women perform in U.S. society.

## PER CAPITA INCOME AND POVERTY OF MEN AND WOMEN

The majority of men and women marry and spend a significant portion of their adult life living with their spouse. Although the percentage of women and men who are currently married has declined, over two thirds of women and men between the ages of 35 and 65 were married in 1990. During the years in which they are married, the financial well-being of the couple and their children are inextricably tied. Any given individual's quality of life is dependent not only on how well he or she does in the labor market, but also on the earnings of those with whom income and assets are pooled. Old-age security, provided by Social Security and pension income, also is determined not only by an individual's own labor force participation but by his or her marital history.

Table 3.13 shows average household, family, and per capita income of women and men, as calculated from the 1960–1990 decennial censuses. Income refers to pretax, posttransfer money income received in the year prior to the census year shown, and all amounts have been adjusted to 1989 dollars. Household income is the sum of money income across all persons who live in the same household. The measure displayed in Table 3.13 assigns the total household income to each individual in the household and averages this amount across all males and females aged 16 and over.

The assignment of household income to all individuals who reside together

TABLE 3.13 Household, family, and per capita income of women and men: 1960–1990 (1989 dollars).

| | 1960 | 1970 | 1980 | 1990 | Percentage Change | | |
| --- | --- | --- | --- | --- | --- | --- | --- |
| | | | | | 1960–1970 | 1970–1980 | 1980–1990 |
| Household Income | | | | | | | |
| Women | $26,913 | $35,601 | $36,008 | $40,680 | +32.3% | +1.1% | +13.0% |
| Men | 28,635 | 38,696 | 39,959 | 45,128 | +35.1 | +3.3 | +12.9 |
| Ratio women/men (per 100) | 94.0 | 92.0 | 90.1 | 90.1 | | | |
| Family Income | | | | | | | |
| Women | $25,903 | $34,642 | $32,734 | $39,212 | +33.7 | −5.5 | +19.8 |
| Men | 27,535 | 37,585 | 35,968 | 43,178 | +36.5 | −4.3 | +20.0 |
| Ratio women/men (per 100) | 94.1 | 92.2 | 91.0 | 90.8 | | | |
| Per Capita Income | | | | | | | |
| Women | $8,458 | $11,484 | $12,633 | $14,916 | +35.8 | +10.0 | +18.1 |
| Men | 8,850 | 12,331 | 13,886 | 16,478 | +39.3 | +12.6 | +18.7 |
| Ratio women/men (per 100) | 95.6 | 93.1 | 91.0 | 90.5 | | | |

SOURCE: Decennial census Public Use Microdata Samples (1 in 1,000) for 1960–1990.

NOTE: Mean income assigned to all persons aged 16 and over, living in households.

assumes that these individuals pool income. This assumption may be particularly suspect for persons sharing a residence who are not related and, hence, a family income measure is also shown. If an individual is related to the householder by blood, marriage, or adoption—the census definition of family ties—he or she is assigned the sum of income of all family members; otherwise, the person's individual income is assigned. As can be seen, trends in household and family income are similar.

Finally, because household and family income measures make no adjustment for the number of individuals who must share a given pool of income, a per capita measure is also shown. Household income is divided by the number of people in the household, and this amount is assigned to each individual.[16]

Whereas the gender gap in earnings of full-time, year-round working women was about 70 percent in 1990, household, family, and per capita income levels of women averaged about 90 percent those of men.[17] The level of per capita, family, or household income of women relative to men did not change greatly over the 1960–1990 period, although women's income declined somewhat between 1960 and 1980 as a greater percentage lived apart from a spouse and had sole financial responsibility for dependent children.

Although women earned more relative to men in 1990 than in 1980 (Figure 3.2), the changes in per capita, family, or household income were comparable for women and men. Per capita improvements for both men and women were greater in the 1980s than in the 1970s, but about one half the size of the increase in the 1960s.

Ratios of per capita income of cohorts of adult women relative to men are shown in Table 3.14. Per capita income of women relative to men is lower at age 55 and over than at earlier ages. Table 3.14 also suggests some deterioration in the relative well-being of women to men over time, although this deterioration seems to have halted and may even be reversing for the baby boom cohorts.

Much concern in recent decades has focused not so much on the relative

TABLE 3.14   Per capita income ratio of women to men (per 100), by age and birth cohort.

| Birth Cohort | Ages | | | | | |
|---|---|---|---|---|---|---|
| | 25–34 | 35–44 | 45–54 | 55–64 | 65–74 | 75+ |
| 1956–1965 Late baby boom | 90 | | | | | |
| 1946–1955 Early baby boom | 87 | 92 | | | | |
| 1936–1945 World War II | 85 | 89 | 93 | | | |
| 1926–1935 Parents of baby boom | 89 | 94 | 94 | 87 | | |
| 1916–1925 Parents of baby boom | | 99 | 99 | 89 | 87 | |
| 1906–1915 Grandparents of baby boom | | | 102 | 91 | 93 | 89 |

SOURCE: Decennial census Public Use Microdata Samples (1 in 1,000) for 1960–1990.

well-being of women and men in the middle or upper end of the distribution—the focus of most of the data presented so far in this chapter—but rather on the changing gender composition of the poverty population. The term *feminization of poverty* gained popularity in the late 1970s and early 1980s as analysts and commentators noted the shift toward more mother-child families among the poor.

Many of the poor are children, as discussed in greater detail in the chapter by Hogan and Lichter in Volume 2, and the likelihood of being poor is much higher for children in mother-child families. But what about adult women and men? How different is the likelihood of living in a family with income below the official poverty level for them?

Figure 3.3 shows that adult women's poverty rates were higher than men's at every age in 1992, the most recent year for which data are available. Poverty rates were closest for individuals aged 35–54, the ages with the most similarity in the proportion of men and women who are married and living together. But even at these ages, women's poverty rates were 25 to 35 percent higher than men's. Among those aged 65 and over, women's rates were 75 percent higher than men's.

Gender disparities in the likelihood of being either poor or "near poor"—with incomes above poverty but less than 50 percent above poverty—are also shown in Figure 3.3. The proportion of women aged 35–54 who had incomes less than 1.5 times poverty was 20 to 23 percent higher than it was for men of the same age. Among the elderly, 33 percent of women and 21 percent of men were poor or near poor. That is, the likelihood of women falling into this low-income category was 60 percent greater than that of men.

What do gender disparities in poverty among the working age population reflect? They result primarily from two factors: Women continue to work less than men, and they earn considerably less than men when they do work for pay. Gender differences in labor force attachment and earnings leave women more vulnerable, particularly those who are not in a household with a male wage earner. Secondly, women who are not living with a husband are much more likely than men who are not living with a wife to be caring for and supporting dependent children. These women must share their own often meager income with children, which drives the family's living standards below the poverty level.

Although father-child families have been increasing in number, only 1.4 million father-child families compared with 6 million mother-child families were enumerated in the 1990 census. In the 1980s the formation of mother-child families slowed. However, the increase that occurred was much more concentrated among never-married mothers than it had been in earlier decades (Bianchi 1994). A large minority of divorced mothers (41 percent in 1989) do not receive child support from the absent father, but the proportion of never-married moth-

FIGURE 3.3    Poverty rates, by gender and age: 1992.

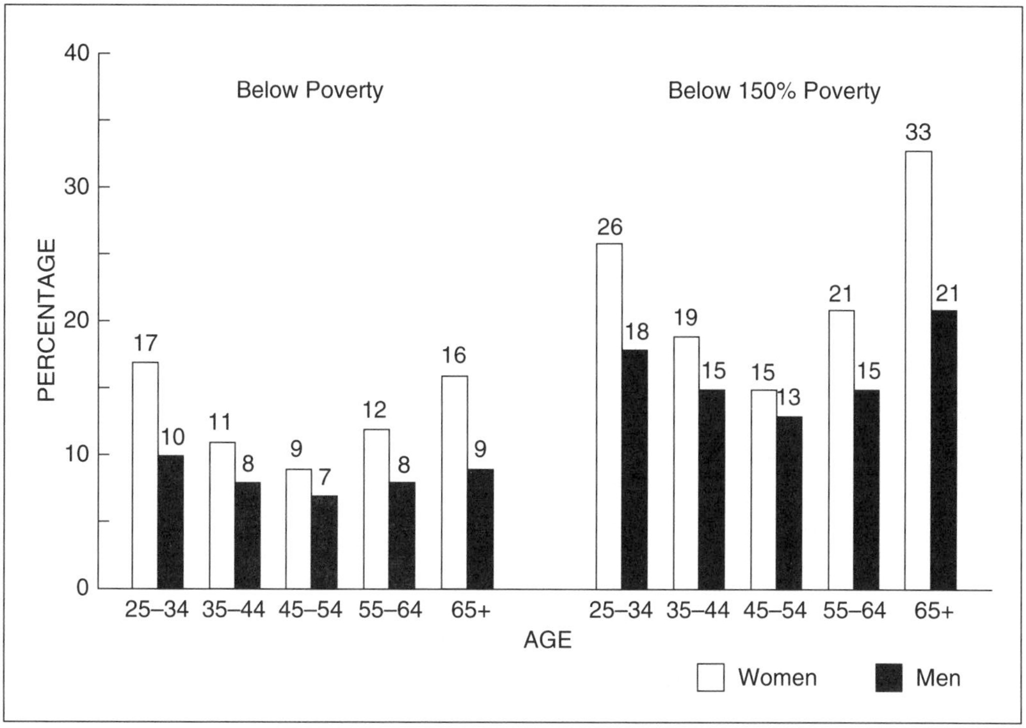

SOURCE: U.S. Bureau of the Census, Current Population Survey, published tabulations.

ers who receive support from an absent father is much lower. In 1989, 82 percent of never-married mothers with children under age 21 received no support from the children's father.[18]

During the 1980s, as shown in Figure 3.4, the employment rates of married women with children essentially caught up with the rates of unmarried women rearing children alone. As more two-parent families contained two breadwinners, one-parent families with one earner—or frequently no earners, given the growth in rates of young, less-educated, never-married mothers—became more disadvantaged. Families became increasingly bifurcated along marital and educational lines.

If women's labor force participation and earnings were more nearly equal to men's in the United States, the gender differential in poverty would be reduced. Also, if absent fathers more often fulfilled their child support obligations, the gender gap would narrow. On the other hand, there would also be a smaller gender poverty gap, at least at younger ages, if adult men and women were much more likely to marry and stay married throughout adulthood (Casper, McLanahan, and Garfinkel 1994).

Men and women may enter more stable marriages in the future, but a large

FIGURE 3.4   Employment rates of married and unmarried mothers
with dependent children: 1964–1989.

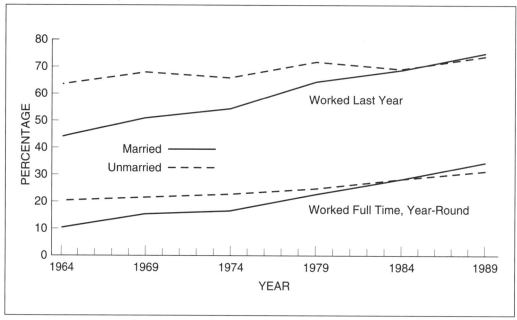

SOURCE: U.S. Bureau of Labor Statistics, Current Population Survey, published tabulations.

shift in this direction seems unlikely. The divorce rate peaked in 1981, declined
by 9 percent in the 1980s, and then leveled out in the early 1990s (National
Center for Health Statistics 1993b). However, it remains high by historical standards. As documented earlier, the trend toward postponing marriage shows no
signs of reversal. Keeping men and women married throughout adulthood would
reduce gender differences in poverty, but seems unlikely to be a workable approach to achieving gender equality in overall economic status in the United
States.

Gender differences in poverty might be reduced in the future through continued movement toward gender equality in the labor force behaviors of women
and men. Such movement would be aided by more father involvement and responsibility for the care and support of children. The paradox—and why we are
unlikely to see any family policy address gender equality in the market—is that
women's move toward equality is intertwined with their move away from marriage and their move toward more independence from men. In some sense,
women's liberation has "caused" more mother-child families. Women shifted
toward more equal work roles with men, but men did not shift so readily to
equalize domestic roles. The movement toward equality was lopsided—with
women adding the responsibility of providing economically for their family

while continuing to provide most of the caregiving for children and doing the majority of household work—and this unbalanced the marital division of labor.

## THE ECONOMIC ROLES OF WIVES AND HUSBANDS

According to England, "a long line of research on marital power has shown that women's employment and the relative earnings of husbands and wives affects the balance of power in marriages. When women's earnings are lower, even when they are making valuable contribution in the form of home management and child rearing, their bargaining power is substantially lower than is their husband's."[19] In 1992, working wives contributed about 30 percent of their family's income—40 percent in those families in which the wife worked full-time, year-round (Hayghe and Bianchi 1994). By the early 1990s, wives' economic contribution to the family represented much more than "pin money" and presumably, if the marital power research is correct, their bargaining power within marriage was rising as was their financial ability to leave an unsatisfactory marriage or not enter into one in the first place.

Iams shows that the trends characterizing women in general, reviewed in previous sections and captured with snapshots from various decennial censuses, typify married women and men of each cohort. Whereas 25 percent of wives born in the early 1930s (mothers of the baby boom) spent no years working outside the home between ages 22 and 31, only 5 percent of late baby boom wives did not work. Conversely, whereas only 14 percent of the mothers of the baby boom had earnings from their participation in the labor force in all (or all but one) of the years between age 22 and 31, over 50 percent of late baby boom wives had such earnings (Iams 1993).

The proportion of wives who had no earnings in their 20s fell from 30 percent for the mothers of the baby boom (born in the early 1930s) to 7 percent for the late baby boom cohort (born in the later 1950s). In 20 percent of the late baby boom couples, wives' earnings in their 20s were equal to or greater than their husbands' earnings, and another 26 percent had earnings that were 50 to 99 percent of their husbands' earnings. These percentages were far higher than among their parents' generation among whom 10 percent of wives had earnings at least equal to their husbands' and another 10 percent had earnings 50 to 99 percent of their husbands' when they were in their 20s (Iams 1993).

Census data allow one to compute a wife's proportional contribution to family income and assess how it varies by characteristics of families. The first column of Table 3.15 shows the net effects of age of children, age or birth cohort, education, and family income (minus wife's earnings; i.e., a measure of how well-off the family is relative to other families if the wife contributes no earnings) on the chances that a wife between ages 25–64 in 1990 was a family breadwinner in 1989. For example, the chances that a woman without children under age 18 in the household is a family earner are three times those of a woman who is similar in age, educational attainment, and other family income but has a child under age 6 in the home. The second column shows the effect of these characteristics on whether those wives who had earnings in 1989 contributed a greater than average percentage of income (the average being about 30 percent of family income in the 1990 census data). Full-time, year-round attachment is added as a predictor of above-average percentage contribution to family income.

TABLE 3.15    Likelihood (odds) of a married woman
              contributing earned income to the family: 1990.

| | Odds Ratios | |
| --- | --- | --- |
| | Contributes Earnings | Earns More than 30 Percent of Family Income |
| Children (odds relative to children under age 6) | | |
| No children under age 18 | 3.0 | 1.7 |
| Children 6–17 | 2.4 | 1.2 |
| (Children under age 6) | 1.0 | 1.0 |
| Cohort/Age (odds relative to ages 55–64) | | |
| Ages 25–34 (late baby boom) | 5.8 | 3.0 |
| Ages 35–44 (early baby boom) | 4.5 | 2.2 |
| Ages 45–54 (World War II) | 2.9 | 1.4 |
| (Ages 55–64 (mothers of baby boom)) | 1.0 | 1.0 |
| Education (odds relative to not high school graduate) | | |
| (Not high school graduate) | 1.0 | 1.0 |
| High school graduate | 2.0 | 1.2 |
| Some college | 2.9 | 1.6 |
| College graduate | 3.5 | 2.7 |
| Postgraduate education | 5.7 | 5.8 |
| Other Family Income (odds relative to $40,000 or more) | | |
| Less than $15,000 | 1.8 | 6.6 |
| $15,000–24,999 | 2.1 | 9.9 |
| $25,000–39,000 | 1.8 | 4.9 |
| ($40,000 or more) | 1.0 | 1.0 |
| Full-Time, Year-Round Worker | — | 15.1 |
| (odds relative to part-year/part-time) | — | 1.0 |

SOURCE: Decennial census Public Use Microdata Samples (1 in 1,000) for 1990.

NOTE: Numbers shown are relative odds ratios. Regressions of likelihood of contributing more than 30 percent of family income are restricted to wives with $1 or more of earnings in 1989.

Not only are married women without children under age 18 more often family earners, but mothers with school-age children are more than twice as likely to contribute to family earnings as mothers of children under age 6. Each younger cohort of married women has higher odds of being a family breadwinner relative to older cohorts. For example, the odds that married mothers among the late baby boom (ages 25–34) were earners in 1990 were six times those of their mothers (ages 55–64).

The chances that a married woman was an earner rose steeply with educational attainment; the odds of paid labor force participation for women with a postgraduate degree were 5.7 times greater than the odds for those who dropped out of high school. Also, other things being equal, the odds were 2 to 1 that wives were earners in families with (other) income less than $40,000 compared with wives in families in the highest income quartile (those with income minus the wife's earnings of over $40,000 in 1989). Since we are describing married couples, most of this other family income comes from the earnings of husbands. This suggests that, other things being equal, economic need continues to be an important factor in married women's decision to participate in the paid labor force. A major source of income in the majority of families continues to be the husbands' earnings. Although the importance of husbands' earnings as a factor propelling married women to work outside the home has declined over time (see Goldin 1990: Table 5.2), other things being equal, wives in 1990 were more likely to be employed if their husbands were not highly paid.

On average, wives who contributed to family income earned about 30 percent of the family's income. Most of the same factors that predicted whether a wife was an earner at all predicted whether a wage-earning wife contributed more than the overall average of 30 percent of family income. Those who worked full-time, year-round were 15 times more likely to contribute more than 30 percent of the family income. On average, wives who worked full-time, year-round contributed 40 percent of income, all other things being equal.

## GENDER EQUALITY IN HOUSEWORK AND CHILDCARE

Wives are increasingly employed (see Table 3.12), and they contribute a sizable share of income in many families. Is there evidence of a compensating move toward gender equality in the domestic sphere? What indications of change, if any, exist in terms of fathers' caring for children and men's sharing of housework? Time budget data collected by J. B. Robinson (1988) suggest a sizable decline in the number of hours that married mothers spend in housework, more so between 1965 and 1975 than between 1975 and 1985. During the 1965–1985 period, married mothers' time spent in housework declined by 10 hours weekly (from about 30 hours to 20 hours). An increase in fathers' time of 5 hours per week (from about 5 hours to 10 hours) compensated for about one half of the decline in mothers' time in the home. By 1985, married mothers continued to do about two thirds of the housework, on average, but this represented a decline from three fourths in 1965 (Robinson 1988; Gershuny and Robinson 1988). Time budget data collected in the late 1970s and 1980s in Utah (and a handful of other states) corroborate the decline in hours that mothers spend on housework, but also show that even with the additional hours of housework done by fathers, the decline does not offset mothers' increased market work (Zick and McCullough 1991; Bryant and Zick 1993).

Household tasks continue to be quite differentiated by gender. Husbands participate most in childcare and yard and home maintenance, assuming about 40 percent of the family workload in these areas according to data analyzed by Goldscheider and Waite (1991: Chap. 7). Husbands do relatively little (less than 25 percent) of the more traditionally female tasks of cooking, housecleaning, dishwashing, and laundry and share in just over 25 percent of the grocery shopping and paperwork associated with family finances.

In families in which the wife works outside the home, husbands do a greater share of domestic tasks and childcare: the higher the wife's percentage contribution to a family's income, the more equitable the division of labor within the home. And couples with more egalitarian views on gender roles share tasks more often than those with more traditional views about marriage and "women's work" (Waite and Goldscheider 1992). Presumably, as younger cohorts of men and women, whose labor force participation and earnings are more similar, replace cohorts in which the economic activity of men and women was more dissimilar, the gender division of labor within the home will become more equal.

To date, the movement toward gender equality in the domestic sphere has been quite gradual. The finding that better-educated wives with higher earnings have a more equitable division of labor within the home suggests that gender earnings equality may be a necessary prerequisite for greater involvement of husbands in childcare and housework. Given that the labor force participation and earnings of husbands and wives in 1990 remained as divergent as indicated in Table 3.12—that is, that married women averaged 900 fewer hours of market work per year and earned almost $6 less per hour than married men—it seems unlikely that men's and women's allocation of time to childcare and housework will converge rapidly.

## RACIAL DIFFERENCES IN ECONOMIC EQUALITY

The discussion in the preceding pages focused on the economic equality of women relative to men without differentiating race or ethnicity. This was done, in part, because the gender story crosscuts racial and ethnic lines. Women of color have also increased their labor force activity over time and increased their earnings relative to men of color. However, important differences characterize racial and ethnic subgroups of women. A much longer time series of information exists on the relative position of black women than on other racial or ethnic minority groups.

The family living arrangements of black and white women are divergent and became increasingly so during the 1980s. Black women are far more likely to be the single parent of dependent children than are white women, and these differences are currently greater than they were a generation ago (Cherlin 1992; Bianchi 1994). Black women are less likely to marry, are more likely to have a marriage end, and are less likely to remarry than are white women. Birthrates are higher for unmarried black women than for white women, and in 1991, 68 percent of black births were to unmarried women compared with 22 percent of white births (National Center for Health Statistics 1993a). Although economic and family trends have moved in the same direction for both racial groups—and, in terms of family formation behavior and economic activity, the behaviors of black women may be leading indicators of the eventual behaviors of white women—the racial differences remain large.

In 1970, when the early baby boom cohort was coming of age, black women, driven in part out of economic necessity, already had far stronger labor force attachment and experience than white women. They also had experienced discrimination, as a group, on the basis of both race and gender and hence their earnings were the lowest of the four race-gender groups. They shared in the compositional shifts that accompanied women's increased labor force participation—the delay in marriage, decline in fertility, and educational and occupational upgrading. Perhaps because black women's labor force participation was already quite high in 1970, there was not the widespread behavioral change (extending beyond compositional shifts) that characterized white women's increased participation.[20]

Although black women were historically more likely to work for pay than white women, the labor force differentials between black and white women narrowed substantially during the 1970s and 1980s. Between 1965 and 1992, the participation rate for white women rose 20 percentage points to reach 58 percent, while the rate for black women rose by only 9 percentage points to reach the same level (U.S. Department of Labor 1993).

Children less often deter married black women from working full-time, year-round. In 1990, for example, almost one half of married black mothers worked full-time, year-round compared with about one third of married white mothers (Hayghe and Bianchi 1994). Married black women have typically worked more hours, on average, and have contributed a greater proportion of family earnings than married white women. In some sense, black women have been less economically dependent on men, in part because of the disadvantaged labor market position of black men.

Beginning in the 1950s for black women and in the 1960s for black men, earnings increased relative to whites of the same sex (Blau and Beller 1992). One of the important reasons that black women increased their earnings relative to white women was that they increasingly shifted out of poorly paid, private household work into clerical and service sector jobs. The movement of black women out of private household work began earlier in the century—the proportion of black women in private household work dropped from 60 percent in 1940 to 36 percent in 1960 and then to 2 percent by 1990.[21] Still, as shown by Blau and Beller, because of gradual cohort replacement, the movement out of private household work continued to explain part of the improvement in earnings of black women relative to white women and men into the 1970s. The retirement of older cohorts of black women in the 1970s, over one quarter of whom were private household workers, significantly increased the average earnings of black women workers.

This movement out of private household work was virtually complete by the end of the 1970s and, according to Harrison and Bennett (see their chapter in Volume 2), the average earnings of black and white women with the same level of educational attainment were within 5 percent of each other by 1980. By 1990, the earnings of comparably educated black and white women had achieved parity, although differences persisted for men.

Table 3.16 shows average hourly earnings in 1989 for white, black, and Hispanic women and men of the early and late baby boom cohorts. Data are shown for two educational groups: those with a high school diploma and those with a college degree. Among the late baby boom cohort, black women's hourly earnings were 93 percent those of white women, whereas the comparable percentages for men were 78 percent among high school graduates and 87 percent among college graduates.

Among the early baby boom cohort, black women's average earnings surpassed those of white women, whereas black men's earnings were 85 percent of those of white men with similar levels of education. Gender equality was not achieved by either racial group in 1989, but black women's hourly earnings were considerably closer to those of black men (90 percent of men's among black college graduates) than white women's earnings were to those of white men.

Blau and Beller (1992) note three problematic trends for black men in the 1980s. Young cohorts stopped doing better relative to older cohorts. The narrowing of racial differences in earnings and wages that had characterized the 1970s stopped. And the amount of time black men spent in the labor force decreased, perhaps because industrial restructuring (which affected the less-skilled) and movement of jobs out of central cities (where residentially segre-

TABLE 3.16   Average hourly earnings of high school and college graduates, by birth cohort, sex, and ethnicity: 1990.

|  | White | Black | Hispanic | Black/ White | Hispanic/ White |
|---|---|---|---|---|---|
|  |  |  |  | Ratio (per 100) | |
| Late Baby Boom (ages 25–34) |  |  |  |  |  |
| Women |  |  |  |  |  |
| High school graduate | $6.71 | $6.25 | $6.73 | 93 | 100 |
| College graduate | 11.36 | 10.58 | 11.06 | 93 | 97 |
| Men |  |  |  |  |  |
| High school graduate | 9.62 | 7.50 | 8.20 | 78 | 85 |
| College graduate | 13.33 | 11.54 | 11.83 | 87 | 89 |
| Ratio women/men (per 100) |  |  |  |  |  |
| High school graduate | 70 | 83 | 82 |  |  |
| College graduate | 85 | 92 | 93 |  |  |
| Early Baby Boom (ages 35–44) |  |  |  |  |  |
| Women |  |  |  |  |  |
| High school graduate | $7.21 | $7.50 | $7.31 | 104 | 101 |
| College graduate | 12.24 | 13.14 | 12.22 | 107 | 100 |
| Men |  |  |  |  |  |
| High school graduate | 11.83 | 9.62 | 10.26 | 81 | 87 |
| College graduate | 17.05 | 14.42 | 14.90 | 85 | 87 |
| Ratio women/men (per 100) |  |  |  |  |  |
| High school graduate | 61 | 78 | 71 |  |  |
| College graduate | 72 | 91 | 82 |  |  |

SOURCE: Decennial census Public Use Microdata Samples (5 percent) for 1990.

gated poorer blacks were concentrated) had a disproportionate effect on young cohorts of black men.

The declining wage-earning ability of less-educated workers had a particularly large impact on the employment and earnings of young black men. They had spent fewer of their adult years married than young white men in 1970 and became even less likely to marry over the course of the ensuing two decades. Hence, the likelihood that a black woman was the sole family support for dependent children increased and remained much higher than that for white women. The likelihood that a young black man could not support a family on his earnings alone also increased. If anything, this augmented the trend away from marriage within the black community.

There is a much shorter time series with which to measure gender differences within Hispanic subgroups. Tienda and her colleagues point out that one Hispanic subgroup—Puerto Rican women—seems to have fared particularly badly in the labor force in recent decades (Tienda, Donato, and Cordero-Guzman 1992). Puerto Rican women's labor force participation was similar to other Hispanics in 1960, but by the mid-1980s participation rates were far below those of all other racial and ethnic groups. The differential was particularly great among those with less than a high school education.

Table 3.16, which aggregates all Hispanics, suggests that, as a group, Hispanic women's earnings were equivalent to those of white women with the same level of education in 1990. As with black men, the average hourly earnings of Hispanic men continued to lag behind those of comparably educated white men. Hispanic women earned less than Hispanic men of similar education, but the gender wage gap was smaller among Hispanics than among whites, in part because of the lower average earnings of Hispanic men.

It is impossible to consider the range of labor force diversity among men and women of different ethnic and racial groups in a relatively short chapter such as this, and, indeed, much of this diversity is discussed in the chapter by Harrison and Bennett in Volume 2. Increased gender equality in economic activity is characteristic of all groups. But the relative importance of women's gains in education, labor force attachment, and earnings versus earnings losses by men varies by racial and ethnic subgroup. Those more concentrated at the bottom of the income distribution were much more subject to the adverse economic conditions that affected the unskilled in the 1980s.

## CONCLUSION

Much of the "true" or "real" movement toward gender equality has been the result of a gradual process of cohort replacement. There were profound changes in educational attainment, occupational choice, labor force attachment, and earnings with the baby boom generation of women. Much greater market equality of women and men has progressively distinguished these cohorts from those who came before. With the baby boom, a tide rose and swept through the 1970s and 1980s and left the economic, if not the domestic, roles of women and men far more similar by 1990 than they had been at any other time in this century.

Many baby boom men and women were raised in affluent families who could afford to send them to college, and go to college they did. The contraceptive revolution also allowed women of this generation far greater sexual freedom and planning of fertility than their mothers had known. The Vietnam War provided an impetus for men of the baby boom to go to college. During the 1970s, the difficulty for the labor force to absorb all of this large cohort provided further incentive for men and women to continue schooling and postpone marriage and children, a trend that continues.

As the baby boom—especially the late baby boom—entered the labor force, wages stagnated and the economy grew at a slower rate than it had in earlier decades. Although the economy absorbed millions of workers, the lack of earnings improvements intensified the economic uncertainty of the times. That uncertainty, in turn, helped discourage young adults from marrying early and starting families.

The continued conflict between labor force participation and marriage and children for women, especially among those with a huge investment in education, also served to lengthen the period of postponement of childbearing. Hence, many women of this generation had 5, 10, even 15 years of uninterrupted labor force experience before they married and had their first child. To contemplate walking away from the labor force, given their sizable investment in education and the fact that their family's standard of living depended on their earnings, was something many could not and did not do. Many women hedged their bets by working part-time after marriage and children. This retarded the trend toward gender earnings equality, but was not as great a drag on earnings as their mothers' "choice" of dropping out of the labor force completely.

Most of what emerged clearly in the 1980s had already started in the 1970s. However, in the 1970s, mothers of the baby boom had not yet reached retirement age. The massive restructuring that so affected younger, less-skilled workers was not complete.[22] Women with continuous work experience had not aged into the years when women's income had in the past declined most relative to men's income. The effects of these changes were still difficult to see by the end of the decade.

During the 1980s, as the early baby boom women aged into mid-career, their mothers aged out of the labor force. The generation of women who parented the baby boom children and who interrupted work to raise them, retired from the labor force. This particular generational replacement added substantially to the narrowing of the gender wage gap in the 1980s. In addition, young workers at the bottom of the skill distribution found an increasingly hostile labor market. Their economic insecurity propelled the less-educated to remain unmarried and delay having children. It also ensured that wives without particularly high earnings would continue to work even after starting a family.

What about the 1990s? It seems unrealistic to expect a repeat of the 1980s, but gender differences in earnings should narrow more than they did in the 1970s. Trends in educational attainment portend continued opening of occupational opportunities for women. The trend toward gender economic equality might accelerate if there were an exceptionally fast movement toward gender equality on the domestic front. However, what seems more likely is that some baby boom (and baby bust) women will drop out of the labor force as their mothers did, and many will work part-time after having children, which will keep men's and women's labor force (and domestic work) experiences dissimilar.

By the end of the 1990s, the cohorts moving toward retirement will be less distinct (in terms of lifetime work experience) from those moving through the labor force than was the case for the baby boom cohorts and their mothers in the 1980s. This may begin to slow the pace of change in women's earnings. If the past is any indication, change is gradual, and permanent transformation results from a process of cohort replacement. When mothers look ahead, they see what looks like great change in their children's lives. Their daughters juggle home and work in ways that seem almost incomprehensible. They are astounded by the number of tasks their sons and sons-in-law do around the house. They see great shifts in gender roles, yet significant differences continue.

Meanwhile, their daughters, especially those now in school and who have recently entered the work force, are impatient with the pace of change, for it is gradual in their lifetimes. Their earnings remain unequal to men's and will likely continue to be so throughout their labor force career. The division of labor in their homes is also unequal, and men's care and responsibility toward children and housework are changing only slowly. But to fail to recognize that change is occurring is to miss the revolution that has indeed transformed the economic activity of women, is beginning to transform the domestic roles of men, and will alter the American family in ways that would have seemed impossible just a generation ago.

---

I am grateful to Lynne Casper, Reynolds Farley, Larry Long, Karen Mason, Martin O'Connell, Arthur Norton, Paul Siegel, Daphne Spain, Cynthia Taeuber, Charles Westoff, and James Wetzel for comments on earlier drafts. Shannon Cavanagh and Andrea Walter provided invaluable research assistance. I owe special thanks to Prithwis Das Gupta who provided the decomposition of the index of occupational segregation and to Claudette Bennett and Roderick Harrison for assistance with the racial differences section of the chapter. I am also appreciative of the support and resources provided by Arthur Norton, Chief of the Population Division, Larry Long, chief of the Demographic Analysis Staff, and Daniel Weinberg, chief of the Housing and Household Statistics Division of the U.S. Bureau of the Census. Of course, the views expressed are my own and not necessarily those of the Census Bureau or of the individuals who have assisted me in this effort.

## ENDNOTES

1. An influential sociologist of that time, Talcott Parsons, in writings on the family, emphasized the functional necessity of the dissimilar (but complementary) roles of husbands and wives. See Parsons (1949, 1955).

2. For a thorough discussion of trends affecting less-educated workers, particularly in manufacturing, see the chapters by Wetzel, Kasarda, and Levy in this volume.

3. The role of World War II in facilitating women's movement into paid work remains controversial. During the war years, women not only filled traditionally female jobs in the economy, but were also employed in male-dominated jobs owing to the

increased production demands of the war and the absence of men, who were fighting abroad. However, upon demobilization after the war, many of the women employed in the more highly paid manufacturing sector were displaced by returning servicemen who were given preference for these jobs. Some argue that the war had little permanent effect on women's employment. Rather, women who were already employed at the start of the war moved into better-paying jobs, but only for a temporary period.

Yet World War II may have raised women's "taste" for market work, which, in turn, facilitated the increase in paid employment among women in later decades. That is, for some who were induced into the labor market during the war and subsequently left paid employment to marry and raise children, the introduction to paid work may have contributed to the greater likelihood that they would return to the labor force after raising their children. Hence, World War II may have been a factor in the acceleration in employment among older, married women during the 1950s and 1960s. For interesting discussions of women's employment during World War II, see Goldin (1991); Honey (1984); and J. G. Robinson (1988).

4. For a review of the trends in delayed marriage, see the chapter by McLanahan and Casper in Volume 2.

5. O'Connell (1993) shows that between 1988 and 1991 there was a significant increase in the proportion of children cared for by their fathers while their mothers worked.

6. Unpublished tabulations by the author from the decennial census Public Use Microdata Samples for 1960–1990: Goldin (1992).

7. See evidence assembled by Mare in the chapter on education in this volume.

8. Danziger and Stern (1990); U.S. Bureau of the Census, "Workers with Low Earnings: 1964 to 1990" (1992).

9. For a discussion of international comparisons in family living arrangements and labor force roles of women, see Chapter 1 in Volume 2.

10. U.S. Bureau of the Census, "Male-Female Differences in Work Experience, Occupation, and Earnings: 1984" (1987).

11. U.S. Bureau of the Census, *Statistical Abstract of the United States: 1993* (1993: Table 622).

12. The coding of occupations changed between 1970 and 1980; 1970 data in the table have been converted to comparable 1980 codes.

13. The author is grateful to Prithwis Das Gupta for providing these calculations. The decomposition method used is detailed in U.S. Bureau of the Census, "Standardization and Decomposition of Rates: A User's Manual" (1993).

14. Acs and Danziger (1990); Blackburn, Bloom, and Freeman (1991); Bound and Holzer (1991); Bound and Johnson (1992); Ryscavage and Henle (1990); U.S. Bureau of the Census, "Studies in the Distribution of Income" (1992).

15. As discussed in the chapter by Mare in this volume, the educational attainment question changed between the 1980 and 1990 censuses. In 1980, respondents indicated the years of school they had completed; in 1990, they reported on the degrees they had earned. In order to ensure that the comparison of earnings by education was not affected by a change in the educational item, March 1980 and 1990 Current

Population Survey (CPS) data are reported in Table 3.10 (and Table 3.11). In both years, the years of school completed question was used to determine educational attainment in the CPS.

16. Per capita income is a frequently used per person measure of income, but makes no adjustment for economies of scale realized by larger households. Other per person measures are often used, such as the ratio of income to the poverty threshold or an income per adult equivalent measure in which children and adults (after the first in the household) are assigned some fraction of one in adjusting income for household size. In general, there is no universally agreed upon household size adjustment. I use the per capita measure because it is easily constructed from census data, and trends are similar to those using other measures.

17. Because in the gender comparisons of household, family, and per capita income the income of the household (or family) in which a man or woman resides is assigned to all individuals in the household, husbands and wives have equal household, family, and per capita income. Hence, if all adult men and women were married, per capita, household, and family income would not differ by gender.

18. Bianchi (1993: Table 4.2); U.S. Bureau of the Census, "Child Support and Alimony: 1989" (1991).

19. England (1992). The research on marital power is reviewed in England and Kilbourne (1990).

20. Black women's increase in labor force participation between 1970 and 1990 can almost entirely be accounted for by compositional shifts in education, marriage, and fertility. Only 40 percent of the increased participation of white women can be "explained" by these factors (Zhan 1992).

21. Malveaux and Wallace (1987); U.S. Bureau of the Census, "Detailed Occupation and Other Characteristics from the EEO File for the United States" (1992).

22. For more detail on the topic, see the chapters by Levy on income and Wetzel on the labor force in this volume.

# 4

# Changes in Educational Attainment and School Enrollment

### ROBERT D. MARE

EDUCATION PLAYS MANY roles in American society. Schools are supposed to teach skills and knowledge as well as attitudes, values, and behaviors and to ready all students to be effective workers, parents, citizens, and consumers. But schools also play a big part in determining who is economically successful and who is not. Young persons pass through school and acquire not only skills and knowledge, but also degrees and certificates that are recognized in the world of work. People vary greatly in how long they stay in school, in what they learn there, and in the credentials that they accrue. Depending in part on their school experiences, people also vary in their economic well-being once they leave school. Persons who do well in school, who successfully go through the system and acquire diplomas and degrees, tend to be attractive to employers and enjoy the greatest chances of economic success. They tend to get the best jobs when they leave school and to be protected from unemployment and downward mobility during times of economic hardship.

If schooling is a contest with winners and losers, everyone does not have an equal chance to do well in school and to leave school with the promise of lifelong economic success. Rather, the quantity and quality of schooling that persons acquire depend in large measure on the advantages or disadvantages that their parents confer on them throughout childhood. Children of economically well-off and well-educated parents enjoy much greater chances of success in school than children of disadvantaged parents. Indeed, these patterns have persisted throughout the twentieth century, even as the average amount of schooling received by all persons has grown immensely. Schooling, in short, plays a key role in maintaining social inequality from one generation to the next.

Yet it would be a mistake to view schooling merely as a corridor through which children of the poor, the middle class, and the rich pass along the way to their predestined stations in adult life. Many Americans believe, correctly, that schooling can be an avenue of social mobility, a means by which the able and hardworking sons and daughters of less well-off parents can rise above the standing of their parents. The educational system in the United States does indeed permit and, to some extent, facilitate social mobility. Thus, schools play a complex and subtle role in the maintenance of inequality and the allocation of persons to positions in America's socioeconomic hierarchy. Inequalities of opportunity and of outcome persist from generation to generation, and schools are important in determining who gets ahead. But the socioeconomic inequalities that children bring to schools are shuffled during the educational process, permitting some individuals and groups to transcend their social origins and some children of well-to-do parents to slide down the socioeconomic ladder.

The 1990 census shows that during the 1980s a century-long pattern of increasing average educational attainment in the American population continued, much of it accomplished by the spread of schooling to social groups that have been traditionally disadvantaged in educational attainment, including women, persons from poor and lower-class families, and members of some racial-ethnic groups. The continued spread of schooling altered, but did not eliminate, many longstanding patterns of educational inequality. Some inequalities were reduced but others persisted, and some new forms of inequality became visible. During the 1980s traditional differences in educational attainment among racial-ethnic groups, for example, largely disappeared at the elementary and secondary school levels, but differences among these groups in access to and progress through institutions of higher education persisted. At the start of the 1980s young adult men and women were equally likely to receive at least some schooling beyond the high school level, but men continued to enjoy an advantage in actually completing college and far outstripped women in their numbers who received advanced professional degrees. By 1990, however, women surpassed men in the rate at which they continued to college, achieved parity with men in completing college, and, in many fields, showed enormous progress in reducing the gap in achieving higher professional degrees. Patterns of inequality among socioeconomic groups were stable during the 1980s, although the continued increase in rates of high school graduation shifted the importance of these inequalities away from the high school years and toward both the college and preschool levels.

The 1980s also witnessed major changes in the ways in which educational attainment affects the economic rewards enjoyed by young adults. Throughout the decade, higher education continued to be a good investment for young persons. Indeed, the gap in wages earned between persons with a college education and those with only a high school education widened. During the 1980s, the average wages of persons with a college degree did not change very much, but the wages of persons without a degree fell dramatically. Most severely hurt were high school dropouts, for whom opportunities for well-paying employment, already poor in 1980, diminished even further by 1990. Educational attainment, always a marker for distinguishing those with good economic prospects from those with poor ones, became an even more powerful discriminator during the 1980s.

Beyond the capacity that schooling plays in helping to prepare persons for adulthood and to sort persons into jobs, it is an ongoing organized activity with a life of its own. Schooling fills a vast portion of the lives of young persons and competes with work, parenthood, recreation, and public service for their time and attention. Students and their parents are also the clients of a vast industry that employs many persons, uses a large portion of public resources, and commands the concern of politicians and administrators at the local, state, and national levels. Thus, it is not surprising that almost every era of American history has been beset with public anxiety and controversy about educational issues. The past decade has been no exception.

## ISSUES IN THE STUDY OF EDUCATIONAL TRENDS BETWEEN 1980 AND 1990

The 1980s and 1990s have witnessed widespread concerns about the quality of American public school education, especially with the ability of schools to provide students with the skills to be effective workers in an increasingly competitive national economy, and about the quality of personnel attracted to the teaching profession. There remain persistent concerns about the capacity of schools to both raise the achievement levels of the very best students and still serve students with weaker academic backgrounds, especially members of traditionally disadvantaged minorities. Ongoing public debates address the issues of how to allocate resources for education between public and private institutions and how schools can be equipped to respond to a changing student population created by changes in family life, by the precarious economic future facing many students, and by new waves of immigrants.

This chapter will focus on seven major aspects of educational attainment:

1. trends in educational attainment throughout the twentieth century, emphasizing differences between men and women and among racial-ethnic groups;
2. trends in educational attainment as a reflection of changes in family socioeconomic circumstances;
3. trends in school enrollment, emphasizing its spread beyond traditional school-attending ages to younger and older age groups;
4. trends in academic performance of elementary and secondary school students;

5. trends in the transition from school to employment for persons with varying levels of educational attainment, emphasizing the varying experiences among racial-ethnic groups;

6. trends in the kinds of occupations open to men and women with varying educational qualifications; and

7. trends in the economic returns to schooling for young workers.

### Racial-Ethnic Groups as Part of this Study

This chapter discusses the racial-ethnic differences in educational attainment, school enrollment, and their economic consequences for five groups: non-Hispanic whites; non-Hispanic blacks; Asian and Pacific Islanders; American Indians, Eskimos, and Aleuts; and Hispanics. (Asian and Pacific Islanders will be referred to as "Asians"; American Indians, Eskimos, and Aleuts will be referred to as either "Indians" or "Native Americans"; and non-Hispanic blacks will be referred to as either "blacks" or "African Americans.")[1] Schooling has traditionally been viewed as an avenue of upward mobility for the economic assimilation of immigrant and disadvantaged minority groups, yet these groups vary widely in the extent to which they have been able to enjoy the benefits of schooling. Compared with majority whites, blacks have traditionally faced severe disadvantages in the quality of schools that they have attended, their level of educational attainment, and the economic rewards that they have derived from their schooling.[2] The educational attainment of some Hispanic groups has substantially lagged behind that of both whites and blacks; yet within levels of education, Hispanics have typically enjoyed higher economic rewards than blacks (Borjas and Tienda 1985; Sandefur and Tienda 1988). Asian Americans have enjoyed unusually high levels of educational and socioeconomic success compared with whites as well as other minorities, despite persistent racial discrimination (Hirschman and Wong 1986; Mare and Winship 1988; Xie 1993). Both Hispanics and Asians, however, are heterogeneous groups that differ widely in their socioeconomic success. Additionally, within racial-ethnic groups, there is substantial variation in the educational and economic attainments of native-born and foreign-born groups. Although immigration often attracts the most educated and ambitious members of foreign populations, such persons often face significant handicaps relative to their native counterparts once they enter the United States.

### Census Data as a Tool for Studying Educational Issues

The decennial census is a unique tool for the assessment of social change because it provides a rich set of data for detailed analysis of social and demographic groups. For example, the census is a uniquely reliable source of data on the educational attainments of small racial-ethnic groups. For the most part, the census employs a constant set of measures for each decade, thereby avoiding the problem of confusing changes in the population with changes in the way that the population is measured. From time to time, however, the Census Bureau does change the way that a phenomenon is measured, either because changes in the phenomenon itself make the old measures obsolete or because users of the census shift their ideas about what is important to measure.

An important change in the 1990 census is the new measure of educational attainment. It resulted from the belief that measures used in prior censuses and many other data sources correspond poorly to widely used educational concepts and that this problem has worsened over time. In the five censuses before 1990, educational attainment was measured in a single number: highest grade of school completed. Users of census data typically inferred whether a person completed major stages of schooling (e.g., high school graduation, college graduation) from whether he or she completed a given number of years of schooling (e.g., 12, 16). Yet this assumption works poorly for persons who attend school part-time, take accelerated or prolonged degree programs, or attend full years but only partially complete degree requirements. For example, many students spend five years or more getting a college degree, whereas others obtain a degree in three years. Nor is this assumption adequate for inferring whether individuals receive specific advanced degrees. To remedy this, the 1990 census asked respondents explicitly about their academic credentials. To offset the increased detail of response categories for higher education, the 1990 schedule requested less detail at lower levels of schooling and in the measurement of school attendance. Table 4.1 shows the three major changes between 1980 and 1990 in the census items on schooling: (1) For educational attainment at the high school level and above, respondents were asked their highest *degree* obtained rather than their number of years or grades completed; (2) they were asked their highest level of schooling *completed* (in a one-part question) rather than their highest level *attended* and whether they completed that level (a two-part question); and (3) they were given detailed response categories for the type of advanced degree that they may have obtained, but broader categories for attainment at the elementary and high school level.[3] One must adopt a variety of strategies to distinguish actual changes in educational patterns from artifacts of change in the measurement of educational attainment. One strategy for assessing changes in the attainment patterns of young adults is to rely on estimates of the joint responses of persons in several surveys in which both the 1990 census and the traditional educational attainment measures have been administered. Using these estimates, one can estimate the response that 1990 census respondents would have supplied had they been given the 1980 education items and the response that the 1980 respondents would have supplied had they been given the 1990 items. A second strategy is to use ancillary data, such as the Census Bureau's October Current Population Surveys (CPSs), which employ measures of schooling that are stable over time.

TABLE 4.1   School enrollment and educational attainment items in 1980 and 1990
censuses.

---

### 1980

---

8. **Since February 1, 1980,** **has this person attended regular school or college at any time?** *Fill one circle. Count nursery school, kindergarten, elementary school, and schooling which leads to a high school diploma or college degree.*

- ○ No, has not attended since February 1
- ○ Yes, public school, public college
- ○ Yes, private, church-related
- ○ Yes, private, not church-related

---

9. **What is the highest grade (or year) of regular school this person has ever attended?**

*Fill one circle.*

*If now attending school, mark grade person is in. If high school was finished by equivalency test (GED), mark "12."*

**Highest grade attended:**

○ Nursery School            ○ Kindergarten

Elementary through High School *(grade or year)*

| 1 | 2 | 3 | 4 | 5 | 6 | | 7 | 8 | | 9 | 10 | 11 | 12 |
|---|---|---|---|---|---|---|---|---|---|---|----|----|----|
| ○ | ○ | ○ | ○ | ○ | ○ | | ○ | ○ | | ○ | ○ | ○ | ○ |

College *(academic year)*

| | 1 | 2 | 3 | 4 | 5 | 6 | 7 | 8 or more |
|---|---|---|---|---|---|---|---|-----------|
| | ○ | ○ | ○ | ○ | ○ | ○ | ○ | ○ |

○ Never attended school —*Skip question 10*

---

10. **Did this person finish the highest grade (or year) attended?**

*Fill one circle.*

- ○ Now attending this grade *(or year)*
- ○ Finished this grade *(or year)*
- ○ Did not finish this grade *(or year)*

---

### 1990

---

11. **At any time since February 1, 1990, has this person attended regular school or college?** Include only nursery school, kindergarten, elementary school, and schooling which leads to a high school diploma or a college degree.

- ○ No, has not attended since February 1
- ○ Yes, public school, public college
- ○ Yes, private school, private college

---

12. **How much school has this person COMPLETED?** Fill ONE circle for the highest level COMPLETED or degree RECEIVED. If currently enrolled, mark the level of previous grade attended or highest degree received.

- ○ No school completed
- ○ Nursery school
- ○ Kindergarten
- ○ 1st, 2nd, 3rd, or 4th grade
- ○ 5th, 6th, 7th, or 8th grade
- ○ 9th grade
- ○ 10th grade
- ○ 11th grade
- ○ 12th grade, **NO DIPLOMA**
- ○ **HIGH SCHOOL GRADUATE**—high school DIPLOMA or the equivalent (For example: GED)
- ○ Some college but no degree
- ○ Associate degree in college—Occupational program
- ○ Associate degree in college—Academic program
- ○ Bachelor's degree (For example: BA, AB, BS)
- ○ Master's degree (For example: MA, MS, MEng, MEd, MSW, MBA)
- ○ Professional school degree (For example: MD, DDS, DVM, LLB, JD)
- ○ Doctorate degree (For example: PhD, EdD)

---

## TRENDS IN EDUCATIONAL ATTAINMENT IN THE TWENTIETH CENTURY

### The Educational History of the Twentieth Century

The 1980 and 1990 censuses provide snapshots of the population for only two years. Yet because most people get their schooling during their childhood, teens, and 20s, the reported average educational attainments of the various age groups observed in each census provide a good indication of the trend in attainment across the birth cohorts represented in the census. For example, the average attainment of persons aged 40–44 in 1990 shows the attainment experienced by persons who were born in 1946–1950 (the early baby boomers) and who attended school between the late 1950s and the early 1970s. To be sure, such measures are affected by the fact that persons with more schooling tend to live longer than those with less schooling and that some persons acquire more schooling at older, nontraditional ages of enrollment. Nonetheless each census provides an informative view of the educational history of the twentieth century.

Figures 4.1–4.4 show percentages of men and women who completed selected levels of schooling by year of birth. A rough indication of the extent to

FIGURE 4.1  Percentage of persons completing 4 years of school or less, by sex and year of birth.

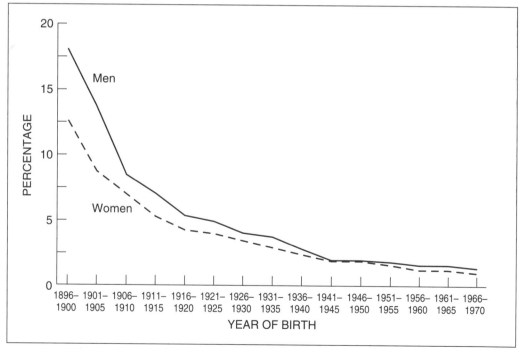

which the population has eliminated functional illiteracy is the percentage of persons who have completed four years of formal schooling or less. As Figure 4.1 shows, about 15 percent of persons born at the turn of the century completed four years or less, a proportion that declined steadily over cohorts born during the next 40 years, reaching a level of about 2 percent. This proportion has held at between 1 and 2 percent of cohorts born since World War II. In pre–World War II birth cohorts, boys were somewhat more likely than girls to complete four years or less, but this differential disappeared as completion of this educational milestone became nearly universal.

Figure 4.2 presents percentages of persons who completed at least a high school education.[4] The trend follows the S-shape that is characteristic of the spread of innovations. Between cohorts born at the turn of the century and those born in the 1960s, the rate of high school graduation grew from approximately 25 percent to more than 80 percent. In cohorts born early in this period, women were somewhat more likely than men to graduate, but this advantage for women disappeared for cohorts born from the 1920s onward. In recent cohorts, however, high school graduation rates for women once again exceeded those of

FIGURE 4.2    Percentage of persons completing at least 12 years of school, by sex and year of birth.

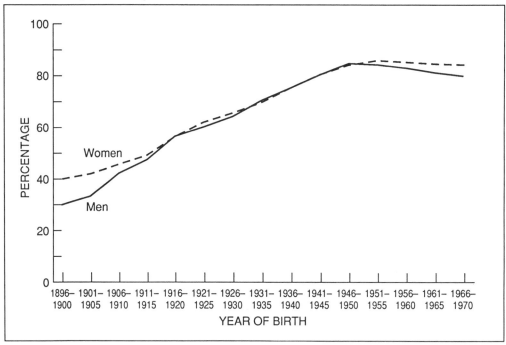

men. For both sexes, rates of graduation declined slightly over cohorts born in the 1950s and 1960s. The erosion of graduation rates for the population as a whole may be the result of the changing makeup of successive cohorts. Over cohorts, educationally disadvantaged minority populations (especially African Americans and Hispanics) have grown relative to the white majority. Although differential population growth among racial-ethnic groups is apparent in cohorts born well before the 1950s, secular increases in high school graduation rates among whites during this earlier period were more than sufficient to offset the negative effect of minority population increase on graduation rates for the whole population. Now that white rates have stabilized, however, the increase of educationally disadvantaged minorities will reduce total graduation rates until educational inequality among racial-ethnic groups is further reduced.

At the college level, the trend in attainment also follows an S-shaped pattern, albeit one in which the acceleration of completion rates occurs somewhat later than for the completion of high school (Figures 4.3 and 4.4). According to 1990 census estimates, the percentage of persons who completed at least some college increased from about 15 percent for men born at the turn of the century to about 60 percent for men in the 1946–1950 birth cohort, and subsided to about 50

**FIGURE 4.3** Percentage of persons completing at least some college, by sex and year of birth.

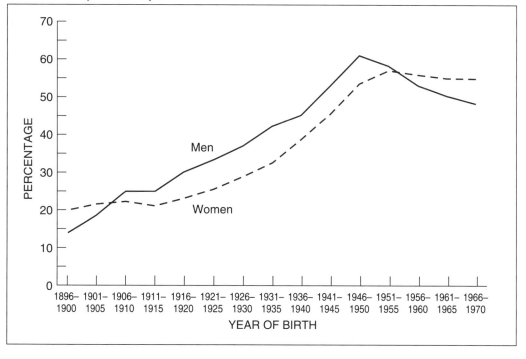

FIGURE 4.4    Percentage of persons completing at least a bachelor's degree, by sex and year of birth.

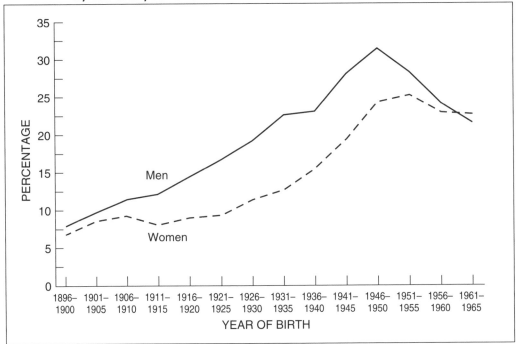

percent for the cohort born in the late 1960s. The percentage of women who completed at least some college increased from about 20 percent for cohorts born at the turn of the century to about 55 percent for cohorts born in the 1950s and 1960s. The 1980 census estimates show a similar trend in rates of completion of some college; but within each cohort, the 1990 estimates were 5 to 10 percentage points higher.[5] To some extent the higher estimates for 1990 occurred because a small proportion of persons continued to obtain further education during their adult years, implying that, within cohorts, average educational attainment increases with age. It is likely, however, that an equally important cause of the difference between the 1980 and 1990 estimates of percentages who completed at least some college is the change in the wording of the 1990 census educational attainment item, which led individuals who attended technical and vocational schools after high school to report that they had attended some college without obtaining a degree. In the 1980 census, such persons were not encouraged to count such schooling as college. Question wording, however, does not have the same impact on our estimates of the proportions of persons who completed a college degree.[6]

Increases in rates of college completion reflect secular changes in the socioeconomic characteristics of families, long-run technological changes in the economy, the increasingly competitive pressure to maintain one's competitive position in the work force, and the nation's dedication to providing postsecondary education for an ever-growing proportion of the population (Mare 1981b). During the late nineteenth and twentieth centuries in the United States each successive cohort has been born to parents who, on average, have higher levels of schooling and higher socioeconomic standing than the parents of previous cohorts.[7] Given the strong effects of parents' schooling and socioeconomic status on the schooling of their offspring, over the long run, secular changes in the family have been an important source of educational growth. Changes in measured characteristics of the family, however, account for only about one third of the growth documented in Figure 4.1. In addition, the emphasis of the American economy and labor market has changed from agrarian to blue collar industrial to white collar service, increasing the demands for a highly educated work force. The extent to which the economy has "needed" workers who have spent increasingly large portions of their early lives in school is, of course, debatable. Even if the educational requirements for jobs did not change, the average educational attainments of successive cohorts would have grown. Because employers often regard formal school credentials as markers for the desirability of workers, individuals are induced to acquire as much schooling as they can. Increases in educational attainment between successive birth cohorts resulted both from the efforts of individuals to compete successfully in the labor market and from large public subsidies of postsecondary schooling.

As Figures 4.3 and 4.4 show, trends in the educational attainment of women have roughly paralleled those of men, although the sexes have differed somewhat in the pace of change. Women born at the turn of the century had about the same chance as men to attend and complete college, but subsequent cohorts of women did not keep pace with their male counterparts. For both completion of some college and a college degree, the gap between the sexes reached a maximum of about 10 percentage points for cohorts born during the Depression and subsequently narrowed. Among cohorts born since the mid 1950s, women have completed at least some college at higher rates than men. There is considerable evidence that rates of college completion for women may have surpassed those of men for cohorts born in the early 1960s. The sex difference in college attendance and completion trends reflects the different role that college has played in the lives of men and women during the twentieth century. Early in the century, a college-educated, professional class was open to small numbers of men and women, albeit one in which women were primarily teachers and men occupied a more diverse set of positions. Professional opportunities grew rapidly for men throughout the middle part of the century, but comparable occupational opportunities were not open to women, who remained primarily housewives and mothers; or if they obtained advanced degrees, they were mainly confined to a small number of female-dominated occupations such as teaching, library science, or nursing (Goldin 1990). The percentage of women who attended college nonetheless grew over this period, first gradually for cohorts born during the first quarter of the century and rapidly thereafter. Many of the women who received higher education did not enjoy its full benefit in the labor market. College did, however, provide them the opportunity to meet and marry men who had similar educational credentials. In many instances, therefore, women derived an economic benefit from increased education, albeit indirectly through marriage (Mare 1991; Goldin 1992). In more recent cohorts, in contrast, as men's and women's positions in the work force have become somewhat more similar, women have experienced more direct economic benefits from their own education. In these cohorts, women have equaled or surpassed men in their college attendance and completion rates.

As with high school graduation rates, college attendance and completion rates have declined over cohorts born since 1950, to a small extent for women and to a much greater extent for men. These changes have two main causes. First, college attendance was unusually high for male cohorts born in the middle and later 1940s, those who were most vulnerable to the Vietnam era military draft and could avoid the draft by obtaining a college deferment. Men who belonged to subsequent cohorts, who entered college when the manpower needs of the armed forces were lower and the draft deferment of college students was eliminated, attended college at lower rates than their earlier counterparts. Second, as with high school graduation rates, college attendance and completion rates for each cohort are affected by the changing racial-ethnic and socioeconomic makeup of the population. Educational attainment for the white majority has not changed a great deal in recent cohorts, but the proportion of each cohort made up of educationally disadvantaged minorities has grown. This has reduced average attendance and completion rates for cohorts as a whole.

## Advanced Degrees for Men and Women

Although trends in educational attainment provide a broad indication of the population's education level, persons with the same numbers of years of schooling often vary considerably in their credentials and skills. This is particularly the case beyond the college level, where advanced specialized degrees provide people with varying qualifications in the labor market. It is, moreover, at this advanced level that changes in educational equality between men and women over the past several decades have been particularly striking. As women have attended and completed college at increasing rates, more and more of them have been eligible to pursue advanced professional degrees. As will be discussed in later sections, higher educational qualifications, combined with reduced discriminatory barriers in the labor market, have enabled highly educated women to make progress in reducing their economic disparity with men.

The number of men and women who earn bachelor's degrees has increased dramatically since 1950. In 1950, about 330,000 men and 100,000 women received them; in 1980, about 475,000 men and 450,000 women received them; and in 1990, about 490,000 men and 560,000 women received them. The growth in the numbers of women who earned bachelor's degrees over this period led to equally impressive gains in the numbers who earned graduate and professional degrees. Figure 4.5 shows the numbers of advanced professional degrees received by men and women during the past four decades in selected fields. In 1960, about 5,000 men were awarded master's degrees in business (M.B.A.s), about 25 times the number that women were awarded. The subsequent 30 years brought about a 10-fold increase in M.B.A.s for men, but almost a 150-fold increase for women. By 1990, about 10 men received M.B.A.s for every 6 women who received them, but this gap is narrowing year by year and shows every sign of disappearing. Similar trends can be seen for law and medicine, two of the most common and best-paying professions. In 1960, about 45 men received law degrees for every woman who received one; by 1990, the ratio was 4 to 3. In 1960, about 9 men received M.D. degrees for every woman who received one; by 1990, the ratio was less than 2 to 1.

Although women have made striking advances in business, law, and medicine, the changes in other, sex-typed professions have been smaller. In 1950, virtually no women received master's degrees in engineering (M.Eng.); about 3,500 did so in 1990. Nonetheless, men still received six times as many engineering degrees as women. Conversely, women still receive far more advanced degrees in education than men, as they have since 1970. The number of master's degrees in education (M.Ed.) declined for both sexes in the 1980s, reversing a long-term trend, but the decline was proportionately greater for men than women, who now receive more than three times as many degrees as men.[8]

These trends reveal a mixed pattern of change in the educational standing of men and women during the 1980s. Both sexes sought and obtained advanced professional degrees in increasing numbers in many fields; however, men still retain substantial advantages in the attainment of valuable post-baccalaureate degrees. These advantages are important because these degrees are often requirements for entering the very top jobs in industry and government and thus are the keys to many of the most stable and high-paying positions in the work force. In business, law, and medicine, as well as other fields, however, women's progress in a relatively short period of time has been revolutionary. The trends toward educational convergence for men and women at the highest levels of schooling show no sign of abating.

FIGURE 4.5 Professional degrees received, by sex, year, and field: 1950–1990.

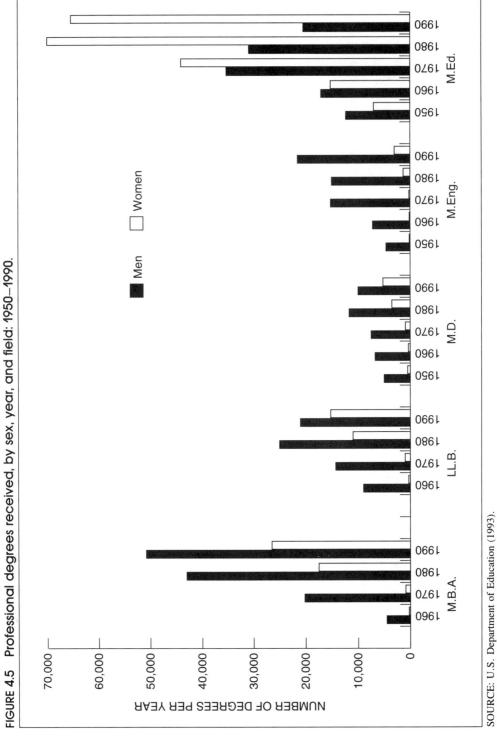

168

### Educational Attainment in the 1980s

To examine trends in educational attainment during the 1980s, it is necessary to examine the behaviors and statuses of young persons, many of whom are still in school. An effective method is to examine the probabilities that persons move between successive stages of schooling for those who have either made these transitions or who have dropped out of school. Because these probabilities are estimated from the educational experiences of all persons aged 7–24 in each census, they describe the experiences of people who were born over an 18-year period. They characterize a hypothetical group of persons who had the school continuation probabilities experienced by census respondents aged 7–24 up to the date of the census. These probabilities are estimated as the ratio of persons who completed a given level of schooling to persons who completed at least the previous level of schooling, excluding persons who are enrolled in school but have not yet completed the given level of schooling. Comparing the experiences of persons aged 7–24 in the 1980 and 1990 censuses provides an indication of recent attainment trends. As noted above, however, because of the change between the censuses in the way that schooling is measured to make comparisons it is necessary to estimate what the 1990-basis education responses would have been for people enumerated in 1980 and what the 1980-basis responses would have been for people enumerated in 1990. Although the 1980 and 1990 censuses do not let one see how the same person would have answered the two questions, several surveys fielded by the Census Bureau between 1980 and 1990 let one observe the joint distribution of educational attainment measures that are similar to the 1980 and 1990 census items.[9]

Figure 4.6 shows school continuation probabilities between 1980 and 1990 using the 1980 basis codes. This figure presents the probability that for each grade of schooling, an individual will complete the subsequent grade of schooling. These estimates show that probabilities of school continuation are near unity throughout the elementary and early secondary years in both 1980 and 1990 and at rates in excess of .95 for the later stages of secondary school. High school dropout rates declined slightly during the decade: At each grade of high school, the rate at which students continue from one grade to the next increased by between 1 and 2 percentage points. This increase is small because high school dropout rates were, on a national basis, already very low at the start of the decade. That the dropout rates nonetheless declined, however, is a reflection of the same secular forces that have driven educational attainments throughout the century, including the rising educational attainments of parents and the dwindling employment prospects for persons who fail to complete high school.

At the transition from high school to college, rates of continuation increased sharply over the 1980s. The probability of progressing from twelfth to thirteenth grade jumped sharply by more than .1 from 1980 to 1990. Inasmuch as only

FIGURE 4.6   School continuation probabilities: 1980 and 1990.

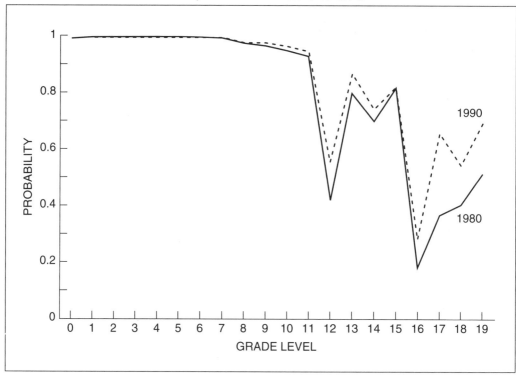

about 42 percent of high school graduates went on to complete a year of college in 1980, this offered the potential for significant growth in school persistence over the decade. In addition, there were modest increases in probabilities of persistence in and graduation from college during the 1980s. Beyond the college level there were large increases between 1980 and 1990 in proportions of persons continuing to advanced degrees. For example, among persons who completed 16 years of schooling, the percentage who completed a seventeenth year increased from about 18 to 28 percent over the decade. To a limited degree this increase may result because increasing numbers of persons took more than four years to complete a bachelor's degree. To a large extent, however, this change, like the changes observed at the lower levels of schooling, reflects a continuation of long-run trends toward increased educational attainment.

### Historical Differences among Racial-Ethnic Groups

Average educational attainments have varied historically among major racial-ethnic groups in the United States, and these differences persist today. They reflect socioeconomic differences among these groups, ethnic-racial discrimination in schools and in the economic rewards to schooling, group differences in the timing of immigration to the United States, and group differences in values placed on formal schooling and in strategies that families use to facilitate the schooling of their offspring. This section reviews historical differences among major racial-ethnic groups. The next section will describe changes during the 1980s.

Figures 4.7–4.10 present rates of completing selected levels of schooling for five major racial-ethnic groups over cohorts born between 1900 and 1970, estimated from the 1990 census. Inasmuch as many Asians and Hispanics are foreign-born, Figures 4.7–4.10 will distinguish between native-born and foreign-born members of these groups. The attainments of native-born and foreign-born persons may differ greatly. On the one hand, immigrants are a selective group and may, relative to their racial or ethnic counterparts who do not come to the United States, acquire more schooling. Indeed, many immigrants may come to this country specifically to obtain further education. On the other hand, compared with native-born members of their group, they may have lacked educational opportunities in their place of birth and have faced considerable economic and linguistic obstacles to schooling on entering the United States.[10]

All racial-ethnic groups follow the trends of increasing rates of school completion observed in the population as a whole, but they differ markedly in their

FIGURE 4.7    Percentage of persons completing 4 years of school or less, by racial-ethnic group and year of birth: 1990.

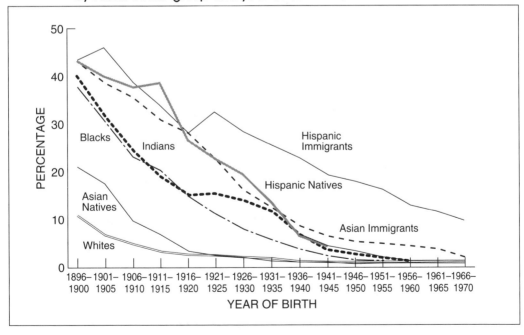

FIGURE 4.8    Percentage of persons completing at least 12 years of school, by racial-ethnic group and year of birth: 1990.

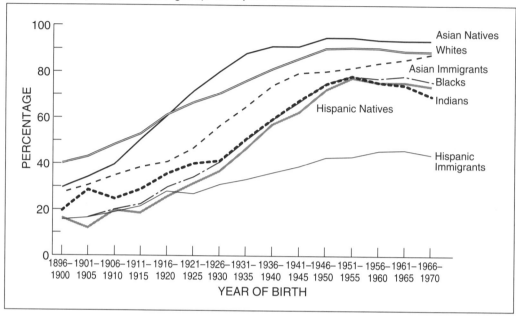

levels of attainment and in the rates at which their attainment levels grow. The size and pattern of change in racial-ethnic differences varies with level of schooling: the higher the level of schooling, the larger the differentials that can be seen in recent birth cohorts. For completion of four years of school or less, racial-ethnic differences were substantial for cohorts born at the turn of the century, favoring majority whites and the small native Asian population. For cohorts born in the 1960s, completion of four years of school or less was nearly universal for all groups except foreign-born Hispanics, many of whom were not living in the United States at the time that they were teenagers. As one considers higher levels of school completion, however, the differentials among cohorts born at the turn of the century are smaller and those for recent birth cohorts are much larger. For completion of at least some college among cohorts born at the turn of the century, only whites enjoyed completion rates in excess of 15 percent. For cohorts born in the 1960s, in contrast, completion rates vary from a remarkably high 70 percent for Asian natives to less than 20 percent for foreign-born Hispanics.

Differences between native-born and foreign-born Asians are very large for cohorts born during the first third of the century, particularly for completion rates at elementary and secondary school. Among recent cohorts, in contrast, native-born and foreign-born Asians enjoy similar levels of attainment. For Hispanics, the trend is the opposite. Native-born and foreign-born Hispanics who

FIGURE 4.9   Percentage of persons completing at least some college, by racial-ethnic group and year of birth: 1990.

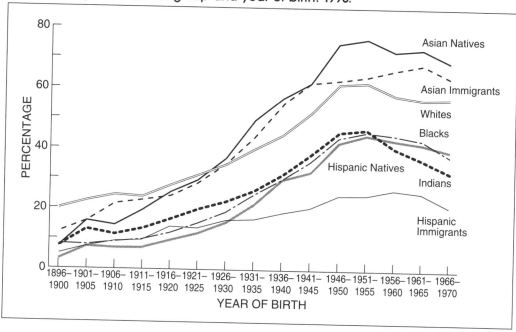

were born early in the century experience similar rates of school completion; in more recent cohorts, natives experience much higher levels of attainment. These differences in the educational histories of native-born and foreign-born Asians and Hispanics result from differences between the two groups in educational opportunities in their countries of origin as well as differences in opportunities to acquire more school once they are living in the United States.

The school completion rates for cohorts born between approximately 1940 and 1970 have determined the educational makeup of most of the current labor force in the U.S. economy. Among such persons there are large racial-ethnic differences in educational attainment, which are a major source of differences in earnings and occupational placement (see Borjas and Tienda 1985; Sandefur and Tienda 1988). Racial-ethnic differences in educational attainment, particularly as indicated by rates of completing some college and completing a college degree, remain substantial for working age adults. Within this broad age group, approximately 70 percent of Asians, 60 percent of whites, 40 percent of blacks and native-born Hispanics, 30 percent of American Indians, and 20 percent of foreign-born Hispanics have completed at least some postsecondary schooling. These differences imply large lifelong differences in socioeconomic welfare among these groups and large differences in the socioeconomic and educational opportunities that these groups can provide to their offspring. Despite the

FIGURE 4.10  Percentage of persons completing at least a bachelor's degree, by racial-ethnic group and year of birth: 1990.

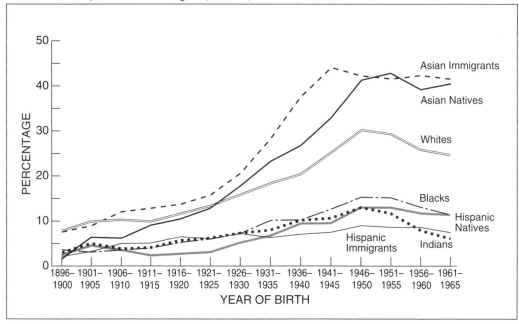

shrinkage of educational differences among racial-ethnic groups in elementary and high school, inequalities in ultimate educational attainment are pervasive and likely to persist for some time to come.

### Racial-Ethnic Differences in the 1980s

To examine more recent trends in racial-ethnic differences in attainment, one can again examine the school continuation probabilities for young persons, some of whom are still in school. Using the educational experiences of persons aged 7–24 in the 1980 and 1990 censuses, one can estimate the probabilities of continuing between successive levels of schooling. Within each census these probabilities taken together describe the educational transitions for a hypothetical group of persons who experienced the probabilities observed at each age level in the census.

Between 1980 and 1990 all major racial-ethnic groups increased their average rates of school continuation and levels of educational attainment. Although historical differentials among these groups compressed to some extent, they nonetheless persisted at some stages of schooling. Figures 4.11 and 4.12 present probabilities of school continuation for five major racial-ethnic groups for 1980

FIGURE 4.11   School continuation probabilities in high school and college, by racial-ethnic group: 1980 (1980 education codes).

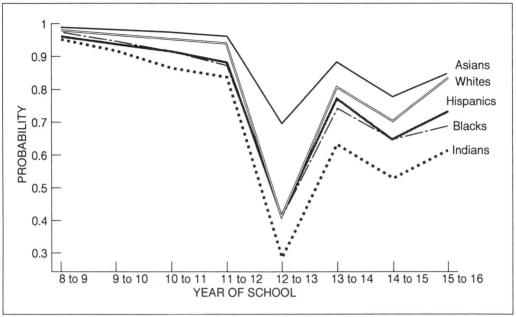

and 1990, respectively, as estimated from 1980-basis education codes for year-to-year transitions at the high school and college levels.[11] Racial-ethnic differences in school continuation probabilities emerge during high school and grow much larger at the transitions into and within college. Among the five groups considered here, Asians continued to enjoy the highest probabilities of school progression at each level of schooling, followed at some distance by whites. Blacks and Hispanics experienced similar progression probabilities, which were somewhat lower than those of non-Hispanic whites. Finally, at almost all transitions, American Indians had the lowest continuation probabilities. These differentials became somewhat smaller at the secondary school level and in the transition between high school and college from 1980 to 1990, but differentials in school progression among persons who reached college persisted. Indeed, at the transition from some college to attainment of a bachelor's degree some racial-ethnic differences grew. Progression probabilities for Asians and whites, which were already much higher than those for the other three groups in 1980, grew substantially between 1980 and 1990, whereas the corresponding probabilities for the other groups were largely unchanged. These trends follow a general historical pattern that applies to socioeconomic as well as racial-ethnic differentials. That is, inequality of educational attainment moves from earlier to later

FIGURE 4.12    School continuation probabilities in high school and college, by racial-ethnic group: 1990 (1980 education codes).

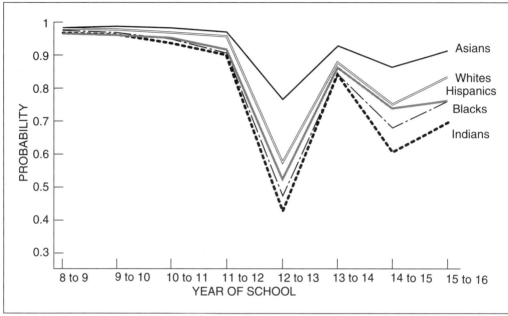

stages of the schooling process as average levels of attainment increase for all groups. As schooling becomes nearly universal at the elementary and secondary levels, inequalities are eliminated there, but inequalities persist or even increase at the postsecondary level (Mare 1981a; Hout, Raftery, and Bell 1993).

## FAMILY EFFECTS ON EDUCATIONAL ATTAINMENT

### Assessing the Effects of Family Background Factors in the 1980s

Children raised in families in which parents are well educated, have high family incomes, and bear small numbers of children go further in school than children of poorly educated, low-income, and high-fertility parents. Children raised in single-parent families tend to have lower high school graduation rates than their counterparts raised in two-parent families (Garfinkel and McLanahan 1986; McLanahan 1985). Secular increases in marital disruptions and in the proportion of births that are to unmarried women tend to increase the proportion of young persons who grow up in families that are unfavorable to educational success. In addition, low levels of growth in real incomes and stable birthrates during the late 1970s and 1980s may have eliminated some of the main sources of educational growth enjoyed by cohorts born earlier in this century. Given these facts, it is valuable to assess the effects of family factors on the chances that young persons remain in school.

*Parents' Schooling.*   Highly educated parents have higher educational expectations for their offspring and provide family environments more conducive to educational attainment. Secular increases in parents' educational attainment are an important component of educational growth in offspring cohorts (see, e.g., Hauser and Featherman 1976; Mare 1979). As parental education levels have increased, their variability has declined, which has tended to reduce the inequality in attainment of offspring. There is some evidence, however, that the educational attainments of mothers and fathers have become more alike in recent years because persons are increasingly likely to meet their mates in college or at work. Thus, successive cohorts of children are increasingly likely to have two parents who are both either highly educated or poorly educated. This trend tends to increase the combined variability of mother's and father's schooling, which may tend to increase the inequality of all children's educational attainment (Hauser and Featherman 1976; Mare 1991).

Among all racial-ethnic groups except Asians, the distribution of mothers' educational attainment shifted unambiguously upward during the 1980s. The largest increases in proportions of persons with mothers who have at least a high school diploma occurred for non-Hispanic blacks, Hispanics, and American Indians, groups with historically the lowest average attainment. Among Asians, a relatively large proportion of mothers have at least a bachelor's degree. This proportion increased markedly during the 1980s. At the same time, however, Asians had a relatively large proportion of mothers who have no high school education. The polarized distribution of maternal education for Asians appears to reflect the high overall average level of educational attainment in that population combined with a large number of recent poorly educated immigrants. Overall, the trends in maternal education between 1980 and 1990 may have been an important component of educational growth over the decade.

*Family Income.*   The socioeconomic standing of families affects the educational achievements of children. Prosperous families have more money to pay educational expenses and are less likely to create pressures upon their teenage members to work. In addition, children raised in such families enjoy better housing, clothing, quality of neighborhood, and so on, that derive from higher incomes and are likely to have the higher socioeconomic aspirations that higher-status families transmit to their children (Sewell and Hauser 1975). Thus, secular change in real family income may have contributed to changes in educational attainment.

Average family incomes did not change greatly between 1980 and 1990, although whites and blacks experienced modest real increases. The cross-section racial-ethnic differentials in family income reflect well-established patterns of relative affluence of whites and deprivation of Indians, blacks, and Hispanics. Whereas it is unlikely that income trends can account for trends in educational attainment, income differences among racial-ethnic groups are an important component of cross-section racial-ethnic differences in attainment.

*Family Structure and Size.*    School attendance and completion are affected by several aspects of family life apart from the socioeconomic characteristics of parents. First, children raised in female-headed families are less likely to graduate from high school than those raised in two-parent families. Single mothers who bear children tend to be economically disadvantaged. Married mothers whose marriages break up also suffer economic hardship and their children experience the disruptive effects of divorce on their social and intellectual development (Garfinkel and McLanahan 1986; McLanahan 1985). Secular growth in the proportion of children raised in female-headed families may have slowed rates of high school graduation and other indicators of educational achievement.

Second, the number of siblings in a family affects educational attainment. Attendance and completion rates vary inversely with family size, presumably because children from large families face more competition for family resources than children from small families. These resources include not only economic benefits but also the socioemotional benefits that parents can provide to their offspring (Blake 1989; Hauser and Sewell 1985; Mare and Chen 1986). Given declines in fertility since the late 1950s and the strong cross-sectional effect of number of siblings on schooling, declining family size may have been an important source of educational growth during the past three decades.

Among most racial-ethnic groups, the proportion of persons living in families headed by women grew between 1980 and 1990, reflecting the well-established pattern of secular growth in such families. Proportions of children who live only with their fathers increased, too, but by small amounts in each group. Given the negative association between single parenthood and educational success of offspring, these trends may have exerted downward pressure on school continuation probabilities between 1980 and 1990, although the quantitative importance of this component is likely to be small.

One of the biggest changes in family characteristics between 1980 and 1990 was the decline in average number of siblings. For all racial-ethnic groups, the proportion of persons with three or more siblings declined between 20 and 25 percentage points. In view of the negative effect of family size on educational attainment, these declines in family size may have been an important component of educational growth in the 1980s.

Variations in the distributions of family characteristics may partly account for levels of educational attainment as well as cross-section variation in school progression among racial-ethnic groups. Because the census obtains information only about coresident members of families and households (and not about kin who live elsewhere), these analyses are mainly restricted to young persons aged 7–24 who were living with at least one biological or step-parent at the date of the census.[12]

***Racial-Ethnic Makeup and Nativity.*** Racial-ethnic groups exhibit important differences in family background composition, both cross-sectionally and in the factors that changed the most between 1980 and 1990. Unlike blacks, whites, and Indians, Asians and Hispanics include a substantial foreign-born population, although the nativity status of the latter two groups differs markedly. Among Asians, the proportion of young persons who were born abroad grew from approximately 50 to 60 percent of the population, whereas among Hispanics the foreign-born share of the population grew from about 25 to 30 percent. The influx of immigrants altered the ethnic makeup of these two populations. Among Asians, the shares of the population made up by Koreans, Indians, Vietnamese, and others grew in the 1980s, while the relative size of the Japanese American population became smaller. Among Hispanics, the Mexican American share grew at the expense of the Cuban share. Because these groups vary considerably in their levels of educational attainment, and immigrants typically have lower levels of schooling, these changes may have exerted downward pressure on attainment levels of Asians and Hispanics.

## Census Measures of Family Background Effects

Schooling can be represented as a sequence of transitions that correspond to major milestones in the formal schooling process. This approach is well suited to the qualitative measure of educational attainment in the 1990 census and can reveal variation in the effects of family background across stages of schooling (Mare 1980). Moreover, this approach allows for the possibility that many people in the sample are only part way through their schooling careers. The analyses of school progression presented here focus on four transitions: (1) completion of ninth grade, (2) completion of a high school diploma or GED given completion of ninth grade, (3) completion of some college given completion of a high school diploma or GED, and (4) completion of a bachelor's degree given completion of some college.[13] Figures 4.13–4.16 display the net effects of family characteristics on the odds of school continuation for each of the four school transitions.

FIGURE 4.13    Effects of family background on odds of completing ninth grade.

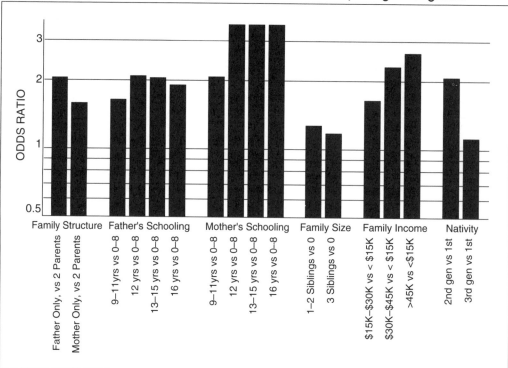

SOURCE: Decennial census for 1980 and 1990.

NOTE: Effects are based on a model that also includes effects of sex and race-ethnicity.

*Parents' Schooling.* Parents' schooling has a strong effect for all four school transitions. For example, persons whose mothers have a high school diploma are more than twice as likely to complete a high school diploma as those whose mothers have less schooling (Figure 4.14). Persons whose fathers or mothers have attended at least some college are nearly twice as likely to complete some college as those whose fathers or mothers did not attend college (Figure 4.15). (The effects of mother's or father's schooling applies only to persons who were living with their mother or father, respectively. Census data do not permit one to assess the effects of a parent's characteristics when the parent is absent.)[14] Typically, the effects of parental schooling exhibit a striking nonlinear pattern. The largest increment to the odds that offspring will make a given transition depends on whether or not the parent made that transition. For example, the largest contrast in odds of ninth grade completion is between those whose mothers attended some high school and those whose mothers had only grade school education; the largest contrast in odds of high school graduation is between those whose mothers were high school graduates and those whose

FIGURE 4.14  Effects of family background on odds of completing high school diploma, given completion of ninth grade.

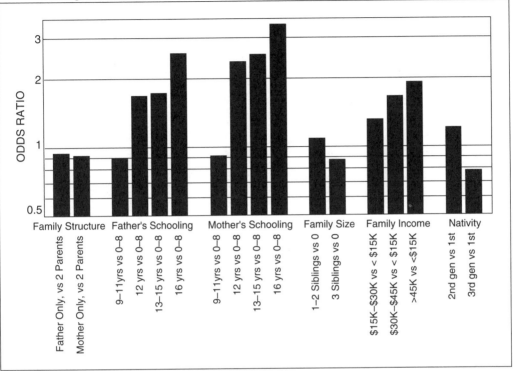

SOURCE: Decennial census for 1980 and 1990.

NOTE: Effects are based on a model that also includes effects of sex and race-ethnicity.

mothers dropped out before graduation; the largest contrast in odds of college attendance is between those whose mothers attended at least some college and those whose mothers had no college; and the largest contrast in the odds of college graduation is between those whose mothers graduated from college and those whose mothers had some college but no college degree (Figures 4.13–4.16). This pattern is somewhat starker for the effects of mother's schooling than of father's schooling, but it is observable for both parents. It strongly suggests that each successive generation constructs an educational "floor," below which its offspring are unlikely to fall, that provides a platform for further intergenerational growth.

*Family Income.* In 1980 and 1990, the effect of family income on the odds of school progression was substantial for all school transitions. Unlike the parental schooling effect, the income effect tends to be linear across broad income strata. The effect of income on the odds of school progression shows some tendency to decline from the earlier transitions to the later ones, suggesting that

FIGURE 4.15    Effects of family background on odds of completing some college, given completion of high school diploma.

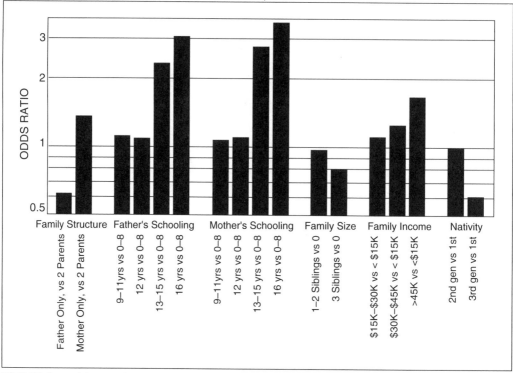

SOURCE: Decennial census for 1980 and 1990.

NOTE: Effects are based on a model that also includes effects of sex and race-ethnicity.

income indicates more than simply a family's capacity to meet the direct expenses of higher education. Income differences also reflect variation in the quality of schools and neighborhoods as well as other, unobserved dimensions of family socioeconomic standing that affect educational aspirations and achievement.

*Family Structure and Size.* The estimated effects on school progression of living with only one parent may be attenuated in census data because family structure is measured only at the census date and not at the stages of life when young persons are at risk to each school transition. Taking the estimated effects at face value, however, suggests that differences in rates of school progression between persons who live with one parent or both parents are limited to specific school transitions. The handicap faced by young persons living in a mother-only family is confined to the transition from high school attendance to high school graduation; in a father-only family, from high school to college.

Offspring with relatively large numbers of siblings have lower educational attainment than those with few siblings because both material and socioemo-

FIGURE 4.16    Effects of family background on odds of completing a college degree, given completion of some college.

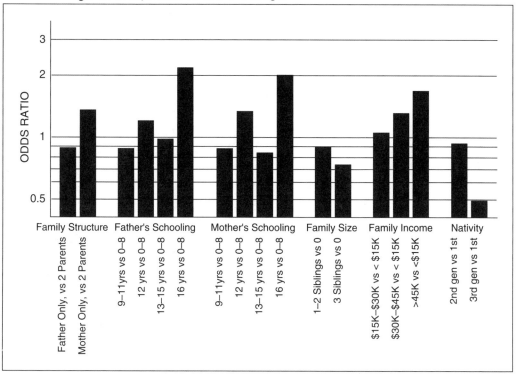

SOURCE: Decennial census for 1980 and 1990.

NOTE: Effects are based on a model that also includes effects of sex and race-ethnicity.

tional resources are spread more thinly in large families than in small ones. Among the school transitions considered here, the effects of sibship size are, for the most part, confined to the transitions from high school to college and from college to college graduation. For example, for persons with three siblings or more the odds of completing some college given high school graduation or of graduating from college given some college completion are only about 60 percent of the corresponding odds for those who are only children (Figure 4.15).

## RECENT TRENDS IN SCHOOL ENROLLMENT

Educational attainment is a characteristic that individuals carry with them throughout their lives, whereas school enrollment is both an activity that may engage an individual at a particular age and a component of eventual educational attainment. School enrollment rates signify the current rate at which schooling is "produced" and "consumed" in the population. This section briefly describes recent trends in school enrollment rates for children and young adults and then focuses on nursery and kindergarten where enrollment has increased significantly during the past decade. Preschool enrollment provides some indication of the extent to which individuals either have access to explicit programs to facilitate elementary schooling, such as Head Start, or are at least exposed to an educational environment at an early age. Because school enrollment rates in the 1980 and 1990 censuses are not comparable, the analyses reported in this section are based on the October 1979, 1980, 1989, and 1990 CPSs. To obtain enough observations for detailed analysis and to obtain measures that corresponded approximately to the census years of 1980 and 1990, the 1979 and 1980 and the 1989 and 1990 CPSs were pooled.[15] In contrast to the census, the CPS does not identify Asian and Native American persons. Thus, the racial-ethnic groups considered are non-Hispanic whites, non-Hispanic blacks, and Hispanics.

Figure 4.17 shows percentages of persons enrolled in school in 1979–1980 and 1989–1990 for two-year age groups for three racial-ethnic groups. During the 1980s school enrollment rates increased at the youngest and oldest ages, continuing a century-long pattern of educational growth from the middle-childhood years toward infancy and young adulthood (Duncan 1968). This trend is particularly strong for whites. For whites aged 3–4, enrollment increased by about 8 percentage points; at the traditional college ages, by about 10 percentage points; and, in the mid-20s and early 30s, by 3–5 percentage points. Blacks and Hispanics in their 20s experienced slightly smaller increases than whites did, while enrollment rates were stable for those in their 30s or in the preschool ages. Increased enrollment beyond the traditional college ages reflects both increasing rates of continuation to advanced degree programs and intermittent and part-time enrollment on the way to obtaining a bachelor's degree. At the preschool level, increased enrollment rates may be a result of increased rates of labor force participation of young mothers, although other social trends may have contributed to this increase as well.

The importance of preschool education for young children prior to ages of compulsory school attendance is now widely accepted, especially as a means of facilitating the achievement of groups who have been traditionally educationally disadvantaged, and has given rise to demands for increases in funding for Head Start and similar preschool programs (U.S. General Accounting Office 1992). While nursery school and kindergarten are enriching educational experiences for many children, for children from single-parent families, families in which both parents work, and families that cannot afford individualized child care arrangements, their function may often be more custodial than educational. Although these children may be more likely to enroll in nursery school and kindergarten, preschool education, much of which is privately funded, is more easily available to children from socioeconomically advantaged families.[16]

FIGURE 4.17 Percentage enrolled in school, by age, racial-ethnic group, and year.

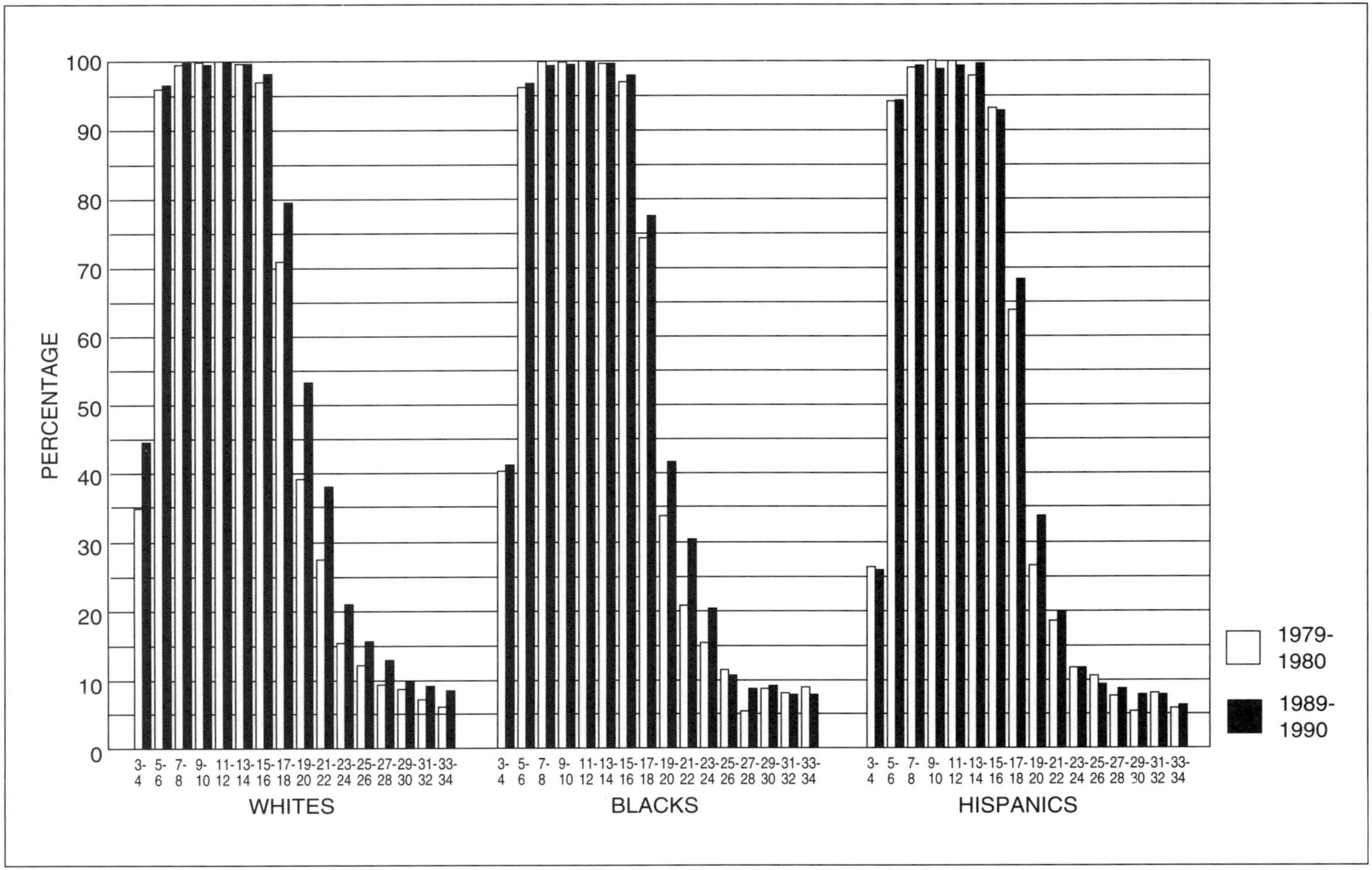

185

Figure 4.18 illustrates the effects of a variety of family factors on the odds of nursery school or kindergarten enrollment for children aged 3–5. In this figure each effect is estimated holding other factors constant.[17] Children whose mothers work were about 40 percent more likely to attend nursery school or kindergarten than children whose mothers do not work. Similarly, children from single-parent families headed by mothers were about 40 percent more likely to attend preschool than children from two-parent families. Larger than the effects of maternal employment and family structure, however, are the effects of family size and the socioeconomic characteristics of the parents. The odds of attendance for only children were about 75 percent higher than the odds for children who have three siblings or more. On the one hand, in larger families older siblings may be available to substitute for nursery school care. On the other, parents with many children may be less able to afford private nursery school. Mother's educational attainment also has a strong positive effect on the odds of preschool enrollment. Children whose mothers were college graduates were almost twice as likely to attend nursery school or kindergarten as children whose mothers graduated from high school but did not attend college. That this effect is so large even among mothers who have the same employment status strongly suggests that better-educated parents are more likely to value formal early childhood education. Finally, children from economically advantaged families were much more likely to attend nursery school or kindergarten. Children from families with incomes over $45,000 were about twice as likely to attend as children from families with incomes under $30,000, suggesting that families are indeed economically constrained in their ability to send their children to preschool. Whatever the educational benefits of preschool attendance, like the benefits of elementary, secondary, and postsecondary schooling, they are enjoyed disproportionately by children from socioeconomically advantaged backgrounds.

Figure 4.19 illustrates changes in the distributions of several family factors that affect nursery and kindergarten attendance. For the most part, the family characteristics of children aged 3–5 changed during the 1980s in similar fashion to families as a whole. The family incomes of young children grew more unequal over the decade, as indicated by the relative growth in the proportion of children from families earning more than $45,000 and less than $15,000 (adjusted to constant 1989 dollars). The average education of mothers of young children increased dramatically during the 1980s, reflecting the large secular increases in college attendance and completion in the cohorts of women who are most likely to be mothers of young children in the late 1980s. The proportion of children whose mothers work also increased sharply during the decade. Finally, the proportion of children who were raised in single-parent families also increased between 1980 and 1990.

When combined with the strong effects of these factors on the likelihood that children are enrolled in nursery school or kindergarten, the changing characteris-

FIGURE 4.18 Effects of selected family factors on odds of enrollment for children aged 3–5: 1980 and 1990.

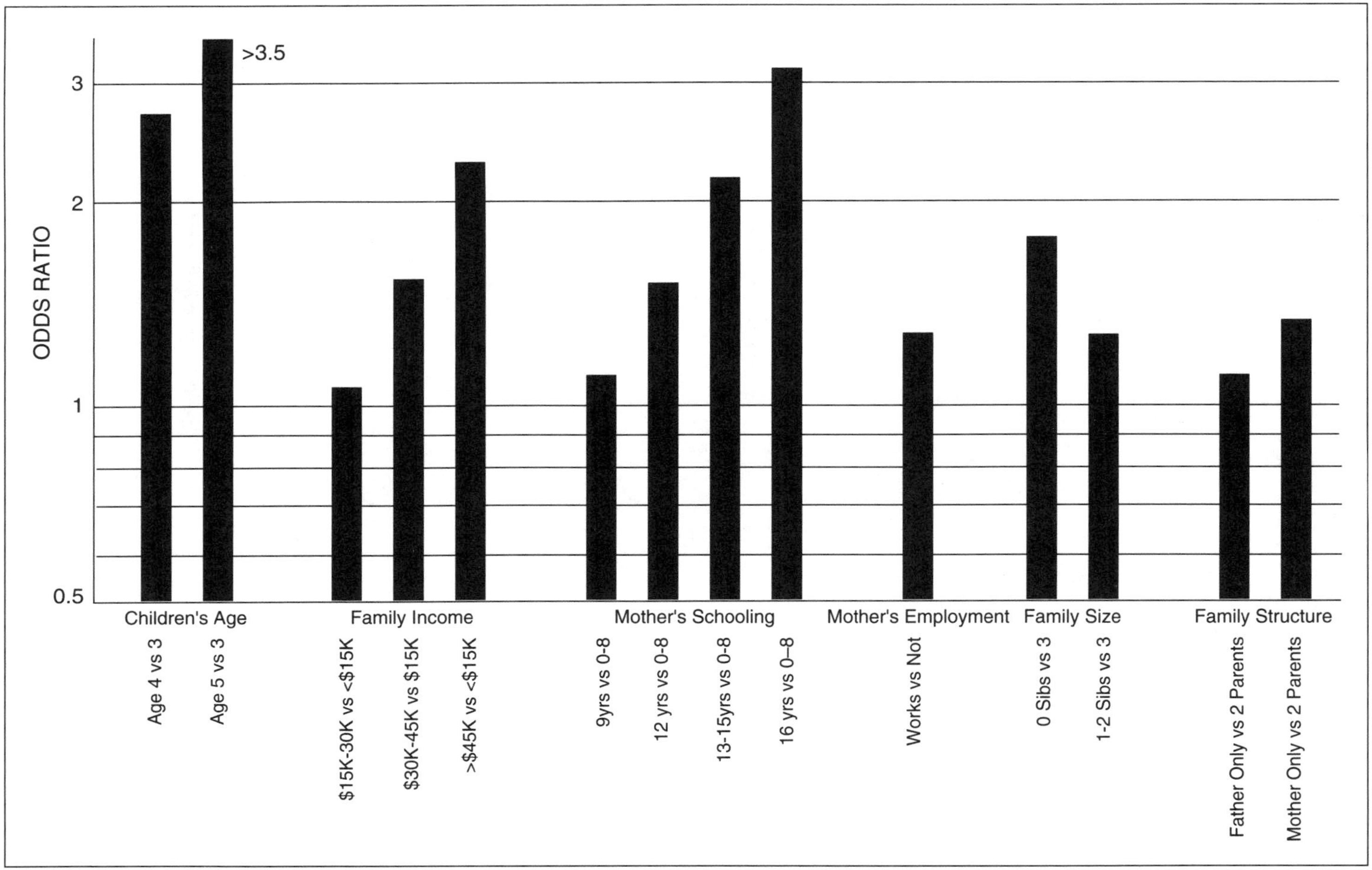

SOURCE: Current Population Survey for October 1979, 1980, 1989, and 1990.

187

FIGURE 4.19   Family characteristics of children aged 3–5: 1980 and 1990.

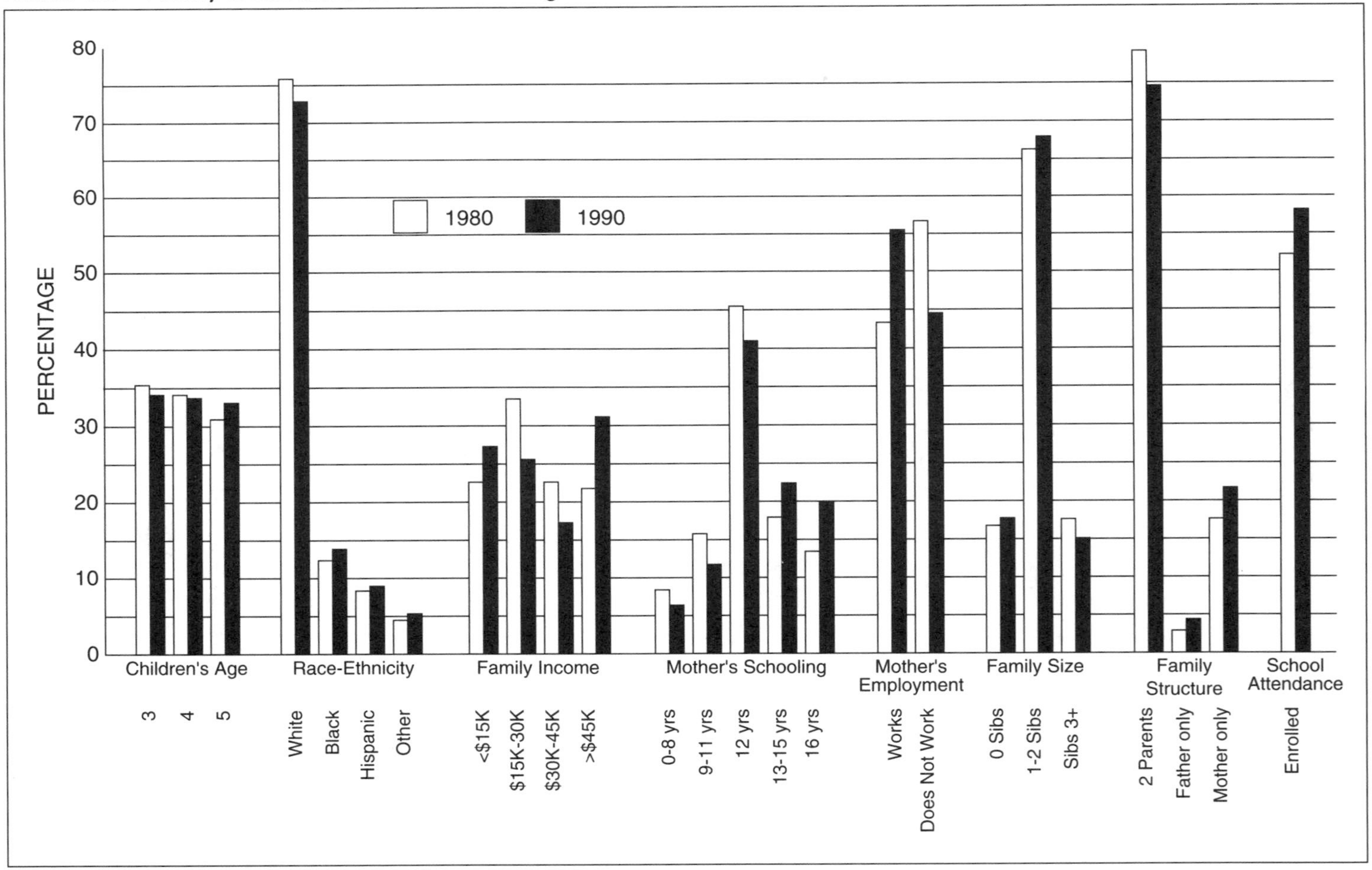

SOURCE: Current Population Survey for October 1979, 1980, 1989, and 1990.

188

tics of families may account for increases in rates of attendance over the decade. Figure 4.20 plots the estimated probability of attending nursery school or kindergarten in 1980 and 1990 for each racial-ethnic group. For each group, the first pair of bars denotes the observed proportion of children aged 3–5 who attended preschool in 1980 and 1990. The second pair of bars denotes the expected proportion who would have attended if all the racial-ethnic groups had the same distributions of the characteristics shown in Figure 4.19 and if these distributions had not changed over the decade. For whites, the actual rate of attendance increased between 1980 and 1990 by about 8 percentage points. If the average characteristics of white children had not changed, then their rate of attendance would have increased by only 4 percentage points. Thus, for white children, changes in family characteristics account for about half of the observed change in attendance rates, and changes in enrollment rates *within* specific categories of the characteristics shown in Figure 4.19 account for the other half of the change in attendance. For blacks and Hispanics, the actual increases in attendance were 5 and 9 percentage points, respectively. When changes in family factors are taken into account, however, all of the observed increases are eliminated, indicating that changes in family characteristics fully account for increases in nursery school and kindergarten enrollment for these groups. In other words, among whites there was a shift toward higher enrollment rates net of family background factors, but among blacks and Hispanics there was not.

Figure 4.20 also illustrates how differences in the distributions of family background characteristics between racial-ethnic groups account for differences in their nursery and kindergarten enrollment rates. In both 1980 and 1990, the actual enrollment rates of Hispanic children were considerably lower than those of white children. For example, in 1990, about 50 percent of Hispanic children were enrolled compared with about 60 percent of white children. If white and Hispanic children had the same family characteristics, however, this gap in enrollment rates would have been much smaller. The enrollment rates of white and black children were in fact similar in both 1980 and 1990. If black children had the same distributions of family characteristics as white children, their enrollment rates would have been markedly *higher* than those of white children. Thus, the rates of preschool attendance for racial-ethnic minorities would be significantly higher if they enjoyed the same favorable levels of family income and maternal schooling as whites.

In summary, levels of nursery school and kindergarten attendance increased markedly in the 1980s, a trend that is largely attributable to increases in mother's schooling, increases in proportions of children whose mothers work, and increasing proportions of single-parent families. Secular increases in mother's schooling are likely to bring about further increases in preschool enrollment, although many families will continue to be unable to afford private nursery schools.

FIGURE 4.20   Observed and adjusted probabilities of nursery or kindergarten enrollment of children aged 3–5: 1980 and 1990.

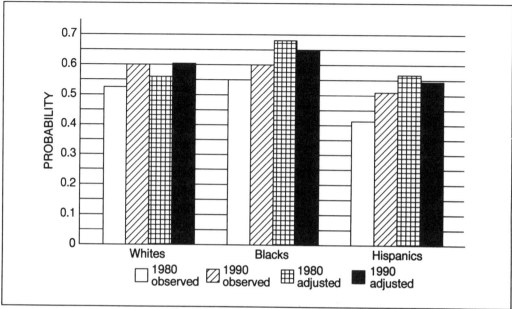

SOURCE: Current Population Survey for October 1979, 1980, 1989, and 1990.

NOTE: Probabilities are adjusted for age, income, mother's schooling, mother's employment, family size, and family structure.

## RECENT TRENDS IN ACADEMIC ACHIEVEMENT

The trends discussed thus far show unambiguously a continued upswing in the quantity of schooling received by young Americans, but is increased schooling accompanied by increased learning? How far one goes in school plays a role in how well one does in the labor market. But technological changes in the workplace and an increasingly competitive international economy have put new pressures on American workers to be literate, numerate, and capable of adapting to change. In recent decades there has been a national outcry about the quality of the nation's schools and adequacy of the skills that young persons bring from schools to their jobs. Compared with their counterparts in other industrialized nations, students in the United States do poorly on tests of mathematics and science knowledge and reasoning. The 1990–1991 International Assessment of Educational Progress provided information on the performance of students aged 9 and 13 on a standardized battery of mathematics and science tests in a number of nations. For example, for 13-year-olds, among the 15 nations with high rates of participation in the study, the United States ranked 14th on mathematics performance. Students from the United States averaged 55 percent correct on the test, lagging behind Korea (73 percent), the former Soviet Union (70 percent), Hungary (68 percent), France (64 percent), Canada (62 percent), and eight other competitors (U.S. Department of Education 1993: 415). This type of result has spurred the development of numerous policies and programs designed to improve the effectiveness of students and their schools. Examples of these efforts include broadened support for Head Start programs that will improve the readiness of young children for elementary school, increased salaries for public school teachers, competency tests for teachers, and more demanding coursework requirements for receiving a high school diploma. Absent carefully designed evaluation studies, it is difficult to assess whether any specific set of programs has affected the academic proficiency of students. Nationwide standardized assessments of student progress, however, that have been conducted since the mid 1970s provide a basis for a general discussion of trends.

Table 4.2 shows average numbers of year-long courses taken during high school for students who graduated in 1982 and 1990. These trends show that students are indeed taking more courses during high school, an average of about 2.5 courses per student per year over the four years of high school. Two aspects of these trends are heartening. First, students are taking more courses in core academic areas—a third of a year of English, a half year of mathematics, a full year of science, and about a half year of history and social science. By contrast, students are taking fewer vocational courses in such areas as business, agricul-

TABLE 4.2   Numbers of courses taken in high school,
              by racial-ethnic group, subject matter, and graduating class.

|  | 1982 | 1990 | Change | 1982 | 1990 | Change |
|---|---|---|---|---|---|---|
|  | All Courses | | | English | | |
| Whites | 21.4 | 23.6 | 2.2 | 3.8 | 4.0 | 0.2 |
| Blacks | 20.5 | 23.4 | 2.9 | 3.9 | 4.2 | 0.3 |
| Hispanics | 20.8 | 23.9 | 3.1 | 3.8 | 4.4 | 0.6 |
| Total | 21.2 | 23.6 | 2.4 | 3.8 | 4.1 | 0.3 |
|  | Mathematics | | | Science and Computer Science | | |
| Whites | 2.6 | 3.1 | 0.5 | 2.4 | 3.3 | 0.9 |
| Blacks | 2.4 | 3.1 | 0.7 | 2.1 | 3.3 | 1.2 |
| Hispanics | 2.2 | 3.1 | 0.9 | 1.9 | 3.0 | 1.1 |
| Total | 2.5 | 3.1 | 0.6 | 2.3 | 3.3 | 1.0 |
|  | History and Social Science | | | Vocational Education | | |
| Whites | 3.2 | 3.6 | 0.4 | 3.9 | 3.3 | −0.6 |
| Blacks | 3.0 | 3.4 | 0.4 | 4.2 | 3.5 | −0.7 |
| Hispanics | 2.9 | 3.5 | 0.6 | 4.6 | 3.2 | −1.4 |
| Total | 3.1 | 3.5 | 0.4 | 4.0 | 3.2 | −0.8 |

SOURCE: U.S. Department of Education (1993).

ture, occupational home economics, and marketing. Second, blacks and Hispanics—groups who are traditionally disadvantaged in the quality of their schooling, academic achievement, and educational attainment—experience a greater increase in total number of courses and in courses in basic academic areas than students as a whole.

A more direct indication of the trend in academic performance is provided by students' average performances on the National Assessment of Educational Progress (NAEP). Table 4.3 reports changes between 1979–1980 and 1989–1990 for reading, mathematics, and science for students aged 9 and 17. With the exception of reading scores for 9-year-olds, the data indicate improved academic proficiency during the 1980s. Paralleling the trend in coursework, the improvement in academic performance was particularly large for black and Hispanic students. Although gaps in performance on standardized tests between these groups and white students persisted, the gaps became significantly smaller during the 1980s. Although it may be tempting to ascribe the trends in Table 4.3 to the changing coursework patterns shown in Table 4.2, it should be stressed that many social changes may have contributed. Some aspects of the family backgrounds of students—such as the average educational attainments of their parents—became more favorable to academic achievement during the 1980s. Tougher coursework requirements for high school students are only one of a number of initiatives that have been taken to improve academic performance. Early childhood education programs, for example, are much more likely to affect the achievements of 9-year-olds than an increasingly rigorous high school program.

From the data presented in Table 4.3, it is difficult to assess the magnitude of the changes observed in the 1980s. On balance, however, these changes should be regarded as small. The possible range of test scores is between 0 and 500. The changes between 1979–1980 and 1989–1990 are, for the most part, small compared with the differences in average scores between racial-ethnic groups and between age groups. These changes, moreover, did not narrow the performance gaps between students in the United States and other nations, which remained large in 1990. Some idea of the size of the changes can be obtained by examining Scholastic Aptitude Tests (SAT), which are taken by a much more selective population—high school students bound for selective colleges—than the NAEP tests, but for which a longer time series is available. Average SAT verbal and mathematics scores increased steadily from World War II until the late 1960s, at which time they began a decline that lasted until about 1980. Since 1980, SAT mathematics scores have increased, returning approximately to their 1974 level, but not yet to their level in the late 1960s. Verbal SAT scores remained essentially unchanged throughout the 1980s. Taken together, the SAT and NAEP trends suggest that the academic proficiency of the high school population as a whole improved modestly in the 1980s.

These qualifications notwithstanding, however, the improvements in test per-

TABLE 4.3  Academic proficiency scores,
by age, racial-ethnic group, and subject matter.

| | Age 9 | | | Age 17 | | |
|---|---|---|---|---|---|---|
| | 1979–1980[a] | 1989–1990 | Change | 1979–1980[a] | 1989–1990 | Change |
| Reading | | | | | | |
| Whites | 221 | 217 | −4 | 293 | 297 | +4 |
| Blacks | 189 | 182 | −7 | 243 | 267 | +24 |
| Hispanics | 190 | 189 | −1 | 261 | 275 | +14 |
| Total | 215 | 209 | −6 | 285 | 290 | +5 |
| Mathematics | | | | | | |
| Whites | 224 | 235 | +11 | 304 | 310 | +6 |
| Blacks | 195 | 208 | +13 | 272 | 289 | +17 |
| Hispanics | 204 | 214 | +10 | 277 | 284 | +7 |
| Total | 219 | 230 | +11 | 299 | 305 | +6 |
| Science | | | | | | |
| Whites | 229 | 238 | +9 | 293 | 301 | +8 |
| Blacks | 187 | 196 | +9 | 235 | 253 | +18 |
| Hispanics | 189 | 206 | +17 | 249 | 262 | +13 |
| Total | 221 | 229 | +8 | 283 | 290 | +7 |

SOURCE: U.S. Department of Education (1993).

[a]Mathematics and science scores are for 1981–1982.

formance by minorities during the 1980s were remarkable. That the overall trajectory is positive, moreover, suggests that students who have recently left high school are better prepared for higher education or for demanding employment than were their counterparts a decade earlier.

## THE TRANSITION FROM SCHOOL TO EMPLOYMENT

### The Age Profile of Employment for Young Adults

Among men, and to an increasing extent among women, young adulthood is a time of transition from full-time schooling to full-time work. The timing and success of a person's transition to employment depends on his or her educational attainment in a number of important ways. First, among persons of a given age who are out of school, those who stayed in school longer have accumulated less work experience than those who left school early. The advantage in work experience of leaving school early, however, dissipates as persons age inasmuch as their better-educated counterparts eventually become highly experienced workers, too. Second, persons who obtain more schooling are able to improve their employment chances because such persons are, on average, more desirable to prospective employers. This also implies that among persons who are out of school, rates of employment will rise with age as persons who have more schooling gradually enter the labor force (Mare, Winship, and Kubitschek 1984). Finally, persons with varying amounts of schooling are prepared to a varying extent for the specific demands of employers. Some postsecondary school programs are occupationally oriented (e.g., teaching or nursing degrees) or at least provide specific credentials that employers seek (e.g., bachelor's degrees in business or engineering). At the secondary school level such specific links are far less common than at either the postsecondary level or the secondary level in other nations. This has given rise to calls for the implementation of apprenticeship programs similar to those in some European nations to provide vocational opportunities for noncollege-bound youths (U.S. General Accounting Office 1992). Given the complex relationship between educational attainment and the transition from school to work, it is instructive to look at the employment and earnings of young men and women at various ages who have acquired varying amounts of schooling. These trends provide a general picture of the relationship between schooling and work and how it has changed over time.

Figures 4.21–4.24 present the percentages of out-of-school persons aged 16–35 who were employed in the week prior to the census by age, educational attainment, sex, and census year.[18] Such estimates provide a rough indication of the "age pattern of employment" experienced by persons with varying levels of educational attainment and work experience. Within each census, however, the way that employment varies with age may reflect not only the effect of aging on employment but also differences in employment between members of different birth cohorts.[19]

Rates of employment vary markedly among young persons with differing amounts of schooling and between men and women. Although men are more likely to work than women, this gap narrowed markedly between 1980 and 1990, a change that occurred to a greater extent among more highly educated persons. Except for high school dropouts, this change occurred only because rates of employment for women increased, not because of a decline in employment for men. Among college-educated women in both censuses, rates of employment appeared to decline with age, albeit to a lesser extent in 1990 than in 1980, largely because each new cohort of adult women participates in the paid labor force at a higher rate. Although it appears that women work less as they grow older, in fact they work at approximately the same rate throughout their early adult years. The women aged 30–35 in Figures 4.21–4.24 were working at about the same rate as when they were in their 20s; the women in their 20s will continue to work at their current rate when they are in their 30s and thus at a higher rate than women who are currently in their 30s. Younger women have higher employment rates than older women not because employment declines with age, but because successive cohorts of women experience secular increases in labor force participation. Within each census women in their 30s

FIGURE 4.21 Percentage employed among out-of-school persons with fewer than 12 years of school.

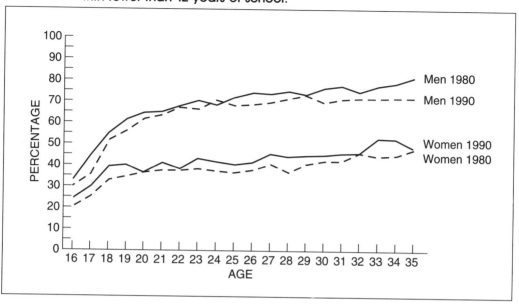

FIGURE 4.22 Percentage employed among out-of-school persons with 12 years of school.

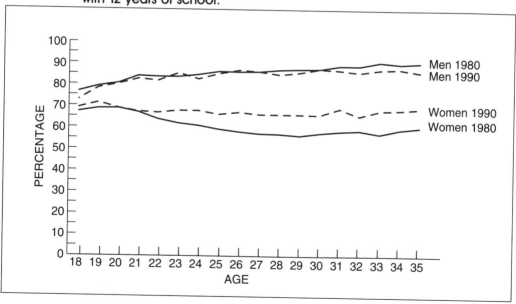

FIGURE 4.23 Percentage employed among out-of-school persons with some college but no degree.

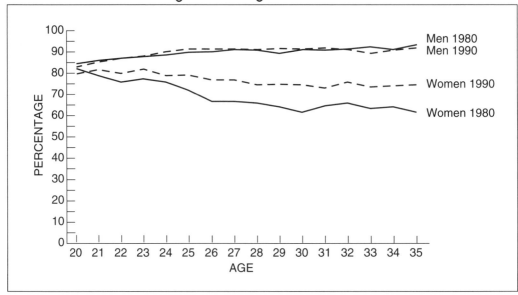

FIGURE 4.24 Percentage employed among out-of-school persons with at least a bachelor's degree.

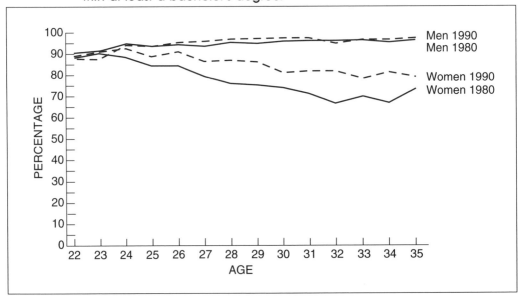

entered the paid labor force at a time when employment opportunities for women were fewer than they were for their younger counterparts. This cohort difference in employment opportunities at the start of women's careers may have persisted over time.[20]

Both the level and the timing of employment vary across educational attainment groups. Out-of-school persons with more schooling are more likely to be employed than their counterparts with less schooling. Among men aged 30, for example, about 70 percent of high school dropouts, 80 percent of high school graduates, 90 percent of persons with some college, and over 90 percent of college graduates were employed. In addition, the transition into employment appears to be much smoother for college-educated persons than for persons with less schooling. The percentage employed of college-educated men is almost constant across ages, suggesting that the transition to employment is smooth and direct. Among men who are high school dropouts and, to a lesser extent, high school graduates, employment varies directly with age during the teens and early 20s. Poorly educated workers have a harder time and take longer to find stable employment than their better-educated counterparts. With the exception of high school dropouts, the level and age pattern of employment for young men was essentially stable between 1980 and 1990. Among dropouts, the percentage employed at most ages declined between 1 and 5 percentage points. Men without a high school diploma, who have become a smaller proportion of successive birth cohorts, fared worse in 1990 than in 1980. Educational attainment at all levels of schooling continues to be a pathway to improved employment prospects for men and women. For men, a high school diploma or better was required to avoid an increasing chance of joblessness during the 1980s.

### Racial-Ethnic Differences in Employment

The patterns shown thus far suggest that persons with a high school diploma are disadvantaged in employment relative to college-educated persons, but this disadvantage has not worsened over time. It nonetheless remains possible that there is additional variation (beyond sex and educational attainment) in the population in the success with which young persons make the transition from school to work and that the transition from school to work has not been stable for all groups. In particular, there was considerable concern during the 1970s and 1980s about the economic prospects for young blacks. Although high school graduation rates have risen for blacks since 1970, during this period young blacks have experienced unprecedentedly high rates of unemployment, suggesting that for at least some African Americans the transition from school to work may have become more difficult since 1980 (Freeman and Holzer 1986; Mare and Winship 1984).

Figures 4.25 and 4.26 show percentage employed by educational attainment,

FIGURE 4.25 Percentage employed among out-of-school men aged 16–35, by racial-ethnic group, educational attainment, and year.

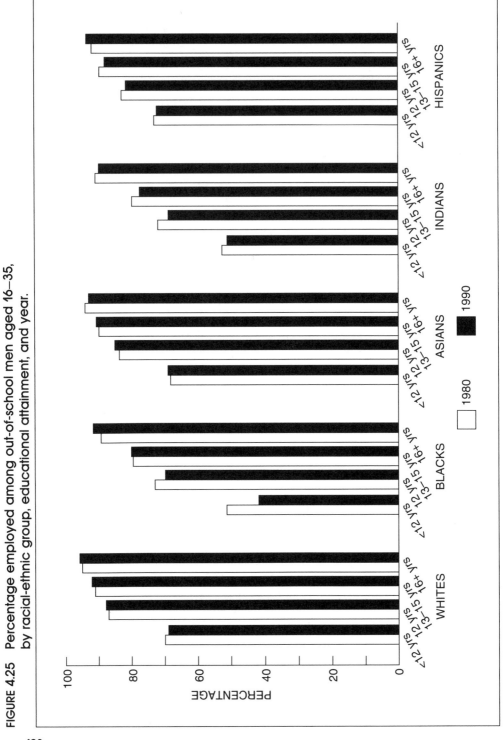

FIGURE 4.26 Percentage employed among out-of-school women aged 16–35, by racial-ethnic group, educational attainment, and year.

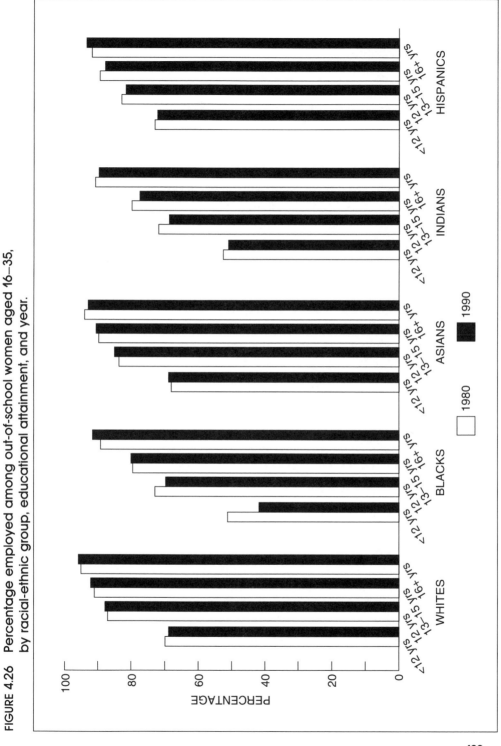

racial-ethnic group, and census year for men and women aged 16–35. Blacks and Indians had the lowest percentages employed in 1980 and experienced unfavorable changes during the 1980s compared with the other three groups. The proportion employed among young black male high school dropouts fell by 10 percentage points during the decade. Data not shown here indicate that this large decline is not restricted to the teenage years, but occurs at virtually every age between 16 and 34. White, Asian, and Hispanic employment rates for male high school graduates were stable over the decade. Among women, black college graduates were more likely to be employed than any other group, including white women, but employment rates for black women with less education grew much more slowly than those for the white majority. Percentages employed were stable for black female high school graduates over this period; in contrast, the female high school graduate population as a whole experienced markedly increased employment rates over the decade. Among blacks with a college degree, employment rates were stable during the 1980s. This stability preserved the employment gap between black men and the rest of the population. For women, however, the employment gap widened as a result of the large increase in employment for college-educated women as a whole. Percentages employed fell sharply for Native American women over the decade.

Using employment as a criterion, the patterns for the population of persons who have recently left school and for blacks in this group indicate a stable transition from school to work for better-educated persons and for the majority of the population, as well as a continuation of the secular trend toward increased employment of women. For persons with low levels of schooling and for the traditionally disadvantaged black and Native American minorities, however, this transition is becoming increasingly difficult. For these persons, the proportion holding jobs shortly after leaving school was lower in 1990 than 1980.

## EDUCATION AND THE OCCUPATIONS OF YOUNG WORKERS

In addition to the employment status of young persons who have recently left school, an important indication of their economic well-being is the *kind* of job held. Persons who are still in school are often aware of the occupational opportunities experienced by those who were just a few years ahead of them in school. These perceptions may affect their decisions about how far to go in school, what fields to major in, and what skills and training to seek. During the 1980s, the occupational structure of the American economy underwent a variety of shifts that resulted from changes in the international economy, in technology, and in women's access to economic opportunity. The U.S. domestic economy increasingly emphasized the provision of services at the expense of manufacturing industries. Global economic competition, combined with the actions of

American corporations to move production to other nations with lower-priced labor led to a decline in manufacturing employment. This trend hurt many American workers who had only a high school education and who for a generation had enjoyed relatively well-paying skilled and semiskilled positions in manufacturing. This change also meant that new cohorts of high school graduates who did not continue to college often had to settle for jobs in the service sector, jobs with less pay and less job security than the blue collar industrial jobs that had employed their counterparts in the previous generation.[21]

The use of computers became important in the 1970s and accelerated in the 1980s. In all sectors of the economy computer technology altered the way that goods were manufactured and sold and that services were delivered. This changed the content of many jobs, typically requiring the adoption of new skills by workers, created new jobs, and eliminated others. It also fueled the computer industry itself, creating new employment for those who design, manufacture, sell, and maintain electronic equipment and the requisite software. These changes created new fields of employment, typically available only to persons with some form of postsecondary education.

During the 1970s and 1980s there was a gradual breakdown of barriers to lucrative employment for women, who received advanced degrees in unprecedented numbers in fields traditionally dominated by men, such as business, law, and medicine. These changes have been both the cause and the consequence of more women achieving employment in these fields. Conversely, proportionately fewer women are working in the less lucrative and traditionally "female" positions. Although the segregation of occupations by sex in the U.S. work force remained in 1990, the 1980s were a decade of substantial change.[22]

Table 4.4 illustrates these patterns by listing the ten leading civilian occupations for out-of-school persons aged 16–34 in 1990, as well as the ranks of these positions in 1980, for both high school and college graduates. It also lists the occupations that dropped out of the top ten between 1980 and 1990. Although the leading occupations did not change greatly between 1980 and 1990 for male high school graduates, some of the larger changes in the economy are nonetheless discernible. The disappearance from the list of machine operators and welders and cutters illustrates the decline in skilled and semiskilled blue collar manufacturing employment. Taking the places of these two occupations are construction laborers, who are typically unskilled workers, and sales supervisors and proprietors. Although sales supervisors are heterogeneous, encompassing positions in both large and small establishments, their growth among high school graduates reflects the substantial growth of service industries such as retail trade.

The leading occupations for male college graduates reveal the dramatic growth of jobs relating to the provision of computers and computer services. The three new entrants to the list—programmers, computer scientists, and elec-

TABLE 4.4 Ten leading occupations of high school and college graduates aged 16–34, by sex, year, and rank: 1980 and 1990.

**Men**

**High School Graduates**

| Occupation | 1980 | 1990 |
|---|---|---|
| Truck drivers | 1 | 1 |
| Carpenters | 4 | 2 |
| Auto mechanics | 5 | 3 |
| Janitors and cleaners | 8 | 4 |
| Supervisors and proprietors, sales | 12 | 5 |
| Laborers, excluding construction | 3 | 6 |
| Construction laborers | 11 | 7 |
| Managers and administrators, nec* | 2 | 8 |
| Cooks | 9 | 9 |
| Assemblers | 7 | 10 |
| (Machine operators, nec*) | 6 | 13 |
| (Welders and cutters) | 10 | 12 |

**College Graduates**

| Occupation | 1980 | 1990 |
|---|---|---|
| Managers and administrators, nec* | 1 | 1 |
| Accountants and auditors | 2 | 2 |
| Supervisors and proprietors, sales | 9 | 3 |
| Lawyers | 5 | 4 |
| Sales representatives, mining, manufacturing, and wholesale | 4 | 5 |
| Computer programmers | 13 | 6 |
| Electrical and electronic engineers | 11 | 7 |
| Physicians | 7 | 8 |
| Computer systems analysts and scientists | 23 | 9 |
| Teachers, elementary school | 3 | 10 |
| (Teachers, secondary school) | 6 | 18 |
| (Managers, marketing, advertising, and public relations) | 8 | 12 |
| (Supervisors, production occupations) | 10 | >25 |

**Women**

**High School Graduates**

| Occupation | 1980 | 1990 |
|---|---|---|
| Secretaries | 1 | 1 |
| Cashiers | 3 | 2 |
| Waitresses | 5 | 3 |
| Nursing aides, orderlies, and attendants | 6 | 4 |
| Bookkeepers, accountants, and auditing clerks | 2 | 5 |
| Supervisors and proprietors, sales | 20 | 6 |
| General office clerks | 4 | 7 |
| Managers and administrators, nec* | 10 | 8 |
| Receptionists | 15 | 9 |
| Cooks | 17 | 10 |
| (Typists) | 7 | 17 |
| (Sales workers, other commodities) | 8 | 13 |
| (Assemblers) | 9 | 12 |

**College Graduates**

| Occupation | 1980 | 1990 |
|---|---|---|
| Teachers, elementary school | 1 | 1 |
| Registered nurses | 2 | 2 |
| Accountants and auditors | 7 | 3 |
| Managers and administrators, nec* | 4 | 4 |
| Secretaries | 5 | 5 |
| Supervisors and proprietors, sales | 12 | 6 |
| Social workers | 6 | 7 |
| Lawyers | 16 | 8 |
| Computer programmers | 20 | 9 |
| Bookkeepers, accountants, and auditing clerks | 10 | 10 |
| (Teachers, secondary school) | 3 | 11 |
| (Clinical laboratory technologists and technicians) | 8 | 23 |
| (General office clerks) | 9 | >25 |

* nec = not elsewhere classified.

trical engineers—illustrate this trend. The rising importance of supervisory positions in sales and the decline of production supervisors also reflect the growth of the service sector and the decline of manufacturing.

Trends for women show that the benefits of reduced barriers to women's employment are largely confined to highly educated women. Among high school graduates, changes in the leading occupations are attributable to the same broad forces that affect men: that is, the rise of service employment (rise of sales supervisors), the decline of manufacturing (decline of assemblers), and the computerization of office work (decline of typists). The occupations of college-educated women, in contrast, show increasing representation of women in well-paying jobs traditionally dominated by men. Although many women continue to be employed in traditional occupations—elementary school teaching, nursing, and secretarial—others are now lawyers and computer programmers, titles that make up a significant share of employment for male college graduates. Conversely, highly educated women are significantly less likely to become laboratory technicians and office clerks than they were, changes which signify that better opportunities are available elsewhere.

## EDUCATION AND THE WAGES OF YOUNG WORKERS

### The Age-Wage Profile for Young Workers

As illustrated in the discussion of occupational trends, schools sort and rank individuals for positions in the labor market. From the standpoint of the individual, the anticipated economic rewards are incentives for persistence in school. Employment signifies attachment to the labor force and, in principle, access to a predictable and independent means of economic support. It does not, however, indicate the level of support that it can provide. To examine the role that schooling plays in determining economic well-being and whether this relationship has shifted over time, it is valuable to examine the wages of young persons with varying amounts of schooling.

Figures 4.27–4.30 show the hourly wage rates of employed out-of-school young men and women in 1979 and 1989, adjusted to constant 1989 dollars.[23] Unlike the trend for employment, which was stable or improving for all persons except male high school dropouts, the wage data indicate a substantially worsening economic condition for most young persons. Among young men who had not completed any college, the median wage dropped by one to two dollars at virtually every age between 18 and 34. The deteriorating wage prospects for young workers, moreover, were not confined to the first few years after leaving school. The real drop in wages was approximately constant from the teenage years into the 30s. The wages of young women who had not completed any

FIGURE 4.27  Estimated median hourly wage for out-of-school employed persons without a high school diploma.

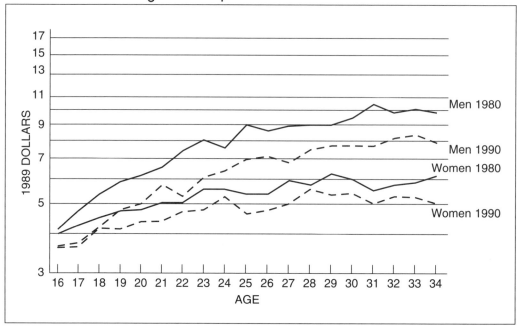

FIGURE 4.28  Estimated median hourly wage for out-of-school employed persons with 12 years of school/high school diploma.

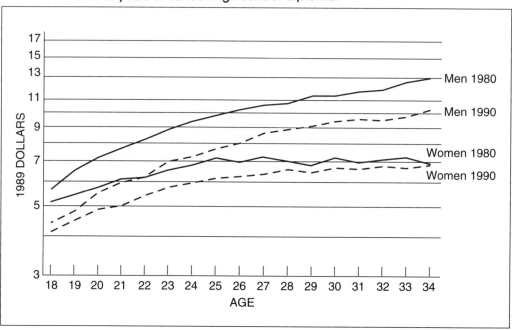

FIGURE 4.29   Estimated median hourly wage for out-of-school employed persons with some college.

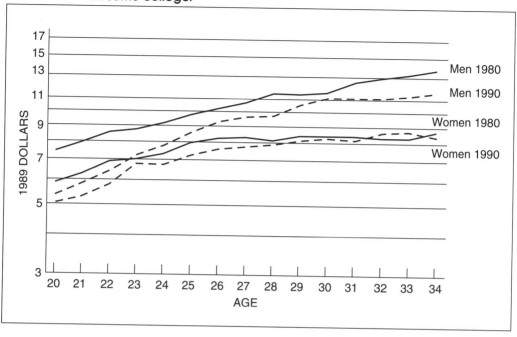

FIGURE 4.30   Estimated median hourly wage for out-of-school employed persons with at least a bachelor's degree.

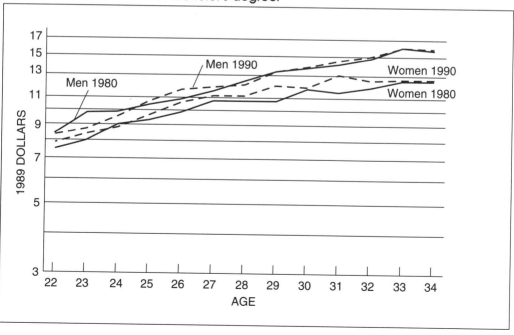

college also fell between 1979 and 1989, albeit not as much as for men. Young women's wages fell between approximately 50 cents and one dollar at most ages. Taken together, these trends imply that for high school graduates, the gap in wages between men and women narrowed somewhat during the 1980s, but only because men's wages fell more than women's. Male high school dropouts fared even worse. They suffered the twofold hardships of a significant drop in their chances of employment combined with a large drop in the wages they earned if they became employed.

For out-of-school employed persons with some college, wages also fell between 1979 and 1989, albeit to a lesser extent than for high school dropouts or persons with only a high school diploma. For both men and women, the data suggest that the erosion of real wages was greater for new entrants into the labor market than for somewhat older workers. It is not possible to tell from these data, however, whether the wages of persons in their early 20s in 1989 will grow as rapidly as the pattern shown in Figure 4.29 implies. The considerably depressed wages of new labor force entrants in 1989 may portend lower real wages than those earned in 1989 by persons ten years older. Only persons who completed at least a college degree were immune to the declines in real wages during the 1980s. For men who earned a college degree, the age profile of wages was almost identical in 1979 and 1989, and for women there is evidence of a slight increase in wage rates. For these workers the gap in wage rates between men and women is smallest in proportionate terms, and it is only for them that whatever reduction in gender inequality in wages has occurred is the result of women's gains rather than greater losses for men.[24]

Taken together, the trends in wages show that the relative economic values of various levels of education changed during the 1980s. Simple estimates of the way that the economic return to schooling changed can be obtained by taking the ratios of median wages of persons with varying amounts of schooling in the two censuses. For the medians plotted in Figures 4.27–4.30, averaged over all ages between 18 and 39, these ratios are as follows:

|  | Men | | Women | |
| --- | --- | --- | --- | --- |
|  | 1979 | 1989 | 1979 | 1989 |
| High school graduate versus dropout | 1.27 | 1.28 | 1.24 | 1.26 |
| Some college versus high school graduate | 1.13 | 1.19 | 1.17 | 1.25 |
| College graduate versus some college | 1.23 | 1.40 | 1.33 | 1.52 |
| College graduate versus high school graduate | 1.09 | 1.18 | 1.14 | 1.22 |

The payoff of additional schooling to young workers increased slightly at lower levels of schooling, but sharply for college graduates during the 1980s. The value of obtaining a college degree over some college with no degree increased from 23 to 40 percent for men and from 33 to 52 percent for women. Yet the increasing "return" to higher education over this period occurs only because higher education has protected some workers against the decline in real wages experienced by the labor force as a whole. The increased return to college results from the declining economic opportunities of those with less schooling.

### Racial-Ethnic Differences in Wage Rates

The trends in age-earnings profiles for the population as a whole mask differences among racial-ethnic groups in wage rates during the 1980s. Not only are traditionally disadvantaged minority groups less likely to be employed than the population as a whole, but they typically earn less when they do work. These patterns, moreover, were reinforced during the 1980s, particularly among persons who did not go beyond high school. Table 4.5 shows the ratios of wage rates for four racial-ethnic groups relative to those for whites by educational attainment among employed out-of-school men and women aged 16–34. Although some of the wage differences among racial-ethnic groups are attributable to their varying average levels of educational attainment, substantial differences in earnings are observable within educationally homogeneous groups. Wages were lower for black and Indian men at every level of educational attainment than they were for white and Asian men in 1980 and declined further over the decade. White, Asian, and Hispanic female college graduates enjoyed substan-

TABLE 4.5   Earnings of racial-ethnic groups relative to whites, by educational attainment, sex, and year.

| | Less Than High School Diploma | | High School Diploma | | Some College | | College Degree | |
|---|---|---|---|---|---|---|---|---|
| | 1980 | 1990 | 1980 | 1990 | 1980 | 1990 | 1980 | 1990 |
| Men Aged 16–34 | | | | | | | | |
| Blacks | .83 | .82 | .79 | .76 | .87 | .90 | .91 | .83 |
| Asians | .93 | .97 | .87 | .93 | .83 | 1.04 | 1.05 | 1.02 |
| Indians | .84 | .86 | .82 | .83 | .88 | .84 | .97 | .85 |
| Hispanics | .92 | .84 | .91 | .86 | .95 | .92 | .94 | .87 |
| Women Aged 16–34 | | | | | | | | |
| Blacks | 1.01 | .96 | 1.00 | .88 | .96 | .94 | 1.04 | .92 |
| Asians | 1.13 | 1.16 | 1.01 | 1.05 | 1.02 | 1.08 | .95 | 1.05 |
| Indians | .93 | .95 | .89 | .86 | .95 | .82 | .94 | .86 |
| Hispanics | 1.04 | .99 | .96 | .98 | .96 | 1.02 | .97 | .99 |

tial increases in their real wage rates over the decade of the 1980s. Unfortunately, similar gains were not enjoyed by black and Indian women.

Census data from 1980 and 1990 paint a bleak picture of the employment and earnings prospects for persons who have recently left school, with the exception of those who have college degrees. Although employment levels of recent school-leavers remained stable for the population as a whole, high school dropouts and traditionally disadvantaged minorities experienced erosion of their employment position in the 1980s. The *quality* of employment available to young American workers, however, eroded dramatically during this period, as indicated by the drop in real wages suffered by workers at all educational levels except college graduates. For wages, as well as employment, moreover, the declines were greatest for persons with no college education and for blacks and Indians at every educational level. Thus, traditionally disadvantaged minorities suffered the twin effects of poorer prospects for employment and poorer wages when they were employed.

## CONCLUSION

During the 1980s the growth and distribution of educational attainment followed trends that have characterized the U.S. population throughout the twentieth century. Successive cohorts of young persons received on average more schooling than their counterparts in previous generations. Access to formal schooling became more widespread at each level of schooling—reducing traditional educational inequalities between men and women, among members of racial-ethnic groups, and among persons from varying socioeconomic backgrounds. Nonetheless, educational opportunities and credentials remained scarce at the highest levels of the educational system. During the 1980s women finally surpassed men in the rates at which they complete college, the culmination of a long-run trend toward the elimination of men's advantage. At the graduate level, women continued to make rapid advances in their completion of advanced and potentially highly rewarding degrees in business, law, and medicine, but each year men still receive considerably more degrees in these fields than women. During the 1970s and 1980s, however, women's progress in attaining professional credentials was revolutionary, and it appears certain that remaining disparities will all but vanish within the next decade or two.

Racial-ethnic differences in educational opportunities and attainments are a persistent feature of the American social landscape. High school graduation rates exceed 90 percent for whites and Asian Americans, whereas only about 80 percent of blacks, Hispanics, and Native Americans complete high school. Dropout rates continued to decline in the 1980s, but racial-ethnic parity in high school completion remains a goal for the future. An important source of further educational growth for racial-ethnic minorities is the intergenerational transmission of educational status. Secular improvements in minority educational status imply that each successive generation of minority parents improves its average level of educational attainment. Inasmuch as parents typically try to ensure that their children attain at least their own educational level, this augurs well for successive generations of minority offspring. The beneficial effects of intergenerational improvement can be offset only when immigration introduces parents with lower educational attainment than those who are native-born. Hispanic immigrants have far lower educational attainment than any major native-born racial-ethnic group. Undoubtedly, the children of recent Hispanic immigrants will have higher educational attainment than their parents, but it will take several generations before their progeny will have attainments rivaling those of native groups.

During the 1980s persons acquired more education not only at the college and graduate levels, but also in nursery school and kindergarten. This trend has been driven by secular increases in numbers of mothers of young children who work full-time, by the spread of Head Start programs, and by a growing belief in the benefits of early childhood education. Although evidence for the effectiveness of Head Start programs is mixed,[25] the importance of early childhood programs for improving the educational prospects of disadvantaged children is part of a national consensus. At the same time, however, the children of highly educated and upper-income families are also receiving early childhood schooling in increasing numbers. It remains to be seen whether preschool education will reduce or increase educational inequalities over the long run.

A review of trends in students' performances on standardized tests of academic achievement during the 1980s brings some hope to those concerned about the capacity of America's schools to prepare students for higher education and an increasingly demanding world of work. Although average test scores for the nation as a whole increased modestly in the 1980s, the scores of black and Hispanic high school students increased sharply. This trend reduced, but far from eliminated, traditional disparities in measured academic performance among major racial-ethnic groups. It is to be hoped that these trends for blacks and Hispanics will reenforce the beneficial effects of secular improvements in parents' educational attainment on their offspring's ability to pursue higher education.

Labor market trends in the 1980s accentuated the importance of educational credentials for young workers. Average wage rates for young persons fell, but this trend differed dramatically for men with varying amounts of schooling. High school dropouts experienced the greatest drop in wages between 1980 and 1990; college-educated workers experienced the least. Only those who had completed a college degree experienced a stable wage rate over the decade. Although a college education provides no guarantee of economic security, its value increased during the 1980s, if only as buffer against downward mobility.

---

This research was supported by grants from the Russell Sage Foundation and the Graduate School of the University of Wisconsin–Madison to the author and from the Office of the Assistant Secretary for Planning and Evaluation, U.S. Department of Health and Human Services, to the Institute for Research on Poverty. Computations were performed using the facilities of the Center for Demography and Ecology at the University of Wisconsin–Madison, which are supported by the Center for Population Research of NICHD (HD-5876). Any opinions expressed are those of the author alone and not of the sponsoring institutions. The author is grateful to Reynolds Farley, Richard Easterlin, Nancy Cunniff, Judith A. Seltzer, Michael Wienstein, and the 1990 Census Project Advisory Committee for helpful comments on earlier drafts, and to Huey-Chi Chang, Barbara Corry, and Julia Gray for research assistance.

## ENDNOTES

1. This classification is mutually exclusive and covers more than 99 percent of the population. Asian and Pacific Islanders and Indians, Eskimos, and Aleuts who also identify themselves as Hispanics are classified as Asians and as Indians, respectively. The terms foreign-born and immigrant are used interchangeably.
2. See, for example, Farley (1984); Lieberson (1980); Jaynes and Williams (1989); and Margo (1990).
3. Studies conducted at the Census Bureau show that measures of educational attainment in the 1980 and 1990 censuses are not strictly comparable. For example, a much smaller percentage of persons identified themselves as "high school graduates" in the 1990 census than claimed to have completed exactly 12 years of schooling in the March 1990 Current Population Survey (CPS). This discrepancy appears to result partly because the 1990 census schedule distinguishes persons who completed 12 grades without a diploma from those who graduated and partly because a greater proportion of 1990 census respondents claimed that they completed "some college but no degree" or "associate degree in college" than March 1990 CPS respondents claimed that they completed 13–15 years of schooling. Because of the broad grouping of attainment categories in the elementary and secondary years in the 1990 census, one can no longer make these inferences about the grade in which a student is currently enrolled from questions on school enrollment status and educational attainment. Estimated school enrollment rates from the 1990 census differ considerably from what one would expect from the 1980 census or recent CPS data. See Kominski (1985, 1988, 1990); Kominski and Siegel (1987, 1992); Siegel (1991); Siegel and Kominski (1986).
4. This is the percentage of persons who reported that they received a high school diploma.
5. The estimates are the percentages of persons who completed "some college but no degree" or any postsecondary degree.

6. The estimates of the percentages of persons who completed at least four years of college are based on percentages of persons who completed a bachelor's or higher degree.

7. Folger and Nam (1967); Duncan (1965, 1968); Hauser and Featherman (1976); Mare (1979).

8. For further evidence of the dramatic increase in the number of women entering the professions, see Bianchi, Chapter 3 in this volume.

9. These surveys include the 1980 Census-Content Reinterview Survey matched file, the third wave of the Survey of Income and Program Participation 1984 panel, the 1986 National Content Test, and the February 1990 CPS. These surveys show that the educational attainment measures used in the 1940–1980 censuses are a poor basis for inferring whether a person achieved a high school diploma, a college degree, or a master's degree. Conversely, the 1990 measures are of limited use in determining the amount of time that a person has spent in school. See Kominski (1985, 1988); Kominski and Siegel (1987, 1992); Siegel (1991); Siegel and Kominski (1986).

   The studies with two measures of schooling provide a way of estimating the 1990 code that 1980 census respondents would have supplied had they been asked the 1990 question, and vice versa. The procedure is to (1) use one of the surveys that obtained both items to cross-classify 1980-basis highest grade of school completed by 1990-basis highest grade or degree completed; (2) from this table, estimate the conditional probabilities of each 1990-basis response given each 1980-basis response; (3) assign 1990-basis codes to 1980 census respondents with probabilities estimated in step 2; and (4) perform the converse of steps 2 and 3 to assign 1980-basis codes to 1990 census respondents. For example, if 73 percent of respondents who report having completed 16 years of school on the 1980-basis measures also report that their highest degree is a bachelor's, (a randomly selected) 73 percent of 1980 census respondents who report having completed 16 years of school are assigned a bachelor's degree and the remaining 27 percent are assigned a different 1990-basis code. Most of the imputation is based on a table reported from the February 1990 CPS, which has the largest sample size (190,730) of the several Census Bureau studies (see Siegel 1991: Table A). The February 1990 CPS included the 1990 census educational attainment question and the CPS schooling item, which is similar but not identical to the 1980 census item. In particular, (1) the CPS top codes educational attainment at six years or more of postsecondary school, whereas the 1980 census top codes attainment at eight years or more of postsecondary school; and (2) the 1980 census distinguishes among persons with no school completed, with nursery school, and with kindergarten, whereas the CPS combines these three groups. To impute the 1990-basis codes for 1980 respondents who had six, seven, or eight years or more of postsecondary schooling, a cross-classification of the 1990 and 1980 items from the 1986 National Content Test was used (Kominski and Siegel 1987: Tables 4 and 5). Here again the conditional probabilities of attaining each 1990-basis schooling level given a 1980-basis response were estimated and used to impute probabilistically a 1990 code to 1980 census respondents. The converse procedure was used to impute 1980 codes to 1990 respondents. This method assumes a homogeneous relationship between 1980 and 1990 measures across sociodemographic groups. Group differences in attainment patterns may result in heterogeneity in this relationship. For example, trends in attainment may cause age groups to vary in the extent to which they are at risk to various types of mismatch between 1980 and 1990 concepts (see Siegel and Kominski 1986).

10. Important factors affecting the educational attainments of foreign-born persons are their age of immigration and whether they entered the United States before or after completing their schooling.

11. Survival probabilities for transitions before high school are not reported because there are only trivial differences among racial-ethnic groups at this level. Survival probabilities for transitions beyond the bachelor's degree are not reported because samples are too small to be reliable for some racial-ethnic groups and it is difficult to construct comparable measures of school continuation from the 1980 and 1990 censuses at this level of schooling.

12. In both 1980 and 1990 more than 95 percent of persons lived with at least one parent until age 18, at which point the percentage dropped precipitously. By age 21, approximately 60 percent of persons had left the home of their parents. From the middle teens onward, rates of school enrollment differ markedly between persons living with and away from their parents. Despite the large proportion of young persons who do not live with parents and the gap in enrollment rates between persons living with and away from their parents, the analysis of educational attainment for young persons who live with parents is informative about the attainments of all young persons. *Rates of school progression* estimated from persons living with parents at the census date are similar to those for persons living away from parents. This suggests that the *timing* of educational attainment differs between these two groups, but the level of attainment is similar. See Mare (1993).

13. The odds of making each school transition are predicted using logistic regression models. Preliminary analyses of the 1980 and 1990 Public Use Microdata Samples showed that there were no systematic changes in the effects of family characteristics on school continuation between 1980 and 1990; although for several racial-ethnic groups and for one or two transitions there is some evidence of an increasing effect of family income between 1980 and 1990. Thus, the results reported in this section are based on additive models for the effects of family characteristics, racial-ethnic group membership, and time on school progression.

14. Figures 4.13–4.16 are based on logistic regression models in which persons who were not living with their father were given a separate code for "father absent" in place of a code for their father's schooling. The "father absent" code, however, is equivalent to the code such persons receive for their family structure. Likewise, persons who were not living with their mother are coded as "mother absent," which is equivalent to their code on family structure.

15. The analyses reported in this section rely on a uniform series of reformatted microdata files for the October CPS prepared by Hauser and his associates. See Hauser, Jordan, and Dixon (1993); and Hauser and Hauser (1993).

16. In October 1990 about 65 percent of nursery school students attended private schools. About 15 percent of kindergarten students attended private schools.

17. The model is a logistic regression model for the log odds of enrollment in nursery school or kindergarten. In addition to the factors shown in Figure 4.18, the model included a dummy variable for year (1979–1980 vs. 1989–1990), a four-category variable for race-ethnicity (white, black, Hispanic, other), and interactions between

year and race-ethnicity. The small number of children aged 3–5 who were attending elementary school were excluded from the analysis.

18. Persons who serve in the armed forces are classified as employed in Figures 4.21–4.26.

19. For a detailed analysis of the transition from school to work using panel data, see Tiemeyer (1993).

20. See Bianchi, Chapter 3 in this volume for further discussion of the distinction between cohort and age patterns of women's labor force participation.

21. For further discussion of these trends, see Levy, Chapter 1 and Kasarda, Chapter 5 in this volume.

22. For further discussion of trends in occupational sex segregation, see Bianchi, Chapter 3 and Wetzel, Chapter 2 in this volume.

23. These data derive from the Public Use Microdata Samples of 1980 and 1990. The wage rate is estimated as the ratio of wage and salary income in 1989 to the product of weeks worked in 1989 and hours worked per week in 1989.

24. For further discussion and interpretation of these wage trends, Chapters 1, 2, and 3 in this volume.

25. For a recent review and analysis, see Currie and Thomas (1993).

# 5

# Industrial Restructuring and the Changing Location of Jobs

## JOHN D. KASARDA

A MERICA'S INDUSTRIAL GEOGRAPHY is constantly changing. New locations of employment routinely rise while others decline as (1) transportation and communication technologies advance; (2) modes of goods processing and services transform; (3) labor and natural resource requirements of business change; (4) federal, state, and local policies play out; and (5) global competition becomes more pervasive. The local supply of jobs, in turn, either facilitates or constrains employment opportunities for residents and their social mobility (Cisneros 1993; Peterson and Vroman 1992; Wilson 1987).

This chapter examines the transforming industrial geography of the United States and its implications for employment and earnings of people at different locations. Focus will be on shifts in jobs and earnings during the 1980s across census regions, metropolitan-nonmetropolitan areas, and central cities and suburbs, and their consequences for skills and spatial mismatches between local labor and available work, structural unemployment, and urban problems.

A number of striking findings will be presented, including the following:

1. Between 1980 and 1990, the Frostbelt (Northeast and Midwest census regions) lost 1.5 million manufacturing jobs and $40 billion (in constant 1989 dollars) in aggregate manufacturing worker earnings, whereas the Sunbelt (South and West) added 450,000 manufacturing jobs and gained $21 billion in manufacturing worker earnings.

2. During the 1980s, the central counties of the Frostbelt's 28 largest metropolitan areas lost nearly 1 million manufacturing jobs and over $28 billion in manufacturing worker earnings.

3. Metropolitan areas captured nearly 90 percent of the nation's employment

growth; much of this growth occurred in booming "edge cities" at the metropolitan periphery. By 1990, many of these "edge cities" had more office space and retail sales than the metropolitan downtowns.

4. The economies and population compositions of older, larger central cities remained on a collision course during the 1980s, with information-processing jobs that typically require higher education replacing low-education jobs, while the city residential bases became increasingly dominated by less-educated minorities and immigrants.

5. Growing skills mismatches between city minority residents and city jobs were exacerbated by widening spatial mismatches as jobs suburbanized, the latter especially impacting less-educated blacks who remained in the cities.

6. As a result, joblessness among less-educated inner-city blacks soared. By the early 1990s, the jobless rate for black males without a high school diploma ranged from 52 percent in southern cities to 63 percent in midwestern cities. Among younger high school dropouts in poverty ghettos, 80 percent, on average, were without work.

7. The 1980s were also characterized by marked declines in the proportion of inner-city blacks who worked full-time and rises in the proportion who did not work at all. In many large cities, the proportion of black male residents who did not work at all in 1989 exceeded the percentage who worked full-time, a dramatic reversal from earlier decades.

Let us now take a more detailed look at these and other features of America's changing employment landscape, which will be followed by an appraisal of associated problems and their implications for policy.

## REGIONAL REDISTRIBUTION TRENDS

Until the 1960s, the metropolitan areas of the Northeast and Midwest contained the majority of the nation's industrial location advantages (excellent deepwater ports, extensive inland rail and waterway systems, well-developed inter- and intrametropolitan highways, rich nearby coal deposits, ubiquitous public utilities, a diverse and relatively well-educated labor force, ready access to investment capital, and strong local markets). Such features provided firms that located in these two Frostbelt regions with competitive cost and market advantages that helped them develop and expand much faster than they could in the relatively less advanced, more rural West and South.[1] As late as 1960, the northeastern and midwestern states were the dominant industrial regions. They contained more than two thirds of the nation's manufacturing jobs, most of which were concentrated in and around the core cities of their largest metropolitan areas (Economic Census of 1963; Kasarda 1976, 1978).

The rapid postwar growth of the aerospace, defense, solid-state electronics, construction, and service industries that did not depend on rail, deepwater, or riverine access, along with the expansion of large-scale commercialized agriculture and western oil field development, spurred the economies of the far West, especially California. Between 1950 and 1970, the western census region added more than 6 million jobs, of which nearly 4 million can be attributed to California alone (U.S. Bureau of the Census 1975).

The West grew at an accelerated pace during the 1970s and 1980s by adding approximately 7 million jobs during each decade, nearly doubling its employment base from 15 million to 29 million. But, as Figure 5.1 shows, the South added more than 9 million jobs during each of the past two decades (growing from 27.6 million to 46.3 million between 1970 and 1990), to lead the nation in absolute employment growth (U.S. Bureau of Economic Analysis 1993). Employment growth was considerably less in the Northeast and Midwest. Between 1980 and 1990 the Northeast added 4.1 million jobs and the Midwest added 4.4 million jobs compared with job growth of 2.2 million and 4.1 million, respectively, in these two regions during the 1970s.

The post-1970 resurgence of the South from an industrially lagging, rural-dominated region to a national force in job creation was largely the result of changes in its accessibility and the relative costs of doing business in the United States. The expansion of airports and multilane highway systems in the South

FIGURE 5.1  Total employment, by region: 1970–1990.

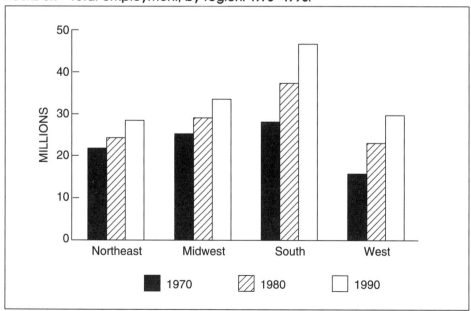

SOURCE: U.S. Bureau of Economic Analysis (1993).

along with a shift from rail to truck transport made southern business locations more accessible. Other factors such as relatively inexpensive land, lower energy costs, reduced wage scales, fewer union restrictions, more modern physical plants, and shifts in manufacturing away from heavy metals to lighter alloys and plastics gave the South an advantage in the highly cost-competitive manu-facturing sector. In addition, there was a reduction in southern racism, substan-tial improvement in public education, and highly favorable state and local gov-ernment attitudes toward industry. The latter were manifest in direct subsidies to relocating firms, lower business taxes, right-to-work laws, fewer regulations, and a peerless form of industrial boosterism by many southern communities (Abbott 1987; Cobb 1982, 1984; Goldfield 1984). Thus, Figure 5.2 reveals that, between 1970 and 1990, while the Northeast lost over 1.5 million manufactur-ing jobs and the Midwest lost nearly 600,000, the South gained 1.1 million and the West gained a similar number.

It would be a mistake, however, to assume that manufacturing was the driv-ing force of either the southern or western economies. Job growth in trade and services far overwhelmed manufacturing employment growth in both regions. The Northeast and Midwest also experienced substantial growth in trade and services during the 1970s and 1980s. As Figure 5.3 shows, the vast majority of the nation's employment growth was captured by the service sector and retail trade between 1970 and 1990.

FIGURE 5.2   Manufacturing employment, by region: 1970–1990.

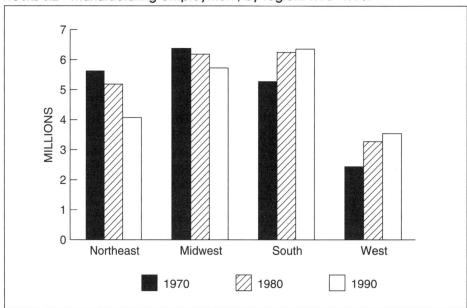

SOURCE: U.S. Bureau of Economic Analysis (1993).

FIGURE 5.3    Employment, by industrial sector: 1970–1990.

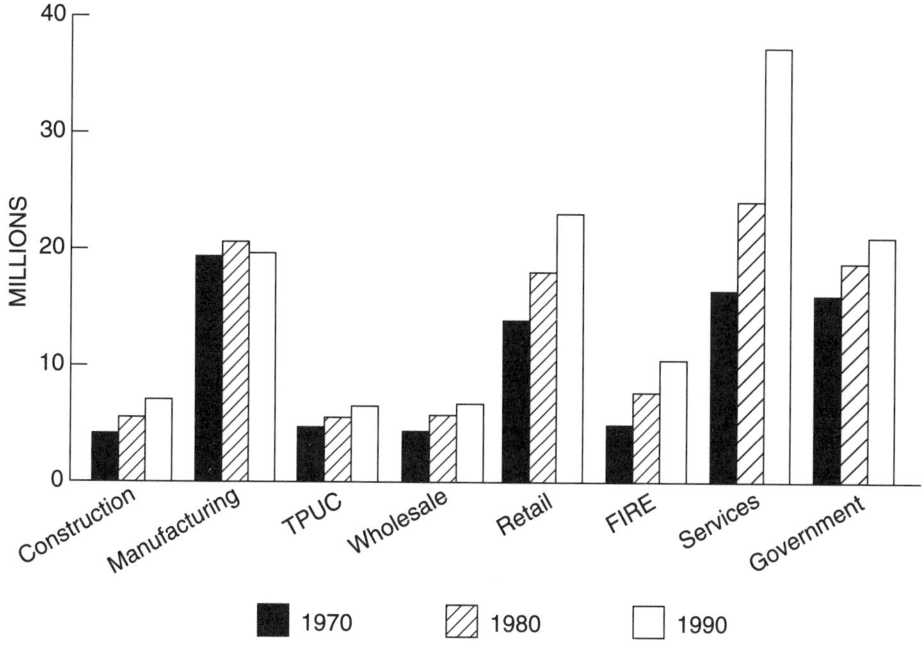

SOURCE: U.S. Bureau of Economic Analysis (1993).

NOTE: FIRE: finance, insurance, and real estate; TPUC: transportation public utilities, and communication.

Regional breakdowns further reveal that all four census regions added consid-erably more service sector jobs during the 1980s than the 1970s. Job growth was spatially uneven within each census region, however, especially for the manufacturing sector. It will now be described, first in terms of basic metropoli-tan-nonmetropolitan growth patterns and then in terms of a detailed classifica-tion of counties along an urban-rural continuum within regions.

## Metropolitan-Nonmetropolitan Patterns

Of the 3,126 counties in the United States, 722 were classified as metropoli-tan by the Bureau of the Census in 1983. To obtain comparable measures of metropolitan-nonmetropolitan employment change during the 1970s and 1980s, each county contained in the Bureau of Economic Analysis *Regional Economic Information System, 1969–1990* (REIS) longitudinal files was tagged with a constant code based on its 1983 Bureau of the Census metropolitan or nonmet-ropolitan designation. All of the nation's counties were thus classified in 1970,

1980, and 1990 based on this 1983 standard, which was used for the 1990 enumeration.

The 2,404 nonmetropolitan counties added 4.5 million jobs between 1970
and 1980 (a 23 percent growth), but their aggregate employment growth slowed
to 3.3 million between 1980 and 1990 (a 14 percent growth). The 722 metropolitan counties added 18 million jobs during the 1970s (a 26 percent growth) and
21.6 million jobs during the 1980s (a 24 percent growth). Thus, while one in
every four jobs added during the 1970s was in nonmetropolitan areas, only one
in every seven jobs added during the 1980s was so located. Stated a bit differently, metropolitan counties, which constitute less than a quarter of all U.S.
counties, captured nearly 90 percent of the nation's employment growth during
the 1980s. A more detailed 11-category classification of counties—from large
metropolitan central counties (with at least 750,000 residents) to small, isolated
nonmetropolitan ones (nonadjacent to metropolitan areas and with no place of
2,500 residents)—revealed that all five metropolitan classifications added overall
employment at faster rates than did any of the six nonmetropolitan classifications.[2]

Table 5.1, which presents these county classifications by Frostbelt (Northeast
and Midwest) and Sunbelt (South and West) regions, shows that the 35 large
metropolitan central counties in the Sunbelt (just 1 percent of all counties) accounted for one quarter of the nation's 24.9 million new jobs between 1980 and
1990. In addition, employment growth *rates* have been highest in suburban
counties of the largest metropolitan areas, whether Frostbelt (30 percent) or
Sunbelt (49 percent). Suburban counties of the largest Frostbelt metropolitan
areas also experienced, by far, the greatest absolute employment increases in
the region, more than double those of any other aggregate county classification.
For example, DuPage County in suburban Chicago added 228,416 jobs during
the 1980s and Middlesex County outside Boston added 165,888 jobs.

Detailed decomposition by industry groups demonstrated that service sector
jobs (particularly white collar service industries) were responsible for the highest
share of employment growth in metropolitan areas in all regions. Retail trade
contributed a considerable number of jobs as well to metropolitan core and suburban counties in both the Frostbelt and the Sunbelt during the 1980s.

On the other hand, Table 5.2 provides data on the heavy loss that Frostbelt
metropolitan counties experienced in manufacturing employment and manufacturing earnings between 1980 and 1990. During the 1980s, the 28 large metropolitan central counties of the Frostbelt lost nearly 1 million manufacturing jobs
while their 65 mid-size metropolitan central counties lost another 350,000 manufacturing jobs. Corresponding to this job loss, aggregate earnings of persons
employed by manufacturing establishments in the 28 large metropolitan central
counties in the Frostbelt declined by a remarkable $29 billion (in constant 1989
dollars) between 1980 and 1990, while manufacturing earnings in mid-size
Frostbelt central counties declined by over $11 billion.

TABLE 5.1 Employment change, by Sunbelt/Frostbelt and county type: 1980–1990.

| County Type | Frostbelt Employment Change 1980–1990 | | | Sunbelt Employment Change 1980–1990 | | |
|---|---|---|---|---|---|---|
| | Number of Counties | (000) | Percentage | Number of Counties | (000) | Percentage |
| Nonmetropolitan | | | | | | |
| Nonadjacent to metropolitan area with small place | 251 | 44 | +6% | 284 | 128 | +16% |
| Nonadjacent to metropolitan area with medium place | 189 | 113 | +8 | 309 | 257 | +11 |
| Nonadjacent to metropolitan area with large place | 82 | 185 | +12 | 125 | 452 | +17 |
| Adjacent to metropolitan area with small place | 89 | 111 | +19 | 214 | 109 | +14 |
| Adjacent to metropolitan area with medium place | 223 | 285 | +12 | 343 | 394 | +13 |
| Adjacent to metropolitan area with large place | 124 | 470 | +14 | 171 | 756 | +19 |
| Metropolitan | | | | | | |
| Metropolitan, in area with population less than 150,000 | 50 | 421 | +18 | 67 | 588 | +20 |
| Suburban, in metropolitan area with population 150,000–749,999 | 64 | 341 | +15 | 93 | 637 | +32 |
| Central, in metropolitan area with population 150,000–749,999 | 65 | 1,604 | +18 | 89 | 3,677 | +32 |
| Suburban, in metropolitan area with population 750,000 or more | 106 | 3,296 | +30 | 125 | 3,371 | +49 |
| Central, in metropolitan area with population 750,000 or more | 28 | 1,634 | +9 | 35 | 6,026 | +27 |
| Total | | 8,505 | +16 | | 16,396 | +28 |

SOURCE: U.S. Bureau of Economic Analysis (1993).

NOTES: Frostbelt includes the Northeast and Midwest census regions; Sunbelt includes the South and West census regions. Rows may not sum to 100 due to rounding.

TABLE 5.2  Employment and earnings change in manufacturing, by Sunbelt/Frostbelt and county type: 1980–1990.

| Area/County Type | Number of Counties | Employment Change 1980–1990 | | Earnings Change 1980–1990 | |
|---|---|---|---|---|---|
| | | (000) | Percentage | (millions) | Percentage |
| Frostbelt Nonmetropolitan | | | | | |
| Nonadjacent to metropolitan area with small place | 251 | +8 | +13% | $+26 | +2% |
| Nonadjacent to metropolitan area with medium place | 189 | +23 | +11 | +168 | +4 |
| Nonadjacent to metropolitan area with large place | 82 | +10 | +4 | −275 | −4 |
| Adjacent to metropolitan area with small place | 89 | +7 | +8 | +152 | +8 |
| Adjacent to metropolitan area with medium place | 223 | +52 | +12 | +717 | +7 |
| Adjacent to metropolitan area with large place | 124 | −40 | −5 | −1,516 | −6 |
| Frostbelt Metropolitan | | | | | |
| Metropolitan, in area with population less than 150,000 | 50 | −12 | −2 | −985 | −6 |
| Suburban, in metropolitan area with population 150,000–749,999 | 64 | −75 | −13 | −3,160 | −16 |
| Central, in metropolitan area with population 150,000–749,999 | 65 | −349 | −16 | −11,150 | −15 |
| Suburban, in metropolitan area with population 750,000 or more | 106 | −124 | −5 | +3,384 | +4 |
| Central, in metropolitan area with population 750,000 or more | 28 | −971 | −26 | −28,558 | −22 |
| Total | | −1,471 | −13 | −41,196 | −11 |

Sunbelt Nonmetropolitan

| | | | | | |
|---|---|---|---|---|---|
| Nonadjacent to metropolitan area with small place | 284 | +23 | +19 | +396 | +18 |
| Nonadjacent to metropolitan area with medium place | 309 | +35 | +9 | +324 | +4 |
| Nonadjacent to metropolitan area with large place | 125 | +4 | +1 | +31 | 0 |
| Adjacent to metropolitan area with small place | 214 | +9 | +8 | +57 | +2 |
| Adjacent to metropolitan area with medium place | 343 | +18 | +3 | +130 | +1 |
| Adjacent to metropolitan area with large place | 171 | +65 | +8 | +1,196 | +6 |
| Sunbelt Metropolitan | | | | | |
| Metropolitan, in area with population less than 150,000 | 67 | −6 | −1 | −580 | −5 |
| Suburban, in metropolitan area with population 150,000–749,999 | 93 | +41 | +10 | +1,691 | +15 |
| Central, in metropolitan area with population 150,000–749,999 | 89 | +120 | +8 | +4,640 | +11 |
| Suburban, in metropolitan area with population 750,000 or more | 125 | +155 | +15 | +6,673 | +23 |
| Central, in metropolitan area with population 750,000 or more | 35 | −17 | −1 | +6,294 | +6 |
| Total | | +446 | +5 | +20,852 | +8 |

SOURCE: U.S. Bureau of Economic Analysis (1993).

NOTE: Earnings are reported in constant 1989 dollars.

Plummeting most precipitously were Cook County (Chicago), where workers in manufacturing earned an aggregate of $5.3 billion less in 1990 than in 1980; Wayne County (Detroit), where aggregate manufacturing earnings declined by $4.7 billion; New York City and Allegheny County (Pittsburgh), where earnings in each declined by $3.2 billion; and Milwaukee, where manufacturing workers earned $1.7 billion less in 1990 than in 1980 (again, in constant 1989 dollars). Conversely, in King County (Seattle) aggregate manufacturing earnings rose by $1.2 billion between 1980 and 1990, in Maricopa County (Phoenix) by $981 million, and in Dallas by $624 million. Regional rates of change in urban manufacturing earnings were similarly opposed: Wayne County (Detroit) lost 32 percent of its manufacturing earnings during the 1980s and Allegheny County (Pittsburgh) lost 51 percent, whereas King County experienced a 21 percent rise and Maricopa County a 27 percent rise.

The data in Table 5.2 hint at average earnings declines per worker in the manufacturing sector during the 1980s in nonmetropolitan areas of the Frostbelt. Aggregate manufacturing earnings grew faster than aggregate employment during the 1970s in all nonmetropolitan classifications within the Frostbelt (data not shown here), whereas the reverse was the case in the 1980s. Nevertheless, manufacturing employment grew in five of the six nonmetropolitan categories in the Frostbelt and major losses were experienced in all the metropolitan categories (large to small; city or suburban), indicating the general centrifugal drift of manufacturing employment away from Frostbelt metropolitan areas.

### Underlying Factors Shaping Uneven Growth

Why has the Sunbelt significantly outperformed the Frostbelt in overall employment growth, and what factors underlie major losses in manufacturing employment and earnings in metropolitan core counties of the Northeast and Midwest? Industrial mixes, interacting with national business cycles and local competitive effects, account for a large portion of the explanation. Using a technique known as *shift-share analysis,* regional scientists have shown that employment changes between two times within any geographic area (region, state, or locality) can be decomposed into three components: (1) national economic conditions (business cycle effects), (2) the area's industrial mix (compositional effects), and (3) special characteristics of the area (competitive effects). The hypothesized determinants of the third component—competitive effects—are numerous and hotly contested. I return to these after briefly describing how the first two components interact to shape local employment change.

Typically, employment in most areas tends to fare better during business cycle upswings than during recessions. Yet some areas almost always do much better than others during all phases of the business cycle.

Industry mix has received the greatest attention in explaining different local employment growth outcomes. It has been shown that areas in which employment bases are dominated by mature, slow-growth, or no-growth industries (such as mining, electrical machinery, or rubber products) perform much worse than areas in which employment bases have greater proportions of rapidly growing newer high-tech manufacturing or advanced service sector industries (such as microelectronics, biotechnology, or business services). Moreover, places where the job bases are dominated by older industries subjected to intense foreign competition (e.g., textiles, steel, machine tools) tend to decline faster during recessions and continue to decline or grow more slowly during national economic recovery than do places with younger, more vibrant industries adapted to the new economic order and less affected by foreign competition.

It has been shown, nonetheless, that numerous localities with *unfavorable* industrial mixes have exhibited marked employment growth during recent national recessions, whereas other localities with *favorable* industrial mixes have experienced considerable employment decline, even during periods of national economic prosperity (Kasarda and Irwin 1991). Such places apparently possess competitive advantages or disadvantages that overcome the effects of national business cycles and their industrial composition in affecting local employment change.

Figure 5.4 provides a model of the process by which the three basic factors—national economic conditions, industrial mix, and competitive effects—shape an

FIGURE 5.4    Model of determinants of local employment growth.

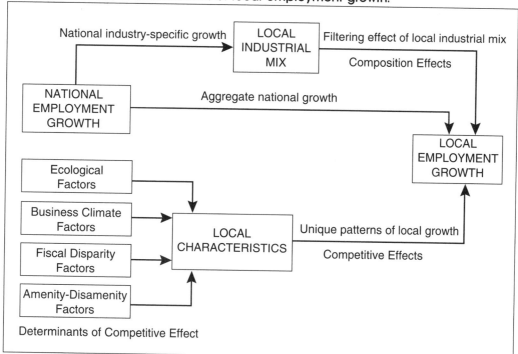

SOURCE: Kasarda and Irwin (1991).

area's employment growth. The first source of local employment growth, national growth (or decline) directly affects employment opportunities in its constituent communities. Fluctuations in national economic conditions (i.e., business cycles) are also transmitted to localities indirectly through the industrial mix of each locality, the latter influencing the degree to which national economic changes affect local employment opportunities. While the first two sources of local employment change originate in the broader economic system, the third source—competitive effects—reflects local features of communities that attract or dissuade business and determine whether localities' "industry-specific" growth rates will be greater or less than the national growth rate of the same industries.

A review by Kasarda and Irwin (1991) revealed more than two dozen separate hypotheses of competitive effects, which they reduced to four theoretical clusters, summarized below.

*Ecological Factors.*    The first cluster is composed of hypotheses that stress the roles of transportation access, density, *agglomeration economies* (a term meaning that proximity gives firms better access to inputs and outputs necessary for production), age of public and private infrastructure, and economic conditions in adjacent, functionally integrated market areas.[3]

The pivotal argument of social ecologists is that modern advances in transportation and communication technologies have reduced the advantages of physical proximity and made compactness unnecessary for conducting many of today's economic and social exchanges. Kasarda (1980) and Hicks (1982), for example, provide detailed discussions of the increasing costs for certain goods-producing industries of locating in large, dense concentrations and the reasons that agglomeration economies are no longer tied to central locations. They further discuss the negative role that aging infrastructure (e.g., old factories, bridges, water systems, and rail lines dating to the nineteenth century) plays in propensities for firm location and business expansion, especially as it has affected the ability of older cities to compete for blue collar jobs.

Economic geographers have also employed traditional ecological variables to explain employment growth and decline of localities. For example, Berry and Cohen (1973:454) argued:

> Concentrated industrial metropolises developed *only* because proximity meant lower transportation and communication costs for these interdependent specialists who had to interact with each other frequently or intensively and could only do so on a face-to-face basis. But shortened distances also meant higher densities and costs of congestion, high rent, loss of privacy, and the like. As soon as technological change permitted, the metropolis was transformed to minimize these negative externalities. The decline of downtown retailing and of central-city manufacturing are manifestations of this fundamental transformation.

Another ecological variable of importance is spatial context. Differential employment growth is predicated not only on the community's own mix of factors, but also on the performance of other communities in its immediate economic area. Such spillover effects can be dramatic, as manifested in one of the nation's fastest-growing counties of over 100,000 population, Gwinnett, Georgia, a suburb of Atlanta, which more than tripled its employment between 1980 and 1990 (from 56,856 to 184,640), despite having an industrial mix *unfavorable* to job growth (Kasarda and Irwin 1991).

*Business Climate Factors.*   A second cluster of hypotheses may be classified under the rubric *business climate*. This construct, often cited but seldom crisply defined, is a product of the local social, political, and economic milieu as it influences the cost and ease of conducting business and has been applied primarily, though not exclusively, to the manufacturing sector.

Thus, a favorable business climate is often equated with limited unionization—little union-organizing activity and the presence of other businesses operating without unions (Harrison and Bluestone 1988; Logan and Molotch 1987). Closely related to unionization, labor costs are often perceived to play a vital role in business climate (Gottdiener 1985). Labor costs are central to the traditional *product cycle theory* of business economists (Burns 1934; Kuznets 1930; Vernon 1960) and to its neo-Marxian update, *profit cycle theory* (Markusen 1985). Both theories postulate spatial decentralization of manufacturing activity (domestically and worldwide) during a product's life course, from initial development in one area or a few core areas by skilled labor to its final standardized, mass-production phase by low-skill labor in outlying areas. Driving the decentralization process are technological change and foreign competition, which force maturing industries to minimize factor costs, especially those of labor. Since standardization and mechanization reduce the need for skilled labor, firms will move their production facilities from higher-wage areas (where product innovation typically occurs) to peripheral locations (sections of the Sunbelt, nonmetropolitan areas, and developing nations) that offer cheaper labor.

Following this reasoning, popularized ratings of state business climate— Grant Thornton's (1985) perhaps being the best known—give heavy weight to hourly manufacturing employee wages. Such ratings, however, have come under increased criticism as the U.S. economy transforms from routinized mass-production manufacturing to flexible high-tech manufacturing and advanced information-processing industries (Blair and Premus 1987; Castells 1988; Erickson 1987). In this transforming arena, it is argued that labor force *skills* are at least as important as labor force *costs* in the locational choice of many of our nation's fastest growing industries (Reich 1991; Siegel 1988). It is further argued that communities offering a better-educated labor force—capable of processing, analyzing, and transmitting information as well as working with technologically advanced machinery—will be most competitive in capturing new growth sectors (Birch 1987; Reich 1991).

A synergistic component often considered central to an area's business climate is the direct support of its local government to private sector initiatives (Schmenner 1985). Of special relevance are taxes and tax credits, infrastructure provision, loans and loan guarantees, and direct cost underwriting (Kenyon 1991). Many states and communities, in fact, have become aggressive "capitalist actors" in competing with other states and communities for industrial investment and jobs by offering tax concessions, infrastructure subsidies, publicly financed worker training programs, and wage subsidies Eisinger 1988; (Logan and Molotch 1987; Mollenkopf 1983). For example, in attracting Mercedes-Benz to Alabama in 1993, the city of Vance and the state offered well over $300 million in incentives, including free land, huge tax reductions, free employee training, worker wage subsidies, and a state promise to purchase over 2,500 new Mercedes sport utility vehicles for public use (Browning and Cooper 1993). In like manner, some states commenced venture capital programs during the 1980s, using public money to make high-risk investments in firms perceived to be innovative and likely to create jobs (Eisinger 1991, 1993).

Government regulations that are exclusionary or that translate into direct costs to firms also influence local employment growth. For instance, manufacturing firms whose production processes generate harmful air emissions or other pollutants may be precluded by law from highly populated areas or find costs of local environmental compliance so great that they seek alternative sites where emission regulations are more lax (Stafford 1985). Likewise, community growth controls and state and local regulatory policies can have a powerful influence on local employment growth, especially new firm ventures (Baldassare 1986; Birch 1987).

In sum, business climate may be characterized as the multidimensional investment milieu offered by local government and local population for the private sector, measured in terms of taxes, unionization, wage structure, labor force skills, capital availability, and regulations. While business climate arguments are usually formulated in terms of manufacturing site choices, these factors, as noted, may be assumed to influence local employment growth across other industries.

*Federal Fiscal Disparity Factors.*    A third cluster of hypotheses focuses on the role of federal bias in state and local redistribution of public funds (certain areas send far more tax dollars to Washington than are returned in federal funds). It has been argued that the Sunbelt's economic growth since 1960 rested, in part, on a highly favorable balance of payments with the federal government (Castells 1985; Mollenkopf 1983).

A number of scholars have stressed the importance of military complexes, defense contracts, and federal research and development expenditures on the growth of local and regional economies during the 1980s and 1990s (Castells 1988; Markusen 1987). Sixty percent of all defense installations and contracts are located in the South and West, along with 80 percent of all defense personnel, implying that shifts in the federal budget toward defense during the first half of the 1980s favored some localities and regions more than others (Logan and Molotch 1987). In turn, the major slump in employment in southern California during the early 1990s has been partially attributed to defense cutbacks (Scott 1993).

Fiscal disparity theorists further emphasize antiurban and regional biases in federal policies that foster disinvestment in older, larger cities and in the Frostbelt (Bluestone and Harrison 1982; Luger 1984; Markusen 1987). The basic argument here is that federal tax codes are skewed toward businesses' investing in new plant facilities in new locations rather than remodeling old plants, and that major federal grants provide the infrastructure for such investments in newly developing areas (e.g., highways, sewage systems, dams). The outcome, they contend, is serious local and regional imbalances in the growth of new employment activity.

*Amenity-Disamenity Factors.* The fourth explanatory cluster reflects the quality of life of an area. In the postindustrial era, people and businesses are increasingly footloose and can often locate where they perceive the physical and social environment as more desirable. Much of the employment growth in Sunbelt states (Florida, California, and Arizona, in particular) has been attributed to the mild, sunny winter climates that have attracted higher-income migrants, tourists, and businesses serving them (Frey and Speare 1988). Harsh winter climates also pose additional costs to firms (such as interrupted production and distribution schedules as well as employee absenteeism from adverse weather) that make them less competitive for certain industries (Gappert 1987; Gutterbock 1987).

High crime rates undoubtedly spur businesses to leave an area and reduce the likelihood that new firms will locate there. Theft, vandalism, and other casualty losses not only pose direct costs to firms and households, but also reduce the overall quality of life for residents, contributing to middle-class flight (Bradbury, Downs, and Small 1982; Gurr and King 1985; Skogan 1977).

Amenity-disamenity factors are also important in attracting migrants or encouraging outmigration, which will have either a positive or a negative impact on local employment change through consumer multiplier effects. Additional residents increase aggregate demand for retail, professional, and government services in nearby areas. More large grocery stores, shopping malls, gas stations, professional office complexes, and schools are built to meet this demand. This has happened not only in growing Sunbelt metropolitan areas, but also at the exurban peripheries of many northern metropolitan areas in recent decades. Conversely, when individuals move away from an area they take their spending patterns (personal income) with them, further deflating commercial markets and demand for certain services in the origin area.

Most evidence suggests that in the past people followed jobs. Today, however, job growth locations are beginning to reflect residential preferences of workers, especially professionals who have multiple location options. Indeed, it has been argued that the rapid growth of knowledge-based industries such as biotechnology and microelectronics has given rise to a new class of technocratic workers, whose emphasis on privatized consumption and quality-of-life has elevated environmental and social amenity factors to prime importance (Kasarda and Irwin 1991).

Ideology and values play key roles in the "new class" theory of industrial relocation. Elite workers and affluent retirees (former elite workers) prefer not to subsidize collective consumption, which they see as benefiting other (typically lower) classes. The new class requires a few "elite services," such as good schools, and prefers to finance transportation, health care, and the like through private means. These people seek mild winter climates, ample outdoor recreational opportunities, and relatively lower housing costs while also seeking to avoid crime (and the costs of controlling it). Rather than fighting urban problems and paying premium costs for better housing in major metropolitan areas, they choose to exit. Their footlooseness (facilitated by modern telecommunications and relatively low-cost airfare) and privileged economic position allow them to relocate to smaller, less-problem-prone cities and towns without losing the benefits and networking of a major metropolitan location.

This "new class" affects the relocation of jobs in two ways. Affluent retirees generate private consumption-related business activity, while elite technocratic workers, because of their critical positions in the new information-age economy, influence firms to locate in areas that meet their lifestyle preferences. As technical knowledge becomes increasingly pivotal to the new economic order, it is hypothesized that these elite workers actually gain influence over the location decisions of some of the nation's fastest-growing industries. In fact, many analysts feel that corporate location decisions have already begun to reflect residential preferences of the new class. Those places offering greater environmental amenities and lower crime rates (e.g., Boulder, Colorado, and Raleigh, North Carolina) are gaining at the expense of those offering fewer amenities, particularly over those areas possessing such "disamenities" as harsh winters, polluted environments, high crime rates, large social welfare burdens, and exorbitant housing costs (Heenan 1991; Kasarda and Irwin 1991).

As wealthier people pour into these amenity-rich areas, not only are more residential and commercial facilities needed to serve them, but corporations also notice the abundant higher-quality labor supply and move to take advantage of it. For instance, between 1980 and 1990, the *working age* population in both Fort Myers and Fort Pierce, Florida, grew at more than four times the national rate. Even higher growth ratios of working age population can be found in and around the booming "edge cities" at the distant periphery of many metropolitan areas.

An increasingly important exogenous factor that affects spatially uneven employment growth is global competition. Most research to date has focused on the effects of foreign competition on manufacturing and the demise of the blue collar production jobs in the Frostbelt. Today, these effects are being felt all the way up to the executive suites of America's largest corporations.

To reduce overall corporate costs and respond more efficiently to competition from abroad, major corporations are undergoing dramatic restructuring of their management staffs. Thus, during the latter half of the 1980s, terms such as *downsizing, delayering,* and *right-sizing* (all euphemisms for white collar layoffs) became corporate buzzwords. Under increased competitive pressures, many of the nation's largest corporations reduced top management staff, removed entire bureaucratic layers, and relocated their trimmed-down headquarter units to much smaller, lower-cost cities. As one example, after slashing its headquarter staff in the late 1980s from 2,000 to 320, Exxon relocated from New York City to Irving, Texas, a Dallas suburb. Such major white collar layoffs could be one reason why Levy reports such sharp drops in the earnings of older men with college degrees between 1989 and 1993 (see Chapter 1 in this volume).

The decline of Frostbelt big-city corporate headquarter locations between 1960 and 1990 is well illustrated in Table 5.3. Observe that as late as 1960 more than 25 percent of all Fortune 500 firms were headquartered in New York City. By 1990, only 8 percent were so located. One may also observe the spatial shift of major corporate headquarters to Sunbelt cities, corresponding to overall employment redistribution from the Frostbelt to the Sunbelt.

Perhaps the sea change of the 1980s, though, was the emergence of small, sometimes quite isolated cities as corporate headquarter locations. Table 5.4

**TABLE 5.3**  Primary locations of Fortune 500 headquarters, by city: 1960–1990.

| | Number of Firms in 1960 | | Number of Firms in 1970 | | Number of Firms in 1980 | | Number of Firms in 1990 |
|---|---|---|---|---|---|---|---|
| New York | 130 | New York | 117 | New York | 81 | New York | 43 |
| Chicago | 43 | Chicago | 39 | Chicago | 25 | Chicago | 22 |
| Pittsburgh | 22 | Cleveland | 15 | Pittsburgh | 16 | Dallas | 15 |
| Cleveland | 17 | Pittsburgh | 15 | Stamford, CT | 15 | Houston | 14 |
| Detroit | 13 | Los Angeles | 13 | Houston | 12 | Cleveland | 13 |
| St. Louis | 13 | Philadelphia | 11 | Los Angeles | 12 | Pittsburgh | 12 |
| Philadelphia | 13 | Milwaukee | 9 | Dallas | 11 | Atlanta | 9 |
| San Francisco | 11 | St. Louis | 9 | St. Louis | 11 | Los Angeles | 9 |
| Los Angeles | 11 | Detroit | 8 | Cleveland | 9 | St. Louis | 9 |
| Dallas | 6 | Minneapolis | 8 | Minneapolis | 8 | Minneapolis | 7 |

SOURCES: Heenan (1991) and information compiled by the author.

TABLE 5.4   Corporate headquarters locations of selected fast-growing
U.S. companies: 1990.

| Company | Primary Business | Location | Population |
|---|---|---|---|
| L.L. Bean | Mail order | Freeport, Maine | 6,905 |
| Ben & Jerry's Homemade | Ice cream | Waterbury, Vermont | 1,702 |
| Cabletron Systems | LAN components | Rochester, New Hampshire | 26,630 |
| Lands' End | Mail order | Dodgeville, Wisconsin | 3,882 |
| Microsoft Corp. | Computer software | Redmond, Washington | 35,800 |
| Mrs. Fields Cookies | Cookies, confectioneries | Park City, Utah | 4,468 |
| Nike, Inc. | Sports shoes | Beaverton, Oregon | 53,310 |
| PC Connections, Inc. | Software and peripherals | Marlow, New Hampshire | 650 |
| SAS Institute, Inc. | Computer software | Cary, North Carolina | 40,926 |
| Universal Electronics | Remote controls | Twinsburg, Ohio | 9,606 |
| U.S. West, Inc. | Telecommunications | Englewood, Colorado | 29,387 |
| Wal-Mart Stores | Retail stores | Bentonville, Arkansas | 11,257 |

SOURCES: Heenan (1991) and information compiled by the author.

lists a number of them. Most exemplary is Wal-Mart, the nation's fastest-growing and most profitable major corporation during the latter half of the 1980s, headquartered in Bentonville, Arkansas (1990 population 11,257). Another striking example is PC Connections, in Marlow, New Hampshire (1990 population 650), which set up its distribution warehouse as part of the Airborne Express complex in Wilmington, Ohio. The company guarantees delivery of its computer software and peripherals the same day for phone orders received by 2:00 A.M. that day. Using advanced telecommunications and air express service to compete on the basis of speed, PC Connections' sales have skyrocketed.

### The Spatial Redistribution of Earnings

Migration (including immigration) and the changing location of jobs across regions and metropolitan-nonmetropolitan areas have altered national earnings patterns considerably. This shift is illustrated in Table 5.5, which shows the spatial redistribution of aggregated total earnings and manufacturing earnings across the four census regions and their nonmetropolitan and metropolitan components from 1970 to 1990. For example, in 1970 the Northeast contributed 27 percent of all dollars earned in the country from public and private employers. Nonmetropolitan counties in the Northeast contributed 2 percent of the nation's earnings, while metropolitan counties in the Northeast contributed 25 percent.

The data in Table 5.5 suggest that the hemorrhage in aggregate earnings that the Northeast experienced during the 1970s ceased during the 1980s, especially for the region's metropolitan counties. Further analysis reveals that figures for the large metropolitan core counties were most significant. For instance, while total constant (1989) dollar private sector earnings in New York City declined

TABLE 5.5  Percentage distribution of all earnings and manufacturing earning, by region and metropolitan status: 1970–1990.

| Region/Metropolitan Status | All Industries | | | Manufacturing | | |
|---|---|---|---|---|---|---|
| | 1970 | 1980 | 1990 | 1970 | 1980 | 1990 |
| Northeast | 27% | 23% | 23% | 29% | 25% | 23% |
| Nonmetropolitan (N = 100) | 2 | 2 | 2 | 2 | 2 | 2 |
| Metropolitan (N = 117) | 25 | 21 | 21 | 27 | 23 | 20 |
| Midwest | 28 | 26 | 23 | 35 | 33 | 31 |
| Nonmetropolitan (N = 858) | 6 | 6 | 5 | 5 | 6 | 6 |
| Metropolitan (N = 196) | 22 | 26 | 19 | 30 | 27 | 25 |
| South | 27 | 30 | 31 | 22 | 26 | 28 |
| Nonmetropolitan (N = 1,061) | 7 | 7 | 6 | 6 | 8 | 8 |
| Metropolitan (N = 333) | 20 | 23 | 25 | 16 | 18 | 20 |
| West | 18 | 21 | 23 | 14 | 16 | 19 |
| Nonmetropolitan (N = 385) | 2 | 3 | 3 | 1 | 2 | 2 |
| Metropolitan (N = 76) | 16 | 18 | 20 | 12 | 15 | 18 |

SOURCE: U.S. Bureau of Economic Analysis (1993).

NOTE: Regional column totals may not sum to 100 due to rounding.

by $9.5 billion between 1970 and 1980, aggregate private sector earnings of persons employed in New York City rose by $32.2 billion between 1980 and 1990. Of this increase in employee earnings, $14.4 billion was accounted for by growth of the city's finance, insurance, and real estate sector ($8.5 billion added earnings by brokers alone) and $8.7 billion from employees of firms providing business services. On the other hand, aggregate manufacturing employee earnings in New York City declined by $3.2 billion during the decade, while transportation and utility employee earnings declined by $1.5 billion and wholesale trade employee earnings by $59 million.

In both metropolitan and nonmetropolitan counties in the Midwest relative earnings steadily declined between 1970 and 1990, especially in the region's metropolitan counties. Note that in 1970 the Midwest produced the highest percentage of the nation's earnings (28 percent) and that their metropolitan counties ranked second only to the Northeast. By 1990, aggregate earnings produced by firms located in midwestern metropolitan counties were surpassed by firms located in the other three census regions. Metropolitan counties in the Midwest still generate the most manufacturing earnings, however (25 percent in 1990), and the region as a whole still contributes 31 percent of the nation's manufacturing earnings.

Driven by the rapid growth of their metropolitan counties, the South and the West steadily captured larger proportions of the nation's earnings. Nevertheless, most of the proportional increase of national earned income by both regions came between 1970 and 1980. In the manufacturing sector, the regional redistribution of aggregate earnings to the Sunbelt continued during the 1980s, reflecting largely the major declines in manufacturing employment in Frostbelt metropolitan areas. Most of these manufacturing job declines occurred in the central cities, an issue to which we now turn.

## INTRAMETROPOLITAN TRENDS

Fueled by an intense interaction of technological, economic, and social forces, the economic and demographic structures of the metropolitan areas were altered significantly during the 1970s and 1980s. Manufacturing dispersed to the suburbs, exurbs, nonmetropolitan areas, and abroad. Warehousing activities relocated to more regionally accessible beltways and interstate highways. Retail establishments followed their suburbanizing clientele and relocated in peripheral shopping centers and malls. The urban exodus of the middle class from the central cities further diminished the number of blue collar service jobs such as gas station attendants and delivery personnel. Many secondary commercial areas of central cities withered as the income levels of the residential groups that replaced a suburbanizing middle class could not economically sustain them.

Although most parts of the central cities continued to experience an erosion of their employment base, pockets of economic vitality emerged offering entertainment, cultural, and leisure services to younger white collar workers who resided in the cities and to growing numbers of tourists and conventioneers (Kasarda 1985). Large infusions of public and private funding led to the development of downtown shopping arcades, convention centers, entertainment complexes, and, as in Baltimore and Cleveland, new ballparks.

The central business districts (CBDs) also experienced an investment surge in high-rise office buildings housing accountants, lawyers, management consultants, bankers, financial analysts, and other information processors. In contrast to the expansive space per worker typically consumed in processing, storing, and selling material goods, the employee space required for processing, storing, and transmitting information is small. Moreover, unlike material goods, information can be transferred vertically as efficiently as it can be transferred horizontally. Those who process information, therefore, can be stacked, layer upon layer, in downtown office towers, the resulting proximity often increasing the productivity of those who require extensive, nonroutine, face-to-face interaction.

The intensive use of prime space by information-processing industries drove up CBD office rents during the 1970s and the first half of the 1980s. This, together with new tax incentives and readily available financing from banks, pension funds, and savings and loans, contributed to severe overbuilding of downtown office space in the mid- to late-1980s. At the same time the downsizing of corporate headquarters staff commenced, and computers increasingly replaced individuals who worked downtown processing information. Thus, by the early 1990s, CBD office building vacancy rates exceeded 20 percent nationally and approached 30 percent in some areas. When service sector employment growth slowed in the late 1980s, particularly in finance, insurance, and real estate, numerous downtown office towers went into bankruptcy.

With metropolitan shoppers continuing to abandon the downtown for newer suburban malls and for mail-order catalogues (e.g., L. L. Bean and Lands' End), CBD retail sales also stagnated or declined. As a consequence, between 1970 and 1990 many landmark downtown department stores such as Hudson's in Detroit and Gimbels in New York City closed.

Manufacturing employment in the largest central cities in the Midwest and Northeast was impacted the most, however. Between 1967 and 1987, Chicago lost 60 percent of its manufacturing jobs; Detroit, 51 percent; New York City, 58 percent; and Philadelphia, 64 percent (Census of Manufacturing 1967, 1987). In absolute numbers, New York City's manufacturing employment declined by 520,000 jobs, Chicago's by 326,000, Philadelphia's by 168,000, and Detroit's by 108,000.

Led by a remarkable expansion in trade and services, overall suburban ring employment growth in northern metropolitan areas was very strong (as shown by the 1967, 1977, and 1987 economic censuses). For example, between 1977 and 1987 the suburban rings of New York City added 472,000 jobs; those of Chicago, 256,000; those of Philadelphia, 249,000, and those of Detroit, 232,000.

Analysis of the major Sunbelt cities reveals that their central cities did not suffer nearly so severely with manufacturing and trade job losses during the 1970s and 1980s as did major Frostbelt cities. In fact, most major Sunbelt cities added manufacturing jobs between 1977 and 1987 and experienced considerable growth in their trade and service sectors. Furthermore, the suburban rings of many Sunbelt cities experienced accelerated job growth in the 1980s compared with the 1970s.

Examination of overall national trends in the suburbanization of employment since 1970 shows that metropolitan employment balance for combined industries shifted to the suburbs during the mid-1970s and has been deconcentrating at a rate of approximately 1 percent per year. Manufacturing employment is now over 70 percent suburban; that of wholesaling and retailing is just under 70 percent. Even the last bastion of central-city employment dominance—business services—succumbed to the powerful suburban pull, with suburban office employment surpassing the central cities during the mid-1980s (Muller 1989).

Also driven by tax incentives and readily available financing, the magnitude of suburban office development during the 1980s was massive. By 1990, the Dallas area contained 120 million square feet (MSF) of office space, 75 percent of it in the suburbs; the Detroit area contained 63.5 MSF, more than 75 percent of it in the suburbs. Northern New Jersey contained 120 MSF of office space. The Washington, DC, suburbs in northern Virginia and Maryland contained 95 MSF and 52.5 MSF of office space, respectively (Appold and Kasarda 1991).

Clayton, outside St. Louis, has 50 percent as much office space as the CBD, while two Atlanta subcenters, Perimeter/Georgia 400 and Cumberland/Galleria, now employ more workers than the city's CBD. Tysons Corner, 12 miles west of Washington, DC—with over 60,000 workers and 15 MSF of offices—contains more office space than downtown Baltimore or Miami. Post Oak Galleria in Houston, if it were freestanding, would be the ninth largest office agglomeration in the country, surpassing downtown Atlanta (Appold and Kasarda 1991).

Many suburban employment centers grew at a rapid pace during the 1980s. For example, the North Dallas Parkway area, 12 to 15 miles north of downtown, now has over 20 MSF of office space, a fivefold increase between 1980 and 1990. The symbolism, if not reality, of suburban metropolitan development dates back at least to 1972 when Nassau-Suffolk became the first totally suburban metropolitan statistical area (MSA) without a core central city.

Not only is urban employment rapidly suburbanizing but, as suggested above, it is often clustering into tight peripheral agglomerations with sales and jobs-to-housing ratios exceeding those of many cities. The relative importance of new suburban mega-retail centers is worth noting here. Woodfield, located in Schaumburg, is the Chicago area's largest suburban retail center (including a 2.3 MSF mall) and ranks second to the Loop in retail sales in the state. Westroads, outside Omaha, accounted for 9.1 percent of the entire metropolitan area's retail trade and four times that of the CBD in 1990. The King of Prussia agglomeration, 15 miles northwest of downtown Philadelphia, more than doubled its retail sales (in constant dollars) during the 1980s and now rivals Philadelphia's downtown (Appold and Kasarda 1991).

Numerous suburban employment centers have become household words. Route 128 and Silicon Valley are perhaps the most recognized industrial addresses today. Tysons Corners, adjacent to the District of Columbia, Atlanta's Perimeter City, and Gallerias in Houston and Dallas, as well as Chicago's Schaumburg, carry almost as much cachet as their respective central cities, and their rents rival those downtown. Nationally prominent firms such as Motorola, McDonald's, Control Data Corporation, and McDonnell Douglas are headquartered in the new suburban "downtowns." Even Sears vacated its famous tower in Chicago's Loop and built its new corporate headquarters in suburban Hoffman Estates, some 35 miles northwest of downtown.

Many of these new agglomerations can barely be thought of as "suburban." North Carolina's Research Triangle Park and its immediate built-up area—employing over 40,000 in 20 MSF of manufacturing, research, and office space—

is actually "downtown" Raleigh-Durham. The park contains the metropolitan area's most prominent corporate employers (e.g., Burroughs Wellcome, Glaxo, IBM, Northern Telecom, and Sumitomo), important cultural institutions such as the National Humanities Center, and the state's public television station, as well as most of the area's showcase architecture (Appold and Kasarda 1991). Such suburban downtowns, or "edge cities," as Garreau (1991) terms them, became the nation's employment growth nodes during the 1980s and continued so during the early 1990s.

Population agglomerations developed in a similar dispersed fashion, with the largest population growth nodes occurring in suburban locations. Table 5.6 lists the ten U.S. cities with a population of 100,000 or more in 1990 that experienced the greatest percentage increase in population during the 1980s. All are in the Sunbelt and all but Bakersfield, California, are suburbs of large metropolitan areas.

With population and jobs rapidly suburbanizing, suburb-to-suburb commuting has become the national norm. Table 5.7 reveals that by 1990 suburb-to-suburb commuters typically outnumbered suburb-to-central-city commuters by at least a 3-to-1 margin. In the Philadelphia PMSA 1.2 million workers commute between

TABLE 5.6   Cities with a population of 100,000 or more in 1990 having the largest percentage increase from 1980.

| City | Population in 1980 | Population in 1990 | Percentage Change |
|---|---|---|---|
| Moreno Valley, California (suburb of Riverside) | 28,309 | 118,779 | 320% |
| Mesa, Arizona (suburb of Phoenix) | 152,404 | 288,091 | 89 |
| Rancho Cucamonga, California (suburb of Los Angeles) | 55,250 | 101,409 | 84 |
| Plano, Texas (suburb of Dallas) | 72,331 | 128,713 | 78 |
| Irvine, California (suburb of Los Angeles) | 62,134 | 110,330 | 78 |
| Escondido, California (suburb of San Diego) | 64,355 | 108,635 | 69 |
| Oceanside, California (suburb of Los Angeles) | 76,693 | 128,398 | 67 |
| Santa Clarita, California (suburb of Los Angeles) | 66,730 | 110,642 | 66 |
| Bakersfield, California | 105,611 | 174,820 | 66 |
| Arlington, Texas (suburb of Dallas) | 160,113 | 261,721 | 64 |

SOURCE: Decennial census for 1980 and 1990 (Summary Tape File 1C).

TABLE 5.7    Commuting times from the suburban ring to the central city
and within the suburban ring for selected metropolitan areas: 1990.

| Metropolitan Area | Suburban Ring to Central City | | Suburban Ring to Suburban Ring | |
|---|---|---|---|---|
| | Number of Commuters (000) | Mean Time (in minutes) | Number of Commuters (000) | Mean Time (in minutes) |
| Baltimore | 179 | 30 | 550 | 21 |
| Boston | 230 | 34 | 748 | 20 |
| Chicago | 435 | 41 | 1,111 | 22 |
| Cleveland | 180 | 28 | 376 | 19 |
| Detroit | 174 | 31 | 1,292 | 22 |
| Los Angeles/Long Beach | 564 | 35 | 1,497 | 23 |
| New York | 146 | 51 | 347 | 19 |
| Philadelphia | 228 | 37 | 1,218 | 20 |
| St. Louis | 195 | 29 | 708 | 21 |
| Washington, DC | 441 | 39 | 1,291 | 26 |

SOURCE: Decennial census Public Use Microdata Samples (5 percent) for 1980 and 1990.

NOTES: Mean commuting time is based on the total time that it takes a person to make a one-way trip from home to place of work. Metropolitan areas are based on MSA/PMSA boundaries.

suburbs compared with 228,000 suburbanites who commute to the central city, and in the Detroit PMSA 1.3 million commute between suburbs compared with only 174,000 who commute to the central city.

Because suburb-to-suburb work trips are nearly 50 percent shorter on average than suburb-to-central-city work trips, the continued suburbanization of employment has resulted in overall gains in urban efficiency. For example, the mean one-way commute time of suburban residents who work in New York City was 51 minutes in 1990 compared with 19 minutes for suburbanites who commute to jobs in the suburbs. Chicago's suburb-to-central-city mean commuting time was approximately double that of the mean suburb-to-suburb commuting time (41 minutes versus 22 minutes).

Several dark clouds, however, hover over suburban growth centers. First, dramatically increased peripheral employment brought congestion, as suburb-to-suburb commuting grew far more rapidly than peripheral road construction. Second, the nucleated pattern of employment combined with dispersed labor sheds makes public transit inefficient, especially exacerbating location-specific shortages of nonmanagerial and lower-skill workers in the suburbs.

In this regard, lack of affordable housing for less-skilled employees near suburban commercial growth nodes has become a serious problem. Compounding the problem of spatial mismatch has been the substantial restructuring of central-city economies (especially in the North) that has dramatically reduced the number of appropriate jobs available for less-skilled residents of these cities. In the next section, the nature and scope of urban industrial restructuring are documented and implications for spatial and skills mismatches and minority joblessness assessed.

## URBAN ECONOMIC RESTRUCTURING AND JOB ACCESSIBILITY

As a place where people work, the American city today is not the city we knew in the 1960s when many of our assumptions about joblessness and poverty were formed. Since then, advances in transportation and communication technologies, interacting with a rapidly changing structure of the national and global economy, have transformed our major cities from centers of manufacturing, retail, and wholesale trade to centers of information processing, finance, and administration. In the process, many traditional goods-processing jobs that once constituted the economic backbone of cities and provided nearby employment for less-educated residents vanished. These industries were replaced, at least in part, by information-processing jobs that require education beyond high school and, hence, are not *functionally* accessible to the poorly educated, even though these new jobs are in relatively close proximity to them (*spatially* accessible).

Cities that lost the largest numbers of goods-processing jobs with lower education requisites between 1970 and 1990 also added large numbers of minorities with no education beyond high school to their working age population. Many of these new labor force entrants were sons and daughters of the millions of southern blacks who had migrated to northern cities during the 25 years following World War II when employment opportunities requiring only limited education were plentiful.

Following the Immigration Act of 1965, black inner-city population growth was demographically supplemented by waves of Hispanic and Asian immigrants, while white migration to the suburbs continued apace. As a result, by 1990 racial-ethnic minorities composed the demographic majority in most of our largest cities—57 percent in New York, 62 percent in Chicago, 63 percent in Los Angeles, 70 percent in Atlanta, 79 percent in Detroit, and 88 percent in Miami. Table 5.8 lists the 1990 minority proportions of central cities with populations of 200,000 or more where minorities composed more than half of the city's population.

Declines in urban blue collar jobs had serious consequences for blacks: As late as the 1968–1970 period, more than 70 percent of all blacks working in metropolitan areas held blue collar jobs at the same time that more than 50 percent of all metropolitan workers held white collar jobs (calculated from pooled Current Population Survey files for 1968–1970). Moreover, of the large numbers of urban blacks classified as blue collar workers during the late 1960s, more than 50 percent were employed in goods-producing industries.

TABLE 5.8   Distribution of racial-ethnic minorities in selected cities: 1990.

| City | Population (000) | Non-Hispanic Black | Hispanic | Total Minority |
|---|---|---|---|---|
| Miami | 359 | 25% | 62% | 88% |
| Newark | 275 | 56 | 26 | 84 |
| Detroit | 1,027 | 75 | 3 | 79 |
| Santa Ana | 294 | 2 | 65 | 77 |
| Honolulu | 365 | 1 | 5 | 75 |
| El Paso | 515 | 3 | 69 | 74 |
| Washington, DC | 607 | 65 | 5 | 73 |
| Oakland | 372 | 43 | 14 | 72 |
| Atlanta | 394 | 67 | 2 | 70 |
| New Orleans | 497 | 61 | 3 | 67 |
| Birmingham | 266 | 63 | 0 | 64 |
| San Antonio | 936 | 7 | 56 | 64 |
| Jersey City | 229 | 28 | 24 | 63 |
| Los Angeles | 3,485 | 13 | 40 | 63 |
| Chicago | 2,784 | 39 | 20 | 62 |
| Baltimore | 736 | 59 | 1 | 61 |
| Houston | 1,631 | 27 | 28 | 59 |
| New York | 7,323 | 25 | 24 | 57 |
| Memphis | 610 | 55 | 1 | 56 |
| San Francisco | 724 | 11 | 14 | 53 |
| Dallas | 1,007 | 29 | 21 | 52 |
| Cleveland | 506 | 46 | 5 | 52 |

(Percentage Distribution spans Non-Hispanic Black, Hispanic, Total Minority)

SOURCE: Decennial census for 1990 (Summary Tape File 1C).

NOTE: Total Minority includes all persons who are not non-Hispanic white.

With the ready availability of urban blue collar jobs (requiring little more than a strong back and a willingness to work), 80 percent of central-city black males (aged 16–64) with less than 12 years of schooling completed were actually working in the 1968–1970 surveys. By the 1990–1992 period, fewer than 50 percent of comparably educated urban blacks were working.

Later in this section I document trends in urban black joblessness and compare them with trends for white residents and others in the same cities. First, however, let us examine the nature and extent of urban economic restructuring, focusing on employment changes between 1970 and 1990 in the largest cities across the four census regions for which Census Bureau *County Business Patterns* data can be used to trace such changes. The nine selected cities (New York, Philadelphia, Boston, Baltimore, St. Louis, Atlanta, Dallas, Denver, and San Francisco) have boundaries either identical to or closely approximating their respective county boundaries. This allows the use of county data to trace employment changes, by industry, for these cities.

Table 5.9 shows that all the older northern cities—New York City, Philadel-

TABLE 5.9   Central-city employment, by sector: 1970–1990.

| Central City/Sector | 1970 (000) | 1970 Percentage | 1980 (000) | 1980 Percentage | 1990 (000) | 1990 Percentage |
|---|---|---|---|---|---|---|
| **New York** | | | | | | |
| Total employment[a] | 3,350 | 100% | 2,883 | 100% | 3,128 | 100% |
| Manufacturing | 864 | 26 | 570 | 20 | 368 | 12 |
| Retail/wholesale | 779 | 23 | 596 | 21 | 616 | 20 |
| White collar services[b] | 1,172 | 35 | 1,201 | 42 | 1,607 | 51 |
| Blue collar services[c] | 424 | 13 | 388 | 13 | 398 | 13 |
| Other | 112 | 3 | 128 | 5 | 138 | 4 |
| **Philadelphia** | | | | | | |
| Total employment[a] | 772 | 100 | 630 | 100 | 611 | 100 |
| Manufacturing | 257 | 33 | 145 | 23 | 85 | 14 |
| Retail/wholesale | 180 | 23 | 134 | 21 | 135 | 22 |
| White collar services[b] | 220 | 29 | 259 | 41 | 302 | 49 |
| Blue collar services[c] | 81 | 11 | 64 | 10 | 63 | 10 |
| Other | 35 | 5 | 28 | 5 | 26 | 4 |
| **Boston** | | | | | | |
| Total employment[a] | 465 | 100 | 439 | 100 | 509 | 100 |
| Manufacturing | 84 | 18 | 57 | 13 | 36 | 7 |
| Retail/wholesale | 111 | 24 | 82 | 19 | 82 | 16 |
| White collar services[b] | 194 | 42 | 219 | 50 | 296 | 58 |
| Blue collar services[c] | 55 | 12 | 59 | 13 | 66 | 13 |
| Other | 21 | 5 | 21 | 5 | 29 | 6 |
| **Baltimore** | | | | | | |
| Total employment[a] | 367 | 100 | 307 | 100 | 310 | 100 |
| Manufacturing | 105 | 29 | 72 | 23 | 42 | 14 |
| Retail/wholesale | 94 | 26 | 67 | 22 | 61 | 20 |
| White collar services[b] | 108 | 29 | 109 | 36 | 152 | 49 |
| Blue collar services[c] | 44 | 12 | 43 | 14 | 39 | 13 |
| Other | 16 | 4 | 16 | 5 | 16 | 5 |
| **St. Louis** | | | | | | |
| Total employment[a] | 376 | 100 | 286 | 100 | 257 | 100 |
| Manufacturing | 133 | 35 | 88 | 31 | 51 | 20 |
| Retail/wholesale | 89 | 24 | 61 | 21 | 58 | 23 |
| White collar services[b] | 96 | 26 | 82 | 29 | 97 | 38 |
| Blue collar services[c] | 44 | 12 | 41 | 14 | 40 | 16 |
| Other | 14 | 4 | 14 | 5 | 12 | 5 |
| **Atlanta** | | | | | | |
| Total employment[a] | 370 | 100 | 390 | 100 | 534 | 100 |
| Manufacturing | 72 | 19 | 58 | 15 | 59 | 11 |
| Retail/wholesale | 122 | 33 | 112 | 29 | 136 | 26 |
| White collar services[b] | 95 | 26 | 116 | 30 | 197 | 37 |
| Blue collar services[c] | 59 | 16 | 79 | 20 | 112 | 21 |
| Other | 23 | 6 | 24 | 6 | 29 | 6 |

TABLE 5.9  (continued)

| Central City/Sector | 1970 | | 1980 | | 1990 | |
|---|---|---|---|---|---|---|
| | (000) | Percentage | (000) | Percentage | (000) | Percentage |
| Dallas | | | | | | |
| Total employment[a] | 584 | 100 | 850 | 100 | 1,111 | 100 |
| Manufacturing | 171 | 29 | 202 | 24 | 181 | 16 |
| Retail/wholesale | 165 | 28 | 244 | 29 | 299 | 27 |
| White collar services[b] | 123 | 21 | 214 | 25 | 388 | 35 |
| Blue collar services[c] | 77 | 13 | 101 | 12 | 159 | 14 |
| Other | 48 | 8 | 89 | 10 | 83 | 8 |
| | | | | | | |
| Denver | | | | | | |
| Total employment[a] | 252 | 100 | 336 | 100 | 332 | 100 |
| Manufacturing | 48 | 19 | 47 | 14 | 34 | 10 |
| Retail/wholesale | 76 | 30 | 94 | 28 | 79 | 24 |
| White collar services[b] | 74 | 29 | 103 | 31 | 135 | 41 |
| Blue collar services[c] | 35 | 14 | 61 | 18 | 62 | 19 |
| Other | 19 | 8 | 30 | 9 | 22 | 7 |
| | | | | | | |
| San Francisco | | | | | | |
| Total employment[a] | 400 | 100 | 487 | 100 | 518 | 100 |
| Manufacturing | 59 | 15 | 55 | 11 | 45 | 9 |
| Retail/wholesale | 101 | 25 | 94 | 19 | 113 | 22 |
| White collar services[b] | 152 | 38 | 192 | 39 | 247 | 48 |
| Blue collar services[c] | 63 | 16 | 109 | 22 | 82 | 16 |
| Other | 25 | 6 | 38 | 8 | 32 | 6 |

SOURCES: U.S. Bureau of the Census, *County Business Patterns* (1953, 1970, 1990); U.S. Department of Labor, *The National Industry-Occupation Employment Matrix 1970, 1978, and projected 1990* (1981).

NOTE: Rows may not sum to 100 due to rounding.

[a]Total classified employment and industry subcategories excluding government employees and sole proprietors.
[b]Services (excluding government, retail, and wholesale) in which more than one half of the employees hold executive, managerial, professional, or clerical positions.
[c]Services (excluding government, retail, and wholesale) in which fewer than one half of the employees hold executive, managerial, professional, or clerical positions.

phia, Boston, Baltimore, and St. Louis—lost well over half of their manufacturing jobs between 1970 and 1990 with the decreases in the 1980s about as great as those in the 1970s.[4] These cities also experienced considerable declines in their retail and wholesale sectors, but most or all of this job loss occurred before 1980. In fact, the three largest cities in the Northeast (New York, Philadelphia, and Boston) either held their own or expanded slightly their retail and wholesale trade employment during the 1980s. White collar service industry growth accelerated in these cities during the 1980s. Nevertheless, with the exception of Boston, absolute employment loss in the goods-processing industries of these cities overwhelmed growth in their white collar service industries, resulting in overall city employment declines between 1970 and 1990. Baltimore, for example, lost

63,000 manufacturing jobs and gained 44,000 white collar service jobs, while St. Louis lost 82,000 manufacturing jobs but gained only 1,000 white collar service jobs.

Conversely, the four major cities in the South and West all exhibited substantial *total* employment growth between 1970 and 1990 and either relatively little loss or actual job growth in manufacturing, retail, and wholesale trade. Moreover, not only did white collar service employment markedly increase during both the 1970s and 1980s in the four southern and western cities, but, excepting San Francisco in the 1980s, blue collar service jobs expanded as well.

Table 5.10 provides an even more vivid illustration of regional differences in post-1970 urban industrial restructuring. This table decomposes total city employment change between 1970 and 1990 for each city into that accounted for by (1) its service sector industries in which more than 60 percent of the employees were classified as executive, managerial, professional, or clerical; and (2) all other industries combined.

All five northern cities experienced substantial employment growth in their predominantly information-processing industries and marked employment decline in their other combined industries. For example, New York City added 494,000 jobs between 1970 and 1990 in its predominantly information-processing industries (a 52 percent increase) and lost 708,000 jobs in all other industries (a 29 percent decrease). More than two thirds of the nearly half million jobs added in New York City's information-processing industries between 1970 and 1990 were added during the 1980s. By 1990, 46 percent of jobs in New York City were in service industries in which executive, managerial, professional, and clerical workers constituted more than 60 percent of the industry's total employment.

Boston's information-processing industries likewise expanded by 51 percent between 1970 and 1990 (most expansion occurring during the 1980s), while its combined other industries declined by 18 percent. Boston, in fact, is the only major northern city that added more jobs to its predominantly information-processing industries than it lost in other industries during this period. By 1990, well over half of Boston's jobs were in information processing.

For the remaining three northern cities—Philadelphia, Baltimore, and St. Louis—job increases in their predominantly information-processing industries were overwhelmed by job losses in their more traditional industries. This is especially true for Philadelphia and St. Louis, which had lost more than two thirds of their manufacturing jobs between 1970 and 1990 (Table 5.9).

In contrast to larger, older cities in the North, Atlanta, Houston, Denver, and San Francisco experienced employment gains in their predominantly information-processing industries and in all other industries combined between 1970 and 1990. Like older cities in the North, however, the older, major cities in the South and West (Atlanta, San Francisco, and Denver) exhibited substantially

TABLE 5.10  Central-city employment, by percentage of employees in information-processing industries: 1970–1990.

| Central City/Industry Type | 1970 | | 1980 | | 1990 | | Change 1970–1990 | |
|---|---|---|---|---|---|---|---|---|
| | (000) | Percentage | (000) | Percentage | (000) | Percentage | (000) | Percentage |
| New York | | | | | | | | |
| Information-processing industries | 946 | 28% | 1,107 | 38% | 1,440 | 46% | +494 | +52% |
| All other industries | 2,404 | 72 | 1,795 | 62 | 1,696 | 54 | −708 | −29 |
| Philadelphia | | | | | | | | |
| Information-processing industries | 208 | 27 | 240 | 38 | 275 | 45 | +67 | +32 |
| All other industries | 564 | 73 | 392 | 62 | 337 | 55 | −227 | −40 |
| Boston | | | | | | | | |
| Information-processing industries | 189 | 41 | 204 | 46 | 284 | 56 | +95 | +51 |
| All other industries | 276 | 59 | 237 | 54 | 226 | 44 | −50 | −18 |
| Baltimore | | | | | | | | |
| Information-processing industries | 95 | 26 | 103 | 33 | 141 | 45 | +46 | +49 |
| All other industries | 272 | 74 | 205 | 67 | 170 | 55 | −102 | −38 |
| St. Louis | | | | | | | | |
| Information-processing industries | 92 | 24 | 76 | 26 | 91 | 35 | −1 | −1 |
| All other industries | 284 | 76 | 211 | 74 | 166 | 65 | −114 | −41 |

| | | | | | | | | |
|---|---|---|---|---|---|---|---|---|
| **Atlanta** | | | | | | | | |
| Information-processing industries | 92 | 25 | 108 | 28 | 185 | 34 | +93 | +101 |
| All other industries | 280 | 75 | 284 | 72 | 351 | 66 | +71 | +25 |
| **Dallas** | | | | | | | | |
| Information-processing industries | 111 | 19 | 192 | 22 | 346 | 31 | +234 | +211 |
| All other industries | 475 | 81 | 664 | 78 | 768 | 69 | +293 | +62 |
| **Denver** | | | | | | | | |
| Information-processing industries | 70 | 28 | 95 | 28 | 123 | 37 | +53 | +76 |
| All other industries | 183 | 72 | 243 | 72 | 209 | 63 | +26 | +15 |
| **San Francisco** | | | | | | | | |
| Information-processing industries | 149 | 37 | 180 | 37 | 226 | 43 | +77 | +51 |
| All other industries | 253 | 63 | 311 | 63 | 294 | 57 | +41 | +16 |

SOURCES: U.S. Bureau of the Census, *County Business Patterns* (1953, 1970, 1990); U.S. Department of Labor, *The National Industry-Occupation Employment Matrix* (1970, 1978, and projected 1990, 1981).

NOTES: Rows may not sum to 100 due to rounding. Information-processing industries are those in which executive, professional, managerial, and clerical workers constitute more than 60 percent of the industry's total employment.

greater absolute and proportional gains in their information-processing industries than they did in their other combined industries. Moreover, the two older western cities, Denver and San Francisco, lost employment during the 1980s in noninformation-processing industries. Dallas, on the other hand, added a great deal of employment across all industries during both the 1970s and 1980s, no doubt reflecting its economic surge during much of that period.

A major difference, then, between large Frostbelt and Sunbelt cities is that between 1970 and 1990 Sunbelt cities added jobs in many other basic industries besides information-processing jobs that contributed to these cities' overall employment growth. Conversely, many Frostbelt cities experienced overall employment decline between 1970 and 1990 because growth in their predominantly information-processing industries did not numerically compensate for losses in their more traditional industrial sectors, especially manufacturing. The 1980s were, in general, more favorable for most major Frostbelt cities, with greater growth in information-processing jobs and less loss in goods-processing jobs than during the 1970s.

## Rising Education Requisites for Employment

The functional transformation of major northern cities from goods-processing centers to information-processing centers since 1970 corresponds to an important change in the education required for employment in these cities. Job losses have been greatest in those northern urban industries in which education requirements for employment tend to be low (a high school diploma may not be required). Job growth has been concentrated primarily in urban industries in which education beyond high school is the norm.

To illustrate this phenomenon, Table 5.11 presents the employment changes between 1970 and 1980 and between 1980 and 1990 in industries classified by mean years of schooling completed by their jobholders in 1982. Two categories of industries were selected: (1) industries in which jobholders in 1982 averaged fewer than 12 years of schooling (most employees typically did not complete high school) and (2) industries in which jobholders averaged 13 years or more of schooling (employees, on average, acquired at least one year of higher education).

Industry employment changes in cities by average education level of jobholders were estimated by synthesizing individual-level data on the schooling completed by jobholders in detailed classified industries with data on the aggregate job changes that occurred within each industry in each city.[5] The figures reveal that the five major northern cities had consistent employment losses in industries with low education requisites, though losses slowed during the 1980s compared with the 1970s, especially in New York and Philadelphia. Between 1980 and

1990 New York City lost 135,000 jobs in industries with low education requisites and added nearly 300,000 in industries with mean employee education levels of at least 13 years of schooling. Philadelphia, Baltimore, and St. Louis also lost substantial numbers of jobs between 1980 and 1990 in industries with typically low education requirements; St. Louis showed only a marginal gain of jobs in its industries with high mean jobholder education levels. Boston, on the other hand, added more jobs in industries with higher education levels than it lost in jobs with lower education levels, contributing to overall city job growth since 1980. By 1990, Boston had nearly twice as many jobs in industries with high mean employee education levels as it had in industries with low mean levels.

Employment growth in industries in which jobholders' schooling averaged 13 years or more in 1982 was also considerable in major cities in the South and West. Yet, in contrast to major cities in the North, three of the four selected cities in the South and West gained jobs in industries with low education levels during the 1970s and 1980s, Atlanta being the exception during the 1970s and Denver during the 1980s.

The increased importance of higher education for working in economically transforming northern cities is further documented by Table 5.12, which presents place-of-work changes between 1980 and 1990 in the number of people working in ten selected central cities, by two categories of education completed (less than high school diploma and college degree). These data refer to all persons working in a central city regardless of their place of residence. The cities selected represent four large transforming cities in both the Northeast and the Midwest, with Los Angeles and Washington, DC, for comparison. Since these data provide individual education levels of all workers in the cities (using place-of-work codes), they tap the actual changing education distribution of the city employment base.

The results from census data for city job changes by education mirror trends calculated from *County Business Patterns* establishment data. Frostbelt cities experienced major declines in the number of workers with less than a high school diploma and substantial increments in the number of workers with a college degree. Some figures are particularly noteworthy. For example, jobs held by high school dropouts declined by more than 50 percent between 1980 and 1990 in Detroit and St. Louis and by nearly 50 percent in Baltimore and Cleveland. Conversely, city jobs held by college graduates increased by more than 50 percent in Boston and New York City and by more than 40 percent in Baltimore, Chicago, St. Louis, and Washington, DC. Los Angeles, which experienced a 50 percent increase in city jobs held by college graduates, also experienced a 15 percent growth in jobs held by those who had not completed high school. The latter no doubt reflects the large

TABLE 5.11 Central-city jobs in selected industries, by mean education of employees: 1970–1990.

| Central City/Education Mean | 1970 (000) | 1980 (000) | 1990 (000) | Change 1970–1980 (000) | Percentage | Change 1980–1990 (000) | Percentage |
|---|---|---|---|---|---|---|---|
| New York | | | | | | | |
| Less than 12 years | 1,552 | 1,112 | 977 | −440 | −28% | −135 | −12% |
| 13 years or more | 1,002 | 956 | 1,253 | −46 | −5 | +297 | +31 |
| Philadelphia | | | | | | | |
| Less than 12 years | 430 | 281 | 226 | −149 | −35 | −55 | −20 |
| 13 years or more | 205 | 191 | 231 | −14 | −7 | +40 | +21 |
| Boston | | | | | | | |
| Less than 12 years | 189 | 148 | 128 | −41 | −22 | −20 | −14 |
| 13 years or more | 185 | 168 | 237 | −17 | −9 | +69 | +41 |
| Baltimore | | | | | | | |
| Less than 12 years | 207 | 146 | 110 | −61 | −29 | −37 | −25 |
| 13 years or more | 90 | 84 | 118 | −6 | −7 | +34 | +40 |
| St. Louis | | | | | | | |
| Less than 12 years | 210 | 145 | 107 | −65 | −31 | −38 | −26 |
| 13 years or more | 98 | 67 | 79 | −31 | −32 | +12 | +18 |

| | | | | | | | |
|---|---|---|---|---|---|---|---|
| **Atlanta** | | | | | | | |
| Less than 12 years | 179 | 162 | 190 | −17 | −9 | +28 | +17 |
| 13 years or more | 92 | 95 | 165 | +3 | +4 | +70 | +73 |
| **Dallas** | | | | | | | |
| Less than 12 years | 337 | 459 | 468 | +123 | +36 | +9 | +2 |
| 13 years or more | 107 | 187 | 334 | +80 | +76 | +147 | +79 |
| **Denver** | | | | | | | |
| Less than 12 years | 120 | 136 | 107 | +16 | +13 | −29 | −21 |
| 13 years or more | 72 | 94 | 120 | +22 | +30 | +27 | +29 |
| **San Francisco** | | | | | | | |
| Less than 12 years | 132 | 167 | 173 | +35 | +26 | +6 | +4 |
| 13 years or more | 135 | 166 | 204 | +31 | +23 | +38 | +23 |

SOURCES: U.S. Bureau of the Census, *County Business Patterns* (1953, 1970, 1990); U.S. Department of Labor, Current Population Survey Annual Demographic File (1982).

TABLE 5.12   Changes in the number of people working in central cities, by education, between 1980 and 1990.

| Central City | Less Than High School Diploma | | College Degree | |
|---|---|---|---|---|
| | (000) | Percentage | (000) | Percentage |
| Baltimore | −55 | −48% | +35 | +49% |
| Boston | −21 | −38 | +76 | +54 |
| Chicago | −97 | −33 | +144 | +46 |
| Cleveland | −35 | −50 | +22 | +33 |
| Detroit | −48 | −55 | +10 | +12 |
| Los Angeles | +44 | +15 | +172 | +51 |
| New York | −169 | −26 | +446 | +54 |
| Philadelphia | −73 | −45 | +61 | +40 |
| St. Louis | −44 | −55 | +25 | +42 |
| Washington, DC | −16 | −25 | +100 | +43 |

SOURCE: Decennial census Public Use Microdata Samples (5 percent) for 1980 and 1990.

immigration of Hispanic workers and other minorities with low education levels.

Table 5.13 describes the changing education distribution of all persons who worked in the ten cities between 1970 and 1990 (regardless of place of residence). At least 25 percent of workers in every city shown held a college degree by 1990, up considerably since 1980. In Boston and Washington, DC, nearly half of all city workers held a college degree in 1990.

The decline in the proportion of city jobholders who lacked a high school diploma is just as striking. The share in Baltimore dropped from 48 percent in 1970 to 15 percent in 1990; in Boston, from 29 to 7 percent; and in Detroit, from 37 to 11 percent.

Of course, portions of the decrease in city jobs held by those without high school diplomas and the increase in jobs held by those with college degrees reflect improvements in the overall educational attainment of the city labor force since 1970. These improvements, however, were not nearly as great as the concurrent upward shifts in the education of city jobholders. As a result, much of the job increase in the "some college" or "college degree" categories for each city was absorbed by suburban commuters, while many job losses in the "less than high school diploma" or "high school diploma" categories were absorbed by city residents.

Moreover, general improvements in city residents' education levels meant that less-educated, jobless blacks fell further behind in the hiring queue (Lieberson 1980). Particularly affected were the large numbers of urban blacks who had not completed high school, especially younger ones. For inner-city black

TABLE 5.13 Percentage distribution of central-city jobs,
by education level of jobholders: 1970–1990.

| Central City | Year | Less Than High School Diploma | High School Diploma | Some College | College Degree |
|---|---|---|---|---|---|
| Baltimore | | | | | |
| | 1970 | 48% | 29% | 10% | 12% |
| | 1980 | 30 | 36 | 16 | 19 |
| | 1990 | 15 | 32 | 26 | 27 |
| Boston | | | | | |
| | 1970 | 29 | 36 | 17 | 18 |
| | 1980 | 13 | 31 | 22 | 33 |
| | 1990 | 7 | 23 | 26 | 44 |
| Chicago | | | | | |
| | 1970 | 38 | 32 | 15 | 15 |
| | 1980 | 23 | 32 | 20 | 25 |
| | 1990 | 14 | 27 | 29 | 31 |
| Cleveland | | | | | |
| | 1970 | 35 | 38 | 13 | 14 |
| | 1980 | 21 | 40 | 19 | 20 |
| | 1990 | 11 | 33 | 30 | 27 |
| Detroit | | | | | |
| | 1970 | 37 | 37 | 14 | 12 |
| | 1980 | 21 | 37 | 22 | 20 |
| | 1990 | 11 | 30 | 33 | 26 |
| Los Angeles | | | | | |
| | 1980 | 22 | 28 | 26 | 24 |
| | 1990 | 19 | 23 | 31 | 28 |
| New York | | | | | |
| | 1970 | 36 | 33 | 13 | 18 |
| | 1980 | 22 | 31 | 19 | 28 |
| | 1990 | 13 | 28 | 24 | 35 |
| Philadelphia | | | | | |
| | 1980 | 23 | 39 | 16 | 22 |
| | 1990 | 12 | 36 | 23 | 29 |
| St. Louis | | | | | |
| | 1970 | 43 | 33 | 11 | 13 |
| | 1980 | 26 | 37 | 19 | 19 |
| | 1990 | 12 | 29 | 32 | 27 |

TABLE 5.13  (*continued*)

| Central City | Year | Less Than High School Diploma | High School Diploma | Some College | College Degree |
|---|---|---|---|---|---|
| Washington, DC | | | | | |
| | 1970 | 23 | 32 | 18 | 28 |
| | 1980 | 11 | 27 | 21 | 41 |
| | 1990 | 7 | 21 | 25 | 47 |

SOURCE: Decennial census Public Use Microdata Samples (15 percent county group file) for 1970; (5 percent) for 1980 and 1990.

NOTES: Rows may not sum to 100 due to rounding. Data for Los Angeles and Philadelphia are not available for 1970.

youths, school dropout rates exceeded 25 percent during the 1970s and 1980s, with case studies of individual schools suggesting considerably higher dropout rates among the ghetto poor (Hess 1986; Kornblum 1985).

### Skills and Spatial Mismatches

Table 5.14 illustrates the structural dilemma facing sizable portions of the black urban labor force. This table compares the 1990 education distributions of those employed by city industries, including the self-employed, with the education distributions of out-of-school city residents, by race-ethnicity. It also shows the index of dissimilarity between the education distribution of jobholders in each city and the education distribution of the out-of-school white, black, and Hispanic residents of each city. The jobs-resident education dissimilarity index, as an indicator of skills mismatch for each racial-ethnic group, is presented for 1980 and 1990. (The index of dissimilarity measures the change necessary in the education distribution of each racial-ethnic resident group to match the education mix of city jobs.)

One quickly observes the weak education distribution of Hispanics. As city economies continue to transform, Hispanic residents appear to be the most structurally disadvantaged. The black resident distributions also look problematic, especially the low percentage of college graduates (the city job category that is expanding most rapidly). In fact, the job-education mismatch for blacks rose between 1980 and 1990 in Baltimore, Chicago, Cleveland, Detroit, Philadelphia, and St. Louis, suggesting a growing skills mismatch between black residents and jobs available in these cities.

A conceptually related but analytically distinct structural barrier to inner-city minority employment is spatial mismatch. Suburbanization of blue collar jobs, particularly manufacturing and services such as fast foods, together with residential confinement of minorities (particularly blacks) near the central-city core, has physically isolated them from the bulk of deconcentrating job opportunities. This is purported to result in higher unemployment rates as well as increasing

TABLE 5.14 Education distribution of city jobs, education of city residents, and job-resident index of dissimilarity, by race: 1990.

| | Education Distribution | | | | Index of Dissimilarity | |
|---|---|---|---|---|---|---|
| | Less Than High School Diploma | High School Diploma | Some College | College Degree | 1980 | 1990 |
| **Baltimore** | | | | | | |
| Jobs | 15% | 32% | 26% | 27% | | |
| Whites | 25 | 32 | 17 | 25 | 13 | 11 |
| Blacks | 32 | 42 | 18 | 8 | 21 | 27 |
| Hispanics | 29 | 33 | 17 | 21 | 21 | 15 |
| **Boston** | | | | | | |
| Jobs | 7 | 23 | 26 | 44 | | |
| Whites | 9 | 28 | 20 | 43 | 14 | 7 |
| Blacks | 23 | 41 | 23 | 13 | 36 | 34 |
| Hispanics | 41 | 32 | 15 | 11 | 43 | 43 |
| **Chicago** | | | | | | |
| Jobs | 14 | 27 | 29 | 31 | | |
| Whites | 14 | 31 | 22 | 33 | 12 | 6 |
| Blacks | 25 | 38 | 27 | 10 | 22 | 23 |
| Hispanics | 53 | 28 | 13 | 6 | 45 | 41 |
| **Cleveland** | | | | | | |
| Jobs | 11 | 33 | 30 | 27 | | |
| Whites | 28 | 43 | 19 | 10 | 22 | 27 |
| Blacks | 30 | 45 | 21 | 4 | 23 | 31 |
| Hispanics | 47 | 35 | 13 | 5 | 41 | 38 |
| **Detroit** | | | | | | |
| Jobs | 11 | 30 | 33 | 26 | | |
| Whites | 27 | 39 | 21 | 13 | 20 | 25 |
| Blacks | 25 | 40 | 27 | 8 | 21 | 24 |
| Hispanics | 47 | 34 | 13 | 6 | 35 | 40 |
| **Los Angeles** | | | | | | |
| Jobs | 19 | 23 | 31 | 28 | | |
| Whites | 7 | 24 | 32 | 37 | 9 | 12 |
| Blacks | 16 | 39 | 33 | 13 | 19 | 18 |
| Hispanics | 63 | 23 | 11 | 4 | 46 | 44 |
| **New York** | | | | | | |
| Jobs | 13 | 28 | 24 | 35 | | |
| Whites | 11 | 31 | 20 | 38 | 7 | 6 |
| Blacks | 23 | 42 | 23 | 12 | 25 | 24 |
| Hispanics | 44 | 33 | 16 | 7 | 38 | 35 |

TABLE 5.14   (*continued*)

| | Education Distribution | | | | Index of Dissimilarity | |
|---|---|---|---|---|---|---|
| | Less Than High School Diploma | High School Diploma | Some College | College Degree | 1980 | 1990 |
| **Philadelphia** | | | | | | |
| Jobs | 12 | 36 | 23 | 29 | | |
| Whites | 17 | 44 | 17 | 21 | 14 | 14 |
| Blacks | 25 | 48 | 19 | 9 | 23 | 24 |
| Hispanics | 48 | 34 | 11 | 6 | 38 | 36 |
| **St. Louis** | | | | | | |
| Jobs | 12 | 29 | 32 | 27 | | |
| Whites | 21 | 33 | 23 | 23 | 13 | 13 |
| Blacks | 31 | 41 | 21 | 7 | 23 | 30 |
| Hispanics | 27 | 36 | 21 | 16 | 17 | 22 |
| **Washington, DC** | | | | | | |
| Jobs | 7 | 21 | 25 | 47 | | |
| Whites | 2 | 7 | 14 | 78 | 27 | 31 |
| Blacks | 26 | 40 | 20 | 14 | 38 | 38 |
| Hispanics | 50 | 21 | 10 | 19 | 29 | 43 |

SOURCE: Decennial census Public Use Microdata Samples (5 percent) for 1980 and 1990.

NOTE: Rows may not sum to 100 due to rounding.

the job search and commuting times of those minorities who do secure appropriate suburban jobs.

To assess the consequences of spatial mismatches I used the *1990 5 percent Public Use Microdata* samples for the same set of selected larger cities to compute the mean one-way commuting times of central-city residents to city jobs and to jobs outside the city, controlling for means of transit (Table 5.15).

In 19 of the 20 sets of comparison figures, blacks had longer commuting times than whites. The one exception was central-city-to-suburb commutes by private vehicle in Los Angeles where the white, black, and Hispanic times were approximately the same. In addition, the central-city-to-suburb one-way commute times by those using public transit were exceptionally long, especially for blacks. Blacks using public transit averaged more than 40 minutes commuting each way to jobs in the suburbs in all ten cities. One-way commuting times to suburban jobs by central-city black residents using public transit exceeded 50 minutes in Chicago, Los Angeles, and New York. Whites' city-to-suburb and intracity commute times were shorter than blacks', suggesting that white central-city residents are able to live closer to city workplaces, as well.

These commuting times, of course, refer only to those who are employed.

TABLE 5.15  Mean commuting times of central-city residents to city jobs and to jobs outside the city, by private and public transit and race-ethnicity: 1990 (in minutes).

| Central City Race-Ethnicity | Private | | Public | |
|---|---|---|---|---|
| | Central City to Central City | Central City to Outside | Central City to Central City | Central City to Outside |
| Baltimore | | | | |
| Whites | 19 | 27 | 31 | 42 |
| Blacks | 23 | 31 | 36 | 45 |
| Hispanics | 20 | 27 | 35 | 44 |
| Asians and Native Americans | 18 | 25 | 32 | 38 |
| Boston | | | | |
| Whites | 19 | 27 | 32 | 35 |
| Blacks | 22 | 32 | 35 | 42 |
| Hispanics | 20 | 27 | 31 | 39 |
| Asians and Native Americans | 20 | 32 | 30 | 39 |
| Chicago | | | | |
| Whites | 24 | 33 | 36 | 43 |
| Blacks | 29 | 40 | 46 | 56 |
| Hispanics | 26 | 38 | 38 | 48 |
| Asians and Native Americans | 25 | 36 | 37 | 40 |
| Cleveland | | | | |
| Whites | 18 | 23 | 32 | 41 |
| Blacks | 22 | 26 | 36 | 47 |
| Hispanics | 17 | 24 | 31 | 24 |
| Asians and Native Americans | 18 | 23 | 32 | 34 |
| Detroit | | | | |
| Whites | 20 | 25 | 35 | 35 |
| Blacks | 21 | 27 | 39 | 45 |
| Hispanics | 18 | 25 | 39 | 28 |
| Asians and Native Americans | 18 | 25 | 26 | 10 |
| Los Angeles | | | | |
| Whites | 24 | 30 | 40 | 45 |
| Blacks | 25 | 29 | 43 | 51 |
| Hispanics | 23 | 29 | 39 | 46 |
| Asians and Native Americans | 23 | 30 | 38 | 48 |
| New York | | | | |
| Whites | 27 | 38 | 42 | 49 |
| Blacks | 32 | 39 | 48 | 52 |
| Hispanics | 29 | 38 | 44 | 49 |
| Asians and Native Americans | 30 | 45 | 46 | 54 |

TABLE 5.15    *(continued)*

| Central City<br>Race-Ethnicity | Private | | Public | |
|---|---|---|---|---|
| | Central City<br>to Central City | Central City<br>to Outside | Central City<br>to Central City | Central City<br>to Outside |
| Philadelphia | | | | |
| Whites | 21 | 30 | 36 | 41 |
| Blacks | 26 | 33 | 39 | 42 |
| Hispanics | 22 | 34 | 33 | 43 |
| Asians and Native Americans | 26 | 34 | 36 | 43 |
| St. Louis | | | | |
| Whites | 16 | 25 | 33 | 40 |
| Blacks | 20 | 26 | 34 | 45 |
| Hispanics | 16 | 25 | 21 | 20 |
| Asians and Native Americans | 17 | 25 | 28 | 60 |
| Washington, DC | | | | |
| Whites | 18 | 28 | 28 | 37 |
| Blacks | 23 | 31 | 37 | 47 |
| Hispanics | 20 | 30 | 32 | 49 |
| Asians and Native Americans | 19 | 29 | 32 | 37 |

SOURCE: Decennial census Public Use Microdata Samples (5 percent) for 1980 and 1990.

NOTE: Mean commuting time is based on the total time that it takes a person to make a one-way trip from home to place of work.

Since 60 percent of black households living in high poverty areas of our nation's largest cities lack access to a private vehicle, such households are especially isolated from dispersing job bases (Kasarda 1993).

What are the consequences of metropolitan industrial restructuring and associated skills and spatial mismatches for joblessness among less-educated city residents? Table 5.16 provides an answer. This table presents the jobless rates of out-of-school white and black males (aged 16–64) who have not completed high school or have only a high school diploma, for major central cities in each census region where comparable pooled *Current Population Survey* data could be obtained for three 3-year time periods (1968–1970, 1980–1982, and 1990–1992).

If a skills mismatch is a major contributor to city resident joblessness, we should see corresponding rises in the jobless rates of less-educated white city residents as well as blacks during this period. This is indeed what we find. For cities in the Northeast, jobless rates for white high school dropouts steadily rose from 15 percent during 1968–1970 to 37 percent during 1990–1992. In the Midwest, jobless rates for white high school dropouts climbed from 12 to 34 percent; in the South, from 7 to 18 percent; and in the West, from 18 to 26 percent. Jobless rates for central-city whites with only a high school diploma

TABLE 5.16    Percentage not working among out-of-school males aged 16–64 residing in the central city, by race, education, and region: 1968–1970 to 1990–1992.

| Region/Race and Education Level | 1968–1970 | 1980–1982 | 1990–1992 |
|---|---|---|---|
| Northeast | | | |
| Whites | | | |
| Less than high school diploma | 15% | 34% | 37% |
| High school diploma only | 7 | 17 | 24 |
| Blacks | | | |
| Less than high school diploma | 19 | 44 | 57 |
| High school diploma only | 11 | 27 | 31 |
| Midwest | | | |
| Whites | | | |
| Less than high school diploma | 12 | 29 | 34 |
| High school diploma only | 5 | 16 | 18 |
| Blacks | | | |
| Less than high school diploma | 24 | 52 | 63 |
| High school diploma only | 10 | 30 | 41 |
| South | | | |
| Whites | | | |
| Less than high school diploma | 7 | 15 | 18 |
| High school diploma only | 3 | 9 | 19 |
| Blacks | | | |
| Less than high school diploma | 13 | 29 | 52 |
| High school diploma only | 1 | 19 | 22 |
| West | | | |
| Whites | | | |
| Less than high school diploma | 18 | 20 | 26 |
| High school diploma only | 10 | 16 | 19 |
| Blacks | | | |
| Less than high school diploma | 26 | 44 | 57 |
| High school diploma only | 13 | 14 | 43 |

SOURCE: U.S. Bureau of the Census, *Current Population Survey*.

NOTE: Cities represented are Boston, Newark, New York, Philadelphia, and Pittsburgh (Northeast); Cleveland, Chicago, Detroit, Milwaukee, and St. Louis (Midwest); Atlanta, Dallas, Houston, Miami, and New Orleans (South); and Denver, Long Beach, Los Angeles, Oakland, Phoenix, San Francisco, and Seattle (West).

(a city job category that has been declining) also steadily climbed, but not as rapidly as those for white high school dropouts. Clearly, a high school diploma is no longer sufficient for employment in today's transformed urban economies.

For central-city black males without a high school diploma, jobless rates soared in these years. During 1968–1970 roughly 80 percent of black male high school dropouts were working. By 1990–1992, jobless rates of central-city blacks without a high school diploma rose to 57 percent in the Northeast, 63 percent in the Midwest, 52 percent in the South, and 57 percent in the West.

Jobless rates for central-city black males with only a high school diploma likewise rose steeply after the late 1960s. In northeastern cities, the rate climbed from 11 to 31 percent; in the Midwest, from 10 to 41 percent; in the South, from 1 to 22 percent; and in the West, from 13 to 43 percent. This again highlights the fact that those central-city residents with no education beyond high school have become increasingly displaced as urban economies have transformed from goods processing to information processing.

## The Role of Entrepreneurship and Self-Employment

If spatial confinement and poor education are such handicaps to gainful employment in industrially transforming cities, why is it that America's newer urban immigrant groups, especially Asians, seem to have so much success in securing employment and climbing the socioeconomic ladder? Selectivity of immigrants is no doubt a contributing factor. Moreover, Bates and Dunham (1992, 1993) document that a large portion of Asian business start-ups are by well-educated, wealthy individuals who draw on traditional financial institutions and provide goods and services to non-Asians.

Nevertheless, many less-educated Asian and Hispanic immigrants have also succeeded in the inner city by using ethnic-based methods to (1) assemble capital, (2) establish internal markets, (3) circumvent discrimination, and (4) generate employment in their enclaves that is relatively insulated from swings in the national economy and urban structural transformation. These ethnic businesses are typically family owned and operated, often drawing on unpaid family labor to staff functions during start-up periods of scarce resources (Bonacich and Light 1988; Aldrich, Waldinger, and Ward 1990) and on ethnic contacts to obtain credit, advice, and patronage (Light, Kwuon, and Zhong 1990). The businesses are characterized by thriftiness and long hours of intense, hard work with continuing reinvestment of profits. As they expand, ethnic-enclave establishments often display strong hiring preferences for their own members, many of whom would likely face employment discrimination by firms outside their enclave (Bailey 1987). They also tend to do business with their own. A San Francisco study found that a dollar turns over five to six times in the Chinese business community, whereas in most black communities dollars leave before they turn over even once (Kotkin 1986; Wartzman 1988).

Kinship and household structures of ethnic immigrants have significantly facilitated their entrepreneurial successes. Among recently arrived Asian immigrants, for instance, "other relatives," those beyond the immediate family, frequently constitute a substantial portion of household sizes. In addition to serving as a valuable source of family business labor, these extended-kin members enable immigrant households to function more efficiently as economic units by sharing fixed household costs such as rents or mortgages, furnishing child care services, and providing economic security against loss of employment by other household members. In short, by capitalizing on ethnic and family solidarity, many new immigrant businesses, ranging from laundries to restaurants to green groceries, started and flourished in once-downtrodden urban neighborhoods, providing employment and mobility options to group members in what in other respects is an unfavorable economic environment.

Native urban blacks, in contrast, have been burdened by conditions that have impeded their entry and success in enclave employment, including discrimination by lenders, family fragmentation, and limited economic solidarity. Regarding the latter, a survey by *Black Enterprise* magazine reported that 70 percent of self-employed blacks consider lack of community support as one of their most formidable problems (Kotkin 1986).

Given the demonstrated importance of family cohesiveness and kinship networks in pooling resources to start businesses, provide day-care assistance, and contribute labor to family business ventures, poor urban blacks are at a distinct disadvantage. Nearly three quarters of black families with children under age 18 living in high-poverty areas of the nation's 100 largest central cities are headed by women (Kasarda 1993). These households are the poorest segment of our society, with female householders earning only a third as much as married male householders. In essence, it takes discretionary resources to start a small business and it requires patrons with money to sustain that business, both of which are in limited supply in poor black neighborhoods.

All the factors mentioned have converged to depress black self-employment rates, especially in the inner cities. Table 5.17 demonstrates the considerably lower rates of self-employment among less-educated blacks compared with whites, Hispanics, and Asians. The one exception is Los Angeles, where Hispanics (mostly Mexican Americans) exhibit the lowest self-employment rates among those with no education beyond high school.

Interesting racial-ethnic contrasts appear in Table 5.17, especially the example of the breakout of two Hispanic groups (Puerto Ricans and Cubans) and two Asian subgroups (Chinese and Koreans). In Miami, Hispanics have self-employment rates more than three times those of blacks, with non-Cuban Hispanics in the city actually having higher rates than Cubans. In Chicago, New York, Philadelphia, and Washington, DC, Koreans have self-employment rates at least five times those of blacks. Even in Los Angeles, where black self-employment is the highest, Koreans have rates nearly four times higher. Indeed,

TABLE 5.17  Percentage self-employed among employed (out-of-school) males aged 16–64, by race-ethnicity and education: 1990.

| City and Education Level | Whites | Blacks | Hispanics | Puerto Ricans[a] | Cubans | Asians | Chinese | Koreans |
|---|---|---|---|---|---|---|---|---|
| Chicago | | | | | | | | |
| All education levels | 10% | 4% | 4% | 9% | NA | 9% | 8% | 25% |
| High school diploma or less | 7 | 3 | 4 | *10* | NA | 7 | 9 | 22 |
| Los Angeles | | | | | | | | |
| All education levels | 20 | 8 | 7 | 15 | 11 | 15 | 12 | *31* |
| High school diploma or less | 18 | 7 | 7 | 14 | 11 | 16 | 10 | 28 |
| Miami | | | | | | | | |
| All education levels | 19 | 4 | 13 | 17 | 7 | 9 | 9 | NA |
| High school diploma or less | 12 | 4 | *13* | *17* | 10 | *13* | *17* | NA |
| New York | | | | | | | | |
| All education levels | 14 | 5 | 7 | 10 | 9 | 12 | 10 | 25 |
| High school diploma or less | 11 | 4 | 6 | 9 | 9 | 11 | 10 | *19* |
| Philadelphia | | | | | | | | |
| All education levels | 8 | 4 | 8 | 9 | NA | *14* | *21* | *30* |
| High school diploma or less | 6 | 4 | 7 | 7 | NA | *19* | *31* | 36 |
| Washington, DC | | | | | | | | |
| All education levels | 11 | 5 | 6 | 6 | 10 | 5 | NA | 28 |
| High school diploma or less | 8 | 4 | 5 | *29* | 9 | 9 | NA | NA |
| Total for 11 cities[b] | | | | | | | | |
| All education levels | 13 | 5 | 7 | *14* | 8 | 12 | 10 | 27 |
| High school diploma or less | 9 | 4 | 6 | *14* | 9 | 12 | *10* | 25 |

SOURCE: Decennial census Public Use Microdata Samples (5 percent) for 1990.

NOTE: Italicized numbers indicate that the self-employment rate for the group is higher than the rate for comparable whites.

[a] In this table, Asian does not include Pacific Islanders. Puerto Ricans and Cubans are included in the Hispanic category and Chinese and Koreans are included in the Asian category.

[b] The six cities above plus five cities with small race-ethnicity sample: Baltimore, Boston, Cleveland, Detroit, and St. Louis.

in Los Angeles and Philadelphia, nearly one of every three Korean males working is self-employed.

For our pooled 11-city sample, 27 percent of Koreans at all education levels and 25 percent with a high school diploma or less are self-employed compared with 9 percent of whites, 4 percent of blacks, 6 percent of Hispanics, and 12 percent of all Asians. An important message here is that with small-business formation becoming the backbone of job creation in our central cities, blacks appear to be far behind in this critical arena.

For the same 11-city sample I used the 1980 and 1990 5 percent Public Use Microdata Samples to determine the percentage of out-of-school white, black, Hispanic, and Asian males aged 16–64 with a high school diploma or less working full-time the previous year (at least 35 hours per week for 48 weeks). Results showed that only 39 percent of blacks had worked full-time compared with 51 percent of Hispanics, 53 percent of Asians, and 57 percent of whites. I also looked at the same groups of males in terms of the percentage reporting no employment at all during the previous year. Here, 16 percent of Asians, 19 percent of whites, 22 percent of Hispanics, and 34 percent of blacks did not work at all during 1989. At the individual city level some striking comparisons emerged between out-of-school black males (aged 16–64) working full-time and those not working at all during the previous year. For example, in Chicago 35 percent worked full-time and 39 percent had no work in 1989; in Cleveland, 34 and 39 percent; in Detroit, 35 and 39 percent; and in Los Angeles, 32 and 39 percent.

Statistics for Cleveland and Los Angeles in 1980 and 1990 illustrate the considerably weakening labor force attachment of inner-city black males with no education beyond high school. In Cleveland 45 percent of these males were employed full-time, year-round in 1980. This dropped to 34 percent in 1990, while the percentage not working at all the previous year rose from 30 to 41 percent between 1980 and 1990. In Los Angeles 41 percent were employed full-time, year-round in 1980 compared with 33 percent in 1990, while the percentage not working at all the previous year rose from 31 to 39 percent. The 1990 percentage of black males in Los Angeles with no work the previous year was more than double that for comparably educated whites, Hispanics, and Asian males.

These figures refer to all out-of-school males with a high school diploma or less. For younger (aged 16–19) high school dropouts, the jobless rate was much greater. Table 5.18 shows that by 1990, two thirds of high school dropouts aged 16–19 residing in the nation's 100 largest central cities were not working. Within the extreme poverty areas of these cities, four fifths were not working. Even in nonpoverty tracts nearly three fifths were not working in 1990, testifying to the special importance of education for work among urban youth.

TABLE 5.18    Percentage not working among high
school dropouts aged 16–19,
by neighborhood poverty status
in the 100 largest central cities: 1970–1990.

| Tracts | 1970 | 1980 | 1990 |
|---|---|---|---|
| All cities | 57% | 64% | 65% |
| Nonpoverty Tracts[a] | 53 | 55 | 57 |
| Extreme Poverty Tracts[b] | 64 | 81 | 79 |

SOURCE: Decennial census for 1970 (fourth count), 1980, and 1990 (Summary Tape File 3A).

[a]Census tracts in which fewer than 20 percent of the residents are below the poverty level.
[b]Census tracts in which 40 percent or more of the residents are below the poverty level.

## SUMMARY AND POLICY COMMENTARY

The restructuring of America's industrial geography continued apace during the 1980s, with the Sunbelt capturing two thirds of the national increase in employment. In all census regions, the majority of job growth was in services and trade, with manufacturing sharply declining in the Northeast and Midwest and expanding moderately in the South and West.

Major suburban employment centers mushroomed during the 1980s in all regions, with some "edge cities" containing more office and retail space than the central-city downtowns. By 1990, suburban ring employment exceeded central-city employment in virtually all industrial sectors, including business services, and suburb-to-suburb commuting was the norm.

Metropolitan areas captured nearly 90 percent of the nation's employment growth during the 1980s (most of which occurred in larger metropolitan areas), while nonmetropolitan areas led in manufacturing growth. Metropolitan areas in the Northeast and Midwest actually lost 1.5 million manufacturing jobs during the 1980s, more than 1.3 million of them in the central cities. As a consequence, aggregate manufacturing earnings in these cities spiraled downward, particularly in major midwestern cities. For example, between 1980 and 1990, aggregate manufacturing earnings in Chicago (Cook County) dropped by $5.3 billion (in constant 1989 dollars), in Detroit (Wayne County) by $4.7 billion, and in Milwaukee by $1.7 billion. These represent proportional constant dollar manufacturing earnings declines of 25 percent in Chicago, 32 percent in Detroit, and 33 percent in Milwaukee. The largest proportional decline in manufacturing earnings occurred in Pittsburgh (Allegheny County), however, where earnings dropped 51 percent during the 1980s.

The manufacturing base of large central cities in the Frostbelt continued to hemorrhage during the 1980s, whereas strong growth characterized their service sectors. Most of this growth was in information-processing industries that require employee education beyond high school. Jobs held by college graduates rapidly expanded in these cities, while those available to persons with a high school diploma or less contracted.

The economies of cities transformed to such an extent that having only a high school diploma was increasingly less likely to lead to work. Thus, jobless rates for both black and white central-city residents with only a high school diploma rose considerably during the 1980s, with those of blacks rising the most.

Analysis showed that black central-city residents are not only increasingly disadvantaged in terms of their education, but also more spatially isolated from both city jobs and suburban jobs than any other racial-ethnic group. The combination of these spatial and skill mismatches contributed to skyrocketing jobless rates among inner-city blacks with limited education. Especially affected were younger persons aged 16–19 who had dropped out of school and resided in extreme poverty areas. By 1990, four fifths were jobless.

Other racial-ethnic minorities were not as affected by urban industrial restructuring. Unlike blacks, these more recent urban arrivals (mostly Asians and Hispanics) were never concentrated in manufacturing and other rapidly declining urban blue collar industries. Thus, industrial restructuring impacted these minority groups less. Moreover, considerably larger percentages of less-educated Asians and Hispanics were able to start and operate their own businesses, further buffering them from the full effects of urban industrial restructuring.

With weakening attachment to the formal economy, less-educated urban blacks increasingly relied on two surrogate economies (the underground economy and the welfare economy) to stay afloat. Given their skill limitations for employment in new urban growth industries as well as low hourly wages for jobs for which they were qualified, many saw themselves better off in the underground economy where incomes are actually, or perceived to be, higher (Freeman 1992). The underground economy also provides substantially more temporal flexibility and personal autonomy than working in mainstream institutions. This may be particularly important to lifestyle choices of teenagers and young adults.

Responding to rising inner-city joblessness and concentrated poverty, certain public assistance programs geared to distressed urban areas were introduced or substantially expanded in the 1970s. These programs were guided by the reasonable principle that public assistance should be targeted to areas where the needs are the greatest as measured by such factors as job loss, poverty rate, and persistence of unemployment. The idea was that the most distressed areas should receive the largest allocation of government funds for subsistence and local support services for the economically displaced and socially disadvantaged.

These policies unquestionably helped relieve pressing problems such as the inability of the poor and jobless to afford private sector housing or to obtain adequate nutrition and health care. They did nothing, however, to reduce the skills or spatial mismatch between urban ghetto labor pools and available metropolitan jobs. In fact, spatially concentrated assistance may have inadvertently worsened these mismatches and the plight of the ghetto poor by binding them to inner-city areas of severe blue collar job decline and to areas that, by program definition, were most distressed.

For those ghetto residents with some resources and for the fortunate proportion whose efforts to break the bonds of poverty succeeded, spatially concentrated public assistance did not impede their mobility, and may have helped others considerably. But for many ghetto poor without skills and few economic options, local concentrations of public assistance and support services can be "sticking" forces. Given the likely low wages they would earn elsewhere with their limited skills, the opportunity cost of giving up their in-place assistance if they were to move would be substantial. And if they were to move to certain growth areas and not find a job, they might be even worse off. Thus, many see themselves as better off remaining unemployed in the ghettos with their marginal but secure government assistance than taking a chance and moving in search of a low-wage job, often to an unfamiliar environment.

The confluence of high rates of joblessness, illicit activities, and welfare dependency in the ghettos generated a powerful spatial interaction. Associated with this interaction were a plethora of concentrated social problems particularly prevalent in black urban ghettos, including persistent poverty, family dissolution, out-of-wedlock births, school dropout, drug abuse, and violent crime. Highly visible concentrations of black joblessness, poverty, and related social problems, in turn, contributed to negative stereotyping and distancing by outsiders (often with racial connotations), resulting in further spatial and social isolation of the ghetto poor from mainstream institutions.

No straightforward policy prescriptions exist for ameliorating this complex predicament. Programs that could reduce skills and spatial mismatches documented in this chapter would be a good start. These include

1. educational upgrading and improved vocational training programs in the inner city;
2. computerized job opportunity information networks about job openings throughout the metropolitan area and beyond;
3. partial underwriting of more distant job searches by the ghetto unemployed;
4. tax incentives to promote affordable housing construction in the suburbs by the private sector, together with strategies to promote residential integration;
5. need-based temporary relocation assistance for ghetto unemployed once a job has been secured;
6. housing vouchers, as opposed to additional spatially fixed public housing complexes in the inner city;

7. stricter enforcement of fair housing and fair hiring laws;

8. public-private cooperative efforts to van-pool unemployed inner-city residents to suburban businesses facing labor shortages; and

9. a thorough review of all public assistance programs to ensure that they are not inadvertently anchoring the ghetto poor in areas where there are few prospects for permanent or meaningful employment.

Let me conclude this policy commentary with some important qualifications and caveats. By focusing much of my analysis and commentary on skills and spatial mismatches, I do not wish to imply that they are the primary reasons for urban black joblessness, but only that they are major contributors. The causes of rising black joblessness are no doubt intertwined with continuing racial prejudice and a host of other factors.

It is unlikely that skills and spatial mismatches resulted only from racially neutral and rational economic decisions that had unforeseen and unintended consequences for blacks. There is good reason to believe that a component—perhaps a substantial component—of geographical industrial restructuring detrimental to blacks was influenced by racial practices and stereotypes. For example, Cole and Deskins (1988) present evidence about the discriminatory siting and hiring practices of Japanese auto-parts manufacturers and suppliers who set up in the United States during the 1980s. These manufacturers and suppliers were found to locate in areas with few blacks in the commuting range and to hire fewer blacks than would be expected from their local labor shed racial composition. Likewise, careful examination of the locations of booming "edge cities" indicates that they tend to be within the labor commuting shed of the metropolis, but at the farthest points from concentrations of black poor (Garreau 1991).

While debate continues over the basic causes of rising inner-city black joblessness, concentrated poverty, and associated social problems, little progress has been made in reducing these problems. Some have called for massive government intervention (a "Marshall Plan" for the cities) to weed out crime, rebuild the inner-city commercial infrastructure, create public service jobs, and upgrade skills as the most effective means to reduce urban black joblessness and revitalize the ghettos.

Yet policy action, no matter how great the scale, should not be confused with accomplishment, since results are what really matter. In this regard, there is little evidence to date suggesting that outside intervention, public or private, can have more than a marginal effect in improving ghetto conditions. Nor do I see any indications that most Americans, the majority now suburban, possess the political will for large-scale, sustained intervention on behalf of cities and the ghetto poor. As discussed in this chapter, they will more likely choose to "exit" and distance themselves from the poor and their problems.

Perhaps just as sobering must be the recognition that government has limited capacity to affect what may simultaneously be the dual-root *and* dual-resolution of the urban predicament—*attitudes* of those outside and *actions* of those within the ghettos. Government cannot legislate away discriminatory stereotyping and other racist views held by outsiders. Positive attitudinal changes will likely occur only as outsiders come to believe through actions of the ghetto poor that, despite their social and economic disadvantages, most value intact families, hard work, responsibility, and normative order, and that they eschew self-destructive behaviors.

Government cannot weave such values back into ghetto communities nor dictate behavior of their residents. More pointedly, government may be able to help open certain doors of opportunity for the ghetto poor, but it cannot develop the behaviors to take advantage of these opportunities and internal values to sustain them. Almost by definition, the moral authority for these tasks must come from *within* the community, from charismatic leadership and local voluntary and religious organizations that emphasize individual responsibility, family cohesiveness, educational achievement, economic self-support, and anti-drug, anti-crime programs. In the absence of such cultural regeneration, I do not see another promising alternative for inner-city black economic progress and ghetto revitalization.

---

Prepared for the 1990 Census Project Committee of the Russell Sage Foundation and the Social Science Research Council. I would like to acknowledge the comments and suggestions of Reynolds Farley and James H. Johnson, Jr., on an earlier draft of this chapter, the computer programming of Andrea Bohlig and Kwok-Fai Ting, and editorial assistance of Lynn Igoe and Pat Zigas.

## ENDNOTES

1. The regions used herein refer to the four conventional regions defined by the Bureau of the Census. The Northeast includes all of New England and the Middle Atlantic states; the South includes all states below the Mason-Dixon line from the East Coast through Texas; the Midwest includes states west of Pennsylvania and New York to the Colorado, Wyoming, and Montana eastern borders; and the West includes all states west of Texas, Oklahoma, Nebraska, and the Dakotas.

2. REIS does not report data for all the county units recognized by the Bureau of the Census in its Census of Population files. Data for some sparsely populated counties (e.g., Yellowstone Park, Montana, and Menominee County, Wisconsin) are reported with an adjacent county. For Virginia counties, the independent cities were treated as part of the county that surrounds them. The counties reported in the REIS were classified according to their 1983 population status as reported by the Bureau of the Census.

Six classifications of nonmetropolitan counties are presented:

Nonadjacent to metropolitan area with small place (fewer than 2,500): N = 535

Nonadjacent to metropolitan area with medium place (2,500–9,999): N = 498

Nonadjacent to metropolitan area with large place (10,000 or more): N = 207

Adjacent to metropolitan area with small place (fewer than 2,500): N = 303

Adjacent to metropolitan area with medium place (2,500–9,999): N = 566

Adjacent to metropolitan area with large place (10,000 or more): N = 295

Five classifications of metropolitan counties are presented:

Metropolitan, in area with population less than 150,000: N = 117

Suburban, in metropolitan area with population 150,000–749,999: N = 157

Central, in metropolitan area with population 150,000–749,999: N = 154

Suburban, in metropolitan area with population 750,000 or more: N = 231

Central, in metropolitan area with population 750,000 or more: N = 63

3. This perspective has its roots in the work of the economic historian N. S. B. Gras (1922) and later studies by social ecologists McKenzie (1933), Bogue (1949), Hawley (1950), Duncan et al. (1960), Duncan and Lieberson (1970), and others of the Chicago School.

4. Baltimore is treated as a northern city because of its border location and because its economic history, demographic and industrial bases, and physical characteristics are more similar to larger, older cities in the North.

5. To measure the average education level of employees in detailed urban industries, the March 1982 *Current Population Survey* files were used to compute the mean years of schooling completed by all central-city residents who were employed in two-, three-, and some four-digit Standard Industrial Classification–coded industries. Mean education levels were then assigned to industries classified in *County Business Patterns*. Aggregate job changes within each educationally classified industry were then traced between 1970 and 1990 for the same nine major cities whose boundaries are either identical to or closely approximate to those for which place-specific industrial employment data are available in *County Business Patterns*.

# 6

# The Polarization
# of Housing Status

## DOWELL MYERS and JENNIFER R. WOLCH

HOUSING AS SHELTER is as basic to human survival as food and clothing. However, housing is much more than mere shelter from the elements, because it interacts with our social and economic lives in many ways. As an economic commodity, housing consumes the greatest single share of the average American's income; among homeowners, it also has come to represent the largest component of wealth. The type of housing one lives in and its very address signify a person's economic and social status more prominently than any other indicator.

Housing also represents the arena for family life and the staging ground for activities—the journey to work or to school, forays to the grocery store, and the relentless cycle of food preparation, eating, and cleanup. Over the life cycle, people pass through a series of housing arrangements, moving from dependent status as children to independent status as young adults. Their early years in the housing market are often the most tenuous, but for many people the launching of careers and formation of stable households lead to increasingly secure housing circumstances. For many, this means the purchase of a home; for others, it simply means a steady income to meet the monthly rent, a stable family life or set of household relations, and a network of support services as a backstop during spells of misfortune.

Housing takes on added importance because the housing progress of the population is so intimately related to the nation's economy. The construction industry is an important sector of the economy, which employed 5.1 million workers in 1990. Added to this number are the large numbers of workers employed in allied industries—the producers of wood products, masonry materials, plumbing supplies, and other construction components—and those employed in the appliance and furniture industries. Thus, expanding housing consumption is a major stimulant to the nation's economy; in turn, rising incomes generated by a healthy economy lead to stronger housing consumption.

For these reasons, housing has figured prominently in the nation's policies. Generous federal tax benefits have aided home buyers and stimulated housing investment with great success. The federal government has also provided direct subsidies to the poor who cannot afford adequate housing on their own.

Our nation has enjoyed decades of housing progress. Following the economic collapse that led to the Great Depression, Americans experienced steadily rising housing quality. The sustained postwar economic boom, along with favorable federal housing policy, gave more and more Americans the opportunity to realize the American Dream. Each new generation of young adults was launched into larger, better-appointed, and more affordable housing, and an ever-rising proportion of Americans was able to purchase a home of their own.

However, much has changed since 1980. A growing homeless population and mounting problems of housing affordability for the middle class underscore a new reality. Moreover, housing problems are not spread evenly across the nation, but concentrated in certain regions, among certain age groups, and in selected other demographic subgroups. For example, while housing values rose dramatically in the western and eastern regions of the country between 1980 and 1990, they plummeted in the nation's heartland. And while older people enjoyed unparalleled increases in housing status, younger persons across the country were increasingly unable to afford homeownership.

Our task in this chapter is to describe housing dynamics in the 1980s. Such an assessment of changes in the nation's housing situation is a challenging exercise, since housing interacts with so many other factors, including economic forces, race-ethnicity, and the demography of household living units. Thus, we focus primarily on the shelter situation of the population and the extent of the mismatch between shelter needs and the supply of dwelling units. As indicators of housing stress, we consider, sequentially, household formation rates, residential overcrowding, affordability, and homeownership rates. Then, as a means of providing an aggregate picture of housing status changes, we analyze changes experienced at both margins of the housing status distribution. Throughout, we emphasize the changing housing market experiences faced by different age groups, racial-ethnic groups, gender divisions, and other key demographic and socioeconomic cleavages.

In addition, housing is characterized by striking geographic contrasts, making knowledge of spatial differences essential for understanding housing dynamics. Housing markets are highly localized, but broad regional patterns are apparent, with (for example) high prices on the coasts and lower prices in the heartland. Accordingly, we explore regional differences in many dimensions to be described, some of them surprising.

Briefly, we find that while many continued to realize the American Dream during the 1980s, it faded and seemed to slip away for others. Increasingly, the decade of the 1980s is recognized as one of *polarization,* as the gap between rich and poor widened owing to globalization of the economy, economic re-structuring, key demographic shifts, and reductions in many welfare state pro-grams. Strong income growth occurred among the more affluent, while people of very modest means saw their economic status spiral downward, best symbol-ized, perhaps, by a rising tide of homelessness.[1]

Changes in the distribution of housing status during the 1980s in many ways reflected the nation's ongoing economic polarization and demographic shifts. In the housing arena, the effects of polarization were spread unevenly, both so-cially and spatially. As younger persons struggled to reach their aspirations, and even to fill the most basic needs, an older generation rose to levels of economic success that were unmatched in this century. And, predictably, minorities, women, and less economically advantaged citizens suffered most.[2] Thus, we find evidence of a growing "generation gap" and "diversity gap" in realization of the American Dream.

Our findings raise pressing equity issues. Why are only some American households sliding backwards in terms of housing status? How have particular groups managed to retain their ability to improve their housing circumstances at the expense of others? And what do these findings imply for public policy?

## AMERICAN HOUSING AND ITS USES

A *housing unit* is defined by the Census Bureau as living quarters with a separate entrance, whether from a hallway or directly from the outside, and cooking facilities. These are typically one-unit detached structures, also known as single-family houses, or multifamily apartment houses. The *tenure* of a hous-ing unit is given by whether it is owned or rented. Whenever a housing unit is occupied we find a *household,* which can consist of one person living alone, several unrelated people sharing the housing unit, or a family with members related by marriage or birth. For statistical reasons, each household is asked to identify one *householder,* that is, the person (or one of the persons) in whose name the housing unit is owned or rented.

Over 97 percent of the population lives in housing units, hence in house-holds, while the remainder live in *group quarters* or *institutions* (such as college dormitories or nursing homes) or are *homeless* (i.e., living on the street or in emergency shelters for the homeless). Housing status can be measured several ways: based on a person's degree of independent living, tenure status, and vari-ous measures of affordability and crowding experienced in the housing unit. The principal measure of *independence,* or autonomous living, is whether or not a person is the householder (as defined above). Alternatively, we will count both householders and their spouses as living in independent quarters, while other household members are considered dependents.

The reader should note that the analysis makes use of different universes drawn from the census data. (A *universe* is the entire set of cases to be divided into subgroups and described.) Part of the analysis that follows derives from a population universe, asking what proportion of people live independently. Other parts of the analysis derive from a housing unit universe, describing the characteristics of the housing stock in existence. However, most of the analysis is conducted on a household (occupied unit) universe, asking what proportion of households, not people, have different housing problems. We will make clear the basis for analysis appropriate to each section.

## Shelter over the Life Cycle

The vast majority of Americans reside in housing units, either as dependent members of households or as maintainers of their own separate living quarters. In 1990, only 2.7 percent lived in institutions or other group quarters, or lacked any shelter. This proportion changed little during the 1980s.

In general, the pattern of living arrangements varies substantially with age and life experience. Over the life course, people move from one relationship in a household to another. Virtually all children are dependents within a household, but in their late teens and early 20s people leave their parents' homes and begin to set up their own separate living quarters. In this transitional period, many persons spend time in the military or in college dormitories. Later, in the retirement years, some people again exit the housing stock and opt for institutional quarters.

Figure 6.1 portrays the life cycle of living arrangements in 1990 with the horizontal sweep of the axis depicting the age span from 0 to 90. The vertical axis records the probability, or incidence rate, from 0 to 100 percent, that persons of each age occupy particular living situations. At each age, the cumulative probability of living in all arrangements shown is 100. Thus, the area of the graph taken up by each status represents the proportion of a lifetime that is spent in each arrangement. The pattern represented here is a snapshot taken from the 1990 census.[3] In general, we can view this as a profile of the typical residential life cycle, provided we acknowledge that all persons need not conform to the typical. Nor should we expect that persons in the future will follow the age-probabilities that were witnessed in 1990.

The incidence of living *outside* housing units, that is, in institutions or group quarters, is depicted as the dark shaded area at the top of the graph. The sharp increase of this status after age 17 is readily apparent, as is its diminishing frequency during the 20s. Only a very small percentage of the population remains outside housing units through the middle years. After age 60, nonhousehold living again increases, closely tracking the failing health of persons in advanced years.

FIGURE 6.1   Living arrangements of the U.S. population at each age in 1990 (percentage of age group in each status).

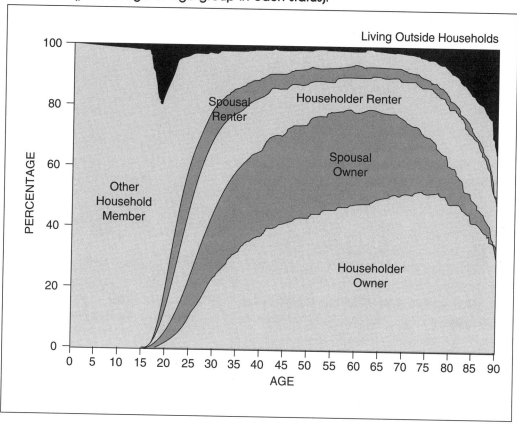

For persons residing in households, status shifts over the life span in two important ways. First, as individuals enter the labor market, they typically advance to their own separate living quarters, signified by their status as either the householder or the spouse of a householder. For accounting reasons, only one householder is designated for each household, even though husbands and wives usually share responsibility.[4] To reflect living arrangements more realistically, we display the proportions of persons who are either the householder or the spouse of the householder.

For obvious reasons, the choice of living arrangements is closely related to changes in marital status and other family composition choices.[5] Figure 6.1 shows that the proportion of spouses of householders sharply rises in the 20s and 30s as couples rent apartments or buy houses together. At older ages, the proportion of spouses shrinks because mortality leaves widows as the sole owner or renter.

For most Americans, a second major shift over the life span is from renting to owning. While the majority of persons begin their independent housing careers as renters, upward economic mobility and efforts to save allow the great majority to become homeowners. Whereas renters move between homes relatively frequently, once households buy a home, their likelihood of moving again drops sharply.[6] This tendency toward lower mobility combines with tax incentives and other factors to discourage transition from owning back to renting (which will be discussed in the next section). As a result, homeownership status is cumulatively attained by a growing number of persons over time, reaching a peak late in the life cycle. Figure 6.1 shows that nearly 90 percent of Americans in their 50s and 60s reside in houses owned by themselves and/or their spouses.

Living arrangements are dependent not only on one's life-cycle stage, but also on the nature of the housing supply, its cost, and the income of each household or individual.[7] Thus, in addition to demographic features, economic circumstances and housing supply strongly influence who can obtain housing of various types, qualities, and prices; the rates at which people move through successive household arrangements (e.g., household formation, homeownership); and the ease with which they can afford a new living arrangement.

## The Evolution and Nature of the Housing Stock

Most American housing has been produced by private sector contractors and builders. In general, the homebuilding industry is composed of many competitive producers, but over the past 60 years, government interventions have altered the framework for housing production, increasingly influencing the functioning of the housing market and the nature of the stock.

Before the Depression the federal government had been sporadically involved in housing production,[8] but after the 1930s major federal programs were put in place to stimulate housing construction and solve housing problems. They included the establishment of a residential savings and loan industry, a variety of agencies to address housing (such as the Federal Home Loan Bank and the Federal Housing Administration), and programs to encourage homeownership and hence residential construction and additions to the stock (including federal mortgage insurance and tax benefits to homeownership).

In addition, major federal actions were directed at improving housing quality and affordability. These efforts were stimulated by the decline of central-city housing stocks during the Depression and World War II and by the growing realization that the private market was unable to meet expanding needs for affordable dwelling units. The landmark National Housing Acts of 1939 and 1949 instituted federal slum clearance programs and launched public housing construction. By 1955, 350,000 public housing units had been erected; with the addition of specialized construction subsidy programs for the elderly and handicapped, and low-income owners and renters, the cumulative total for federally assisted units had risen to 425,000 by 1960 and to almost 1 million by 1970 (see Listoken 1991; Sternlieb and Listoken 1987).

During the 1970s and 1980s, annual federal outlays for assisted housing grew to over $1 billion per year; during the 1940–1990 period, the federal government spent $124 billion (in 1989 dollars) and assisted 5.1 million housing units/households (Listoken 1991:167). After 1974, an increasing share of this assistance was in the form of rental subsidies (Section 8 vouchers/certificates); public housing construction virtually stopped during the 1980s.

The evolution of the nation's housing stock has also been influenced by federal tax policy. This is particularly true with respect to the mix of owned and rented units, owing to the deductibility of mortgage interest payments and property taxes (as discussed below). In addition, tax policy has influenced construction of low-income rental units. After decades of a tax code structure that effectively discouraged investment in low-income housing, the 1981 Economic Recovery Act allowed for accelerated depreciation and a shorter depreciable life for low-income units, thus spurring low-cost rental construction. In 1986 these provisions were largely repealed; instead, special tax credits were provided to investors in low-income housing. (Instituted temporarily in 1986, these credits were made permanent in 1993.)

Despite federal involvement in housing, and growing housing activity by state and local governments, during most of the postwar years new subsidized units constituted less than 10 percent of all new housing unit starts. After 1971, substantial numbers of rehabilitated units began receiving assistance; new and rehabilitated subsidized stock ranged from 20 to 40 percent of total new starts. But after 1983, following policy changes of the Reagan administration, this share plunged to less than 10 percent (Sternlieb and Listoken 1987: Table 2.2).

*Bricks and Mortar.*   As of 1990, there were 106 million housing units in the United States.[9] Sixty million were occupied by homeowners, 34 million by renters, and 12 million were vacant.[10] The median age of the American housing stock was 26 years (i.e., built in 1963), but there was quite a bit of dispersion: Almost 30 percent were built after 1975 and almost 25 percent were built before 1940. Only a small share of pre-1920 units were still in service.

American housing in 1989 was predominantly single-family and low-rise multifamily. Two thirds of all housing units were single-family dwellings; homeowners were more apt to be living in single-family units than renters.[11] Only 10 percent of housing units were located in structures of four stories or more. The Northeast had the highest proportion of units in such buildings, whereas the South was almost entirely dominated by low-rise structures.

Over the decade of the 1980s, the number of housing units grew by 16 million, for an average of 1.7 million housing starts per year. This rate was much lower than that prevalent during the 1970s, when almost 2.1 million units were added to the stock annually. As well, new multifamily units, particularly in larger structures (with five units or more), were more slowly absorbed into the market than they had been during the 1970s. Almost half of the new stock was built in the South. Strikingly, the average size of single-family homes sharply increased over the course of the decade, from 1,720 to 2,080 square feet (a 21 percent increase).

*Housing Quality and Cost.*    As a result of federal and local housing policies, as well as rising housing construction standards, the quality of the housing stock has increased dramatically in the postwar years. After World War II, more than 40 percent of the housing units in the United States did not have complete plumbing facilities—that is, indoor faucets and toilets (many of these were rural housing units)—but this deficiency fell to less than 1 percent by 1980 (Clemmer and Simonson 1983).

Housing quality continued to rise during the 1980s, mostly because of the high quality of new construction rather than the elimination or upgrading of substandard units. Deficient or dilapidated housing was only slowly eliminated from the stock; the number of substandard units declined only 6 percent between 1974 and 1985, mostly because of removals from the stock.[12] And although the proportion of inadequate units renting for under $300 (in 1988 dollars) also declined during this period (by over 46 percent, again due to rapid removal of this stock), such units still constituted approximately two thirds of the total unsubsidized rental stock in this price range (see Apgar 1991: Table 4).

During the 1980s, the composition of the stock shifted, in terms of both unit types and, in particular, distribution of rents. Small affordable units disappeared from the stock (especially single-room-occupancy hotel rooms), while the number of more upscale units grew (Hoch and Slayton 1989). The number of occupied one-room rental units fell 41 percent during 1985–1989 alone, curtailing the availability of some of the most affordable units in the nation.[13] The loss of such units, many located in single-room-occupancy hotels, resulted in homelessness for many individuals unable to accumulate resources for more expensive dwellings (Hoch and Slayton 1989). Their rents also climbed precipitously; median rents in unsubsidized one-room units rose from $229 in 1979 to $317 in 1989, a 38 percent rise,[14] at a time when income growth was stagnating (growing less than 10 percent between 1980 and 1986). Overall, between 1974 and 1985 the number of privately owned, unsubsidized dwelling units renting for less than $200 (in 1988 dollars) fell from 3.2 million units to 1.7 million, while the number of units renting for $200–$299 fell from 5.3 million to 4.0 million, so that the units under $300 lost during this period totaled 2.8 million (Apgar 1991). Although there was growth in the number of subsidized units (by 2.1 million), total dwellings renting for less than $300 still fell markedly.

Much of this loss was due to removals from the rental stock (through demolition or conversion to another use); 1.4 million units renting for less than $200—16 percent of all unsubsidized rental units—were removed during the 1974–1983 period, while only 5.1 percent of units above this rent level were removed. In contrast, numbers of higher-rent units (above $350 in 1988 dollars) grew by 4.5 million during the same time period. Part of this was due to upward filtering: rents on over 800,000 units rose from below $300 to above $300 between 1974 and 1985 (Apgar 1991).

### The Mismatch between Housing Demand and Supply

Paradoxically, while the nation's housing supply improved in quality over the 1980s, a disturbing mismatch developed between housing supply and effective household demand. In particular, many demographic groups experienced stagnating or falling incomes over the course of the decade, sharply limiting their ability to secure or maintain housing (see Levy's chapter in this volume for details on income trends). The mismatch was especially acute at the lower tiers of the housing ladder: Small, affordable units disappeared just as more and more households faced economic difficulties, forcing them to compete for less expensive shelter. In addition, upward filtering and rapid rates of high-quality, upscale dwelling construction meant expanding choices for more affluent households, thus further widening the gap between rich and poor.

This mismatch, in turn, created problems for Americans attempting to make the basic transitions in living arrangement during the 1980s. Moreover, some Americans were unable to afford any type of shelter at all. Thus, the operation of housing markets in the 1980s constituted a root cause of the rising tide of homelessness.

### HOUSEHOLD FORMATION RATES

Following a period of rapidly rising household formation rates during the 1950s, 1960s, and 1970s, rates slowed dramatically. The reasons for this slowdown are complex and beyond the purview of our analysis—involving, for example, poor economic prospects for many young people, trends toward postponed marriages, and macroeconomic forces and fiscal policies influencing housing construction patterns. (See other chapters in these volumes, such as McLanahan and Casper's, for details.) However, falling household formation rates (especially among youthful portions of the age distribution) clearly reveal that for an increasing number of Americans, establishing independence was either beyond their capability entirely or would have required consumption sacrifices that they were unwilling to make.

## Age Polarization in Housing Autonomy

Household formation rates determine the proportion of "autonomous" individuals—namely, those who are either independent householders living on their own or spouses of householders. During the 1960s and 1970s, this proportion increased rapidly, owing mostly to a growing ability of young (often single) people to move into their own living quarters. This trend stopped abruptly during the 1980s, however, at a time when the numbers of young adults was growing relative to earlier periods.

At a national level, the percentage of all persons aged 20–24 who were autonomous fell from 48 to 36 percent. This is not surprising, since these persons who had become householders during the 1980s saw their real cash income fall,[15] and marriage rates (which boost household formations) continued to slow down. The proportion of those aged 25–29 who were autonomous fell over the course of the decade from 79 to 69 percent and declines continued through age 55 (Figure 6.2). In contrast, the likelihood of independent living (either as householder or spouse of householder) among the elderly increased by as much as 7 percentage points (e.g., in the 85–89 age group, the proportion autonomous rose from 60 to 67 percent).

Thus, as Figure 6.2 illustrates, the left "shoulder" of the figure dropped to the left for younger cohorts, and the right shoulder bulged to the right for the older ones. These shifts reveal that while older people were increasingly able to maintain independent dwelling units, stagnating or declining incomes and slowing marriage rates of young and middle-aged individuals sharply reduced their ability to establish or maintain their housing autonomy.

## Differences Across Race-Ethnicity and Gender

These shifts in independent living varied substantially by race-ethnicity and gender. Among young adults aged 25 and over, blacks experienced twice as great a decrease in the proportion autonomous than did whites (e.g., proportions for whites aged 30–34 fell from 91 to 85 percent, but for blacks the drop was from 80 to 67 percent). Similarly, among the elderly, blacks experienced smaller increases than whites in the proportions autonomous. Differences between whites and Hispanics closely paralleled those found between whites and blacks.

The pattern for Asians was altogether different. The proportion of autonomous Asians in all age groups (save one) declined over the 1980s. The magnitude of declines tended to be moderate, however. One possible explanation for such a continuous drop is a rapid influx of elderly foreign-born Asians arriving to take up residence with children who had already become established in this country, magnifying deeply ingrained cultural patterns of two- and three-generation households.

FIGURE 6.2    Percentage who were householders or spouses of householders, by age: 1990 and 1980.

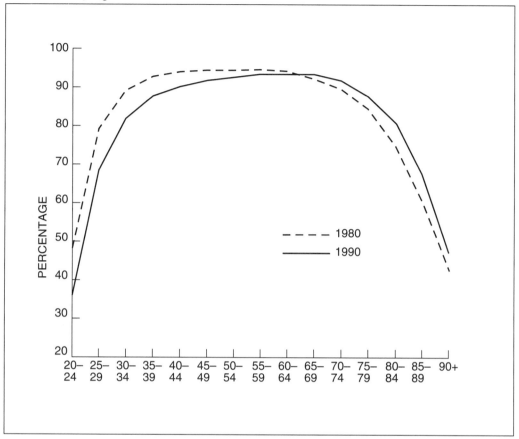

Gender-related differences were modest but intriguing. The proportion of women in their 20s who were either householders or spouses dropped about 8–10 percentage points over the decade. For example, proportions of autonomous women aged 20–24 fell from 55 to 43 percent. Men in these age groups also registered declines; for men in their late 20s the drop was from 75 to 62 percent. In the older age groups, the proportion of autonomous women grew much more rapidly than that of men. This is linked to general trends toward independent living among older people and gender differences in marital status among the elderly. Women are far more apt to be widowed than men, and while in times past widowed persons commonly joined the households of their children, growing preferences for independent living and greater access to Social Security and private pensions meant that women were maintaining their own living quarters longer than they had been in past decades.

In sum, household formation rates slowed during the 1980s. Differences in household formation rates over the 1980s by age groups, race-ethnicity, and gender are complex and warrant further analysis. However, our brief investigation reveals that for individuals in their 20s and people of color (especially Hispanics) household formation rates slowed most dramatically.

## RESIDENTIAL OVERCROWDING

Residential overcrowding, one of the primary measures of housing quality, is also an indicator of the extent to which individuals experience trouble establishing or maintaining autonomous dwelling units. This is because crowding can result from more than one family sharing the same dwelling unit and from households restricting their housing consumption owing to income constraints. Over the 1980s, Americans on average became more spaciously housed, but at the same time a persistent and growing minority became overcrowded.

Judgments about what constitutes overcrowding have changed over the course of the twentieth century. At the turn of the century high levels of immigration produced extreme crowding in major East Coast cities, but with the assimilation of immigrants and steady declines in the level of crowding, the official standard for what constituted overcrowding was made more stringent (Baer 1976). In 1940, the first census of housing recorded 20 percent of all occupied housing units as overcrowded, that is, more than one person per room.[16] From that date the incidence of overcrowding has steadily declined to about 11 percent in 1960 and to less than 5 percent in 1980.

It appeared that overcrowding was about to disappear until the 1990 census results became known. For the first time in 50 years, overcrowding showed an increase, rising to 5 percent. Crowding rates were far higher for renters, for Hispanics and immigrants, and in portions of the country that experienced rapid inflows of international arrivals during the 1980s. Even controlling for income and household size, however, whites and blacks evince lower tolerance for overcrowding—and the sharing of housing space—than do Asians and Hispanics, in the process trading off housing affordability.

### Polarization in Overcrowding Rates between Owners and Renters

As shown in Table 6.1, the increase in overcrowding was much greater among renters, rising from 7.0 to 8.9 percent of rental units. In fact, among owners, overcrowding continued to decline, falling to only 2.7 percent.

In addition to this overall difference between owners and renters, it can be seen in Table 6.1 that the bulk of the increase among renters occurred in the most extreme category of overcrowding, more than 1.50 persons per room (i.e.,

TABLE 6.1  Percentage change in overcrowding, by tenure: 1980–1990.

| | Ratio of Persons per Room | | |
| --- | --- | --- | --- |
| | Total (1.01 or more) | Moderate (1.01–1.50) | Extreme (1.51 or more) |
| All Households | | | |
| 1990 | 5.0% | 2.9% | 2.1% |
| 1980 | 4.5 | 3.1 | 1.4 |
| Change | +0.5 | −0.3 | +0.7 |
| Renters | | | |
| 1990 | 8.9 | 4.7 | 4.3 |
| 1980 | 7.0 | 4.4 | 2.7 |
| Change | +1.9 | +0.3 | +1.6 |
| Owners | | | |
| 1990 | 2.7 | 1.9 | 0.9 |
| 1980 | 3.2 | 2.4 | 0.7 |
| Change | −0.5 | −0.5 | +0.2 |

SOURCE: Decennial census for 1980 and 1990 (Summary Tape File 1C).

NOTE: Numbers may not add to totals because of rounding.

five persons or more living in three rooms or seven or more living in four rooms). The number of renters in the extreme category of crowding is nearly equal to the number in the moderate category and if the pattern of change continues, the extreme group will soon surpass the moderate group. This is evidence of an acute imbalance in the distribution of housing space.

## Variation across the States

The incidence of overcrowding in 1990 was much higher in some states than in others. Given the rising trend among renters, we focus specifically on that tenure group. Figure 6.3 depicts the incidence of overcrowding as the sum of renters who are moderately and extremely overcrowded, with the two components separately indicated in a stacked bar format.[17] From this figure it is clear that overcrowding levels in California and Hawaii are far above those in the other states. In the Midwest, only Illinois rises above the national level; in the Northeast, New York and New Jersey stand out. In the South, overcrowding is uniformly higher, but Texas, Florida, Mississippi, and Louisiana stand out. The extreme level of overcrowding is prominent in the states with the highest incidence of overcrowding, making up more than half of California's 19.6 percent overcrowding level.

FIGURE 6.3   Overcrowding prevalence for renters, ranked within region, sum of moderate and extreme overcrowding: 1990.

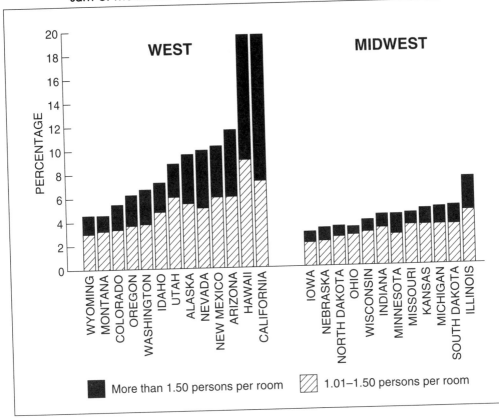

Myers and Choi (1992) tested a number of explanations for the state-specific level of rental overcrowding, finding no effect of rent on crowding levels, but instead a large effect of Hispanic and Asian concentrations. Choi (1993) then researched the determinants of overcrowding variation across 305 metropolitan areas in 1990. The correlation of rent with overcrowding was weaker ($r = 0.27$) than was the correlation of poverty ($r = 0.51$), but the concentration of Hispanics was more important than either economic variable ($r = 0.84$). The percentage immigrants was also highly correlated ($r = 0.78$). Choi's multivariate analysis of the metropolitan variation found that the percentage Hispanic population was the most important in both 1980 and 1990, but that the immigration coefficient increased sharply between 1980 ($b = 0.06$) and 1990 ($b = 0.24$). This implies that immigrants who arrived in the decade prior to the 1990 census were more susceptible to overcrowding than those who arrived in the decade before the 1980 census.

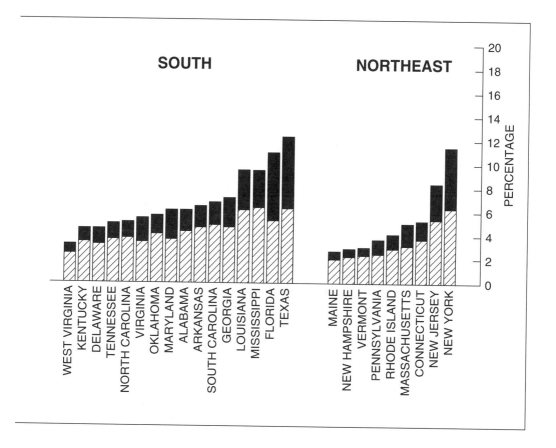

## Cultural Tolerance for Crowding

In a multicultural society, different levels of crowding are judged acceptable by different ethnic groups.[18] These differences are strikingly portrayed in data from the 1990 census. Figure 6.4 shows the percentages of households that are overcrowded (more than one person per room) among separate racial and Hispanic-origin groups, controlling for household income and household size. Both renters and owners are included to capture the full income distribution. The figure controls household size by examining only households with five persons, since it is likely that different ethnic groups have different household sizes, and hence different susceptibility to being crowded. These five-person households would be considered overcrowded if they occupied four rooms or fewer.

Figure 6.4 depicts two strong relations with regard to overcrowding. First, it is clear that the incidence of overcrowding declines for higher-income households. The decline is fairly gradual across the income range and continues to

FIGURE 6.4   Percentage of five-person households that are overcrowded, by relative income level and racial-Hispanic origin: 1990.

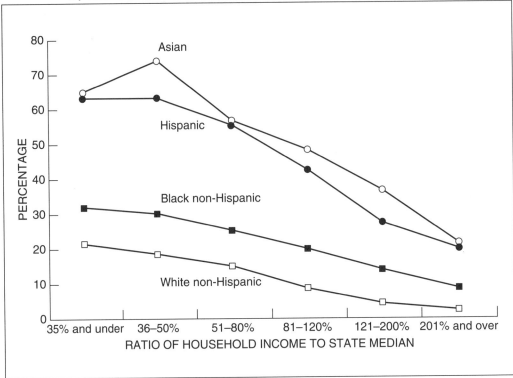

the highest income levels. (The reader should note that the compression of the scale caused by wider intervals above 120 percent may lend the impression of accelerated decline above that point.) Were overcrowding something to be strongly avoided, we might expect to see sharper declines from the lowest income category to the next. Even at the highest income level, a surprising 20 percent overcrowding persists among Hispanic and Asian households. Controlling for four- or three-person households yields a similar pattern of results: Although the overall level of overcrowding is lower, the incidence of overcrowding is slow to diminish with rising income.

A second relationship in Figure 6.4 is the clear stratification by race-ethnicity. Controlled for income and household size, there is a markedly lower incidence of overcrowding among white, non-Hispanic households, and even among the black households, than among the Asian and Hispanic households. Choi (1993) explains this greater propensity for overcrowding by these groups on the basis of their cultural heritage in "close-contact" societies, leading to much greater tolerance for crowding in the home.

Some members of these ethnic groups are recent immigrants, and the immigrant members do have the highest rate of overcrowding, but further analysis of California residents not shown here discloses persistent interethnic differences even among longtime U.S. residents and native-born persons. After two or three generations it is very possible that Asians and Hispanics would converge toward the middle-class space norms held by whites and blacks, but in the meantime cultural differences persist.

Do housing affordability problems lead to increased overcrowding, as households try to economize by either sharing their quarters with others or finding smaller quarters? Or are households willing to pay more for rent in order to avoid being overcrowded, even if they are already burdened by housing costs? If households do trade off overcrowding against payment burdens, we might find equal levels of crowding at all payment levels; alternatively, households might accept overcrowded conditions or opt to pay more of their income for rent and gain more space.

Figure 6.5 presents data for renters in 1990, measuring their incidence of overcrowding in relation to their payment burden (ratio of rent to household

FIGURE 6.5  Percentage of renter households that are overcrowded, by rent burden and racial-Hispanic origin: 1990.

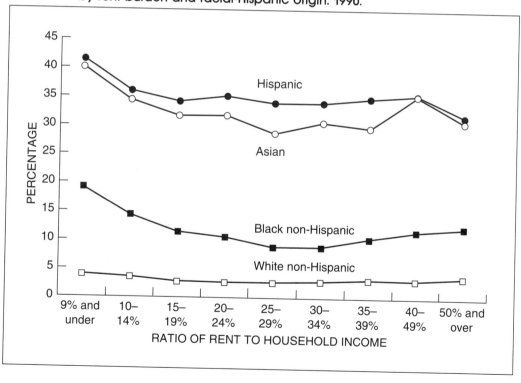

income). Again, we find striking differences in the incidence of overcrowding according to race-ethnicity. What may be more surprising is that there is no apparent relation to payment burden: Households with extreme payment burdens face roughly the same likelihood of overcrowding as those with light burdens. (The upturn among the renters with lightest payment burdens may reflect the doubling up of multiple earners.) Overall, the pattern reflects an equilibration of crowding and affordability. A certain portion of the households in each race-ethnicity are willing to accept overcrowding; the rest distribute themselves upward to higher rent levels and higher payment burdens.

## AFFORDABILITY

Problems of housing affordability hamper the transition from dependent household member to independent householder. Households with affordability problems are forced to devote a disproportionate share of their income to rent or mortgage payments to maintain their own dwelling units. Lack of affordability, particularly for low-income households, has become the dominant housing problem in the United States, particularly as problems of substandard housing quality have receded from importance.

Although trends in prices and rents give some indication of affordability, the relation between incomes and rents must also be captured in measures of housing affordability. Such measures first emerged during the 1930s, when the common rule of thumb was that "a month's rent should not exceed a week's pay,"[19] or rent should not account for more than 25 percent of income. This became accepted into government practice, as most housing subsidy programs of the 1960s and 1970s defined as excessive rent burdens over 25 percent. During the 1980s, however, this standard threshold was raised to 30 or 35 percent in most housing assistance programs. (And, in turn, numbers of households deemed to have an affordability problem were lowered.)

Currently, there are several widely used affordability measures.[20] Here we focus on the direct measure used by the Bureau of the Census: the proportion of current income that households actually spend on housing. The census provides an opportunity for greater geographic coverage of affordability and reflects actual experience, not hypothetical relationships. Rental costs, owner costs, and median household incomes are all recorded in the census. (Housing payments are calculated as gross expenditures: rent or mortgage, plus property taxes, insurance, and utilities.) As we will see, most households pay much less than 30 percent for housing.

FIGURE 6.6    Expenditure burdens of renters and owners in 1990.

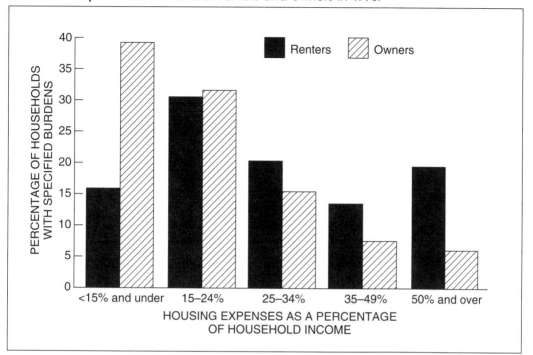

## Polarization between Owners and Renters

Figure 6.6 presents the distribution of housing payment burdens for all house-holds in the United States in 1990. Owners and renters are treated separately because their circumstances are so different. Nearly 40 percent of homeowners have light payment burdens, paying less than 15 percent of their income for housing. Barely 16 percent of renters reach this low a level. Instead, renters are clustered in the high-payment categories. Nearly one fifth pay over half their income for rent. Overall, nearly a third of renters have an affordability problem (paying 35 percent or more of income for rent). Many fewer homeowners suffer this high a burden.[21]

Payment burdens also vary substantially over the life cycle. The proportion of owners with excessive payment burdens is highest among the youngest households, declines in middle age to near 10 percent, and then rises again in the elderly years. Among renters, the proportion with high burdens is substantial for the youngest households, drops in middle age, and then rises greatly in the elderly years.

This increase in payment burdens among renters is due in part to the fixed incomes of the elderly, and the same effect occurs for homeowners, but it also reflects the changing composition of the renter population. As more households switch to homeowning, those who remain as renters have progressively lower incomes. Selection of the better-off renters into homeowning leaves the remaining renters more likely to have an affordability problem. With the approach of retirement, homeowners are also better insulated against current increases in housing prices than are renters. Homeowners also have accumulated equity in their homes, which they can draw upon for financial support. For all these reasons, elderly renters face a much higher incidence of excessive payment burdens than do homeowners.

## Contrasts in Affordability by Race-Ethnicity

Among both renters and owners, minority groups typically face greater problems with housing affordability than whites, and the gap has been widening. In 1980, 29 percent of white renters faced payment burdens in excess of 35 percent of income, which rose by only about 1 percentage point over the decade. In contrast, over 36 percent of black renters and 35 percent of Hispanic renters faced excessive payment burdens, which rose by 3 percentage points between 1980 and 1990 for both blacks and Hispanics, thus magnifying the earlier disparity. Among Asians, the rate of payment burdens rose by more than 5 percentage points, bringing them closer to the high levels of other minority groups (almost 36 percent in 1990).

Even greater inequities of payment burdens are found among homeowners. Just over 12 percent of white owners faced excessive payment burdens in 1980 and in 1990, whereas 23 percent of blacks, 17 percent of Asians, and 17 percent of Hispanics faced payment burdens. Over the decade, the incidence of excessive burdens among black owners fell by almost 2 percentage points, but among Asians the incidence increased by over 7 percentage points, and among Hispanics by almost 4 percentage points. As a result, in 1990 minority homeowners were about twice as likely as white homeowners to suffer excessive payment burdens.

## Change in Affordability over Time and Variation by State

The experience of householders aged 25–34 in 1990 provides a clear measure of recent affordability problems, since these late baby boom birth cohorts include the most recent entrants into the housing market and thus the most exposed to changing market conditions. Focusing on this group, we also control for differences in age composition that occur over time and between places. In the nation as a whole, affordability problems grew for both owners and renters in this key age group. The proportion of households with a payment burden under 15 percent declined from 20 to 17 percent of renters and from 21 to 18 percent of owners. Conversely, the proportion of households with a payment burden of at least 35 percent grew from below 26 percent to over 27 percent of renters, and from 15 to 16 percent of owners.

This national average of change for the group aged 25–34 disguises much variation between locations. Historically, some states have had higher housing costs and higher payment burdens. The 1980 and 1990 levels of affordability problems in each state are moderately correlated: for owners, $r = 0.65$ and, for renters, $r = 0.55$. Nevertheless, some states that formerly had lower affordability problems moved upward, and vice versa. We also note a moderate association between rental and owner affordability problems, measured in 1990 as $r = 0.48$. States with greater problems for owners tended to also have greater problems for renters, but there was by no means a one-to-one correspondence.

A high incidence of renter affordability problems is found in most states (see Figure 6.7). The Midwest tends to be a little lower than other regions, but only in North Dakota do fewer than 20 percent of renters aged 25–34 have an affordability problem. In contrast, the incidence of owner affordability problems is much lower across the nation, but with sharply higher incidence in California and parts of the Northeast (see Figure 6.8).

The variation in owner affordability problems bears close relation to the pattern of housing prices: States with high house values had high affordability problems, and vice versa ($r = 0.87$). In fact, states in which housing prices rose most rapidly in the 1980s had the greatest owner affordability problems in 1990.[22] This is consistent with expectations. As we will see in the next section, ownership rates also increased for young households in the face of price increases. Apparently, young households stretch themselves to buy homes when prices are rising, creating a higher proportion with excessive payment burdens, whereas when prices are falling fewer buy and they pay a smaller proportion of their income when they do.[23]

Renter affordability for households aged 25–34 in 1990 was much less correlated with current rent levels ($r = 0.37$). The added effect of the trend in rents from 1980 also made no significant contribution; owner affordability, in contrast, was impacted by the trend in house values. The best model explaining renter affordability includes the current level of rents in each state, plus the change in the ownership rate for households aged 25–34.[24] A positive association of ownership change with higher renter payment burdens indicates the selection effect created when more advantaged renters are drawn into home buying, leaving a greater concentration of payment-burdened renters behind.

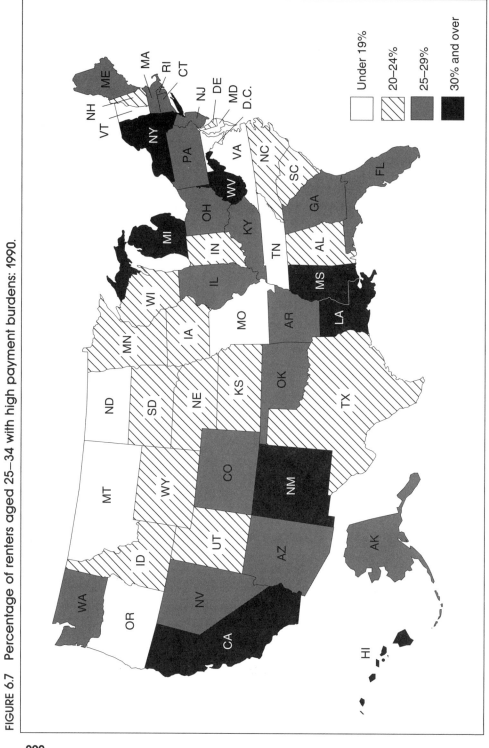

FIGURE 6.7 Percentage of renters aged 25–34 with high payment burdens: 1990.

Under 19%
20–24%
25–29%
30% and over

FIGURE 6.8   Percentage of owners aged 25–34 with high payment burdens: 1990.

Legend:
- Under 19%
- 20–24%
- 25–29%
- 30% and over

## HOMEOWNERSHIP

Both surveys of housing preferences and analysis of lifetime housing behavior indicate homeownership as a goal of most Americans.[25] Indeed, homeownership is often equated with the American Dream. Homeowners enjoy greater security of tenure and acquire important financial and housing advantages. Homeowners also enjoy advantages with regard to the quality of housing itself. Rental units are usually not as large and have less private outdoor space than owner-occupied units, and on average provide significantly fewer amenities (such as porches, decks, balconies, or patios; garages or carports; dishwashers, kitchen sink disposals, fireplaces, or central air conditioning; additional living or recreation rooms, or separate dining rooms).[26] Although it is possible to rent spacious quarters, these are only rarely available. Homeowners also have the pleasure of customizing their homes to personal tastes, through remodeling, landscaping, and so on.

So great is the public sentiment favoring homeownership, that owners have been rewarded with important tax advantages. Because most of their housing expenses can be deducted from their income prior to taxation,[27] their out-of-pocket expenditures are substantially reduced after taxes.[28] Homeowners also may benefit from escalating housing prices, and their growing equity in the home often represents the majority of the family's wealth (Kane 1985). When households sell their homes, their capital gains are deferred provided they buy another home within less than two years. (This is an important incentive, making homeownership status cumulative over the lifetime.) Once they have reached age 55, homeowners who choose to sell may elect a one-time capital gains exemption sheltering them from taxes on that amount. This provision was instituted in the hope that it would stimulate a recycling of large homes from elderly residents to young families.

In general, the rate of homeownership depends on the level of household income and the amount of liquid assets available (needed to make a down payment), and on the differential costs of homeownership versus renting. In addition, various demographic groups have different propensities for ownership; for example, younger households that are more mobile have lower ownership rates, holding other factors constant.

For most of this century, less than 50 percent of all households were able to achieve homeownership. Following the economic collapse that led into the Great Depression, homeownership tumbled to less than 44 percent of households. However, this collapse set the stage for reforms of financial institutions that would support a dramatic increase in ownership during the coming decades. With the introduction of federally backed mortgage insurance, and the Veterans Administration (VA) and Federal Housing Administration (FHA) housing programs, lenders reduced the required down payments from the 40 percent characteristic in the 1920s to 10 percent or even 5 percent of the purchase amount. In addition, the repayment period was lengthened to 30 years, thereby reducing the required monthly payment. The result of these two changes was to enable families to purchase homes with lower incomes than were needed before and to permit young adults to buy homes much earlier in their housing careers. After World War II, these reforms stimulated a high rate of home buying, leading to a total homeownership rate of 55 percent by 1950 and 62 percent by 1960. Since the 1960s, the percentage of households owning homes grew more slowly, peaking at 64.4 percent in 1980.

In the most recent decade, however, the homeownership rate slipped slightly to 64.2 percent.[29] This downward shift, although small, represents the first time in more than 50 years that the rate has fallen. Part of this downward shift can be explained by federal monetary policy, which led mortgage interest rates to climb dramatically during the first half of the decade before falling back to 1980 levels in 1985. However, even when mortgage rates subsequently fell considerably, ownership rates failed to achieve their earlier levels. Rather, stagnating incomes among the young and rapid increases in the costs of owning relative to renting exerted downward pressure on homeownership rates through the end of the decade,[30] which is reflected in comparisons of homeownership rates derived from the census. Although the interest rate surge occurred *after* the 1980 census and ended *before* the 1990 census, home buyers were unable to enter the market quickly enough to bring ownership rates back to their former level. Young first-time buyers of modest means in particular faced a problematic economic climate that dampened their ability to purchase housing. The most recent plunge in interest rates occurred *after* the 1990 census, and so the stimulative impact of low rates on homeownership was not reflected in the 1990 rates.

The fall in ownership rates was not uniform with respect to geography and demography. While certain population groups and regions of the country continued to enjoy rising rates of homeownership, rates for other groups and in other regions fell precipitously. The sharply uneven patterns of homeownership constitute an important dimension of housing status polarization during the 1980s.

### The Polarization of Homeownership Patterns

The decade of the 1980s followed rapid increases in house values during the latter half of the 1970s. Mortgage interest rates reached the highest level in the postwar period: Effective monthly mortgage rates climbed from 9.58 percent in 1978 to 12.95 percent in 1980, then to 15.12 percent in 1981 and 15.38 percent in 1982 (Crellin and Kidd 1990:48). The interest rate surge was accompanied by a recession that lasted through 1983. The result of these calamitous conditions was a sharp slowing of household formations in 1983 (down to a net increase of 500,000 from 1,700,000 two years earlier) and an abrupt drop of the homeownership rate by almost 2 percentage points from its peak in 1980 to 1985 (Devaney 1992:42, 46). On a nationwide basis, the homeownership rate slowly increased during the remainder of the decade, as interest rates dropped to 12.85 percent in 1983, and then gradually subsiding to 9.28 percent by 1987 (Crellin and Kidd 1990:48). But it never fully recovered.

*The "Generation Gap" in Homeownership.* Progress toward homeownership achievement—a central element in the American Dream—became starkly polarized by age during the 1980s as a "generation gap" opened up between younger and older Americans. Rich and poor have always had different opportunities to buy houses, and minorities have fared less well than others, but for the first time a gap opened up within the same families, that is, between elderly parents and their grown children. After decades of postwar progress, young adults found themselves slipping below previous levels of homeownership expected by their age group. At the same time, older Americans moved forward to historically high levels of homeownership.

An analysis of changes in homeownership by age group between 1980 and 1990 shows that only changes in the 45–64 age group over the decade mirrored the national average. Younger persons (aged 25–34), whose ownership rates stood at over 51 percent in 1980, experienced a 6 percentage point decline in their ownership rate, whereas the elderly group experienced a 5 percentage point increase (to over 75 percent). What had been a generation gap of about 18 percentage points in 1980 between the elderly and those aged 25–34 became a gap of nearly 30 percentage points by 1990.[31]

How is it possible that the elderly could increase their ownership rate by so much at the same time as others were declining? It would indeed be surprising to find large numbers of retirees out house shopping, supposedly an activity dominated by younger adults. The explanation is that the households who became elderly during the 1980s, the beneficiaries of the long post–World War II boom, acquired their homes at younger ages and sustained that higher level of homeownership as they aged into the elderly bracket.

Figure 6.9 shows the progress of cohorts of households, tracing their path as they aged ten years between 1980 and 1990. For example, in 1980, the homeownership rate at ages 55–59 was just over 78 percent. In 1990, when they would have been ages 65–69, the ownership rate is slightly higher.[32] The incoming cohorts in these elderly ages are overreaching their predecessors by a substantial margin.

In contrast, for those under age 55 in 1990, the incoming cohorts are arriving at lower levels of homeownership than their predecessors. The cohort shortfall becomes progressively greater at younger ages, amounting to 8 percentage

FIGURE 6.9   Trajectories of home ownership: 1980–1990.

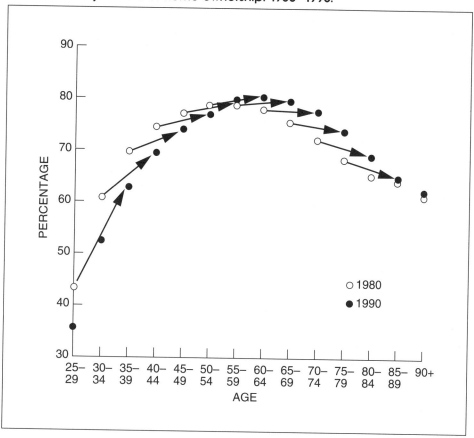

points at ages 30–34. The flattened trajectories of these younger cohorts represent a diminished progress toward the American Dream.

The difference between the generations reflects the different historical circumstances within which they have made their housing careers. Older Americans of 1990 established themselves in the housing market during the favorable
years after World War II, as described above. Persons aged 60 in 1990 would
have been 20 in 1950, ideally positioned to take advantage of the favorable
home-buying years to come. Figure 6.9 shows that the peak cohorts for homeownership in this century were about age 60 in 1990. As these persons continue
to arrive in the elderly age group, the homeownership rate of the elderly will
continue to rise through the coming decade.

In contrast, homeownership prospects for younger Americans, including the
large baby boom generation, have been dampened by much less favorable economic conditions: high housing prices in the 1970s and 1980s, historically high

interest rates for much of the 1980s, and incomes that have stagnated since 1973. Although homeownership trajectories have still moved upward and will continue to do so into the elderly years, it is unlikely that the younger cohorts can close the gap between themselves and older cohorts, making up for their lost progress. Failure to establish equity in the housing market early on reduces household wealth and makes future home buying less possible.

*Polarization by Race and Hispanic Origin.*     White households had the highest homeownership rate at each age, followed by Asian and then Hispanic and black households. Over the course of the 1980s, this pattern of inequality intensified, as Hispanic and black homeownership rates became further differentiated from those of whites. When combined with the strong and pervasive historical imprint of age cohorts in the housing market, racial-ethnic differences became even more magnified.

Table 6.2 summarizes the changes in homeownership attainment at selected ages by householders of different races or ethnicities, showing how already-pronounced differences between the races became even more evident for younger persons. For example, in 1990, the black homeownership rate at ages 25–34 was less than half that of white, non-Hispanic households, a gap of over 28 percentage points. Among those aged 65–74, the black ownership rate was three quarters that of whites, and the gap between white and black was 10 percentage points less than for the younger cohort.

In the 1980s blacks and Hispanics fared less well than whites: Their ownership rate at ages 25–34 fell more, both in proportional terms and in absolute percentages. Similarly, their gains in the elderly years were less than those for white non-Hispanics. What is most alarming in these data is the growing difference in ownership rates between elderly and young black households. All the other racial-ethnic groups show generation gaps of about 30 percentage points, mirroring the national average, whereas the black generation gap soared from 28 percentage points in 1980 to 40 points in 1990. This signifies the relatively greater struggle that young black householders are facing in their effort to enter the middle-class mainstream.

Segregation remains an important feature of minorities' housing careers (Frey and Farley 1993). Spatially restricted searches for housing limits opportunities for both renting and homeownership. Massey and Denton (1993) conclude that this segregation contributes to the long-term economic disadvantage of blacks. Even if current segregation barriers are weaker than they were in earlier periods (although there is widespread evidence that significant barriers remain), past segregation has cumulative effects across generations. As shown by Henretta (1984), the failure of blacks to achieve homeownership in the past reduces the chances for intergenerational transmission of wealth. As a result, young black

TABLE 6.2    Homeownership attainment, by race and
Hispanic origin, at selected ages:
1980 and 1990.

|  | 1980 | 1990 | Change |
|---|---|---|---|
| Ages 25–34 | | | |
|    Whites, non-Hispanic | 57% | 52% | −5 |
|    Blacks | 30 | 24 | −6 |
|    Asians | 38 | 36 | −2 |
|    Hispanics | 35 | 29 | −6 |
|      Total | 52% | 46% | −6 |
| | | | |
| Ages 65–74 | | | |
|    Whites, non-Hispanic | 76% | 82% | +6 |
|    Blacks | 59 | 64 | +5 |
|    Asians | 63 | 66 | +3 |
|    Hispanics | 56 | 59 | +3 |
|      Total | 74% | 80% | +6 |

SOURCE: Decennial census Public Use Microdata Samples–A sample (5 percent, 1-in-5 subsample).

householders have inherited an economic legacy that harms their position in today's housing market.

*Geographic Polarization in House Values and Ownership Trends.*    The national portrait of change in the 1980s averages out substantial differences across the nation. Housing values varied greatly among the states and these, in turn, could be expected to strongly influence the local trend in homeownership.[33] Figure 6.10 portrays the geographic pattern of change in house values between 1980 and 1990, with values measured in constant dollars.[34] In California and the northeastern states house values sharply increased. The greatest increases were recorded in New England, particularly Massachusetts with a 112 percent increase in house values in constant dollars.[35] The New England boom was quite extraordinary (Case 1986), and even though it came to an abrupt halt in 1988, the 1990 census records the cumulative impacts of the decade. In stark contrast, much of the middle of the nation experienced declines in house values over the decade.

Presumably, homeownership became much more affordable in states with falling home values than in states with rising values. Thus, one might expect that homeownership rates would have held up better in the states with falling values. However, the geography of housing price change, and its relation to homeownership rates, is far from straightforward.[36] For example, changes in homeownership rates must be viewed in relation to rents: Ownership rates may rise where the costs of renting and ownership converge. Economists utilize the

FIGURE 6.10 Percentage change in median house value: 1980–1990 (constant 1990 dollars).

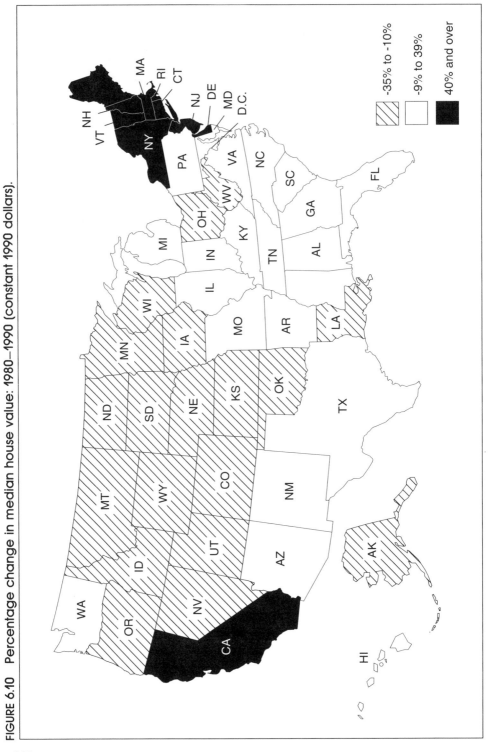

-35% to -10%

-9% to 39%

40% and over

FIGURE 6.11 Percentage change in homeownership: 1980–1990.

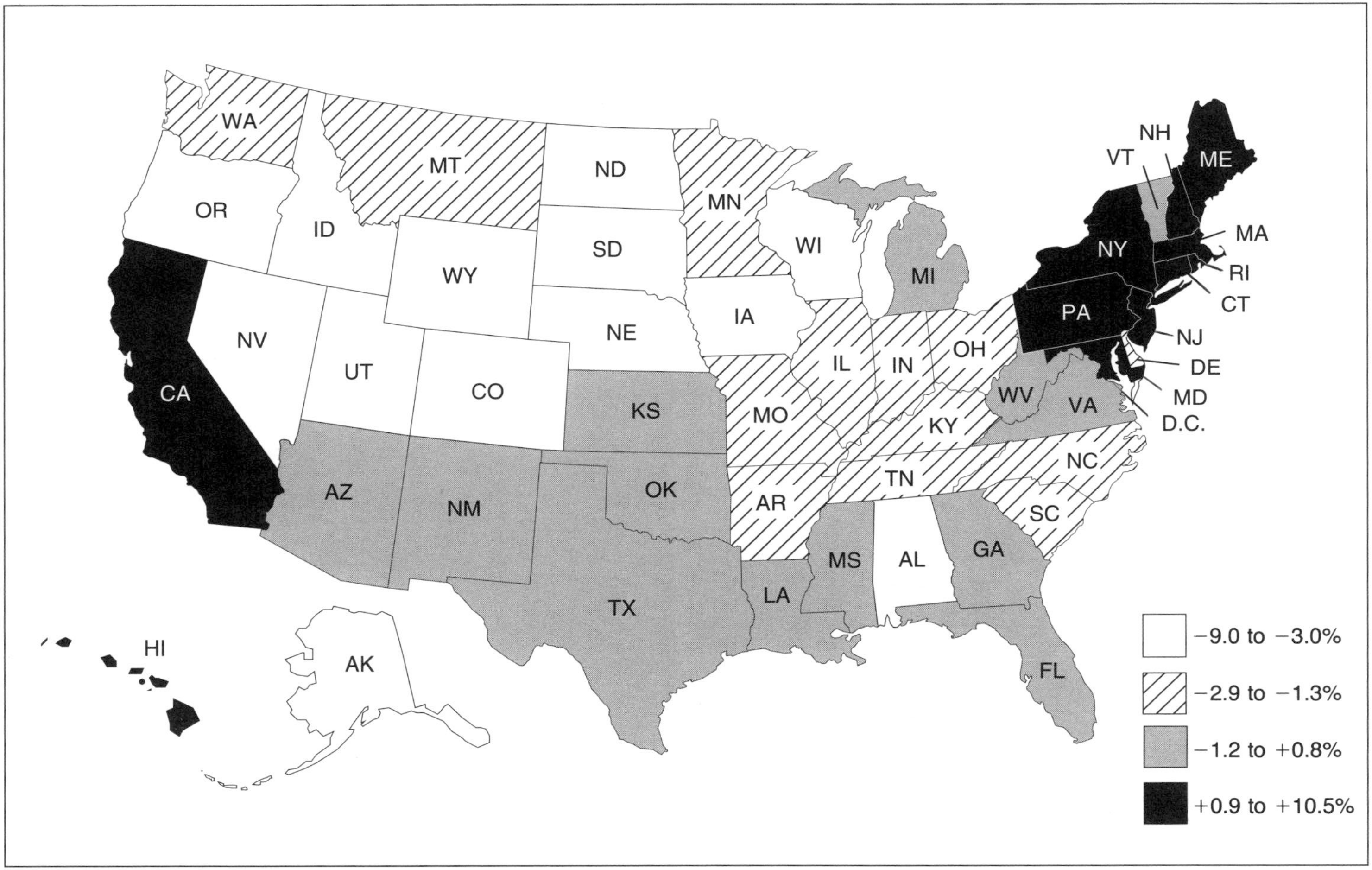

Legend:
- −9.0 to −3.0%
- −2.9 to −1.3%
- −1.2 to +0.8%
- +0.9 to +10.5%

concept of the "user cost of homeownership" to compare costs of renting relative to owning a dwelling unit. User costs include mortgage initiation fees, payments, mortgage interest, property tax, and home maintenance, offset by tax savings due to interest and property tax deductibility, and home value appreciation. When appreciation is rapid, user costs decline, thus spurring homeownership; when home values decline, user costs rise and make ownership a less attractive option. This means that expectations concerning future returns from investments in owner-occupied homes have a major influence on home-buying behavior.[37] For example, Myers et al. (1993) found that states with price decreases also tend to have greater declines in homeownership. But the analysis was based on homeownership of all age groups combined, with the possibility that high homeownership rates of older persons based on purchases in earlier decades could obscure the more recent relationship. For that reason, we should look more specifically at young persons whose ownership attainment would directly reflect recent conditions. The prime home-buying years are usually regarded as ages 25–34. Figure 6.1 showed that the percentage of persons who are either a homeowner or the spouse of a homeowner soared from 20 percent at age 25 to nearly 60 percent by age 34.[38] Homeownership of persons in this young age bracket in 1990 would largely have been attained since 1980. Accordingly, we can best judge the relationship of house value trends to ownership by studying the 25–34 age group.[39]

Figure 6.12 displays the relationship of housing value change and ownership rate change for the 50 states. The horizontal axis marks the percentage change in median house value (in constant dollars) in each state between 1980 and 1990. The vertical axis shows the change in the ownership rate for households aged 25–34, measured simply as the difference between the 1990 and 1980 ownership rates. Relatively few of the states approximate the national average of decline for this age group. Instead, the majority of states show even larger declines. Most of these are lightly populated states of the mountains or plains regions. The handful of states with less decline in ownership, and even gains, include some of the most populous states, such as New York and California.

Figure 6.12 shows the strong positive association between change in ownership and change in house values (r = 0.74). States where prices rose the most actually witnessed less of an ownership decline than states where prices plummeted. In a curvilinear pattern, ownership turned sharply downward in states where house values fell more than 20 percent. Once again, the explanation for this seeming paradox is that home purchases are based on the user cost of ownership rather than the nominal cost, and so the investment potential of the house very strongly affects buyer behavior (Case and Shiller 1988). With prices falling over 20 percent in real terms, why would a young household in North Dakota invest its money in buying a home? It would be far better to delay a purchase

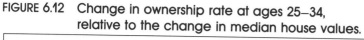

FIGURE 6.12   Change in ownership rate at ages 25–34,
relative to the change in median house values.

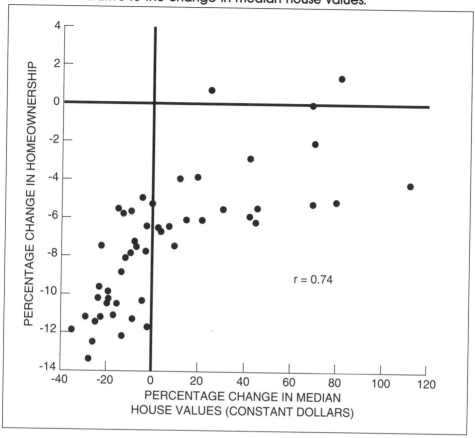

until the price dropped further, avoiding a loss in value; thus, few renters bought homes. Conversely, in Massachusetts, with its 112 percent price increase, young householders stretched to buy homes because the rising prices were a strong incentive for investment and led to reduced real costs of ownership.[40] That is, they often went into debt to buy a home believing that the trend toward higher home prices would give them greater future equity. In this manner, rapid rises in home prices were associated with increases in homeownership.

Each state has its own particular story rooted in its economic base, income patterns, migration trends, and housing market dynamics. The lower corner of Figure 6.12 includes economically troubled states such as the oil states of Texas, Louisiana, and Oklahoma; the timber states of Oregon and Washington; and the farm states of Iowa, Nebraska, and Wisconsin. Young households in these states faced a very different housing market than those in the booming states of California and Massachusetts.[41] However, the relationships between employment and income change, on the one hand, and house value and home-ownership rate changes, on the other, are mediated by migration patterns and their age selectivity, and rates of natural population increase. Regional economic growth tends to push up incomes and tighten housing markets, thereby spurring house values and homeownership due to expectations of continued appreciation. But high home prices have been shown to deter prospective interregional migrants, thereby dampening run-ups in housing prices in high-growth areas and moderating influences on homeownership (see Gabriel, Shack-Marquez, and Wascher 1992). In addition, the lasting imprint of such regional dynamics on specific age cohorts depends on the duration of the downturns and the rate at which interregional migration and natural increase rotate the membership of cohorts in particular states. These relationships are complex and warrant further exploration.

## MEASURING THE MARGINS OF HOUSING STATUS

Most Americans continued to enjoy decent and affordable housing over the course of the 1980s. But our analysis of conventional measures of housing suggests that polarization occurred—namely, that the absolute numbers and relative share of households at the extremes of the overall distribution of housing status increased. Perhaps the most dramatic evidence of polarization is, on the one hand, the trend toward *mansionization* and "mega-homes," with spas, gyms, and tennis courts, witnessed in most urban centers, and on the other, the burgeoning number of *homeless people* on the streets of American cities and towns.

In this section, we tie our previous themes together through a multidimensional analysis of housing status, which joins income, housing tenure, affordability, and crowding in order to define the most and least advantaged Americans in terms of housing well-being.

There are virtually no estimates of the size or composition of the upper tier of the housing market.[42] Instead, most research on housing problems has focused on the rapidly expanding lowest rungs of the housing ladder.[43] When faced with personal hardship (such as a health, mental health, or substance abuse problem), some of those at the bottom of the housing market became homeless. Economic and housing market shifts included structural forces at work during the 1980s, such as economic restructuring and associated job and wage losses for low-skill workers (see the chapters by Levy and Kasarda in this volume); welfare reforms entailing benefit reductions; and housing supply dynamics, especially rising rates of gentrification and urban renewal and growing community-level intolerance of low-income housing (e.g., NIMBY) that in most major cities removed the most affordable housing options (Wolch and Dear 1993).

In the following sections, we develop a methodology using Public Use Microdata Samples (PUMS) to estimate the number of households with significant housing problems, as well as those that enjoy the most comfortable housing circumstances. We term these two groups at the extremes the *precariously housed* and the *generously housed*. Our purpose is to gauge the extent to which these two groups grew over the course of the 1980s. The analysis reveals sharp trends toward polarization in housing status, along lines of socioeconomic class, demographics, and the national geography.

### Precariously and Generously Housed Populations

The concept of precariously housed populations is now common in the literature on housing affordability; it is also utilized in homeless research since precariously housed individuals face a heightened risk of homelessness. Definitions of precariousness differ, however. Typically, they focus on income and poverty, under the assumption that the poor will experience difficulties in maintaining private sector housing.[44] A second definition, resting on "rent burden," or the percentage of income consumed by rent, is also common, although it has obvious shortcomings: For example, the measure does not account for total income (see Dolbeare 1990), the size of the household to be supported, or differential tax treatment of owners and renters as discussed earlier.[45] Living in overcrowded conditions, particularly doubled up, is yet another aspect of precariousness.

Since there has been almost no research on those who are generously housed or "shelter rich," there are no precedents to guide a definition. It is reasonable to assume that those who command generous housing resources are more apt to be homeowners than the precariously housed, have light housing cost burdens, and enjoy levels of space consumption well beyond the standard for uncrowded conditions.[46]

### Developing Measures Based on Public Use Microdata Samples

The PUMS data are well suited to the analysis of housing circumstances. Using 1980 and 1990 PUMS data, we define the precariously and generously housed populations using three criteria relating to income, rent burden, and space consumption. Our analysis is at the household rather than person level, since rent burden and space consumption measures are primarily related to housing units and hence households.

For reasons of data limitations and necessary comparability, our analysis is further restricted to 1980 definitions of "specified" owner and renter universes. In 1980, housing costs were reported only for certain standard configurations of housing units, that is, those in the "specified" universes. The major effect is to exclude renters who are living rent-free and owners who are not occupying a standard, single-family detached house.[47] Because mobile homes and condominiums are removed from the sample, growth in the generously housed population is likely to be underestimated.

Measurement of the generously housed is complicated by several additional factors that may influence the rate of change of this group over time. Homeowner housing cost burdens reported in PUMS reflect before-tax burdens, while after-tax burdens may be much lower and form the basis for home-buying behavior. During periods of rapid house price inflation and income growth among the more affluent, households tend to leverage themselves highly owing to expectations of home value appreciation and increasing need for tax shelter. Thus, households can see their after-tax income and wealth situation improve dramatically at the same time that their out-of-pocket housing cost burdens increase.

Yet another challenge is how to define income in ways useful for geographically disaggregated comparisons. Most other studies have used poverty indices as the basic screen for economic circumstances. However, although the poverty line is adjusted by family size, it does not vary geographically.[48] For comparative geographical analysis, the use of poverty-based measures is misleading and produces results counter to information derived from other sources. We therefore used an alternative income measure that, to some extent, reflects cost-of-living differentials: household income as a proportion of a state's median household income (since median income and cost of living are strongly correlated). However, household size variations are not taken into account if a simple income measure is used, seriously biasing any subsequent analysis. Accordingly, we adapted the approach of the Department of Housing and Urban Development (HUD) to distinguish economic status of households (for purposes of allocating housing subsidies).

HUD adjusts median family income in a geographical area by a series of scalars to account for varying family size. A scalar of 1.0 is used for a four-person family; the scale declines with declining family size (to 0.7 for a one-person family), and increases with larger families (to 1.4 for a family of nine). Since we are concerned with households, we use household income as our base, in conjunction with HUD-defined scalars for family size and income categories. We employ state-level medians as our reference figures, since our geographic analysis disaggregates to the state level. This approach has the virtues of being sensitive to large cost-of-living differences as reflected in variation in median incomes and taking household size into account.

### Identifying the Precariously and Generously Housed

In identifying the *precariously housed* population, the first requirement is that households must be "extremely poor," with household incomes of 50 percent or less than their state median household income level (adjusted for household size). A second requirement is that they must also be renters, since a majority of poor homeowners are retirees who, despite having low incomes, hold significant equity (i.e., in their homes). A third requirement is that households must pay at least 50 percent of their income on housing. Although almost half of all the extremely poor renters pay between 35 and 50 percent of their incomes on rent (and thus are defined by HUD as rent burdened), our goal is to identify those in the very worst housing circumstances.[49] Presumably, poor persons who pay more than 50 percent of their income for housing reside at the threshold of homelessness, and it is from this group that the homeless might emerge. A final criterion distinguishes between households that are severely overcrowded (more than 1.5 persons per room) and those that are not.

Accordingly, we define two progressively severe levels of the precariously housed, namely:

Group 1: renter households that are extremely poor, *and* rent burdened, but *not* extremely crowded, or

Group 2: renter households that are extremely poor, *and* rent burdened, *and* extremely crowded.

The *generously housed* population is similarly identified on the basis of income, rent or mortgage burden, and space consumption. To be considered generously housed, households must have incomes at or above 120 percent of the state median household income (adjusted for household size). Both owners and renters are eligible, since there are substantial numbers of better-off renters. In addition, we focus on households with very low housing payment burdens—less than 15 percent of income. The final criterion is the amount of space per person; those with extra space are measured as having 0.33 persons per room or less (i.e., at least three rooms per person).

Accordingly, we define two progressively more generous levels of the generously housed, namely:

Group 1: owner and renter households that are economically better-off, *and* with a rent or mortgage burden of less than 15 percent, but *not* with extra space, or

Group 2: owner and renter households that are better-off, *and* with light rent or mortgage payments, *and* with extra space.

Thus defined, the generously housed not only have incomes greater (often significantly greater) than the average American household, but they also spend a small share of their incomes for housing, leaving significant amounts of disposable income for consumption and other uses. Some portion of this group also commands substantial space resources.

## THE HOUSING STATUS DISTRIBUTION IN 1990

More than three times as many householders were generously housed as were precariously housed in 1990. Together, these two margins of the housing status distribution constituted 22.2 million householders, or just over a quarter of all U.S. householders.[50] Among the precariously housed, only a small share were extremely crowded, but among the generously housed over one third also had abundant space resources.

This estimate of the precariously housed does not include the 459,215 homeless persons, found in emergency shelters or visible in street locations, who were counted in a separate Census Bureau effort. Because the homeless do not have regular addresses they are much harder to count, and uncertainty about the count has generated substantial controversy.[51]

### Relative Population Size

In 1990, approximately 5.2 million households were precariously housed, 5.1 percent of total households.[52] The precariously housed were a much larger share of total renter households—almost 16 percent. Of the precariously housed total, almost 5 million (95 percent) were extremely poor and heavily rent burdened; only about 5 percent of that total were also extremely crowded (Table 6.3). At the national level, crowding was not a problem for most of these households. This reflects our earlier finding that after some threshold of (tolerable) crowding, households are willing to accept higher rent burdens rather than further crowding.

The generously housed constituted a much larger share of total households (over 17 million, or almost 19 percent). Almost two thirds had light rent or mortgage burdens; and just over a third also had extra housing space. More than 75 percent were homeowners; and in turn, almost 30 percent of all U.S. homeowners were generously housed. By definition, the generously housed had light housing cost burdens; if the tax benefits of homeownership were to be calculated into owners' housing cost burdens, such burdens would be significantly lowered, and even more homeowners would qualify as generously housed.

TABLE 6.3    Housing characteristics of the precariously and
generously housed: 1990.

| | Precariously Housed | Total Households | Generously Housed |
|---|---|---|---|
| Tenure | | | |
| Own | — | 64% | 78% |
| Rent | 100% | 36 | 22 |
| | | | |
| Rent Burden | | | |
| Under 15% | — | 16 | 100 |
| 15–29% | — | 43 | — |
| 30–34% | — | 8 | — |
| 35–49% | — | 13 | — |
| 50% and over | 100 | 19 | — |
| | | | |
| Owner Cost | | | |
| Under 15% | — | 39 | 100 |
| 15–29% | — | 41 | — |
| 30–34% | — | 6 | — |
| 35–49% | — | 8 | — |
| 50% and over | — | 6 | — |
| | | | |
| Crowding (persons per room) | | | |
| Under .34 | 33 | 37 | 36 |
| 0.34–1.0 | 56 | 58 | 61 |
| 1.01–1.5 | 6 | 3 | 2 |
| 1.51 and over | 5 | 2 | 1 |

SOURCE: Decennial census Public Use Microdata Samples (5 percent).

NOTE: Percentages may not add to 100 because of rounding.

## Demographic and Socioeconomic Composition

Table 6.4 gives a breakdown of the demographic and socioeconomic composition of the generously and precariously housed.

*Age.*    The age of the precariously housed reflects both the demographic bulge in the young adult cohorts related to the baby boom and poorer economic prospects facing young people and people of color, especially new immigrants. Differences are extreme: Forty-six percent of the precariously housed were under age 35 compared with 15 percent of the generously housed.

*Gender and Household Type.*    Sixty-five percent of the precariously housed were women compared with 19 percent of the generously housed. Seventy-three percent of the generously housed were married-couple households, while 62

TABLE 6.4  Demographic and socioeconomic characteristics
of the precariously and generously housed: 1990.

| Characteristic | Precariously Housed | Total Households | Generously Housed |
|---|---|---|---|
| **Age** | | | |
| Under 25 | 19% | 5% | 2% |
| 25–34 | 27 | 21 | 13 |
| 35–44 | 17 | 22 | 21 |
| 45–54 | 9 | 15 | 23 |
| 55–64 | 8 | 13 | 22 |
| 65–74 | 9 | 13 | 14 |
| 75–90 and over | 11 | 9 | 6 |
| **Sex** | | | |
| Female | 65 | 33 | 19 |
| **Household Type** | | | |
| Married-couple family | 17 | 56 | 73 |
| Male-headed family | 3 | 3 | 3 |
| Female-headed family | 31 | 12 | 7 |
| Other male-headed household | 18 | 13 | 10 |
| Other female-headed household | 31 | 17 | 7 |
| **Race-Ethnicity** | | | |
| White non-Hispanic | 59 | 80 | 87 |
| Black non-Hispanic | 23 | 11 | 7 |
| American Indian | 1 | <1 | <1 |
| Asian–Pacific Islander | 3 | 2 | 2 |
| Hispanic | 13 | 6 | 4 |
| **Nativity** | | | |
| Not foreign-born | 83 | 90 | 93 |
| Arrived 1980 or after | 7 | 3 | 1 |
| Arrived before 1980 | 9 | 7 | 6 |
| **Income** | | | |
| Public assistance | 29 | 5 | 1 |
| **Labor Force Status** | | | |
| Not in labor force | 52 | 30 | 22 |
| Employed[a] | 39 | 67 | 76 |
| Unemployed | 9 | 3 | 2 |
| **Total Number (millions)** | 5.2 | 91.7 | 17.2 |

SOURCE: Decennial census Public Use Microdata Samples (5 percent).

NOTE: Percentages may not add to 100 because of rounding.

[a]Category includes "employed" and "not working," which refers to people absent from work during the census week (e.g., due to illness or vacation).

percent of the precariously housed were either families headed by women (31 percent) or female heads of nonfamily households (31 percent); only 14 percent of generously housed households were either of these types.

*Race-Ethnicity and Nativity.* Eighty-seven percent of the generously housed were white compared with 59 percent of the precariously housed, of which 23 percent were black and 13 percent Hispanic. Hispanics and immigrants were much more likely to be extremely crowded; whites were more apt to have extra space. And although a large majority of both types of householders had been born in the United States, the proportion among the precariously housed was 10 percentage points lower. Not surprisingly, precariously housed immigrants were far more likely to be recent arrivals than generously housed immigrants.

*Labor Force Status and Income.* Seventy-eight percent of the generously housed were in the labor force, virtually all employed, while 48 percent of the precariously housed were either employed or looking for work. Given their employment circumstances, not surprisingly 29 percent received public assistance income during the previous year.

## Geographical Pattern

The precariously and generously housed were unevenly distributed across the national geography. The average precariously housed rate was almost 6 percent, but proportions rose to more than 9 percent in New York and 8 percent in California (Figure 6.13). Other states well above the national mean included two western states with particularly poor economic circumstances (Nevada and Hawaii); three midwestern industrial states (Illinois, Ohio, and Michigan); Louisiana, hard hit by the energy bust in the 1980s; and Massachusetts, Rhode Island, and New Jersey, where the housing cost surge was among the most rapid in the nation.

In contrast, the generously housed, averaging almost 19 percent of all U.S. households, constituted a larger share of households in the southern and midwestern states than in either of the two large coastal regions (Figure 6.14). Over 80 percent of midwestern states and over 65 percent of southern states were at or above the national norm. Rates were over 22 percent in Indiana, Iowa, Ohio, Michigan, and West Virginia. In the West, only the mountain states of Idaho and Utah had average or above proportions of generously housed. And in the East, only Pennsylvania had a relatively large generously housed population. On the low end, California and Nevada had rates in the 14 percent range, as did Vermont and New Hampshire. No states in the South or Midwest had rates this low.

States with high rates of precarious housing did not also have high rates of

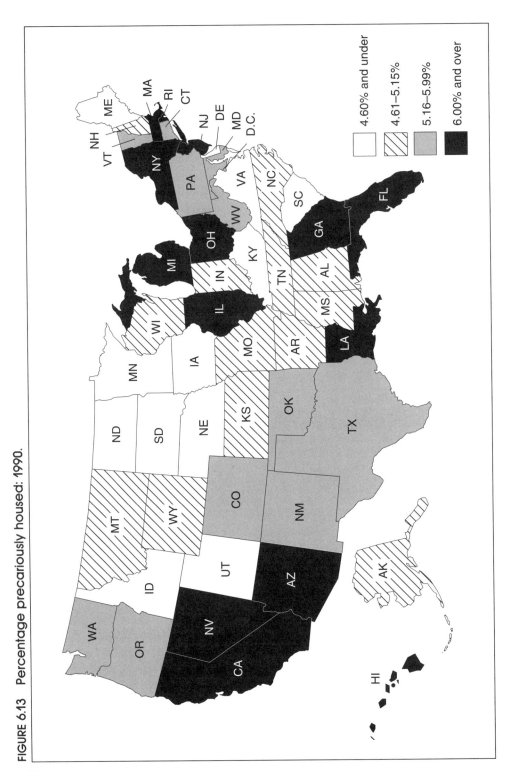

FIGURE 6.13    Percentage precariously housed: 1990.

4.60% and under

4.61–5.15%

5.16–5.99%

6.00% and over

FIGURE 6.14  Percentage generously housed: 1990.

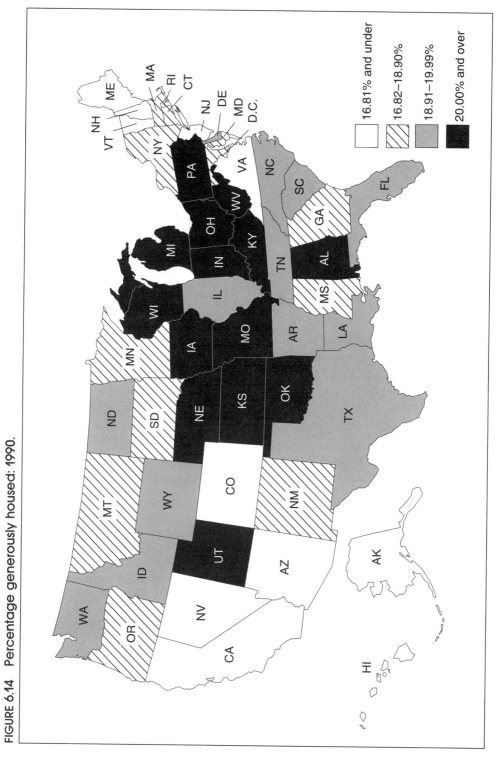

16.81% and under

16.82–18.90%

18.91–19.99%

20.00% and over

generous housing. In fact, the correlation between the proportions precariously and generously housed in 1990 is negative ($r = -0.24$). This relationship is even stronger if we consider only the "extra space" segment of the generously housed ($r = -0.45$). Thus, as one might expect, states with the most severe housing problems also had lower shares of the generously housed.

## THE POLARIZATION OF HOUSING STATUS DURING THE 1980S

Trends between 1980 and 1990 suggest that the margins of the housing status distribution were growing larger. Within the renter population, a greater share of households fell into precarious housing circumstances and more were apt to be faced with crowded living conditions. On the other hand, the proportion of all households that were generously housed with extra space grew rapidly (although the total proportion of generously housed dropped slightly). Moreover, in terms of absolute numbers, both tails of the housing status distribution expanded. This growth was particularly rapid on the precariously housed end.

Significantly, the demographic and socioeconomic mix became more polarized, with earlier patterns becoming increasingly stark by 1990: An increasing share of the precariously housed consisted of young, black, single-parent, and immigrant households, while an increasing share of the generously housed consisted of elderly, white, native-born, and nonfamily households. For some of these groups, the risk of becoming precariously or generously housed shifted dramatically.

Beneath this national portrait were rapidly shifting state housing markets. Patterns of polarization and other types of state-level change in housing status are discussed below.

### Aggregate Trends

At the national level, there was polarization at the margins of the housing status distribution, although the picture for the generously housed is, as expected, made more complex by measurement problems and housing market dynamics of the period. In terms of absolute numbers, both groups expanded, particularly the precariously housed, which grew by over 1 million households, for a growth rate of 29 percent. It is noteworthy that this rate corresponds closely to some of the lower estimates of growth in the homeless population during this same time period.[53] The proportion of extremely overcrowded households doubled, but still amounted to only 5 percent of all precarious households.

Number of U.S. households at extremes of housing status.

|      | All Precariously Housed | All Generously Housed | Generous with Extra Space | Total |
|------|-------------------------|-----------------------|---------------------------|-------|
| 1990 | 5,160,000               | 17,170,000            | 6,250,000                 | 91,750,000 |
|      | 5.6%                    | 18.7%                 | 6.8%                      | 100%  |
| 1980 | 4,120,000               | 16,540,000            | 4,620,000                 | 80,470,000 |
|      | 5.1%                    | 20.6%                 | 5.7%                      | 100%  |

The number of generously housed rose by 4 percent, but their proportion of all households declined slightly. As suspected, limitations of the census data imply that both the number and proportion are underestimated, because the data do not reflect the growth of condominium owners. Moreover, although incomes among this group rose, potentially increasing the generously housed group, two factors mitigated against such growth. First, home prices rose faster than incomes, so that even many better-off people faced housing prices that were higher relative to their incomes than they had been in 1980; in turn, this could have increased the probability of their spending more than 15 percent on housing.[54] Second, because of this rapid housing price appreciation, better-off households could have been increasingly willing to accept a slightly larger housing cost burden because of their expectations for large returns from home investments. Again, this would have induced a greater proportion of households to allocate more than 15 percent of their income for housing.

Indeed, a shift to higher payment burdens did cause some middle-income households to drop from generously housed status. The overall proportion of all households that were income-qualified for this status and carried a housing cost burden under 30 percent grew modestly over the 1980s. In absolute terms, this group expanded by almost 5 million households over the decade. Thus, nominal housing burdens increased among the better-off, whether for housing cost or investment incentive reasons.

In fact, there is clear evidence that polarization occurred within the ranks of the generously housed, as the most advantaged group in the housing distribution increased. The proportion of the generously housed who were concentrated in the upper tail of the income distribution (over 200 percent of state median) rose from 50 to 54 percent over the decade. More important, the proportion of the generously housed with extra space grew rapidly, constituting 28 percent of the generously housed in 1980 and 36 percent in 1990.

The precariously housed constituted a substantial proportion of all renter households in both years, but the share expanded by almost 8 percent between 1980 and 1990. In contrast, generously housed renters, who constituted almost 12 percent of U.S. renter households in 1980, fell by over 2 percentage points, or almost 17 percent; at the same time, generously housed owners also fell as a share of all U.S. homeowners.

## Changes in Composition

What happened to the mix of people who were precariously and generously housed between 1980 and 1990? In general, over the course of the decade the demographic mix of both margins of the housing status distribution became more sharply polarized. The precariously housed grew even younger, and more dominated by female-headed family households, minorities, and the working poor.

*Age.*    The age distribution of the precariously housed shifted, with a greater share being drawn from the early and late baby boom cohorts (persons 25 to 44 in 1990). The share of elderly dropped. In contrast, the generously housed lost households from the 15–24 and 25–34 age cohorts, gained very slightly in the 35–44 group (again, a baby boom effect), and the proportions in the groups aged 65 and over expanded.

*Gender and Household Type.*    The share of precariously housed female householders as opposed to male householders rose fractionally, but the share of generously housed women rose by almost 6 percentage points, reflecting the increasing ability of elderly women to remain autonomous and stay in family homes. The proportion of single-parent householders (both male and female) rose among the precariously housed, while the share of married-couple and non-family householders fell slightly. Notably, the proportion of married-couple householders fell among the generously housed, and the share of single-parent and nonfamily households rose. This is most likely indicative of an age effect: As married-couple households aged, they were more apt to be generously housed, but also more likely to have experienced death of a spouse (most often the male spouse), separation, or divorce. In households with children, women are more likely to retain the family home.

*Race-Ethnicity and Nativity.*    The racial-ethnic composition of the gener-ously housed group remained quite stable. However, among the precariously housed, the share declined by over 5 percentage points for whites and rose by almost 3 points for Hispanics. In addition, the proportion of native-born among the precariously housed group fell, while the share that were immigrants rose.

*Labor Force Status and Income.*    More of the generously housed were not in the labor force by 1990, again reflecting the aging of this population. In contrast, the share of the precariously housed participating in the labor force rose slightly over the decade, and more of those in the labor force were looking for work rather than in a job. The share of the precariously housed who received public assistance remained stable. Virtually none of the generously housed received public assistance in either 1980 or 1990.

### Shifting Risks of Becoming Precariously or Generously Housed

The information on composition of the two housing status groups does not reflect the underlying differences in the sizes of demographic and socioeconomic subpopulations. For example, there may be many more white householders among the generously housed simply because there are many more such householders in the householder universe. To control for underlying differences in population sizes, we must analyze the incidence rates of being precariously or generously housed. This reveals the differential chances faced by members of specific demographic and socioeconomic groups of falling into one of the two categories.[55]

In this section, we consider how the risks of becoming precariously housed shifted over the 1980s for various subgroups of the population, and how chances of being generously housed changed over the decade as well. In general, householders under age 25, female-headed households, minorities, and immigrants stood a far greater chance of being precariously housed than older people, married-couple families, whites, or citizens. Their risks of becoming precariously housed grew throughout the decade of the 1980s (Table 6.5). In contrast, prospects for becoming generously housed rose for women and older householders; while they fell for most other groups, the most precipitous declines were among recent immigrants, Asians and Hispanics, and young people.

*Age-Specific Risks.* Over the 1980s, the risk of becoming precariously housed jumped dramatically for households in the youngest age group—the group that already faced the highest risk (Figure 6.15). Only 15 percent of householders under age 25 were precariously housed in 1980, but more than 20 percent were in this situation by 1990. In the two oldest age cohorts risks were lower in 1990 than in 1980. As cohorts moved through the age distribution their chances of being precariously housed fell (especially by early middle age). However, householders passing from the under-age-25 group to the 25–34 group over the course of the decade ended up at greater risk of being precariously housed than those aged 25–34 had been in 1980. This result has alarming implications: Unless the cohort now under age 25 is able to make up for lost ground over the next ten years, given its higher starting point, it will face dramatically higher risks of precarious housing status than the cohort aged 25–34 in 1990.

Not surprisingly, householders under age 25 had lower chances of being generously housed; by 1990 their rate had fallen to about 6 percent (see Figure 6.16). The chances of the younger groups being generously housed plunged

TABLE 6.5  Changing rates of precarious and generous housing status,
by subgroup: 1980–1990.

| Characteristic | Precariously Housed Rate | Difference 1980–1990 | Generously Housed Rate | Difference 1980–1990 |
|---|---|---|---|---|
| Age | | | | |
| Under 25 | 20% | +5 | 6% | −2 |
| 25–34 | 7 | +1 | 12 | −2 |
| 35–44 | 4 | +1 | 17 | −5 |
| 45–54 | 3 | +1 | 28 | −6 |
| 55–64 | 3 | 0 | 30 | −2 |
| 65–74 | 4 | −1 | 20 | +4 |
| 75–90 | 6 | −1 | 13 | +3 |
| | | | | |
| Sex | | | | |
| Female | 11 | −1 | 5 | +1 |
| | | | | |
| Household Type | | | | |
| Married-couple family | 2 | 0 | 25 | −2 |
| Male-headed family | 6 | +2 | 19 | −4 |
| Female-headed family | 15 | +1 | 11 | 0 |
| Nonfamily | 9 | −1 | 11 | +1 |
| | | | | |
| Race-Ethnicity | | | | |
| White non-Hispanic | 4 | 0 | 20 | −2 |
| Black non-Hispanic | 12 | +1 | 13 | −1 |
| American Indian | 9 | +1 | 12 | −1 |
| Asian–Pacific Islander | 8 | +1 | 16 | −3 |
| Hispanic | 12 | +1 | 11 | −2 |
| | | | | |
| Nativity | | | | |
| Not foreign-born | 5 | 0 | 19 | −2 |
| Arrived in past 10 years | 16 | +4 | 9 | −2 |
| Arrived more than 10 years ago | 6 | +1 | 17 | −1 |

SOURCE: Decennial census Public Use Microdata Samples (5 percent), specified households only.

NOTE: Percentages may not add to 100 due to rounding.

over the decade. In contrast, for the elderly, generously housed rates in 1990 surpassed those in 1980. Significantly, rates for those with extra space grew for virtually all age groups, indicating polarization within the generously housed group.

*Risk by Household Type.*  Rate differentials by household type were sharp in 1990, but in some instances moderated over the course of the decade. Married-couple families faced less than a 2 percent risk of being precariously housed, but this was up slightly from 1980. Conversely, married-couple families' chances of being generously housed fell somewhat. The greatest risks in

FIGURE 6.15    Percentage of each age group that is precariously housed: 1980 and
1990.

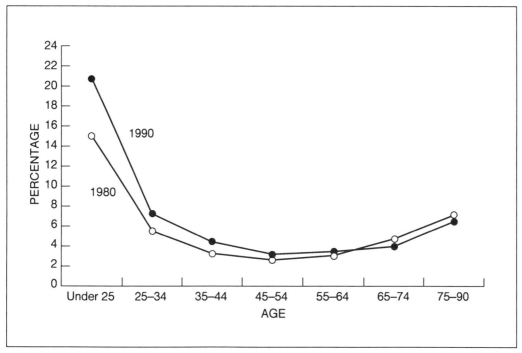

1990 were faced by female-headed family households (15 percent), the rate
rising 11 percent over the decade. (Male-headed families had a rate one third
that of female-headed families, although their risk of precarious housing rose
sharply between 1980 and 1990.) Female-headed families were also relatively
unlikely to be generously housed; their chances were half (or less) of those
faced by married-couple families. Prospects for being generously housed fell for
all household types except nonfamily households, reflecting the growing presence of the elderly (many widowed) among the generously housed.

*Racial-Ethnic Group Risks.*    For both demographic and socioeconomic reasons, the rates of becoming precariously housed rose three to six times as fast
for minorities as for whites. Blacks and Hispanics had the highest 1990 precarious housing rates, up from 1980. Immigrants in general, but recent arrivals in
particular, had the steepest rate increases. The prospects of becoming generously housed declined most for Asians, Hispanics, and recent immigrants. Both
trends underscore the slowdown in upward mobility for immigrants, with the
newest arrivals most affected.

*Risks by Labor Force Status.*    While prospects of being generously housed
increased for those not in the labor force, owing to the growing presence of the

FIGURE 6.16   Percentage of each age group that is generously housed: 1980 and 1990.

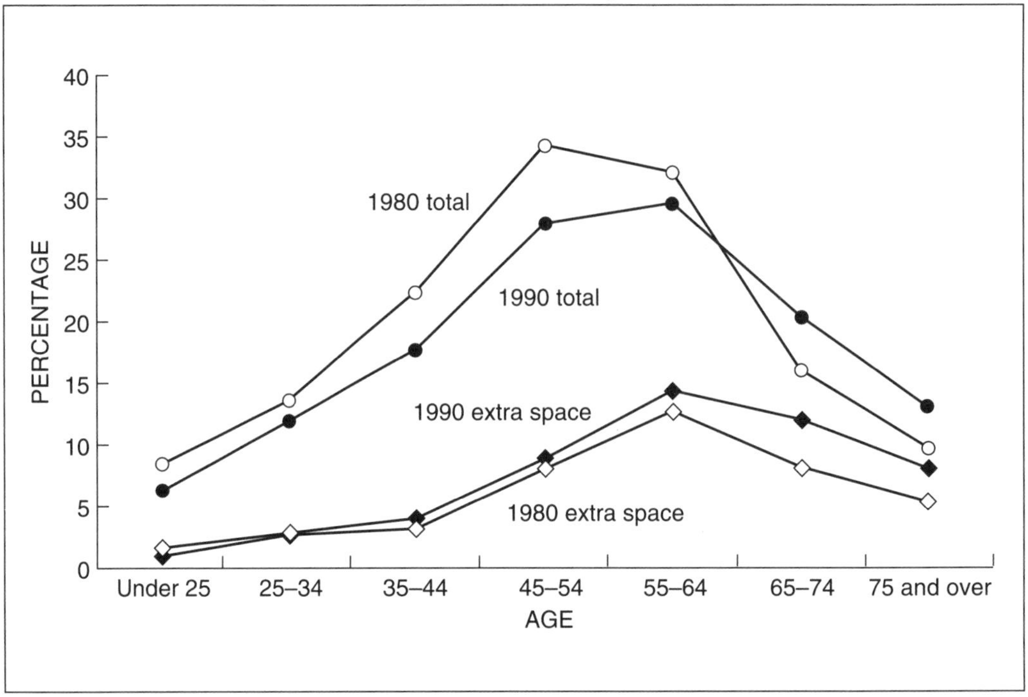

elderly in this housing group, working and unemployed people faced substantially higher risks of being precariously housed over the 1980s. This was particularly true for those looking for work.

### Uneven Development of Polarized Housing Conditions

We have seen how much the chances of being precariously or generously housed depend on the age of the householders, with very young householders much more likely to be precariously housed and elderly householders more likely to be generously housed. Accordingly, differences in age structure between states may cause some states to have higher or lower overall rates of each housing status. Even more relevant, changes in age structure over the decade of the 1980s—principally the middle-aging of the baby boom generation—would be expected to reduce the incidence of precariousness in most states. Therefore, in order to compare the 50 states over time, we have standardized their incidence rates of precariousness and generousness by assuming a common age structure for all states in both 1980 and 1990.[56]

More than 80 percent of all states experienced statistically significant gains in the percentage precariously housed between 1980 and 1990 (see Figure 6.17).[57]

FIGURE 6.17 Change in the percentage precariously housed: 1980–1990.

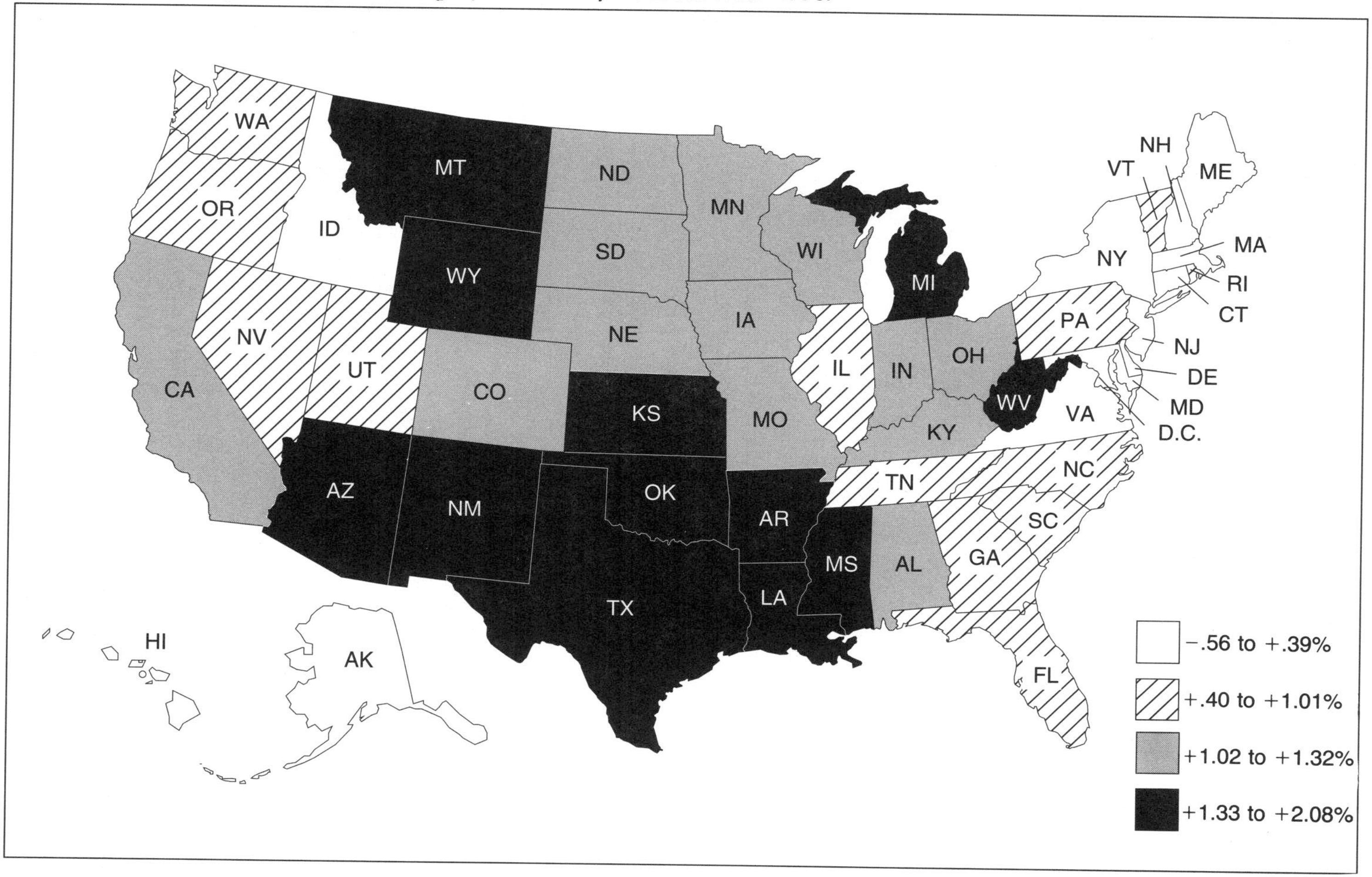

Legend:
- −.56 to +.39%
- +.40 to +1.01%
- +1.02 to +1.32%
- +1.33 to +2.08%

The only significant loss was in New Jersey, but it was small. The biggest percentage point increases were in the South (Louisiana, West Virginia, and Oklahoma) and in the Midwest (Michigan and Kansas); the most extreme proportional shifts (over 50 percent) were in Wyoming, Kansas, West Virginia, and Oklahoma. Shares of the generously housed fell slightly, as expected, the largest declines being in the South and West (especially California, whose share dropped from 19 to 15 percent—for a decline of almost 25 percent). Small but insignificant losses occurred in Wyoming, Alaska, Mississippi, Massachusetts, and Rhode Island. Several states did register minor gains (Idaho, Nevada, North and South Dakota, Alabama, and Kentucky), and Iowa experienced a statistically significant increase.

If we consider changes among the most advantaged group, that is, generously housed with extra space, a radically different picture emerges (see Figure 6.18). Only one state registered a drop in the proportion of households in the "extra space" group, while proportions in all other states rose. The largest jumps occurred in the mountain states (Wyoming, Montana, and Idaho), the plains (Iowa, North Dakota, South Dakota, and Nebraska), West Virginia, and Kentucky. Many of these states had aging populations and high rates of outmigration of younger people, leaving behind older "empty-nester" households with low cost burdens.

Polarization occurs when states gain both precariously housed and generously housed populations; convergence occurs when losses are experienced in both groups. Only one state—New Jersey—experienced such a convergence. In eight other states, there was a *weak polarization,* that is, the precarious housing rate rose while the generous housing rate remained stable. Three additional states experienced no changes in either rate. Thus, in three quarters of all the states, precariousness grew but total generousness fell. Correlation analysis of the two trends across the 50 states indicates a weak polarization pattern ($r = 0.12$).

Once again, the picture changes dramatically when the most advantaged, "extra space" segment of the generously housed is considered. Here we find that *all but 12 states polarized* (see Figure 6.19); the correlation coefficient is positive and reasonably large ($r = 0.48$). The exceptions are states in which rates for the precariously housed rose, but those for the generously housed with extra space did not (California and Hawaii, both states with high housing prices, and Vermont and Delaware); and states in which precariousness was either stable or declined (New Jersey and Maryland in the mid-Atlantic; New Hampshire, Rhode Island, and Maine in New England; and Idaho, Alaska, and Virginia). Some of the most extreme instances of polarization were registered in the plains and mountain states and in the South (Figure 6.19).

FIGURE 6.18  Change in the percentage generously housed (extra space group): 1980–1990.

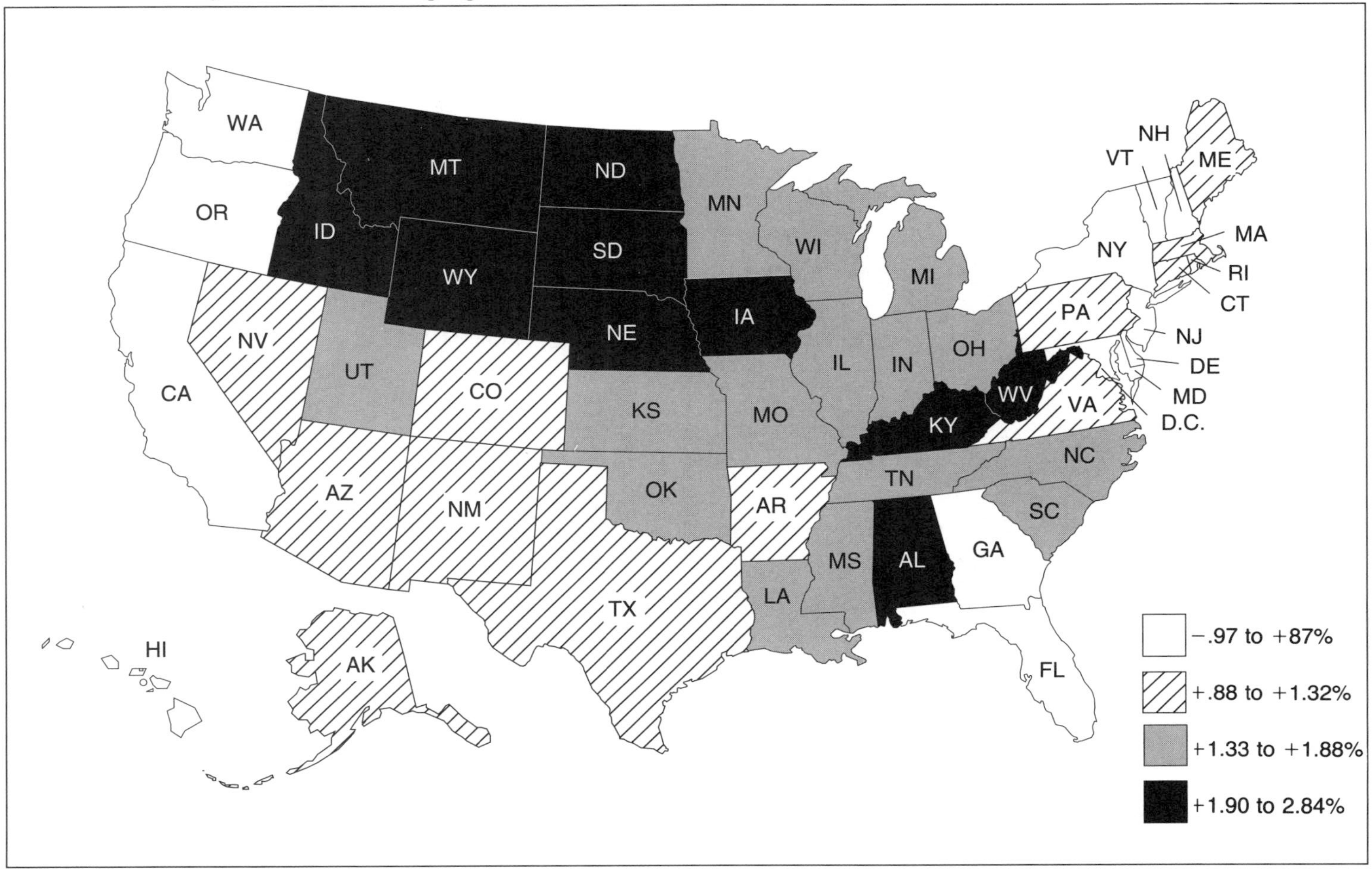

Legend:
- −.97 to +87%
- +.88 to +1.32%
- +1.33 to +1.88%
- +1.90 to 2.84%

321

FIGURE 6.19   Polarization in housing status: 1980–1990.*

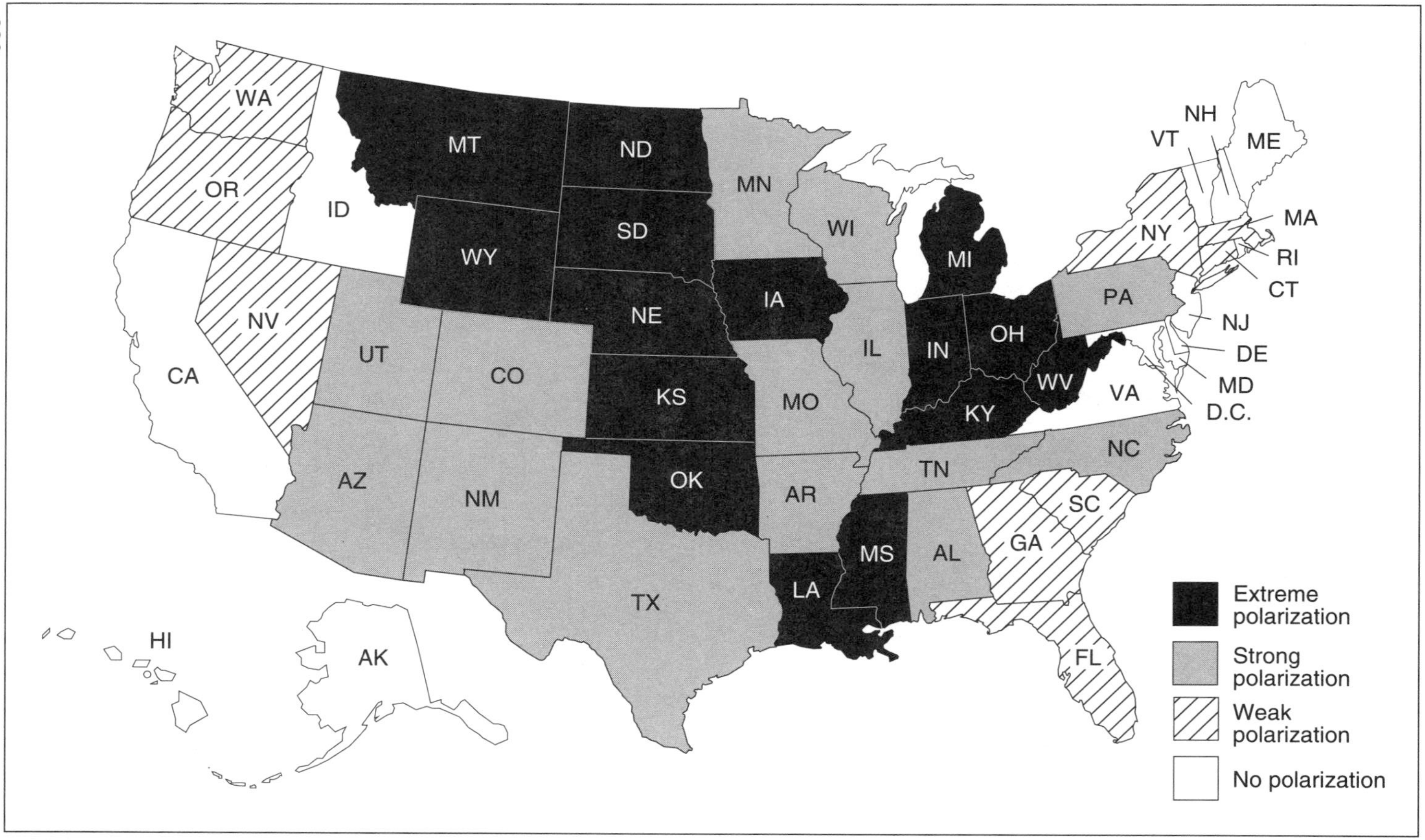

NOTES: Polarization is defined as percentage point change in precariously housed plus percentage point change in generously housed (extra space group only). Map categories are defined as follows: *extreme polarization* = growth in polarization of 3 or more percentage points; *strong polarization* = growth in polarization between 2.1 and 2.9 percentage points (national average rate of polarization was 2.1); *weak polarization* = growth in polarization between 0.1 and 2.0 percentage points; and *no polarization* = growth in either percentage precariously housed or percentage generously housed statistically insignificant.

## CONCLUSION

After decades of steadily improving housing conditions for the majority of Americans, the 1980s marked the first reversal since the Great Depression.

Polarization of housing status must be seen as the overarching story of housing during the 1980s. We have placed this polarization in a broader theoretical context, one emphasizing the longitudinal experiences of cohorts struggling to move through their expected life cycle in the housing market, and the negative effects of changing historical circumstances including economic globalization and restructuring, a redefinition of the social contract and weakening of social safety net programs, and profound demographic and lifestyle shifts.

The most at-risk Americans were those with the most tenuous foothold: those newest in the housing and labor markets—newly launched young households and immigrants—and those placed at the economic margins by virtue of their race-ethnicity, gender, or lack of employment. In contrast, the most successful Americans were those with more advantaged race-ethnicity or gender characteristics and superior labor market position and those who established themselves in earlier decades, at a time when income growth was strong and housing prices were lower.

### Summary of Findings

This chapter has reviewed trends and geographic patterns across a great many dimensions of housing experience. Our major findings are:

1. Individuals' housing experience conforms to a well-defined life-cycle pattern, with age-demarcated transitions from dependent to autonomous living arrangements, from renting to owning, and along other dimensions. These transitions, along with demographic trends and economic factors, generate demand for housing. During the 1980s, the demand for relatively small, affordable housing units rose, but such units were rapidly vanishing from the housing supply. The result was a mismatch between effective housing demand and housing supply that impacted the living arrangements and housing status of American households.

2. One result of the housing mismatch was that between 1980 and 1990 fewer young persons were able to establish independent households. In contrast, the elderly were increasingly able to maintain independent living quarters.

3. Partly as a consequence of declining autonomy among the young, overcrowding increased. This was the first registered increase since the Great Depression and followed decades of steep declines in crowding rates. All of this increase was found among renters, concentrated especially in the most extreme category of crowding.

4. Levels of crowding were strongly related to race-ethnicity, even control-

ling for income and household size, or controlling for the rent burden of a household. This reflects different cultural tolerances for crowding and may indicate the relative willingness to share housing space.

5. In general, census-reported affordability problems were far greater for renters than for owners. Small as they are, owners' problems are exaggerated in the census data because gross payments need to be adjusted for tax savings and expected appreciation, benefits not available to renters.

6. The proportion of owners with excessive payment burdens relative to incomes was higher in states where house values were higher, as might be expected. Payment burdens were higher in states where house values have increased the most since 1980—representing the "stretch" that young adults have made when the investment incentive was strong.

7. The proportion of renters with excessive payment burdens was higher in states where rents were higher and where ownership increased the most—representing a selection effect as the most financially capable renters were skimmed off into owning, leaving a concentration of more-burdened renters behind.

8. The overall ownership rate of the nation declined for the first time since the Great Depression; however, this small overall decline is the sum of major losses concentrated among the young while ownership rates soared for the elderly. This dynamic results from the momentum of more advantaged cohorts— the parents of the baby boomers—aging into their elderly years and bringing with them record-high ownership levels. The result was an increase in the gap between older and younger ownership rates from 18 percentage points in 1980 to 30 points in 1990.

9. Ownership rates for the young have plunged most in the states with greatest price declines—where housing should be most affordable. This apparent anomaly arises because the decision to buy a home is based on actual costs of owning, which go down as housing appreciates in value, leading to greater tax benefits and returns from home equity. Conversely, when values fall, the real cost of ownership increases and people put off buying a home since they expect its value to go down.

10. Overall, minority households fared much worse than white households. Among both owners and renters, affordability problems, already substantially higher than for whites, increased more rapidly than for white households during the 1980s. Moreover, the ownership rates of young black householders fell even more than the rest, creating an even greater generation gap between older and young blacks (40 percentage points) than was found for other racial-ethnic groups. Given that older blacks already had substantially lower ownership rates than whites, this underscores the lagging position of young blacks.

11. Synthesizing these various dimensions of housing well-being, we have proposed measures of the two extremes of the housing status distribution: the precariously housed and the generously housed. Defined on the basis of income,

tenure, payment burden, and level of crowding, these two measures provide rough indicators for estimating the growing polarization in the housing market.

12. The precariously housed and generously housed constituted approximately 5 and 19 percent, respectively, of all American households in 1990. The numbers of those at either margin of the housing status distribution grew over the 1980s. Proportions of precariously housed rose, but those of generously housed apparently fell slightly. Homeowners spent more for housing because home prices rose faster than incomes and because buyers expected growing returns from home equity appreciation, thus edging some out of the generously housed category. However, both the numbers and proportions of the most generously housed (those with light burdens and extra space) rose.

13. The housing status distribution was sharply segmented by age, race-ethnicity, gender and marital status, household type, nativity, and labor market status. In general, the young, minorities, female-headed households, immigrants, and those not in the labor force or unemployed were overrepresented among the precariously housed and faced the greatest risks of becoming precariously housed. For most groups, these risks increased over the decade of the 1980s.

14. The generously housed were more likely to be older, white, married-couple, native-born, and employed persons. The prospects of becoming generously housed rose among women, especially older widows, and older households in general. In most cases, however, chances of becoming generously housed fell for other demographic groups over the decade, especially for recent immigrants.

15. Eastern and western portions of the country had the highest precarious housing rates as of 1990 (especially California and New York), while the southern and midwestern states had some of the highest generous housing rates. Over the 1980s, most states experienced gains in proportions of precariously housed and slight declines in proportions of generously housed. Proportions of the most generously housed, however, grew in almost all states. If the changes in the precariously housed and the most generously housed are added together, all but 12 states became more polarized with respect to housing status over the course of the decade.

## Implications for Public Policy

Our findings have implications for national debates around homelessness, welfare reform, housing assistance, and tax policy. First, policies to alleviate homelessness have centered on responding to the needs of people already on the streets, through the provision of emergency shelters and associated services. Much less attention has focused on preventing homelessness in the first place. In an increasingly stressful housing market, more and more people with marginal financial resources will find themselves unable to compete. Although the precipitating causes of homelessness extend beyond the housing realm (i.e., loss of income or welfare benefits; personal vulnerabilities such as mental disability or substance abuse), analysis of the precariously housed enables policymakers to identify those groups most at risk of homelessness due to housing status and to target them for homelessness prevention efforts. Moreover, comparative analysis of precariously housed and homeless populations would allow service providers to channel assistance to those among the precariously housed at heightened risk of homelessness due to nonhousing circumstances.

Second, proposals for welfare reform contain at their heart further welfare reductions and time limits on welfare receipt. These proposals ignore the growing difficulties in the housing market. They also ignore the fact that economic restructuring over the 1980s meant that more of the precariously housed were forced to depend on public assistance even though greater proportions were looking for work. At the same time, the fall in real welfare benefit levels over the 1980s put increasing numbers of young people (especially female-headed households and people of color) at risk of becoming precariously housed. In the absence of high-quality and accessible child care, job training, and, if necessary, public employment programs, further welfare reduction and/or time limits are apt to simply push additional households into precarious housing circumstances and bring more families to the brink of homelessness.

Third, federal housing assistance programs remain far below their pre-1980 levels, and the gap between numbers of households eligible for assistance and assistance opportunities has widened. This is despite the fact that declining federal involvement in affordable housing during the 1980s contributed to rising precariousness in housing circumstances and spreading homelessness. Although rates of nonprofit housing development increased over the decade, the production capability of nonprofits remains far below that of the public sector. Moreover, even nonprofit efforts increasingly rely on packaging a variety of public housing subsidies in order to render projects financially viable, so that the contraction of such subsidies and restrictions on their utilization threaten to limit the supply of affordable housing units.

Fourth, by far the largest housing subsidy program in America remains the homeowners' benefit program, carried out largely by the Internal Revenue Service through the generous provisions for income tax deductibility of home mortgage interest payments and property taxes. Although homeownership may be a national goal of urgent importance, these subsidies must be periodically reevaluated in light of the full spectrum of housing needs. In spite of the large size, affluence, and growing numbers of the generously housed population, contrasting with the mounting problems for precariously housed Americans, we have yet to engage in serious public debate over the fairness of a federal tax policy that subsidizes homeowners so disproportionately.

Finally, it may be time to consider the benefits to be gained from better management of the private housing market. Volatile housing prices benefit only a few well-positioned individuals, largely those older persons who are most likely to be generously housed. Younger adults are discouraged from home buying by falling prices, and they are induced to make great sacrifices when prices are rising. Certainly price controls would be impractical and even counterproductive. However, there are a number of ways in which government—federal, state, and local—can help to stabilize housing prices. Encouraging a more rapid response of new construction to rising demand would help reduce excessive inflation. For example, rapid response would require lessening of the typical delays incurred in gaining development approvals from local authorities. It also may require greater coordination among major real estate institutions in forecasting economic trends, required infrastructure, and necessary loan commitments. (Failure to coordinate is also one cause of the massive savings and loan bailout of the late 1980s paid by the taxpayers.) Finally, planning agencies should monitor more closely the changing housing inventory and how well it serves the full spectrum of the population. Although the great majority of housing units in the nation are produced as a private business venture, leaving government to pick up the tab for any mistakes, oversights, or unmet needs, greater cooperation between the public and private sectors is already being required as we rethink the nation's housing policies.

## Continuing Inquiry

The nation's housing varies enormously, not only between states and regions, but also within cities and neighborhoods in the same state (Adams 1987). Housing problems are often highly localized. The census provides a rich reservoir of data for more spatially disaggregated analyses of the nation's diverse locales. Scholars and public officials can delve into information pertaining to housing problems in far more detail than we have been able to in the present analysis. Such studies have the potential to more sharply illuminate the dimensions of housing, and in so doing increase our understanding of housing problems and contribute to the design of appropriate public policies and private development initiatives.

Many of the topics addressed in this chapter deserve further scrutiny, given their relevance to both national policy debates and the immediate problems faced by countless localities. The census is an invaluable tool for the investigation of the detailed connections between housing status, the changing circumstances of individuals and households over their life cycles, social diversity, and economic well-being. Its value is greatest for the systematic comparison of states and localities, and in-depth analysis of local changes over time. Given the turbulence of the past decade in economic, political, and social terms, and persistent uncertainties, the complex interactions among demographic forces, labor market dynamics, social differences, and housing need to be continually reexamined.

---

Research funding from the Russell Sage Foundation is gratefully acknowledged. The authors also thank Nancy Cunniff and Reynolds Farley of the Foundation's Census Monograph Project for their advice and guidance during the course of the project. Catherine Walsh provided superior research assistance, for which we are most grateful. William Butz and his colleagues at the U.S. Bureau of the Census, Jorge Chapa, Reynolds Farley, and other participants in the Census Research Project provided insightful comments on an earlier draft. Stuart Gabriel also made numerous suggestions which improved our work. The Population Research Center at the University of Michigan, Ann Arbor, especially Lisa Neidert and Ricardo Rodriguez, assisted with data file construction, and Jill Fox at the USC University Computing Service helped to solve a variety of technical data-processing problems. Jong-Gyu Lee and Jianchun Yi created the cartographic exhibits, and Michael Najjar assisted with other research tasks. All responsibility for errors remains our own.

## ENDNOTES

1. For example, see Levy (1987) and his chapter in this volume; Harrison and Bluestone (1988); Phillips (1990); Braun (1991); Danziger and Gottschalk (1993); Ellwood (1988); Brown (1989); Katz (1989); Rossi (1989); Burt (1992); and Wolch and Dear (1993).

2. Easterlin and his colleagues argue that young adults of the baby boom generation are struggling to stay on track—maximizing their income relative to their parents in order to achieve generational progress—by adjusting their family composition and labor force behavior. See Easterlin (1987) and Easterlin, Schaeffer, and Macunovich (1993); converting total household income to an "adult equivalent" scale, they find that the baby boomers from the top economic quintile have managed to sustain their cohort's progress above preceding generations through such adjustments as delaying marriage, having fewer children, and relying more heavily on multiple wage earners. However, Easterlin et al. (1993) find that the poorest segment of the baby boomers has been less successful in its adjustments. Thus, some of the younger generation are still achieving great economic success, even as others are falling further behind.

3. The data are taken from the Public Use Microdata Sample 1 percent file.

4. Prior to 1980, the Census Bureau convention was to identify the husband as the head of household. With the 1980 census, either spouse could be declared as householder, although at that time 95 percent of the married couples named the husband as householder. For discussion of past controversy over this issue, and for evidence of wives' rapidly growing claims of householder status, see Myers (1992:50–52).

5. For in-depth discussion of these marital and family factors in living arrangements, and their changes over time, see Sweet and Bumpass (1987).

6. For a broad overview of mobility behavior, see Long (1988).

7. For a recent example of the economic perspective that emphasizes the role of real rents and potential personal earnings in household formation, see Haurin, Hendershott, and Kim (1993).

8. For example, almost 1 million dwellings for defense workers and military service personnel were produced by the federal government during World War II; see Jacobs et al. (1982) for a review of wartime and other early federal housing programs.

9. Unless otherwise noted, the figures cited in this section are derived from Devaney (1992).

10. Approximately 4.5 million units were condominiums (3.6 million of which were occupied by owners and renters); most of these units were in the South (1.8 million) and West (1.2 million). In addition, there were 870,000 cooperatives, most in the Northeast, and 6.9 million mobile homes, most located in rural areas; almost half were in the South (Devaney 1992: 6).

11. Almost nine tenths of homeowners lived in single-family units compared with one third of renters.

12. This figure is based on Annual Housing Survey and American Housing Survey data from 1973 and 1985; see Apgar (1991).

13. Figures tabulated by David Rhodes, as reported in Jencks (1994).

14. Rents are quality-adjusted; from Jencks (1994).

15. Between 1980 and 1986, real cash incomes of household heads under age 25 fell by more than 4 percent (Gabriel 1988).

16. In this ratio, all rooms are counted except bathrooms, hallways, closets, and porches.

17. This figure design was first presented in Myers and Choi (1992).

18. Norms of personal space are highly variable across different cultures. See Hall (1966).

19. Baer (1976:381); and Feins and Land (1981). This rule seems to have been based on the practices of factory owners with worker housing, who charged their employees a week's pay for a month's rent.

20. The widely used National Association of Realtors index combines readily available summary measures in a hypothetical formula that describes affordability of home purchase; an index of 100 signifies that a buyer with the median family income could just afford the median-priced house. In practice, this index has proven extremely sensitive to current interest rates; see Crellin and Kidd (1990:48). A second widely used index computed by the National Association of Home Builders (1991) describes affordability not as the share of income that would be required to afford a standard mortgage, but as the share of houses actually sold that could have been afforded by a household with the median family income for a local area. A third index prepared by the Joint Center for Housing Studies (1992) provides an alternative series that covers both owners and renters and uses statistical estimation techniques to measure the expected percentage of income that a household would need to devote to housing. Their home buyer index is calibrated on the incomes of young, potential first-time buyers and uses as a base the median value of units actually purchased by first-time buyers aged 25–29 and deducts expected appreciation that offsets the gross out-of-pocket expenditures of home buyers.

21. In fact, these data actually overestimate the affordability problem for owners. The census calculates expenditure burdens based on gross, out-of-pocket payments for rent or mortgage, plus payments for utilities, property taxes, and other housing expenses. In the case of homeowners, this calculation disregards compensating financial benefits, principally reimbursements from tax deductions and gains in home equity. Even if we consider only the tax advantages, it is clear that the net payment burden to homeowners may be substantially lower than indicated in the census tabulation of gross housing affordability. If homeowners deduct the bulk of their expenses (mortgage interest and property taxes), their after-tax expenses would be substantially lower than reported in the census. That adjustment could move owners down one category or more in the burden distribution—say, from 30–34 percent to the 25–29 percent category of burden.

22. A regression of percentage of young owners with excessive payment burdens on 1990 and 1980 median house values (in $1,000s) for the 50 states yields a 1990 coefficient of 0.14 (se $= 0.014$) and a 1980 coefficient of 0.05 (se $= 0.02$), with a total R-squared of 0.79, F value of 86.4, and model standard error of 2.7 (47 degrees of freedom). Clearly, the 1990 house values are most important, with a 1.4 percentage point increase in owners with excessive payments for every $10,000 increment in house values, but states that started from lower values in 1980 had significantly greater affordability problems in 1990 (0.5 percentage point rise in burdened owners for each $10,000 growth in values between 1980 and 1990).

23. During the 1970s and 1980s young households adjusted their labor force behavior and family lifestyles in order to buy into a housing market with rising prices. See, for example, Myers (1985).

24. The best model of percentage of young renters with excessive payment burdens has the highest R-squared and smallest standard error of those tested; however, the coefficients of the two predictor variables are significant only at the 10 percent level. Contract rent in 1990 has a coefficient of 0.011 (se $= 0.007$), while the percentage point change in ownership rate at ages 25–34 has a coefficient of 0.319 (se $= 0.183$), with a total R-squared of 0.191, an F value of 5.56, and a model standard error of 3.93 (47 degrees of freedom). Clearly, the renter affordability model offers weaker explanation than was found for owners. However, based on this evidence it appears that a $100 difference in rents is associated with a 1.1 percentage point increase in renters with affordability problems, while a 3.0 percentage point decrease in the ownership rate reduces the incidence of renter affordability problems by about 1 percentage point. The latter result is consistent with the fact that, with one third of renters payment burdened, adding would-be owners back to the renter population (presumably to the denominator and not the numerator of the problem incidence ratio), the ratio of payment-burdened households would decline in a 1-to-3 ratio.

25. The evidence is reviewed in Myers (1982).

26. See Devaney (1992:5) for a detailed comparison of amenities provided in owner-occupied versus rental housing units.

27. Allowable deductions include, most importantly, mortgage interest and property taxes.

28. The potential inequity of this favoritism toward homeowners has been long debated among housing economists and policy analysts. For the most recent discussion, see Follain, Ling, and McGill (1993).

29. The question wording in the census questionnaire also changed between 1980 and 1990, with the probable result that the level of homeownership actually slipped slightly more than was measured. In 1990, the question added an extra response category, replacing the choice of "owned or being bought by you or someone else in this household" with two separate line entries: "owned by you or someone else in this household with a mortgage or a loan" and "owned by you or someone else in this household free and clear (without a mortgage)." The potential effect of the extra category is to capture more responses. Although a test of the alternative wording before the 1990 census "did not produce conclusive findings . . . the expanded version appeared more likely to result in higher owner occupancy rates" (U.S. Bureau of the Census, "Housing: Occupancy and Structural Characteristics" 1990:22).

30. Merrill Lynch (1990). Real home prices began to outpace rents in the mid-1970s, with the gap widening in the 1980s.

31. This gap was first identified in Myers et al. (1993).

32. Consistent with the base of analysis for this section, these cohorts are defined on the basis of householders, not all persons. At the youngest ages, new persons joined the householder cohort as they formed new households; whereas after age 75 the householder cohort began to shrink, not only through mortality, but also because some persons left the housing stock and moved to nursing homes and the like (see Figure 6.1). In addition, divorce and mortality cause changes in the householder cohort membership. Mortality has an additional probable effect in that homeowners are likely to live longer than renters, causing ownership rates to stay high in old age because of greater attrition among renters. No data are known to exist that directly correlate tenure with mortality; however, evidence from the attrition of survey panels indicates greater mortality among males who began the panel as lower-income, late-middle-aged renters. See Jianakoplos, Ammon, Menchick, and Irvine (1989).

33. It is important to note that the Public Use Microdata Sample housing value information is not quality-adjusted. When prices are quality-adjusted, the regional price distribution varies somewhat (Gabriel, Shack-Marquez, and Wascher 1992). In addition, the Census Bureau tabulates home value estimates only for a specified universe of houses that are single-family detached structures on a lot of less than ten acres and without a business on the property (thus excluding mobile homes, condominiums, and farm properties). Values themselves are derived through respondents' self-estimate of their home's value, a surprisingly accurate assessment on average; see Kish and Lansing (1954) and Kain and Quigley (1972). However, a new study by Goodman and Ittner (1993) found that respondents consistently overestimated the value of their homes relative to the eventual sale price by about 10 percent. Nevertheless, this overestimate remained unbiased in the sense that it was found to bear no systematic relation to characteristics of the respondent, the home, or the market.

34. The national consumer price index was used as a deflator. Data are taken from U.S. Bureau of the Census, *Housing Highlights: Financial Facts* (1992: Table 1).

35. For more detailed analysis, see Myers et al. (1993).

36. Problems are especially acute for a census-based analysis, since census measures of house value are not quality-adjusted, leading to biases in price change estimates. Shifts in the quality of the housing stock affect price level changes, since areas with rising quality would, all things being equal, experience rising home values.

37. See also Case and Shiller (1988).

38. This cross-sectional pattern may differ somewhat from the longitudinal experience of a cohort starting at age 25 in 1990, but even if the eventual attainment level at age 34 falls short of the mark set by an older cohort in 1990, it is still likely that this age range will represent the cohort's steepest ascent into homeownership.

39. It would be preferable to consider homeownership rates of those aged 25–34, a proxy for first-time home buyers, with the prices of "starter homes"; however, this is not possible using census data. For such an analysis, see Joint Center for Housing Studies (1993).

40. The 4 percentage point drop in young adults' ownership rates recorded by the Census Bureau is much less than in most states, and it likely would have declined even less if the census were taken near the height of the boom. In the two years since prices peaked, a fifth of the households in the 25–34 age group moved on to the next age group, to be replaced by a younger cohort who would not be enticed into buying a home in the face of the suddenly depressed outlook for house values. However, the reports of house values in the census do not reflect this negative outlook, because the existing homeowners probably were sticking to values recorded near the peak even though they knew values were no longer rising but edging downward. Thus, the ownership rate of the 25–34 age group was probably lowered at the very end of the decade even though the rate of value increase remained high.

41. Now that those two states have also met recession, their homeownership attainment patterns may converge with those of other depressed states shown in Figure 6.12.

42. This lack of research on the upper tier of the housing market is due to directions in housing policy. Housing policy has taken two fundamental forms: (1) subsidies to homeowners via tax code provisions for mortgage interest and property tax deductibility and (2) a variety of housing assistance programs in aid of low- and moderate-income households (through both direct assistance to households, i.e., demand-side subsidies, and indirect subsidy to affordable housing providers, i.e., supply-side programs). In recent years, supply-side programs have been eclipsed by demand-side approaches (e.g., vouchers). Since two thirds of all households own homes, and a far higher proportion of voters are homeowners than are renters, tax deductibility provisions that subsidize the more affluent are frequently mentioned but seldom the subject of serious policy debate or extensive research (but see Follain, Ling, and McGill 1993). Housing assistance for low-income households, in contrast, has been a constant focus of policy attention.

43. See, for example, Schwartz, Ferlauto, and Hoffman (1988); Gilderbloom and Appelbaum (1988); Stone (1993); and special issue of *Housing Policy Debate* (1990).

44. For example, Rossi (1989) suggests that the precariously housed, or those "having a tenuous hold on housing of the lowest quality," should be defined as the "extremely poor," that is, individuals receiving an annual income equal to 75 percent of the poverty line or below. Other definitions of the precariously housed highlight smaller proportions of this population. Examples of such groups include people who trade sex for shelter (see, e.g., Dennis 1991); those who have been homeless in the recent past; those awaiting departure from an institution such as a hospital or jail with no financial resources and no place to go; and those living in boarding or halfway houses or single-room-occupancy hotels. Standard data sources such as the

Census of Population and Housing and the Current Population Survey either do not collect information about these groups or do not separate them out from larger categories (e.g., group quarters population). Consequently these subgroups must often be excluded from analysis by default. Smaller scale survey projects may obtain demographic information about such groups, but these data sources are not easily integrated with more extensive ones such as the census.

45. In response to some of these problems, Stone defined a "shelter poverty" measure derived from Bureau of Labor Statistics estimates of the cost of the nonshelter-related necessities of a family of four. This amount is subtracted from household income, and what remains is the amount of disposable income available for housing. The notion underlying this definition of the shelter poor is that if housing payments are too high, other *necessities* will be sacrificed. Unfortunately, this sort of measure cannot be derived using Public Use Microdata Sample data (see Stone 1993).

46. A finer-grained definition would also distinguish the precise mortgage situation of a homeowner, since owners who are highly leveraged or who have unfavorable loan terms are clearly more vulnerable to housing loss than those who own their homes outright, for example.

47. In 1980, the Census Bureau did not publish data on the home value or housing cost burden for all owner-occupied housing (or for a very small proportion of renter-occupied stock). Specifically, condominiums and mobile homes were omitted, as were a variety of other housing types (such as single-family homes that also included a business). As the number of condominiums grew rapidly, this was recognized as a source of bias in estimates of home value and cost burden. Thus, in 1990, the Census Bureau differentiated between "specified" and "unspecified" housing units, the latter including condominiums and other unit types not covered in 1980. In order to consistently compare housing cost burdens in 1980 and 1990, the only recourse is to restrict the investigation to "specified" units. While this restriction does not affect estimates of the precariously housed (all of whom are renters), there is a high probability of underestimating growth in the generously housed. Over 13 percent of 1990 unspecified owner households were generously housed; since the proportion of condominiums (and their owners) grew rapidly between 1980 and 1990, our estimates of the growth in generously housed population are almost certainly too low.

48. Thus, in high-cost-of-living states such as Connecticut (where median household income was over $41,000 in 1990), the poverty population is underestimated, while in low-cost-of-living states (such as Mississippi, where median household income was just over $20,000), overestimates are inevitable.

49. HUD also uses the 50 percent or more rent burden category to define worst-case housing needs (U.S. Department of Housing and Urban Development 1993).

50. As described above, the universe of households for the analysis of precariousness and generousness is limited to what the Census Bureau terms *specified* households.

51. The Census Bureau made special efforts to include the nation's homeless people in the 1990 census, during the shelter and street enumeration, the standard enumeration of group quarters, and the enumeration of persons doubled up in housing units. Their operations were not designed to produce a count of the homeless population per se; rather, they aimed to add persons to the census who were potentially missed

in other census operations. During the evening of March 20 and the early morning hours of March 21—so-called "S-Night"—persons were counted in shelters, voucher motels and hotels, single-room-occupancy hotels, missions, theaters, parks, and transportation terminals, as well as coming out of abandoned buildings or from behind buildings, under bridges, in parking structures, on sidewalks, and visible on the streets. The Bureau's estimate was 190,406 people in emergency shelters and 49,734 in pre-identified street locations, for a combined total of 240,140. If the 219,075 individuals in Special Place Enumeration (drug or alcohol treatment centers, group homes, etc.) with "no usual home elsewhere" are included in this count, the total is 459,215. These estimates remain controversial; for descriptions and critiques, see U.S. General Accounting Office (1991); Cousineau (1991); Burt (1992); Schwede and Siegel (1990); Martin (1992, 1993); and Cecco (1993).

52. If S-Night estimates are included as potential householders, this figure increases to 5.6 million.

53. Estimates of the increase in numbers of homeless persons during this period are notoriously controversial. For useful discussions, see Burt (1992) and Jencks (1994).

54. Between 1980 and 1990, the personal consumer expenditure portion of the Fixed Weighted Price Index rose from 72.6 to 115. The housing portion of the index, in contrast, rose much more quickly, from 63.8 to over 115 (see U.S. Bureau of the Census, *Statistical Abstract of the United States* 1992: Table 750).

55. The difference between these two analysis strategies is described as "rates and shares" in Myers (1992:256–260).

56. The common age structure used for the standardization is based on the nation in 1980. Each state retains its observed rates of precariousness or generousness at each age in 1980 and 1990. The state's age-specific rates are weighted by the proportion of all householders in each age group in the nation. Thus, the standardization retains actual state differences in age-specific rates, with separate rates in 1980 and 1990, but with a common age structure assumed for comparison.

57. Statistical significance (95 percent confidence level) is estimated from a difference of proportions test that takes account of the sampling fraction utilized in compiling the PUMS–A sample. The test is applied to the standardized aggregate percentages in the precarious or generous housing status, treating these in the same manner as the observed aggregate percentages. Given the very large sample sizes contained in the PUMS file for most states (the smallest unweighted sample is 8,338 households in Wyoming in 1980), differences of less than 1 percentage point are usually statistically significant.

# Bibliography

Abbott, Carl. 1987. *The New Urban America: Growth and Politics in Sunbelt Cities.* Chapel Hill: University of North Carolina Press.

Abowd, John M., and Richard B. Freeman. 1991. *Immigration, Trade, and the Labor Market.* Chicago: University of Chicago Press.

Acs, Gregory, and Sheldon Danziger. 1990. "Educational Attainment, Industrial Structure, and Male Earnings, 1973–87." *Population Studies Center Research Report* No. 90-189. Ann Arbor: University of Michigan.

Adams, John S. 1987. *Housing America in the 1980s.* New York: Russell Sage Foundation.

Aldrich, Howard, Roger Waldinger, and Robin Ward. 1990. *Ethnic Entrepreneurs: Immigrant Business in Industrial Societies.* Newbury Park, CA: Sage.

Allan, Emile Andersen, and Darrell J. Steffensmeier. 1989. "Youth, Underemployment, and Property Crime: Differential Effects of Job Availability and Job Quality on Juvenile and Young Adult Arrest Rates." *American Sociological Review* 54:107–123.

Apgar, William C., Jr. 1991. "Preservation of Existing Housing: A Key Element in a Revitalized National Housing Policy." *Housing Policy Debate* 2:187–210.

Apgar, William C., Jr., and George S. Masnick. 1991. "Some Simple Facts about the Demand for New Residential Construction in the 1990s." *Journal of Real Estate Research* 6:267–287.

Appold, Stephen J., and John D. Kasarda. 1991. "The Implications of Demographic and Job Shifts for Future Real Estate Investment Performance." Paper presented at the Prudential Real Estate Strategy Conference, May 14–16, Pinehurst, NC.

Baer, William C. 1976. "The Evolution of Housing Indicators and Housing Standards." *Public Policy* 24:361–393.

Bailey, Thomas R. 1987. *Immigrant and Native Workers: Contrasts and Competition.* Boulder, CO: Westview Press.

Baily, Martin Neil, and Margaret M. Blair. 1988. "Productivity and American Management." In *American Living Standards: Threats and Challenges.* Edited by Robert E. Litan et al. Washington, DC: Brookings Institution.

Baldassare, Mark. 1986. *Trouble in Paradise: The Suburban Transformation in America.* New York: Columbia University Press.

Bancroft, Gertrude. 1958. *The American Labor Force: Its Growth and Changing Composition.* New York: Wiley.

Bates, Timothy, and Constance R. Dunham. 1992. "Facilitating Upward Mobility through Small Business Ownership." In *Urban Labor Markets and Individual Opportunity.* Edited by George E. Peterson and Wayne Vroman. Washington, DC: Urban Institute Press.

————. 1993. "Asian-American Success in Self-Employment." *Economic Development Quarterly* 7(2):199–214.

Bergmann, Barbara. 1986. *The Economic Emergence of Women.* New York: Basic Books.

Berman, Eli, John Bound, and Zvi Griliches. 1993. "Changes in the Demand for Skilled Labor within U.S. Manufacturing Industries: Evidence from the Annual Survey of Manufacturing." NBER Working Paper No. 4255. Cambridge, MA: National Bureau of Economic Research.

Bernheim, Douglas. 1991. *The Vanishing Nest Egg: Reflections on Savings in America.* New York: Priority Press.

Berry, Brian J. L., and Yehoshua S. Cohen. 1973. "Decentralization of Commerce and Industry." In *The Urbanization of the Suburbs* (pp. 431–455). Edited by Louis H. Masotti and Jeffrey K. Hadden. Beverly Hills, CA: Sage.

Bianchi, Suzanne M. 1993. "Children of Poverty: Why Are They Poor?" In *Child Poverty and Public Policy.* Edited by Judith Chafel. Washington, DC: Urban Institute Press.

————. 1994. "The Changing Demographic and Socioeconomic Character of Single-Parent Families." In *Single-Parent Families: Diversity, Myths, and Realities.* Edited by S. Hanson et al. Binghamton, NY: Haworth.

Bianchi, Suzanne M., and Daphne Spain. 1986. *American Women in Transition.* New York: Russell Sage Foundation.

Bielby, William T., and James N. Baron. 1984. "A Woman's Place Is with Other Women: Sex Segregation within Organizations." In *Sex Segregation in the Workplace: Trends, Explanations, Remedies.* Edited by Barbara F. Reskin. Washington, DC: National Academy Press.

Birch, David L. 1987. *Job Creation in America: How Our Smallest Companies Put the Most People to Work.* New York: Free Press.

Blackburn, McKinley L., David E. Bloom, and Richard B. Freeman. 1991. "Changes in Earnings Differentials in the 1980s: Concordance, Convergence, Causes, and Consequences." NBER Working Paper No. 3901. Cambridge, MA: National Bureau of Economic Research.

Blair, John P., and Robert Premus. 1987. "Major Features in Industrial Location: A Review." *Economic Development Quarterly* 1:72–85.

Blair, Margaret M., and Martha A. Schary. 1993. "Industry-Level Pressures to Restructure." In *The Deal Decade* (pp. 149–191). Edited by Margaret M. Blair. Washington, DC: Brookings Institution.

Blake, Judith. 1989. *Family Size and Achievement.* Berkeley: University of California Press.

Blank, Rebecca M. 1991. "Why Were Poverty Rates So High in the 1980's?" NBER Working Paper No. 3878. Cambridge, MA: National Bureau of Economic Research.

Blank, Rebecca M., and David Card. 1994. "Poverty, Income Distribution and Growth: Are They Still Connected?" *Brookings Papers on Economic Activity.* Washington, DC: Brookings Institution.

Blau, Francine D., and Andrea H. Beller. 1992. "Black-White Earnings Over the 1970s and 1980s: Gender Differences in Trends." *Review of Economics and Statistics* 74(2):276–286.

Blau, Francine D., and W. E. Hendrichs. 1979. "Occupational Segregation by Sex: Trends and Prospects." *Journal of Human Resources* 14:197–210.

Blau, Francine D., and Lawrence M. Kahn. 1992. "The Gender Earnings Gap: Some International Evidence." NBER Working Paper No. 4224. Cambridge, MA: National Bureau of Economic Research.

Bluestone, Barry, and Bennett Harrison. 1982. *The Deindustrialization of America: Plant Closings, Community Abandonment, and the Dismantling of Basic Industries.* New York: Basic Books.

———. 1986. *The Great American Job Machine: The Proliferation of Low Wage Employment in the U.S. Economy.* Joint Economic Committee Report. Washington, DC: U.S. Government Printing Office.

Bogue, Donald J. 1949. *The Structure of the Metropolitan Community: A Study of Dominance and Subdominance.* Ann Arbor: Horace H. Rackham School of Graduate Studies, University of Michigan.

Bok, Derek. 1993. *The Cost of Talent.* New York: Free Press.

Bonacich, Edna, and Ivan Light. 1988. *Immigrant Entrepreneurs: Koreans in Los Angeles, 1965–1982.* Berkeley: University of California Press.

Borjas, George, and Marta Tienda. 1985. *Hispanics in the U.S. Economy.* Orlando, FL: Academic Press.

Borjas, George, Jr., Richard B. Freeman, and Lawrence F. Katz. 1992. "On the Labor Market Effects of Immigration and Trade." In *The Economic Effects of Immigration in Source and Receiving Countries.* Edited by George Borjas, Jr., and Richard B. Freeman. Chicago: University of Chicago Press.

Bound, John, and Richard Freeman. 1992. "What Went Wrong? The Erosion and Relative Earnings and Employment of Young Black Men in the 1980s." *Quarterly Journal of Economies* 107(1):201-232.

Bound, John, and Harry J. Holzer. 1991. "Industrial Shifts, Skill Levels, and the Labor Market for White and Black Males." *Population Studies Center Research Report* No. 91-211. Ann Arbor: University of Michigan.

Bound, John, and George Johnson. 1992. "Changes in the Structure of Wages during the 1980s: An Evaluation of Alternative Explanations." *American Economic Review* 82(3):371–392.

Bradbury, Katherine L., Anthony Downs, and Kenneth A. Small. 1982. *Urban Decline and the Future of American Cities.* Washington, DC: Brookings Institution.

Braun, Denny. 1991. *The Rich Get Richer.* Chicago: Nelson-Hall.

Brown, Michael, ed. 1989. *Remaking the Welfare State: Retrenchment and Social Policy in America and Europe.* Philadelphia: Temple University Press.

Browning, E. S., and Helene Cooper. 1993. "Ante Up. States' Bidding War over Mercedes Plan Made for Costly Chase. Alabama Won the Business, but Some Wonder If It Also Gave Away the Farm. Will Image Now Improve?" *Wall Street Journal* (November 24):A1, A6.

Bryant, Keith, and Kathleen Zick. 1993. "Historical Trends in Time Spent with Children." *Consumer Economics and Housing Research Paper* No. RP92-9. Ithaca, NY: Cornell University.

Bumpass, Larry L. 1990. "What's Happening to the Family? Interactions between Demographic and Institutional Change." *Demography* 27:483–498.

Bunda, Michael C., and Stefan Gerlach. 1992. "Intertemporal Prices and the U.S. Trade Balance." *American Economic Review* 82(5):1234–1253.

Burns, Arthur F. 1934. *Production Trends in the United States Since 1870.* New York: National Bureau of Economic Research.

Burt, Martha. 1992. *Over the Edge: The Growth of Homelessness in the 1980s.* New York: Russell Sage Foundation and Washington, DC: Urban Institute Press.

California Association of Realtors. 1990. *California Real Estate Trends* 11 (October). Los Angeles: California Association of Realtors.

Cancien, Maria, Sheldon Danziger, and Peter Gottschalk. 1993. "Working Wives and Family Income Inequality among Married Couples." In *Uneven Tides: Rising Inequality in America.* Edited by Sheldon Danziger and Peter Gottschalk. New York: Russell Sage Foundation.

Card, David, and Alan B. Krueger. 1993. "Trends in Relative Black-White Earnings Revisited." *American Economic Review* 83(2):85–93.

Carliner, Michael. 1987. "Is Homelessness a Housing Problem?" In *The Homeless in Contemporary Society.* Edited by Richard D. Bingham, Roy E. Green, and Sammis B. White. Beverly Hills, CA: Sage.

Case, Karl E. 1986. "The Market for Single-Family Homes in Boston." *New England Economic Review* (May-June):38–48.

Case, Karl E., and Robert J. Shiller. 1988. "The Behavior of Home Buyers in Boom and Post-Boom Markets." *New England Economic Review* (November-December):29–45.

Casper, Lynne M., Sara McLanahan, and Irwin Garfinkel. 1994. "The Gender Poverty Gap: What Can We Learn from Other Countries?" *American Sociological Review* 59 (August):594–605.

Castells, Manuel. 1985. "High Technology, Economic Restructuring and the Urban-Regional Process in the United States." In *High Technology, Space, and Society* (pp. 11–40). Edited by Manuel Castells. Newbury Park, CA: Sage.

———. 1988. "High Technology and Urban Dynamics in the United States." In *The Metropolis Era: A World of Giant Cities* (pp. 85–110). Edited by Mattei Dogan and John D. Kasarda. Newbury Park, CA: Sage.

Castro-Martin, Theresa, and Larry L. Bumpass. 1989. "Recent Trends and Differentials in Marital Disruption." *Demography* 26(1):37–51.

Cecco, Kevin. 1993. "Evaluating the Governmental Unit Participation from the 1990 Shelter and Street Night Operation." *1990 REX Memorandum Series* No. P-14. Washington, DC: U.S. Bureau of the Census, Decennial Statistical Studies Division.

Cherlin, Andrew J. 1988. "The Changing American Family and Public Policy." In *The Changing American Family and Public Policy* (pp. 1–29). Edited by Andrew J. Cherlin. Washington, DC: Urban Institute.

———. 1990. "Recent Changes in American Fertility, Marriage, and Divorce." *Annals of the AAPS* 510:145–154.

———. 1992. *Marriage, Divorce, Remarriage*. Cambridge, MA: Harvard University Press.

Chevan, Albert. 1989. "The Growth of Home Ownership: 1940–1980." *Demography* 26:249–266.

Choi, Seong Youn. 1993. "The Determinants of Household Overcrowding and the Role of Immigration in Southern California." Doctoral dissertation, University of Southern California, Los Angeles.

Cisneros, Henry G., ed. 1993. *Interwoven Destinies: Cities and the Nation*. New York: Norton.

Clemmer, R. B., and J. C. Simonson. 1983. "Trends in Substandard Housing, 1940–1980." *Journal of the American Real Estate and Urban Economics Association* 10:442–464.

Cobb, James C. 1982. *The Selling of the South: The Southern Crusade for Industrial Development, 1936–1980*. Baton Rouge: Louisiana State University Press.

———. 1984. *Industrialization and Southern Society, 1877–1984*. Lexington: University Press of Kentucky.

Cohen, Susan. 1993. "White-Collar Blues." *Washington Post Magazine*, January 17, p. W10.

Cole, Robert E., and Donald R. Deskins, Jr. 1988. "Racial Factors in Site Location and Employment Patterns of Japanese Auto Firms in America." *California Management Review* 3(1):9–22.

Commission on Youth and America's Future. 1989a. *The Forgotten Half: Non-College Youth in America*. Washington, DC: WT Grant Foundation.

———. 1989b. *The Forgotten Half: Pathways to Success for Youth and Young Families*. Washington, DC: WT Grant Foundation.

Cotter, David, JoAnn DeFiore, Joan Hermsen, Brenda Marsteller Kowalewski, and Reeve Vanneman. 1994. "Occupational Gender Segregation and the Earnings Gap: Changes in the 1980s." Paper presented at the annual meeting of the American Sociological Association, August 5–9, Los Angeles.

Cousineau, Michael. 1991. *An Evaluation of the 1990 Census of the Homeless in Los Angeles*. Los Angeles: Homeless Health Care Project.

Crandall, Robert W. 1993. *Manufacturing on the Move*. Washington, DC: Brookings Institution.

Crellin, Glenn E., and Phillip E. Kidd. 1990. *Home Sales Yearbook*. Washington, DC: National Association of Realtors.

Crystal, Graef S. 1992. *In Search of Excess: The Overcompensation of American Executives.* New York: Norton.

Currie, Janet, and Duncan Thomas. 1993. "Does Head Start Make a Difference?" NBER Working Paper No. 4406. Cambridge, MA: National Bureau of Economic Research.

Danziger, Sheldon, and Peter Gottschalk, eds. 1993. *Uneven Tides: Rising Inequality in America.* New York: Russell Sage Foundation.

Danziger, Sheldon, and Jonathan Stern. 1990. "The Causes and Consequences of Child Poverty in the United States." *Innocenti Occasional Papers* No. 10. Florence, Italy: UNICEF International Child Development Centre.

Da Vanzo, Julie, and M. Omar Rahman. 1994. "American Families: Trends and Correlates." *Population Index* 59(3):350–386.

Davis, Steven J. 1992. "Cross-Country Patterns of Change in Relative Wages." In *NBER Macroeconomics Annual 1992.* Edited by Olivier Jean Blanchard and Stanley Fischer. Cambridge, MA: MIT Press.

Davis, Steven J., and John Haltiwanger. 1991. "Wage Dispersion Between and Within U.S. Manufacturing Plants, 1963–86." *Brookings Papers on Economic Activity: Microeconomics.* Washington, DC: Brookings Institution, pp. 115–180.

Denison, Edward M. 1985. *Accounting for Slower Growth.* Washington, DC: Brookings Institution.

Dennis, Michael. 1991. "Changing the Conventional Rules: Surveying Homeless People in Nonconventional Locations." *Housing Policy Debate* 2:701–732.

Devaney, F. John. 1992. *Housing in America: 1989/90.* H123/91-1. Washington, DC: U.S. Bureau of the Census.

Doeringer, Peter B., and Michael J. Piore. 1971. *Internal Labor Markets and Manpower Analysis.* Lexington: Lexington Books.

Dolbeare, Cushing N. 1991. *Out of Reach: Why Everyday People Can't Find Affordable Housing.* Washington, DC: Low Income Housing Information Service.

Donohue, John H., III, and James Heckman. 1991. "Continuous Versus Episodic Change: The Impact of Civil Rights Policy on the Economic Status of Blacks." *Journal of Economic Literature* 29:1603–1643.

Duncan, Beverly. 1965. *Family Factors and School Dropout: 1920–1960.* Cooperative Research Project No. 2258. Ann Arbor: Office of Education, University of Michigan.

———. 1968. "Trends in Output and Distribution of Schooling." In *Indicators of Social Change* (pp. 601–674). Edited by E. B. Sheldon and W. E. Moore. New York: Russell Sage Foundation.

Duncan, Beverly, and Stanley Lieberson. 1970. *Metropolis and Region in Transition.* Beverly Hills, CA: Sage.

Duncan, Otis D., Stanley Lieberson, Beverly Duncan, and Hal. H. Winsborough. 1960. *Metropolis and Region.* Baltimore: Johns Hopkins University Press for Resources for the Future.

Easterlin, Richard A. 1987. *Birth and Fortune: The Impact of Numbers on Personal Welfare.* Chicago: University of Chicago Press.

Easterlin, Richard A., Christine M. Schaeffer, and Diane J. Macunovich. 1993. "Will the Baby Boomers Be Less Well Off Than Their Parents? Income, Wealth, and Family Circumstances over the Life Cycle." Paper presented at the annual meeting of the Population Association of America, Cincinnati.

Eberts, Randall W. 1989. "Accounting for the Recent Divergence in Regional Wage Differentials." *Economic Review, Federal Reserve Bank of Cleveland* 25(3):14–26.

Edsall, Thomas, and Mary D. Edsall. 1991. *Chain Reaction: The Impact of Race, Rights and Taxes on American Politics.* New York: Norton.

Eisinger, Peter K. 1988. *The Rise of the Entrepreneurial State: State and Local Economic Development Policy in the United States.* Madison: University of Wisconsin Press.

———. 1991. "The State of State Venture Capitalism." *Economic Development Quarterly* 5:64–76.

———. 1993. "State Venture Capitalism, State Politics, and the World of High-Risk Investment." *Economic Development Quarterly* 7:131–139.

Ellwood, David T. 1988. *Poor Support: Poverty in the American Family.* New York: Basic Books.

England, Paula. 1982. "The Failure of Human Capital Theory to Explain Occupational Sex Segregation." *Journal of Human Resources* 17:358–370.

———. 1992. "Trends in Women's Economic Status." *Sociological Perspectives* 35:17–51.

England, Paula, and Barbara Stanek Kilbourne. 1990. "Markets, Marriages, and Other Mates: The Problem of Power." In *Beyond the Marketplace: Rethinking Economy and Society* (pp. 163–189). Edited by Roger Friedland and A. F. Robertson. New York: Aldine de Gruyter.

Erickson, Rodney A. 1987. "Business Climate Studies: A Critical Evaluation." *Economic Development Quarterly* 1:62–71.

Farber, Henry S. 1993. "The Incidence and Costs of Job Loss: 1982–1991." *Brookings Papers on Economic Activity.* NSI: 73-132. Washington, DC: Brookings Institution.

Farley, Reynolds. 1984. *Blacks and Whites: Narrowing the Gap?* Cambridge, MA: Harvard University Press.

Feenberg, Daniel R., and James M. Poterba. 1992. "Income Inequality and the Incomes of Very High Income Taxpayers: Evidence from Tax Returns." NBER Working Paper No. 4229. Cambridge, MA: National Bureau of Economic Research.

Feins, Judith, and Terry Saunders Land. 1981. *How Much for Housing? New Perspectives on Affordability and Risk.* Cambridge, MA: Abt Books.

Folger, John K., and Charles B. Nam. 1967. *The Education of the American Population: A 1960 Census Monograph.* Washington, DC: U.S. Government Printing Office.

Follain, James R., David C. Ling, and Gary A. McGill. 1993. "The Preferential Income Tax Treatment of Owner-Occupied Housing: Who Really Benefits?" *Housing Policy Debate* 4:1–24.

Follett, Robert S., Michael P. Ward, and Finis Welch. 1993. "Problems of Assessing Employment Discrimination." *American Economic Review* 83(2):73–79.

Forestall, Richard L. 1991. "Regional and Metropolitan/Nonmetropolitan Trends in the United States." Paper presented for meeting of the Association of American Geographers, April 14, Miami, Florida.

Frank, Robert, and Phillip Cook. 1993. "The Rise of Winner-Take-All Markets." *Working Paper*. Palo Alto, CA: Center for the Advancement of Behavioral Science.

Freeman, Richard B. 1973. "Changes in the Labor Market for Black Americans, 1948–72." *Brookings Papers on Economic Activity* 1:67–120.

———. 1976. *The Overeducated American*. New York: Academic Press.

———. 1992. "Facilitating Upward Mobility Through Small Business Ownership." In *Urban Labor Markets and Job Opportunity* (pp. 201–237). Edited by George E. Peterson and Wayne Vroman. Washington, DC: Urban Institute Press.

———. 1993. "How Much Has De-Unionization Contributed to the Rise in Male Earnings Inequality?" In *Uneven Tides: Rising Inequality in America* (Chap. 4). Edited by Sheldon Danziger and Peter Gottschalk. New York: Russell Sage Foundation.

Freeman, Richard B., and Harry J. Holzer, eds. 1986. *The Black Youth Employment Crisis*. Chicago: University of Chicago Press.

Frey, William H. 1990. "Metropolitan America: Beyond the Transition." Population Reference Bureau. *Population Bulletin* 45(2):3–49.

Frey, William H., and Reynolds Farley. 1993. "Latino, Asian and Black Segregation in Multi-Ethnic Metro Areas: Findings from the 1990 Census." *Research Report* No. 93-278. Ann Arbor: Population Studies Center, University of Michigan.

Frey, William H., and Alden Speare, Jr. 1988. *Regional and Metropolitan Growth and Decline in the United States*. New York: Russell Sage Foundation.

Gabriel, Stuart A. 1988. "Briefing Report." Washington, DC: Board of Governors, Federal Reserve.

Gabriel, Stuart A., Janet Shack-Marquez, and William L. Wascher. 1992. "Regional House-Price Dispersion and Interregional Migration." *Journal of Housing Economics* 2:235–256.

Gallo, Dean. 1993. "Who's Really Poor?" *Northeast-Midwest Economic Review* (July):4–7.

Gamber, Edward M., and Frederick L. Joutz. 1993. "The Dynamic Effects of Aggregate Demand and Supply Disturbances." *American Economic Review* 83:1387–1393.

Gappert, Gary, ed. 1987. *The Future of Winter Cities*. Newbury Park, CA: Sage.

Garfinkel, Irwin, and Sara McLanahan. 1986. *Single Mothers and Their Children: A New American Dilemma*. Washington, DC: Urban Institute.

Garreau, Joel. 1991. *Edge City: Life on the New Frontier*. New York: Doubleday.

Gershuny, Jonathan, and John P. Robinson. 1988. "Historical Changes in the Household Division of Labor." *Demography* 25:537–552.

Gilderbloom, John I., and Richard P. Appelbaum. 1988. *Rethinking Rental Housing*. Philadelphia: Temple University Press.

Gittleman, Maury B., and David R. Howell. 1992. *Job Quality, Labor Market Segmentation, and Earnings Inequality: Effects of Economic Restructuring in the 1980s*. Annandale-on-Hudson, NY: Jerome Levy Economics Institute.

Goldfield, David R. 1984. *Cotton Fields and Skyscrapers: Southern City and Region, 1607–1980*. Baton Rouge: Louisiana State University Press.

Goldin, Claudia. 1990. *Understanding the Gender Gap: An Economic History of American Women*. New York: Oxford University Press.

———. 1991. "The Role of World War II in the Rise of Women's Employment." *American Economic Review* 81:741–756.

———. 1992. "The Meaning of College in the Lives of American Women: The Past One Hundred Years." NBER Working Paper No. 4099. Cambridge, MA: National Bureau of Economic Research.

Goldscheider, Frances K., and Linda J. Waite. 1991. *New Families, No Families?: The Transformation of the American Home*. Berkeley, CA: University of California Press.

Goodman, John L., Jr., and John R. Ittner. 1993. "The Accuracy of Home Owners' Estimates of House Value." Paper presented at the annual meeting of the American Real Estate and Urban Economics Association, Anaheim, CA.

Gottdiener, Mark. 1985. *The Social Production of Urban Space*. Austin: University of Texas Press.

Gramlich, Edward, Richard Kasten, and Frank Sammartino. 1993."Growing Inequality in the 1980s: The Role of Federal Taxes and Cash Transfers." In *Uneven Tides: Rising Inequality in America*. Edited by Sheldon Danziger and Peter Gottschalk. New York: Russell Sage Foundation.

Grant Thornton Company. 1985. *The Sixth Annual Study of General Manufacturing Climates in the Forty-Eight Contiguous States of America*. Chicago: Grant Thornton.

Gras, N. S. B. 1922. *Introduction to Economic History*. New York: Harper.

Green, Patricia. 1993. "High School Seniors Look to the Future, 1972 and 1992." *Statistics in Brief*. NCES No. 93-473. Washington, DC: U.S. Department of Education, National Center for Education Statistics.

Groshen, Erica L., and Donald R. Williams. 1992. "White- and Blue-Collar Jobs in the Recent Recession and Recovery: Who's Singing the Blues?" *Economic Review* 4:2–12.

Gross, Edward. 1968. "Plus ça Change? The Sexual Structure of Occupations over Time." *Social Problems* 16:198–208.

Gueron, Judith M., and Edward Pauly. 1991. *From Welfare to Work*. New York: Russell Sage Foundation.

Gurr, Ted Robert, and Desmond S. King. 1985. "The Post-Industrial City in Transition from Private to Public." In *State and Market: The Politics of the Public and Private* (pp. 271–293). Edited by Jan-Erik Lane. London: European Consortium for Political Research.

Gutterbock, Thomas J. 1987. "The Effect of Snow on Urban Density Patterns in the United States." Paper presented at the annual meeting of the American Sociological Association, Chicago.

Hall, Edward T. 1966. *The Hidden Dimension.* Garden City, NY: Doubleday.

Harper, Lucinda. 1993. "Higher Taxes Unlikely to Hurt Recovery." *Wall Street Journal,* December 22, p. A2.

Harrison, Bennett, and Barry Bluestone. 1988. *The Great U-Turn: Corporate Restructuring and the Polarizing of America.* New York: Basic Books.

Haurin, D. R., Patric H. Hendershott, and D. Kim. 1993. "The Impact of Real Rents and Wages on Household Formation." *Review of Economics and Statistics* 75:284–293.

Hauser, Robert M., and David L. Featherman. 1976. "Equality of Schooling: Trends and Prospects." *Sociology of Education* 49:99–120.

Hauser, Robert M., and Taissa S. Hauser. 1993. "Current Population Survey, October Person-Household Files, 1968–1990: Cumulative Codebook." Madison: Center for Demography and Ecology, University of Wisconsin.

Hauser, Robert M., Linda Jordan, and James A. Dixon. 1993. "Current Population Survey, October Person-Household Files, 1968–1990." Madison: Center for Demography and Ecology, University of Wisconsin.

Hauser, Robert M., and William H. Sewell. 1985. "Birth Order and Educational Attainment in Full Sibships." *American Educational Research Journal* 22:1–24.

Hawley, Amos H. 1950. *Human Ecology: A Theory of Community Structure.* New York: Ronald Press.

Hayghe, Howard V., and Suzanne M. Bianchi. 1994. "Married Mothers' Work Patterns: The Job-Family Compromise." *Monthly Labor Review* 117 (June):24–30.

Heenan, David A. 1991. *The New Corporate Frontier: The Big Move to Small Town, USA.* New York: McGraw-Hill.

Henretta, John C. 1984. "Parental Status and Child's Home Ownership." *American Sociological Review* 49:131–140.

Hernandez, Donald J. 1993. *America's Children: Resources from Family, Government and the Economy.* New York: Russell Sage Foundation.

Herz, Diane E. 1991. "Worker Displacement Still Common in the Late 1980s." *Bureau of Labor Statistics Bulletin* No. 2382. Washington, DC: U.S. Government Printing Office.

Hess, Alfred G., Jr. 1986. "Educational Triage in an Urban School Setting." *Metropolitan Education* 2:39–52.

Hicks, Donald A., ed. 1982. *Urban America in the Eighties.* New Brunswick, NJ: Transaction Books.

Hill, Anne M., and June E. O'Neill. 1992. "Intercohort Change in Women's Labor Market Status." *Research in Labor Economics,* Vol. 1. Edited by R. G. Ehrenberg. Greenwich, CT: JAI Press.

Hill, Martha S., and Mary Corcoran. 1983. "Unemployment among Family Men: A Ten-Year Longitudinal Study." *Monthly Labor Review* 2(11):19–28.

Hirschman, Charles, and Morrison G. Wong. 1986. "The Extraordinary Educational Attainment of Asian-Americans." *Social Forces* 65:1–27.

Hoch, Charles, and Robert Slayton. 1989. *New Homeless and Old: Community and the Skid Row Hotel*. Philadelphia: Temple University Press.

Honey, Maureen. 1984. *Creating Rosie the Riveter: Class, Gender, and Propaganda during World War II*. Amherst: University of Massachusetts Press.

Hout, Michael, Adrian Raftery, and Eleanor O. Bell. 1993. "Making the Grade: Educational Stratification in the United States, 1925–1989." In *Persistent Inequality: Changing Educational Attainment in Thirteen Countries*. Edited by Y. Shavit and H. P. Blossfeld. Boulder, CO: Westview Press.

Iams, Howard M. 1993. "Earnings of Couples: A Cohort Analysis." *Social Security Bulletin* 56:22–33.

Jacobs, Barry G., et al. 1982. *Guide to Federal Housing Programs*. Washington, DC: Bureau of National Affairs.

Jacobs, Jerry A. 1989. "Long-Term Trends in Occupational Segregation by Sex." *American Journal of Sociology* 95:160–173.

Jacobson, Louis S., Robert J. LaLonde, and Daniel G. Sullivan. 1993. "Earnings Losses of Displaced Workers." *American Economic Review* 83:685–709.

Jaynes, Gerald David, and Robin M. Williams, Jr., eds. 1989. *A Common Destiny: Blacks and American Society*. Washington, DC: National Academy Press.

Jencks, Christopher. 1994. *The Homeless: Why They Are Everywhere and What We Can Do About It*. Cambridge, MA: Harvard University Press.

Jianakoplos, Nancy Ammon, Paul L. Menchick, and F. Owen Irvine. 1989. "Using Panel Data to Assess the Bias in Cross-Sectional Inferences of Life-Cycle Changes in the Level and Composition of Household Wealth." In *The Measurement of Savings, Investment, and Wealth*. Edited by Robert E. Lipsey. Chicago: University of Chicago Press.

Johnson, Clifford M., Andrew M. Sum, and James D. Weill. 1989. *Vanishing Dreams: The Growing Economic Plight of America's Young Families*. Washington, DC: Children's Defense Fund.

Joint Center for Housing Studies. 1992. *The State of the Nation's Housing: 1992*. Cambridge, MA: Harvard University.

———. 1993. *The State of the Nation's Housing: 1993*. Cambridge, MA: Harvard University.

Jones, Landon Y. 1980. *Great Expectations: America and the Baby Boom Generation*. New York: Coward, McCann & Geoghegan.

Joskow, Paul, Nancy Rose, and Andrea Sheppard. 1992. "Regulatory Constraints on Executive Compensation." *Brookings Papers on Economic Activity*.

Kain, John F., and John M. Quigley. 1972. "Note on Owner's Estimate of Housing Value." *Journal of the American Statistical Association* 76:803–806.

Kane, Edward J. 1985. "Microeconomic Evidence on the Composition of Household Savings in Recent Years." In *The Level and Composition of Household Saving*. Edited by Patric H. Hendershott. Cambridge, MA: Ballinger.

Karoly, Lynn A. 1993. "The Trend in Inequality among Families, Individuals and Workers in the United States: A Twenty-Five Year Perspective." In *Uneven Tides:*

*Rising Inequality in America.* Edited by Sheldon Danziger and Peter Gottschalk. New York: Russell Sage Foundation.

Kasarda, John D. 1976. "The Changing Occupational Structure of the American Metropolis: Apropos the Urban Problem." In *The Changing Face of the Suburbs.* Edited by Barry Schwartz. Chicago: University of Chicago Press.

———. 1978. "Urbanization, Community, and the Metropolitan Problem." In *Handbook of Contemporary Urban Life* (pp. 27–35). Edited by David Street. San Francisco: Jossey-Bass.

———. 1980. "The Implications of Contemporary Redistribution Trends for National Urban Policy." *Social Science Quarterly* 61:373–400.

———. 1985. "Urban Change and Minority Opportunities." In *The New Urban Reality.* Edited by Paul E. Peterson. Washington, DC: Brookings Institution.

———. 1993. "Inner-City Concentrated Poverty and Neighborhood Distress: 1970 to 1990." Paper presented at the Fannie Mae Annual Housing Conference, June 23, Washington, DC.

Kasarda, John D., and Michael D. Irwin. 1991. "National Business Cycles and Community Competition for Jobs." *Social Forces* 69:733–761.

Katz, Lawrence F., and Kevin M. Murphy. 1992. "Changes in Relative Wages, 1963–87: Supply and Demand Factors." *Quarterly Journal of Economics* 107:35–78.

Katz, Michael B. 1989. *The Undeserving Poor: From the War on Poverty to the War on Welfare.* New York: Pantheon.

Kaus, Mickey. 1992. *The End of Equality.* New York: Basic Books.

Kenyon, Daphne A. 1991. *Interjurisdictional Tax and Policy Competition: Good or Bad for the Federal System?* Washington, DC: Advisory Commission on Intergovernmental Relations.

Kish, L., and J. Lansing. 1954. "Response Errors in Estimating the Value of Homes." *Journal of the American Statistical Association* 49:520–528.

Klein, Bruce W., and Philip L. Rones. 1989. "A Profile of the Working Poor." *Monthly Labor Review* 112(10):3–13.

Kominski, Robert. 1985. "Evaluation of 1980 Decennial Census Education Questions." *1980 Census Preliminary Evaluation Results Memorandum* No. 104. Washington, DC: U.S. Bureau of the Census.

———. 1988. "Education and Earnings: Empirical Findings from Alternative Operationalizations." Proceedings of the Social Statistics Section, American Statistical Association, pp. 82–87.

———. 1990. "Estimating the National High School Dropout Rate." *Demography* 27:303–311.

Kominski, Robert, and Paul M. Siegel. 1987. "Measuring Educational Attainment in the 1990 Census." Paper presented at the meeting of the American Sociological Association.

———. 1992. "Measuring Educational Attainment in the Current Population Survey." Manuscript. Washington, DC: U.S. Bureau of the Census.

Kornblum, William S. 1985. "Institution Building in the Urban High School." In *The*

*Challenge of Social Control: Citizenship and Institution Building in Modern Society.* Edited by Gerald Suttles and Mayer Zald. Norwood, N.J.: Ablex.

Kotkin, Joel. 1986. "The Reluctant Entrepreneurs." *Inc.* 8(9):81–86.

Kristol, Irving. 1982. "Comment" on Alan Blinder's "The Level and Distribution of Economic Well-Being." In *The American Economy in Transition.* Edited by Martin Feldstein. Chicago: University of Chicago Press.

Krueger, A. 1991. "How Computers Have Changed the Wage Structure." Manuscript. Princeton, NJ: Princeton University.

Krugman, Paul R., and Maurice Obstfelt. 1987. *International Economics: Theory and Policy.* Glenview, IL: Little Brown.

Kuttner, Robert. 1983. "The Declining Middle." *Atlantic* (July):60–72.

Kuznets, Simon. 1930. *Secular Movements in Production and Price: Their Nature and Their Bearing upon Cyclical Fluctuations.* Boston: Houghton Mifflin.

Landes, David. 1965. "Technological Change and Development in Western Europe: 1750–1914." In *Cambridge Economic History of Europe from the Decline of the Roman Empire.* Edited by H. J. Habbakuk. Cambridge, MA: Harvard University Press.

Lawrence, Z., and Matthew J. Slaughter. Forthcoming. "Trade and U.S. Wages: Great Sucking Sound or Small Hiccup?" *Brookings Papers on Economic Activity.*

Levy, Frank. 1987. *Dollars and Dreams: The Changing American Income Distribution.* New York: Russell Sage Foundation.

Levy, Frank, and Richard C. Michel. 1987. "Education and Earnings: Recent U.S. Trends." Working paper. Washington, DC: Urban Institute.

Levy, Frank, and Richard J. Murnane. 1992. "U.S. Earnings Levels and Earnings Inequality: A Review of Recent Trends and Proposed Explanations." *Journal of Economic Literature* 30:1333–1381.

Lichter, Daniel T., and Janice A. Costanzo. 1987. "How Do Demographic Changes Affect Labor Force Participation of Women?" *Monthly Labor Review* 110(11):23–25.

Lieberson, Stanley. 1980. *A Piece of the Pie: Blacks and White Immigrants Since 1880.* Berkeley: University of California Press.

Light, Ivan, Im Kwuon, and Deng Zhong. 1990. "Korean Rotating Credit Associations in Los Angeles." *Amerasia* 16(2):35–54.

Listoken, David. 1991. "Federal Housing Policy and Preservation: Historical Evolution, Patterns, and Implications." *Housing Policy Debate* 2:157–186.

Logan, John R., and Harvey L. Molotch. 1987. *Urban Fortunes: The Political Economy of Place.* Berkeley: University of California Press.

Long, Larry H. 1988. *Migration and Residential Mobility in the United States.* New York: Russell Sage Foundation.

Long, Larry H., and Diana DeAre. 1988. "U.S. Population Redistribution: A Perspective on the Nonmetropolitan Turnaround." *Population and Development Review* 14(3):433–450.

Luger, Michael I. 1984. "Federal Tax Incentives and Industrial and Urban Policy." In

*Sunbelt/Snowbelt: Urban Development and Regional Restructuring*. Edited by Larry Sawers and William K. Tabb. New York: Oxford University Press.

McKenzie, Roderick D. 1933. *The Metropolitan Community*. New York: McGraw-Hill.

McLanahan, Sara. 1985. "Family Structure and the Reproduction of Poverty." *American Journal of Sociology* 90:873–901.

McLanahan, Sara, and Gary Sandefur. Forthcoming. *Uncertain Childhood, Uncertain Future*. Cambridge, MA: Harvard University Press.

McNeil, John M. 1993. "Census Bureau Data on Persons with Disabilities: New Results and Old Questions about Validity and Reliability." Mimeographed. Washington, DC: U.S. Bureau of the Census.

Malveaux, Julianne, and Phyllis Wallace. 1987. "Minority Women in the Workplace." In *Working Women: Past, Present, Future* (pp. 265–298). Edited by Karen Shallcross Koziara. Washington, DC: Bureau of National Affairs.

Mare, Robert D. 1979. "Social Background Composition and Educational Growth." *Demography* 16:55–71.

———. 1980. "Social Background and School Continuation Decisions." *Journal of the American Statistical Association* 75:205–305.

———. 1981a. "Change and Stability in Educational Stratification." *American Sociological Review* 46:72–87.

———. 1981b. "Trends in Schooling: Demography, Performance, and Organization." *Annals of the American Academy of Political and Social Science* 453:96–122.

———. 1991. "Five Decades of Educational Assortative Mating." *American Sociological Review* 56:15–32.

———. 1993. "Family Effects on Educational Attainment among Race and Ethnic Groups in the United States, 1980–1990." Paper presented at the meeting of the Population Association of America, Cincinnati, Ohio.

Mare, Robert D., and Meichu. D. Chen. 1986. "Further Evidence on Number of Siblings and Educational Stratification." *American Sociological Review* 51:403–412.

Mare, Robert D., and Christopher Winship. 1984. "The Paradox of Lessening Racial Inequality and Joblessness among Black Youth: Enrollment, Enlistment, and Employment, 1964–1981." *American Sociological Review* 49:39–55.

———. 1988. "Ethnic and Racial Patterns of Educational Attainment and School Enrollment." In *Divided Opportunities: Minorities, Poverty and Social Policy* (pp. 173–195). Edited by Gary D. Sandefur and Marta Tienda. New York: Plenum Press.

———. 1989. "Socioeconomic Change and the Decline of Marriage for Blacks and Whites." In *The Urban Underclass*. Edited by Christopher Jencks and Paul E. Peterson. Washington, DC: Brookings Institution.

———. 1993. "Family Effects on Educational Attainment among Race and Ethnic Groups in the United States." Paper presented at the Population Association of America, Cincinnati, Ohio.

Mare, Robert D., Christopher Winship, and Warren N. Kubitschek. 1984. "The Transition from Youth to Adult: Understanding the Age Pattern of Employment." *American Journal of Sociology* 89:326–358.

Margo, Robert A. 1990. *Race and Schooling in the South, 1880–1950: An Economic History*. Chicago: University of Chicago Press.

Markusen, Ann Roell. 1985. *Profit Cycles, Oligopoly, and Regional Development*. Cambridge, MA: MIT Press.

———. 1987. *Regions: The Economics and Politics of Territory*. Totowa, NJ: Rowman & Littlefield.

Martin, Elizabeth. 1992. "Assessment of S-Night Street Enumeration in the 1990 Census." *Evaluation Review* 16:418–438.

———. 1993. "Using Unobtrusive Observation to Assess Street Enumeration in the 1990 Census." Paper presented at the American Statistical Association Annual Meeting (August).

Massey, Douglas S., and Nancy A. Denton. 1993. *American Apartheid: Segregation and the Making of the Underclass*. Cambridge, MA: Harvard University Press.

Meisenheimer, Joseph R. 1992. "How Do Immigrants Fare in the United States Labor Market?" *Monthly Labor Review* 115(12):3–19.

Merrill Lynch. 1990. "Real Estate Economics Special Report." *Merrill Lynch Capital Markets,* July.

Mincer, Jacob. 1974. *Schooling, Experience and Earnings*. New York: Columbia University Press.

———. 1991. "Human Capital, Technology, and the Wage Structure: What Do Time Series Show?" NBER Working Paper No. 3581. Cambridge, MA: National Bureau of Economic Research.

Mishel, Lawrence, and Jared Bernstein. 1993. *The State of Working America; 1992–93*. Armonk, NY: Economic Policy Institute/M. E. Sharp.

Mollenkopf, John H. 1983. *The Contested City*. Princeton, NJ: Princeton University Press.

Mueller, Dennis C., and Elizabeth A. Reardon. Forthcoming. "Rates of Return on Corporate Investment." *Eastern Economic Review*.

Muller, Peter O. 1989. "The Transformation of Bedroom Suburbia into the Outer City: An Overview of Metropolitan Structural Change Since 1947." In *Suburbia Re-Examined*. Edited by Barbara M. Kelly. New York: Greenwood Press.

Murphy, Kevin, and Finis Welch. 1992. "The Role of International Trade in Wage Differentials." In *Workers and Their Wages* (pp. 39–69). Edited by M. Kosters. Washington, DC: AEI Press.

Murray, Charles. 1984. *Losing Ground: American Social Policy, 1950–1980*. New York: Basic Books.

———. 1993. "The Coming White Underclass." *Wall Street Journal,* October 12, p. A13.

Myers, Dowell. 1982. "A Cohort-Based Indicator of Housing Progress." *Population Research and Policy Review* 1:109–136.

———. 1985. "Wives' Earnings and Rising Costs of Homeownership." *Social Science Quarterly* 66:319–329.

————. 1986. "Reliance upon Wives' Earnings for Homeownership Attainment: Caught between the Locomotive and the Caboose." *Journal of Planning Education and Research* 4:167–176.

————. ed. 1990. *Housing Demography: Linking Housing Markets with Demographic Structure*. Madison: University of Wisconsin Press.

————. 1992. *Analysis with Local Census Data: Portraits of Change*. New York: Academic Press.

Myers, Dowell, and Seong Youn Choi. 1992. "Growth in Overcrowded Housing: A Comparison of the States." *Applied Demography* 7:1–4.

Myers, Dowell, Richard Peiser, Gregory Schwann, and John R. Pitkin. 1993. "Retreat from Homeownership: A Comparison of the Generations and the States." *Housing Policy Debate* 3:945–975.

National Association of Home Builders. 1991. *The Future of Home Building: 1991–1993 and Beyond*. Washington, DC: National Association of Home Builders.

National Center for Health Statistics. 1993a. "Advance Report of Final Natality Statistics, 1991." *Monthly Vital Statistics Report,* Vol. 42, No. 3, Supplement. Washington, DC: U.S. Government Printing Office.

————. 1993b. "Annual Summary of Births, Marriages, Divorces, and Deaths: United States, 1992." *Monthly Vital Statistics Report,* Vol. 41, No. 13. Washington, DC: U.S. Government Printing Office.

Newman, Catherine. 1993. *Declining Fortunes*. New York: Basic Books.

O'Connell, Martin. 1993. "Where's Papa? Father's Role in Child Care." *Population Trends and Public Policy* No. 20. Washington, DC: Population Reference Bureau.

O'Neill, June, and Solomon Polachek. 1993. "Why the Gender Gap in Wages Narrowed in the 1980s." *Journal of Labor Economics* 11(Pt. 1):205–228.

Oppenheimer, Valerie Kincade. 1970. *The Female Labor Force in the United States*. Westport, CT: Greenwood Press.

Parsons, Talcott. 1949. "The Social Structure of the Family." In *The Family: Its Function and Destiny*. Edited by Ruth N. Anshen. New York: Harper.

————. 1955. "The American Family: Its Relation to Personality and to the Social Structure." In *Family, Socialization, and Interaction Process*. Edited by Talcott Parsons and Robert F. Bales. New York: Macmillan.

Peterson, George E., and Wayne Vroman, eds. 1992. *Urban Labor Markets and Job Opportunity*. Washington, DC: Urban Institute Press.

Phillips, Kevin. 1990. *The Politics of Rich and Poor: Wealth and the American Electorate in the Reagan Aftermath*. New York: Random House.

Presser, Harriet B. 1989. "Can We Make Time for Children? The Economy, Work Schedules, and Child Care." *Demography* 26:523–543.

Preston, Samuel H. 1984. "Children and the Elderly: Divergent Paths for America's Dependents." *Demography* 21(4):435–457.

Quigley, John R. 1990. "Does Rent Control Cause Homelessness? Taking the Claim Seriously." *Journal of Policy Analysis and Management* 9:88–93.

Rainwater, Lee, and William L. Yancey. 1967. *The Moynihan Report and the Politics of Controversy*. Cambridge, MA: MIT Press.

Reich, Robert B. 1991. *The Work of Nations: Preparing Ourselves for 21st-Century Capitalism*. New York: Knopf.

Rexroat, Cynthia. 1992. "Changes in the Employment Continuity of Succeeding Cohorts of Young Women." *Work and Occupations* 19:18–34.

Ricketts, Erol, and Isabel V. Sawhill. 1988. "Defining and Measuring the Underclass." *Journal of Policy Analysis and Management* 7(2):316–325.

Riesman, David, with Nathan Glazer and Reuel Denney. 1976. *The Lonely Crowd: A Study of the Changing American Character*. Abridged edition with the 1969 preface. New Haven: Yale University Press.

Robinson, James Gregory. 1988. "A Cohort Analysis of Trends in the Labor Force Participation of Men and Women in the United States: 1890 to 1985." Doctoral dissertation, University of Pennsylvania.

Robinson, John P. 1988. "Who's Doing the Housework?" *American Demographics* 12:24–28.

Roos, Patricia A., and Barbara F. Reskin. 1992. "Occupational Desegregation in the 1970s: Integration and Economic Equity?" *Sociological Perspectives* 35:69–91.

Rossi, Peter H. 1989. *Down and Out in America: The Origins of Homelessness*. Chicago: University of Chicago Press.

Rydzewski, Leo G., William G. Demming, and Philip L. Rones. 1993. "Seasonal Employment Falls over Past Three Decades." *Monthly Labor Review* 116(7):3–14.

Ryscavage, Paul, and Peter Henle. 1990. "Earnings Inequality in the 1980s." *Monthly Labor Review* 113:3–16.

Ryscavage, Paul, Gordon Green, and Edward Welniak. 1992. "The Impact of Demographic, Social, and Economic Change on the Distribution of Income." In Ryscavage, Paul, Gordon Green, Edward Welniak, and John Coder. "Studies in the Distribution of Income." *Current Population Reports,* Series P-60, No. 183. Washington, DC: U.S. Government Printing Office.

Sandefur, Gary D., and Marta Tienda. 1988. *Divided Opportunities: Minorities, Poverty and Social Policy*. New York: Plenum Press.

Sattinger, Michael. 1993. "Assignment Models of the Distribution of Earnings." *Journal of Economic Literature* 31(2):831–880.

Sawhill, Isabel V. 1988. "Poverty in the U.S.: Why Is It So Persistent?" *Journal of Economic Literature* 26(3):1073–1119.

Scharfstein, David S., and Jeremy C. Stein. 1990. "Herd Behavior and Investment." *American Economic Review* 80(3):465–479.

Schmenner, Roger W. 1985. "How Corporations Select Communities for New Manufacturing Plants." In *The Economics of Firm Size, Market Structure, and Social Performance* (pp. 182–198). Edited by John J. Siegfried. Washington, DC: Bureau of Economics, Federal Trade Commission.

Schwartz, David C., Richard C. Ferlauto, and Daniel N. Hoffman. 1988. *A New Housing Policy for America*. Philadelphia: Temple University Press.

Schwede, Laurel, and Paul M. Siegel. 1993. "Coverage of (Not in) Emergency Shelters in S-Night 1990." Paper presented at the American Statistical Association Annual Meeting (August), Boston.

Scott, Allen J. 1993. "The New Southern Californian Economy: Pathways to Industrial Resurgence." *Economic Development Quarterly* 7:296–309.

Sears, David O., and Jack Citrin. 1982. *Tax Revolt: Something for Nothing in California*. Cambridge, MA: Harvard University Press.

Sewell, William H., and Robert M. Hauser. 1975. *Education, Occupation, and Earnings*. New York: Academic Press.

Siegel, Paul M. 1991. "Note on the Proposed Change in the Measurement of Educational Attainment in the Current Population Survey." Manuscript. Washington, DC: U.S. Bureau of the Census.

Siegel, Paul M., and Robert Kominski. 1986. "The Quality of Census Data on Educational Attainment." Paper presented at the meeting of the Census Advisory Committee on Population Statistics, Arlington, VA.

Siegel, Peggy M. 1988. *Education and Economic Growth: A Legislator's Guide*. Denver, CO: National Conference of State Legislatures.

Silvestri, George T. 1981. *The National Industrial-Occupation Employment Matrix, 1970, 1978, and Projected 1990*. Bulletin 2086. Washington, DC: Bureau of Labor Statistics, U.S. Department of Labor.

Skogan, Wesley G. 1977. "The Changing Distribution of Big-City Crime: A Multi-City Time-Series Analysis." *Urban Affairs Quarterly* 13:33–48.

Slemrod, Joel. 1991. "Taxation and Inequality: A Time-Exposure Perspective." In *Tax Policy and the Economy*, Vol. 6. Edited by James Poterba. Cambridge, MA: MIT Press.

Smith, James P., and Michael Ward. 1989. "Women in the Labor Market and the Family." *Journal of Economic Perspectives* 3:9–23.

Smith, James, and Finis Welch. 1989. "Black Economic Progress after Myrdal." *Journal of Economic Literature* 27(2):419–564.

Sorenson, Elaine. 1989. "The Wage Effects of Occupational Sex Composition: A Review and New Findings." In *Comparable Worth: Analyses and Evidence*. Edited by M. Anne Hill and Mark Killingsworth. Ithaca, NY: ILR Press.

Stafford, Howard A. 1985. "Environmental Protection and Industrial Location." *Annals of the Association of American Geographers* 75:227–240.

Sternlieb, George, and David Listoken. 1987. "A Review of National Housing Policy." In *Housing America's Poor*. Edited by Peter D. Salins. Chapel Hill: University of North Carolina Press.

Stone, Michael. 1993. *Shelter Poverty*. Philadelphia: Temple University Press.

Sweet, James A., and Larry L. Bumpass. 1987. *American Families and Households*. New York: Russell Sage Foundation.

Thurow, Lester C. 1976. *The Zero Sum Society*. New York: Basic Books.

———. 1987. "The Disappearance of the Middle Class." *New York Times*, February 5, p. E2.

Tiemeyer, Peter E. 1993. "Racial Differences in the Transition from School to Stable Employment among Young Men." Doctoral dissertation, University of Wisconsin–Madison.

Tienda, Marta, Katherine Donato, and Hector Cordero-Guzman. 1992. "Schooling, Color, and the Labor Force Activity of Women." *Social Forces* 71(2):365.

Topel, Robert. 1993. "What Have We Learned from Empirical Studies of Unemployment and Turnover?" *American Economic Review* 83(2):110–115.

U.S. Bureau of the Census. 1975. U.S. Department of Commerce. *Historical Statistics of the United States, Colonial Times to 1970.* Bicentennial ed. Washington, DC: U.S. Bureau of the Census.

———. 1981. "Characteristics of the Population Below the Poverty Level: 1979." *Current Population Reports,* Series P-60, No. 130. Washington, DC: U.S. Government Printing Office.

———. 1981. "Money Income of Families and Persons in the United States: 1979." *Current Population Reports,* Series P-60, No. 129. Washington, DC: U.S. Government Printing Office.

———. 1983. *Current Population Survey . . . Annual Demographic File.* [CD-ROM.] Washington, DC: User Services Division, Bureau of the Census, U.S. Department of Commerce.

———. 1987. "Male-Female Differences in Work Experience, Occupation, and Earnings: 1984," by John M. McNeil and Enrique J. Lamas. *Current Population Reports,* Series P-70, No. 10. Washington, DC: U.S. Government Printing Office.

———. 1989. "Labor Force Status and Other Characteristics of Persons with a Work Disability," by Robert L. Bennefield and John M. McNeil. *Current Population Reports,* Series P-23, No. 160. Washington, DC: U.S. Government Printing Office.

———. 1990. "Housing: Occupancy and Structural Characteristics." *Content Determination Report* No. 11. Washington, DC: U.S. Bureau of the Census.

———. 1990. *Women-Owned Businesses.* Washington, DC: U.S. Government Printing Office.

———. 1991. *Characteristics of Business Owners.* Washington, DC: U.S. Government Printing Office.

———. 1991. "Child Support and Alimony: 1989," by Gordon H. Lester. *Current Population Reports,* Series P-60, No. 173. Washington, DC: U.S. Government Printing Office.

———. 1991. "Money Income of Households, Families, and Persons in the U.S., 1988 and 1989." *Current Population Reports,* Series P-60, No. 172. Washington, DC: U.S. Government Printing Office.

———. 1991. "Poverty in the United States: 1988 and 1989." *Current Population Reports,* Series P-60, No. 171. Washington, DC: U.S. Government Printing Office.

———. 1992. "Detailed Occupation and Other Characteristics from the EEO File for the United States." *1990 Census of Population, Supplementary Reports.* CP-S-1-1. Washington, DC: U.S. Government Printing Office.

———. 1992. "Educational Attainment in the United States," March 1991, by Robert

Kominski and Andrea Adams. *Current Population Reports,* Series P-20, No. 462. Washington, DC: U.S. Government Printing Office.

———. 1992. "Extended Measures of Well-Being," by Larry M. Radbill and Kathleen Short. *Current Population Reports,* Series P-70, No. 26. Washington, DC: U.S. Government Printing Office.

———. 1992. *The Foreign Born Population in the United States: 1990.* CPH-L-98. Washington, DC: Population Statistical Information Office.

———. 1992. *Housing Highlights: Financial Facts.* CH-S-1-1. Washington, DC: U.S. Government Printing Office.

———. 1992. "Marriage, Divorce and Remarriage in the 1990s," by Arthur J. Norton and Louisa F. Miller. *Current Population Reports,* Series P-23, No. 180. Washington, DC: U.S. Government Printing Office.

———. 1992. "Measuring the Effect of Benefits and Taxes on Income and Poverty: 1979 to 1991." *Current Population Reports,* Series P-60, No. 182. Washington, DC: U.S. Government Printing Office.

———. 1992. "Money Income of Households, Families and Persons in the United States: 1991." *Current Population Reports,* Series P-60, No. 180. Washington, DC: U.S. Government Printing Office.

———. 1992. "Poverty in the United States: 1991." *Current Population Reports,* Series P-60, No. 181. Washington, DC: U.S. Government Printing Office.

———. 1992. "School Enrollment—Social and Economic Characteristics of Students: October 1990." *Current Population Reports,* Series P-20, No. 460. Washington, DC: U.S. Government Printing Office.

———. 1992. *Statistical Abstract of the United States.* Washington, DC: U.S. Government Printing Office.

———. 1992. "Studies in the Distribution of Income," by Paul Ryscavage et al. *Current Population Reports,* Series P-60, No. 183. Washington, DC: U.S. Government Printing Office.

———. 1992. "Studies in Household and Family Formation," by Donald J. Hernandez. *Current Population Reports,* Series P-23, No. 179. Washington, DC: U.S. Government Printing Office.

———. 1992. "Workers with Low Earnings: 1964 to 1990," by John M. McNeil. *Current Population Reports,* Series P-60, No. 178. Washington, DC: U.S. Government Printing Office.

———. 1992. *1990 Census of Population and Housing: Public Use Microdata Sample Technical Documentation.* Washington, DC: U.S. Bureau of the Census.

———. 1993. *Nursing Home Population: 1990.* CPH-L-137. Washington, DC: Population Statistical Information Office.

———. 1993. "School Enrollment—Social and Economic Characteristics of Students," by Robert Kominski and Andrea Adams. *Current Population Reports,* Series P-20, No. 474. Washington, DC: U.S. Government Printing Office.

———. 1993. "Standardization and Decomposition of Rates: A User's Manual," by Prithwis Das Gupta. *Current Population Reports,* Special Studies, Series P-23, No. 186. Washington, DC: U.S. Government Printing Office.

———. 1993. *Statistical Abstract of the United States: 1993*. Washington, DC: U.S. Government Printing Office.

U.S. Bureau of Economic Analysis. 1981. *National Income and Product Accounts of the United States: 1929–76*. Washington, DC: U.S. Government Printing Office.

———. 1993. *REIS: Regional Economic Information System*, CD-ROM. [Washington, DC]: Regional Economic Measurement Division, Bureau of Economic Analysis, Economics and Statistics Administration, U.S. Department of Commerce.

U.S. Council of Economic Advisers. 1993. *Economic Report of the President: 1992*. Washington, DC: U.S. Government Printing Office.

U.S. Department of Education, National Center for Education Statistics. 1991. *Digest of Education Statistics 1991*. Washington, DC: U.S. Government Printing Office.

———. 1993. "National Assessment of Educational Progress." *Digest of Education Statistics 1993*. Washington, DC: U.S. Government Printing Office.

U.S. Department of Housing and Urban Development. 1993. *The Location of Worst Case Needs in the Late 1980s: A Report to Congress*. Washington, DC: Office of Policy Development and Research.

U.S. Department of Labor, Bureau of Labor Statistics. 1980. *Employment and Earnings*. Washington, DC: U.S. Government Printing Office.

———. 1988. *Labor Force Statistics Derived from the Current Population Survey*. Bulletin No. 2370. Washington, DC: U.S. Government Printing Office.

———. 1990. *Employment and Earnings*. Washington, DC: U.S. Government Printing Office.

———. 1991. *Displaced Workers, 1985–1989*. Bulletin No. 2382. Washington, DC: U.S. Government Printing Office.

———. 1993. *Employment in Perspective: Women in the Labor Force*. Report No. 860. Washington, DC: U.S. Government Printing Office.

———. 1993. *A Profile of the Working Poor, 1988–1990*. Washington, DC: U.S. Government Printing Office.

U.S. General Accounting Office, Office of the Comptroller General. 1992. "Education Issues." *Transition Series* Report No. GAO/OCG-93-18TR.

U.S. House of Representatives, Committee on Ways and Means. *Overview of Entitlement Programs: 1993 Green Book*. Washington, DC: U.S. Government Printing Office.

Vernon, Raymond. 1960. *Metropolis 1985: Interpretation of the Findings of the New York Metropolitan Region Study*. Cambridge, MA: Harvard University Press.

Waite, Linda J., and Frances K. Goldscheider. 1992. "Work in the Home: The Productive Context of Family Relationships." In *The Changing American Family*. Edited by Scott J. South and Stewart E. Tolnay. Boulder, CO: Westview Press.

Waldinger, Roger. 1986. *Through the Eye of the Needle: Immigrants and Enterprise in New York's Garment Trades*. New York: New York University Press.

Wartzman, Rick. 1988. "St. Louis Blues: A Blighted Inner City Bespeaks the Sad State of Black Commerce." *Wall Street Journal*, May 10, A1.

Wellington, Alison. 1993. "Changes in the Male/Female Wage Gap, 1976–85." *Journal of Human Resources* 28:383–411.

Wetzel, James R. 1990. "American Families: 75 Years of Change." *Monthly Labor Review* 113(3):4–13.

Wilson, William J. 1987. *The Truly Disadvantaged: The Inner City, the Underclass, and Public Policy*. Chicago: University of Chicago Press.

Wolch, Jennifer R., and Michael J. Dear. 1993. *Malign Neglect: Homelessness in an American City*. San Francisco: Jossey-Bass.

Wolff, Edward N. 1993. "The Rich Get Increasingly Richer: Latest Data on Household Wealth in the 1980's." Briefing Paper. October 30. Washington, DC: Economic Policy Institute.

Xie, Yu. 1993. "Social Mobility of Asian American Youth." Manuscript. Ann Arbor: University of Michigan.

Zelnik, Melvin, and John F. Kanter. 1980. "Sexual Activity, Contraceptive Usage, and Pregnancy among Metropolitan Area Teenagers: 1971–1979." *Family Planning Perspectives* 12(5):230–237.

Zhan, Li. 1992. "Family Demographic Change and Labor Force Participation of Black and White Women, 1970–1990." Manuscript. Population Research Center, Pennsylvania State University.

Zick, Kathleen D., and Jane L. McCullough. 1991. "Trends in Married Couples' Time Use: Evidence from 1977–78 and 1988." *Sex Roles* 24:459–487.

# Name Index

# Subject Index

remarriage: likelihood of, 68

renters: affordability of housing, 287–289, 324; mortality, 331*n;* overcrowding, residential, 280–281; payment burdens, 285–286, **287,** 289, **290,** 303, 305, 306, 313, 324

reorganizations, 11

residential overcrowding. *See* overcrowding, residential

retirees: population of, 64

retraining, 102

rich. *See* wealth

*Roe* v. *Wade,* 113

rural renaissance, 19, 26–27, 45

"Rustbelt," 19

sales occupations, 12

Scholastic Aptitude Tests (SATs), 192

school enrollment: African Americans, 184; census data, **160;** changes in, 155–213; family and, 212*n;* Hispanics, 184; race differences, 184, **185;** recent trends in, 183–190

science: academic achievement, 190

seasonal unemployment, 91, 94

segregation: homeownership, 296

self-employed, 78–79; poverty, 99–100; race differences, **260;** urban economic restructuring and, 258–262

semi-skilled labor: demand for, 132; demand for, 1970s, 41; immigrants, 64; manufacturing, restructuring of, 51*n,* 108; oversupply of, 46, 76, 201; rural renaissance and, 19; suburban commercial growth centers and, 238; technological change and, 86; unemployment, 11–12. *See also* blue collar workers, 91, 99

service sector: employment growth, 235; expansion of, 111; occupations, 124

sex differences: average hourly earnings, **149;** earnings, 6–19, 13–18, 101, 110, 118, 127–131, 206; economic roles, 107–154; educational attainment, **161–164,** 165–168, 166–168; households, 278–280; housing, 307–309, 314; labor force participation, **119, 198–199;** nonparticipation in labor force, **97;** occupations, 122–127; per capita income, **139;** poverty, 140, **141,** 142; professional degrees, **167;** unemployment, **94;**

work experience, **79,** 117–122; workweek, **84;** young adults' employment, 194

sex role: working mothers and, 5

shelter poverty, 333*n*

shopping malls, 234–235

siblings: number of. *See* family size

single-father families: educational attainment and, 178, 212*n;* poverty, 40, 140; precariously housed populations, 317

single-mother families: educational attainment and, 178, 182, 212*n;* income, 3, 21–22, 25, 55*n;* labor force participation rates, **142;** poverty, 37, 40, 103, 140–142; poverty rate, 96; precariously housed populations, 317; welfare benefits, 47–48

single-parent families: educational attainment, effect on, 176; increase in, 186; poverty, 102

single persons: households, income distribution, 22; increase in numbers of, 5; living with parents, 49*n*

single women: average annual earnings, 83; service sector, 111

skills mismatch: urban economic restructuring, 252–258, 265

S-Night persons, 334*n*

social changes: labor force participation, 67; labor force participation of women, 101

social mobility: educational attainment and, 156

Social Security benefits: changes in, 38–39; expansion of, 9–10; fringe benefit, as, 81; income from, 137; value of, 54*n*

social services as a profession, 75

socioeconomic composition: housing, 307–309

South. *See* Sunbelt

Soviet Union: academic achievement, 191

spatial context: job location and industrial restructuring, 227

spatial mismatch: urban economic restructuring, 252–258, 265

spending: growth in, 74

Sputnik, 69

standardized tests, 192, 209

standard of living: baby boom cohorts, 68; family and household income distribution, 24–25; farmers, 53*n;* households, decrease in size of, 25–26; inequality, 4–6, 24–25; productivity growth and, 45–46